D0505487

Off-message

New Labour, New Sketches

Also by Matthew Parris:

Great Parliamentary Scandals
Look Behind You! Sketches and Follies from the Commons
I Couldn't Possibly Comment . . . More Sketches from the Commons

With Phil Mason:

Read My Lips – A Treasury of the Things
Politicians Wish They Hadn't Said

Published by Robson Books

Off-message

New Labour, New Sketches

Matthew Parris

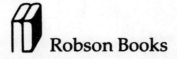

Robson Books

First published in Great Britain in 2001 by Robson Books,
10 Blenheim Court, Brewery Road, London N7 9NY

A member of the Chrysalis Group plc

Copyright © 2001 Matthew Parris

The right of Matthew Parris to be identified as the author
of this work has been asserted by him in accordance with the
Copyright, Designs and Patents Act 1988.

The author and the publishers have made every reasonable effort to
contact all copyright holders. Any errors that may have occurred are
inadvertent and anyone who for any reason has not been contacted is
invited to write to the publishers so that a full acknowledgement may
be made in subsequent editions of this work.

British Library Cataloguing in Publication Data
A catalogue record for this title is available from the British Library.

ISBN 1 86105 479 3

All rights reserved. No part of this publication may be reproduced,
stored in a retrieval system, or transmitted in any form or by any
means, electronic, mechanical, photocopying, recording or otherwise,
without the prior permission in writing of the publishers.

Typeset by SX Composing DTP, Rayleigh, Essex
Printed by Butler & Tanner Ltd, Frome & London

To my friends in The Times *room*
at the House of Commons.

Acknowledgements

My thanks, not just for the last five years but for the last thirteen, to all *The Times* team at the House of Commons, to Phil Webster and Peter Riddell for some of my best facts, and to James Landale for some of my best jokes. Thanks, too, to Julian Glover, now of the *Guardian*, for organising my election campaigns.

The Times and its editors have throughout been my faithful sponsor and (in occasional scrapes) ally. All the sketches in this collection, many abridged, appeared first in *The Times* unless otherwise indicated. To my newspaper, and to the *Spectator* and the *Sun*, thanks.

It's hardly a secret that sketchwriters confer. Over tea in the press gallery canteen, Simon Hoggart (of the *Guardian*), Frank Johnson (of the *Daily Telegraph*), Quentin Letts (of the *Daily Mail*), and, most recently, Simon Carr (of the *Independent*) and I, have colluded regularly. Like some kind of comic version of a witches' coven (is it a pack, a gang, a posse, or perhaps a *sneer* of sketchwriters?), we try out our jokes on each other – and occasionally divide up and share the fruits of our deliberations. Sometimes, disgracefully, we have to agree that this heckle or that snort did come from (say) Dennis Skinner (Lab, Bolsover) or that (say) the morning after a difficult day for Tony Blair, Gordon Brown really did look hung-over as though from a night of celebration. Passing our tittering table, serious journalists shudder and hurry by. To present and many former colleagues as sketchwriters, thanks.

And thanks finally, as ever, to my tireless secretary, Eileen Wright.

Introduction

Many years ago, not long after Tony Blair had become leader of the opposition, 'messages' were things found in bottles, or left in terse form on your telephone answering machine. The idea that a party like new Labour had a 'message' and that the art of political presentation lay in perfecting and controlling the expression of that message, was still in its infancy.

One afternoon in the House of Commons, an 'old' Labour MP who had not quite grasped the point used the banned expression 'socialist' while praising his front bench. The Tories laughed and Tony Blair looked distinctly put out.

I was writing about this for my sketch for the following morning. 'Point out,' suggested *The Times*'s political editor, Phil Webster, 'that the guy was *off-message*. We need to educate our readers in the new jargon.'

Strange as it may seem today, the phrase mystified me. I had no idea what he meant. But Phil had been talking to Alastair Campbell, and explained to me how Tony Blair's press secretary was using the fashionable new terminology in his conversations with lobby correspondents. Utterances by Labour MPs were judged by the party hierarchy according to whether they were 'on' or 'off' message: helpful or otherwise in projecting the image and the ideas which Tony Blair's transformed Labour Party wanted to present.

It dawned on me at once that for a seriously ambitious political party, humour – humour, that is, at their own expense – is off-message. Show the parliamentary sketchwriters the message, and from now on we would do our best to stay off it.

I do hope we have. For it so happens that during the period since, the period covered by the sketches in this collection, humour has often been almost the only weapon to which our governing class has been vulnerable. Only hilarity had succeeded at their expense. Only laughter has ever made them look uncomfortable.

For let's be honest. It has been hard for most of us seriously to argue against the modernisation Blair has sought and achieved for his party, and hard to argue that his government has been a disaster. The few short years leading up to Mr Blair's 1997 general election victory, followed by his first term in office and then his party's triumphant re-election in June this year, have seen a Labour Party with almost everything going for it – except satire. In cold logic they have had the better of the debate.

But boy have they been pompous about it. Smirking self-satisfaction has reached heights undreamed of even under the Tories. Like Peter Pan, Tony Blair has the most unappealing tendency to crow. Around him, many of his most ambitious ministers have been stiff-necked and unsmiling. Men and women of high (presumed) intelligence and minds (we imagine) of their own, have parroted agreed verbal formulae like speak-your-weight machines. Jokes? 'We make the jokes around here,' has been their attitude.

Everywhere there have been balloons to prick. In these circumstances, to giggle, mimic and mock has been more than tempting – it has become a positive civic duty. Of all the slogans with which the Conservative Party tried to score at the last election, 'Wipe the smile off Tony Blair's face' was the only one which drew blood.

For their part, the Tories have been better confronted by mockery than by argument. The party has been disfigured by what many of us see as an obsession with Europe. Their arguments have often held water and their Euro-scepticism has been hard to rebut: it is the single-issue, swivel-eyed fanaticism which has so perverted opposition politics. There is therefore no point *arguing* with this Tory tendency. When in a totally spoof report one of my sketches alleged a series of sinister connections between the pro-European Tory, Chris Patten, and 666 (the number of the Beast), some Conservative MPs asked me which of my allegations were actually serious. In the face of zealotry, what can you do but laugh?

'So why,' readers of *The Times* have sometimes asked me, 'don't you try writing a comic political novel?' The answer is simple. There's no need to make it up.

How could mere fiction be as wacky, as ludicrous or as cute as the real House of Commons? Any made-up story that pushed the unlikely as far as Westminster does would be denounced by critics as too absurd to be funny.

Imagine a political novel in which the Foreign Secretary in the departure lounge at Heathrow is ordered by the Prime Minister's Press

Secretary over the mobile phone to choose between his mistress and his wife. Imagine that same man later, wounded by a television impersonator's take-off of his squeaky voice, turning up for questions in the chamber with a voice which has been lowered by half an octave, and grunting and growling through the afternoon like Daddy Bear. Imagine a former prime minister, the Baroness Thatcher, hitting an Essex supermarket during a general election campaign, only to discover that to complete her purchase she needed something of which she had never heard: a cheque guarantee card.

Imagine the Liberal Democrats' Northern Ireland spokesman opening a debate on the dangers of the world being hit by a rogue asteroid. Imagine a huge national row over the Lord Chancellor's new wallpaper; or the octogenarian Father of the House on the edge of his seat as he chairs the election of a new Speaker, impatience yielding to despair as his prospects of getting off the chair and onto the loo within the next six hours dwindle. Imagine the House of Peers solemnly discussing buggery, from lunch until dinner, in the most lurid terms . . .

'Or imagine,' as I wrote on 24 April this year, 'that at 4.30p.m. in committee room 15 yesterday the select committee on public accounts was to interview experts as part of its inquiry into "Tackling obesity in England" and that it had chosen for its witnesses a Mr Nigel Crisp and a Mr Podger.'

No self-respecting novelist would dare.

Chance has sent me such wonders to report over the recent years covered in this collection, that I begin to think I shall push my luck if I continue much longer. As I write this, it is my plan to quit the parliamentary sketch at the end of the year and not long after this book will be published.

That's not because I'm weary. Anything but. As my fourteenth party conference season beckons, reporting all this seems more fun than ever. The view, I hope, is still fresh. And that's the time to quit.

l'Avenc, Catalunya, August 2001

Prescott Goes Off-message

5.10.96

New Labour wind up their last conference before the election, which they would win.

It was a pretty loud bang and everybody thought a bomb had gone off. The music stopped. Delegates dancing in the aisles froze. There was complete silence as people stared around in alarm.

Then from above came a rain of little leaflets – *Vote Labour* – fired from the Winter Gardens' balcony. There was a brave 'three cheers'. Labour's composure returned but it took time. Until the music restarted, people milled distractedly around, the mood of celebration shattered.

It was the first and only big blunder in a week otherwise almost without incident, and it came in the closing minutes. As delegates and journalists left Blackpool, it remained unclear how the mistake could have been made. Why was the explosion so loud? Why did they halt the music?

Everything about the closing rally had been going so well. John Prescott had been welcomed with a standing ovation even before he spoke.

There were moments during his patter when we wondered whether we had wandered into the wrong arena at Blackpool and found ourselves watching Frank Carson, with Eddie Large's voice.

Labour's deputy leader did his best to keep to his pre-released text – Mr Prescott's controllers now steer him away from all unscripted encounters with Britain – but there was one stumble and it proved the bit delegates loved best. Losing the crib sheet of Labour's promises he had planned to hold up, Prescott exploded: 'I knew this would happen. You know me. I'm old Labour. Got to use my own words.'

Everybody cheered. Spin-doctors' video-pagers flashed 'off-message' warnings to new Labour's command-control centre on the Planet Vanilla. 'Off-message' is the PR-speak for signals out of line with the desired image. 'We believe in socialist principles!' declared Prescott. *Off-message – Beep – Urgent – Abort.*

Yet some of the best of Labour's conference has been off-message – or superfluous to the gloss which some want to project. For this is still a party with kindness and idealism in its ranks.

Off-message or not, delegates gave Prescott a rousing ovation. But what a change that explosion wreaked! The edgy confidence the party has exuded all week evaporated instantly. One bang, one bad stumble, and it was as though delegates feared they had only been dreaming and the game was up. Would a giant spectre of Baroness Thatcher come winging, bat-like, through the hall, as everyone ran screaming for cover?

Confidence returned. Cameramen ambushed a toddler dancing to *Things Can Only Get Better*. Scared by the camera flashes, the child stopped and began to cry. Image of weeping babe. *Off-message! Off-message!* The toddler was hauled away.

The Word Was 'Formidable'   20.9.96

I watched Tony Blair, opposition leader at The Times/Dillons *forum.*

To watch Tony Blair in impromptu performance is to search for the right word to describe his appeal. Charm? Not quite. The audience is impressed but not seduced. At times his competence is almost chilling.

Effective, then? The Labour leader is more than that. The word does not do justice to his personal skills, which are formidable. Blair spoke last night with something which fell short of warmth and never quite amounted to real passion, but which engaged most beguilingly with his questioners. He is the opposite of wooden. He looks at you directly and leaps to answer your inquiry with apparent frankness and flattering informality.

Poised, courteous and convinced, this is a man only too pleased to explain what he can do for you. Even when engaged in evasive action his instinct is never to go on to the defensive. The style stays relaxed, peppered with the occasional 'you know', 'well', 'look', or 'let me give you an example'. One has the impression of a floor salesman with complete confidence in his product. He would prove superlative at shifting life assurance, landmines, patent mousetraps, or personal salvation.

Which was it, then, last night? The language and imagery are a curious mixture of the everyday and the grandiose. Mr Blair had said 'I mean' 27 times and 'you know' 93 times by the time I left and seemed often to flail around clutching at thoughts, yet neither entirely mastering nor properly marshalling them. He has his favoured phrases – I noted 'ethical socialism', 'modern global economy', 'social cohesion' and 'reclaiming the Labour Party as a party of values' – and he gives the impression of lurching for these as might a man trying to traverse a marsh and zigzagging from reed-clump to reed-clump pausing on each as long as it will bear the argument without sinking – then striking out for the next clump of abstract nouns.

'Traditional values in a modern setting,' he declared. One could not help thinking of the wording of modern menus in north London: 'Ocean-gathered prawns on a raft of beanshoots' – yet there is no doubt the audience last night responded approvingly. Mr Blair has the knack of couching observations of quite blinding fatuity in terms of a confiding informality which flatters its audience.

I noted: 'I do believe we have an unrivalled opportunity, you know, to make major changes to the common agricultural policy because, you know, there are lots of consumers all around Europe who want this to happen.' A light tenor, an engaging diffidence and a liberal sprinkling of 'I really do believe' can give reflections a weight which, on cold examination, they should hardly bear. 'I think the closer you get to common sense, you know, the better – I think.'

While calling for a 'real debate' – 'engaging with the issues' – Mr Blair deftly avoids the debate. I know of nobody but Tony Benn more adept at cloaking his rabbit-punches at his rivals' kidneys beneath a mantle of amiability. Answers on the railways, the future of Europe, a single currency and Labour splits were all avoided by attacks on the Conservatives. Shrewdest of all was Mr Blair's complete refusal to engage with the question (which more than one *Times* reader posed) of whether and why socialism was now to be discarded.

These are, however, the reflections of only one observer: *The Times* audience (a remarkable proportion of whom were between the ages of 25 and 35) was overwhelmingly sympathetic.

I started this sketch searching for the right word. It is undoubtedly 'formidable'.

It Keeps Them Cheerful

24.9.96

'Skin cancer is rocketing!' cried Matthew Taylor, MP, Liberal Democrat environment spokesperson. The news was received without panic by party delegates ambling back into the Brighton Conference Centre after lunch.

'One in eight children now suffers the misery of asthma.' Mr Taylor surveyed the hall: a sea of empty plastic chairs, sprinkled Liberally with goodly folk. Ladies with their hair in buns are making a big comeback this year in Brighton. One was knitting.

'An environmental catastrophe is on the way!' Taylor yelped. A few of his audience looked up in mild interest. 'But I'm not here to be gloomy.' That was a relief. One wondered what Mr Taylor would have been like had he come to be gloomy. 'Vast areas of fertile land will all turn to desert!' A bun or two bobbed in gentle surprise. It struck us that, deployed tactically like Agent Orange, Mr Taylor's speeches could be used to transform whole continents into deserts. I fled the defoliating oratory.

At Least the Lib Dems Can Titter

25.9.96

With memories of his brief extra-marital fling in their minds, Liberal Democrats assemble to hear their leader.

Just before Paddy Ashdown spoke to his conference at Brighton yesterday I came close to joining his party. This was when its delegates began to giggle at their leader's own video curtain-raiser. To the strains of Elgar we saw Paddy on a building site; to the strains of Smetana we observed him in a cornfield; and Beethoven accompanied him into a conservatory. For five minutes Mr Ashdown bounced through the British Isles to gentle rhythms and in soft focus, looking tough but tender. His speech pledged to help his countrymen 'find the hero in themselves'. Happily for the Liberal Democrat leader, a camera crew, sound crew, producer, video-editor and PR adviser had helped us to find the hero in Mr Ashdown.

'I want to take a long, hard look,' cried the brave marine, eyes narrowed to flinty slits, 'at some unfashionable subjects.' We wondered which. Flares? Kipper ties? But no: Courage, Leadership and Patriotism were his chosen taboos and the Liberal leader was about to appropriate all three to himself. In doing so, Captain Ashdown had the delicacy to observe that he was only embodying *our* courage, leadership and patriotism – doing it by proxy, so to speak, for the nation. Modestly he acknowledged that Churchill had had much the same thought. Deploring the debauching of patriotism by Tories he added that a true patriot would vote for the opposition parties.

'My next wish,' he declared, 'is for Sally.' A nervous hush descended upon the audience. 'I met her on the Hartcliffe and Withywood estate in Bristol.' You could have heard a pin drop. 'She is a young mother.' A thousand Liberal Democrats groaned inwardly. This was taking honesty too far. Then it dawned on us that Sally was being cited only as an illustration of the benefits-trap. We breathed again.

Bees Collide in Lib Dem Bonnets

26.9.96

Four causes rouse special passion in a Liberal breast. One is local government. They really care about pavement politics and their voice in town halls nationwide is jealously guarded.

Another is disability. To a Liberal Democrat, if the struggle is not about protecting the disadvantaged, it is about nothing.

The third is race. Liberals will bend over backward to show consideration to anyone from a minority ethnic group.

The fourth cause is more selfish: every Liberal's ceaseless search for free food. Some never enter the conference hall but spend their days wandering, like buffalo over the African plain, from nosh to nosh. A foodless debate risks an empty room.

Hold in your mind those four great goals; pavement politics, anti-racism, pro-disability and free nosh. A clash within Liberal Democracy between any two of these impulses would bring turmoil. A clash between all four would be emotional agony.

That clash occurred yesterday at the Sheridan Hotel in Brighton, around lunch. In defence of their local government heritage, Liberal Democrats found themselves obliged to miss lunch, shout down a man with a speech defect, and then rough up a black man.

The pain this caused them was pitiful to observe.

But to begin at the beginning . . . the Urban Campaign Network plus bearded Tony Greaves, old-fashioned liberal and famous wild man of the local government undergrowth, had fronted a lunch-time fringe entitled: 'Why We Don't Want To Get Into Bed With Labour.'

'A meeting for all activists who *don't* see Labour through rose-tinted spectacles!' said the handout. Greaves, a canny old owl, knew the topic was hot and saw his chance to save money on sausage rolls, so (in smaller print) dismayed delegates read 'no free food or drink – but plenty of free expression'.

Fighting the urge to graze at a rival meeting – 'energy from waste (*free refreshments!*)' – scores turned up. They were in a mood to kill.

They think Ashdown is plotting to sell their heritage for a mess of Blairite pottage. As the meeting progressed they grew angrier. 'I don't like the word "consensus". I prefer "suspicion"!' barked an Islington lady councillor. Greaves told them Labour was 'rotting from within' and everyone cheered. 'Don't sell the faith!' shouted one councillor, and they cheered some more. 'Labour will naff up, make no mistake!' yelled another, to supporting whoops. Then an articulate young black delegate rose. Paddy was right, he said, to think about a pact. There was a confused growl from the floor. 'Careerist!' shouted someone, surprising himself. 'Are we serious about power?' demanded the youth. 'Rubbish!' shouted someone else.

'We may need to deal with Labour.'

'Join'm then!' 'Turn off the TV cameras!' 'He only came for the TV!' Soon the black man was being barracked on all sides. He found himself in a smaller minority than the ethnic one. A minority of two, as it turned out, for now a man arose, a thoughtful man, with a stammer. 'To be f-f-fair to Labour . . .' he began. 'Why?' shouted someone. Soon, hindered by his stammer, he too was being interrupted cruelly.

These gentle people became like wild beasts. As I left, the black man was being attacked on the stairs. Someone was jabbing a finger at his chest shouting: 'People like *you* . . .' and then, ''Ow much did Paddy pay you?'

I ran for cover.

A Pink Rinse But Darker Roots

1.10.96

Labour's new stage at the Winter Gardens hovers between the neo-fascist and the neolithic. White Stonehenge-like structures mingle with ramps, kerbs and pillars, and the orators emerge from caves.

Red has been banished from the platform's focus but an anaemic pink floods eerily in from the margins. Spin doctors have achieved a technical miracle: the view from the conference floor is framed in pink but the area immediately behind the speaker's head is neutral and forms the surround for most television soundbites.

Thus the nation's news-watchers are seeing a different picture from what confronts Labour delegates – each designed to please its target audience best. And in what amounts to a parable of modern Labour, it is impossible to be sure whether the pink bits really are pink or just lit by 'mood' spotlighting, a chameleon's dream, changeable at the stage manager's whim.

Electric lecterns rise and fall at the touch of a button. The suspicion grows that if any orator were to speak beyond his allotted time, a trap-door would whisk open beneath him, plucking him from the scene. Perhaps debaters who depart from Labour's new line might be zapped by laser, like those electric-blue fly incinerators we see in butchers' shops: 6,000 volts – *fzt!* – and he's gone. A faint smell of singeing suffuses the hall.

That sense of ruthless orthodoxy – consensus by diktat – permeates the whole conference scene. The party's organisational techniques are redolent of the worst excesses of the Zanzibar police. 'STAGE MANAGEMENT' says the notice on one door, just beside the platform. The door next to it says 'Autocue operations. Strictly no entry.' Officials have now banned me from the corridor – 'a restricted zone', they say.

Flanked by a new-look Clare Short resembling Eva Peron relaunched in Clinique, Gordon Brown spoke yesterday with humanity and intelligence, but to a strangely sour Winter Gardens. For Labour, the nature of the orthodoxy changes but not the habit of orthodoxy. The party is getting less silly but not any nicer.

Glum Tories Gather in Bournemouth

7.10.96

As at the Vatican, where ambitious cardinals crowd the corridors around an ailing Pope, so at Bournemouth do aspirants for the leader's crown linger by the bedside of a sick party, mouthing concern for the Prime Minister's political health.

The most honest bulletin we could issue from Bournemouth yesterday was that the patient's condition was grave, but stable. Bewildered Tories (the geek-quotient increases every year and this is the only party where you see conferencegoers attending with their mothers) met mixed signals on their first day.

They were confronted by a science fiction stage set: *Eurovision Song Contest* meets *Star Trek*. On to blank, futuristic screens, video projections remind us what the debate is about: for Farming we had combine-harvesters, ladybirds, par-baked buns, and a plum.

Platform parties float in space, safe within two lifeboat-like vessels. Between the boats a lonely speaker thrashes about like a swimmer in trouble. Bald heads peer over the boats' sides in concern. We half expect the occupants to start throwing each other overboard, or eating the cabin-boy.

Into one of these boats the Baroness Thatcher bustled before noon. Her familiar royal blue outfit and little partridge-like steps were reassuring. We held our breath, and – yes! – she kissed John *and* Norma Major. And sat next to William Hague, the Welsh Secretary. Could this be an omen?

Mr Hague gave the day's best speech. With conviction and fluency the young prodigy tore into devolution plans, Lady Thatcher gazing adoringly on. Hague's well-placed Yorkshire grind ('millions of uzz') verges on the robotic and comes oddly from a chap resembling a Cow-&-Gate baby competition winner – like one of those horror movies where the voice of an alien body-invader emerges from an abducted toddler – but the conference loved him.

They loved Michael Forsyth (the Scottish Secretary) too. Forsyth has a hunched, jagged delivery, faintly demonic, and played shamelessly to the gallery by waving altered images of the Union Flag. Finally he and Hague held a huge, real Union Flag between them: grinning poison-dwarf and alien body-invader, our poor flag stretched between.

The repellent spectacle was cheered wildly.

But then no conference speech succeeds, these days, without the gimcrack. Videos, postcards from old ladies in Liverpool, near-sobbing references to deaths in the family or among friends, politicians piggy-backing on to the emotional aftermath of national tragedy . . . It is not enough to inform: we must be whammied.

Stephen Dorrell's whammy was to replace his speech with a marathon question-and-answer session. People could ask anything they liked. The ostentatiously competent Health Secretary coped well, so the session was without interest. Nobody asked the real questions: 'Why don't you get a suntan, you whey-faced bap?' 'Why do you scowl like a ghoul and shout all the time?' and 'Reincarnated, which animal would you choose?'

Still, Dorrell's gimmick succeeded, like Forsyth's flag. Soon will come the ultimate conference speech. A host of hologram angels flock from the ceiling, dry ice puffs from the platform, lasers scissor, video-images dance around the walls and, to deafening disco music, politicians rollerskate around the conference floor, miming to quadraphonic repeats of a killer soundbite.

Douglas Hogg, the Agriculture Minister, did none of these things yesterday. He waved nothing, failed to sing – failed even to produce an anecdote about his dear old auntie. Instead he just explained doggedly how difficult it all was. Thus, Hogg missed the point. Some of us love him the better for it.

Lilley Pecks While Portillo Gropes

10.10.96

John Major's question-and-answer session worked well yesterday at Bournemouth. Hand on hip and shirt in need of tucking, he leaned against the podium as a neighbour might lean on the garden fence, chatting with Tory representatives.

Alongside him, however, the masterful Brian 'Don't mess with me' Mawhinney was ill-advised to roll up his sleeves without warning. The intended impression was of chummy informality, but one felt a sudden anxiety that he was about to glass somebody. At least he proved that, contrary to rumour, there were no tattoos.

After lunch, even the Environment Secretary got into the act, proving quite a hit in his new role as Oprah. How long before people start weeping in the aisles? Still, the idea crowned a day which lifted Tory spirits.

Or, rather, *most* Tory spirits. Not Ted Heath's. In aspect and shape, Sir Edward increasingly resembles the cartoonist Giles's 'Grandma'. On the platform party he contributed an intense localised depression. All through Malcolm Rifkind's cautiously Euro-sceptical speech, Sir Edward – Europhile and Euro-Blobby – sat slouched in a total grump, chair pulled back from table. At applause at the name of Margaret Thatcher, he clasped his hands together, immobile, face like frozen puff pastry.

In a separate enclosure sat another Euro-Blobby, Kenneth Clarke. The Chancellor seemed at times to be spilling over into the seat of the much trimmer Michael Portillo. Why do all Euro-enthusiasts go pear-shaped? Is federalism fattening? Or does being fat make one a federalist?

The Tory rank and file want speakers to thump the lectern and bash Brussels bureaucracy; but go further and they get nervous.

Peter Lilley judged his audience shrewdly yesterday, offering more anti-EU rhetoric than substance.

The Social Security Secretary gains every year in assurance and poise. This year he was rewarded by the arrival of his wife, Gail, who bounded up and planted a smacker on the back of his neck.

This is a new kind of conference kiss. Such a kiss is vaguely suggestive without implying an immediate proposition. The Lilleys may have been offering a metaphor for Mr Lilley's approach to his own leadership prospects.

Where Michael Heseltine has stroked the Tory thigh, John Redwood grabbed the Tory knickers, as Michael Portillo lunged (last year) at the Tory bra, Peter Lilley was merely, so to speak, kissing the Conservative Party on the back of its neck.

For now.

Houdini of Love Sees Ken Perform

11.10.96

The Chancellor faced what may have been an historic challenge yesterday. On the success of his speech rode the hopes of his wing of the party. Had this conference sent Kenneth Clarke packing, we would have said the Tory Centre Left was finished for some time.

After the speech, it becomes possible to believe it has only just started. For once, he made an effort and, frankly, walked it. If a man can receive a stomping ovation for promising *not* to cut taxes, how might he be received when he cuts them?

I watched Steven Norris, watching him. Mr Norris was suspended in a tiny TV studio hung from the wall: the third commentator to spend a day interpreting for BBC viewers.

On Tuesday it was David Mellor: a sideshow of his own beneath the television lights. Perspiring, teeth glinting through the thick sound-proofing glass, mouth opening and closing, goldfish-like, without sound, Mr Mellor resembled a show-trial serial killer in a maximum-security glass box. Representatives craned their necks up in horror and fascination.

Wednesday brought Edwina Currie, in sequinned electric blue such as might be worn by the lady the conjuror saws in half. An illuminated exhibit floating in space, she stole the show like minor royalty in an opera box.

And, for yesterday's freak show, Steven Norris. Roll up! The Houdini of Love, exhibited in a box. Norris was there to explain the conference to the world. But the world stared back, more interested in the explanation for Mr Norris.

14.10.96

Any Word Will Do

With the exception of the Prime Minister, they all seem to be at it. One page of Michael Portillo's speech to the Tory conference last week contained little more than a hundred words, arranged in paragraphs, none of which contained more than one sentence. Only two paragraphs contained more than a dozen words. A week earlier in Blackpool, Andrew Smith, Labour's Transport spokesman, followed his Leader's lead into short, verbless sentences, one passage of his speech running:

'Traffic jams on the M1.

'Road congestion.

'Changing at Preston.'

As with so many attempts by politicians to be modern, the style is actually about half a step behind the times. You see the same grasping at what was modern yesterday in the design of today's conference stage sets, which were the sort of look in vogue for the television set designs of the Eighties.

As in the visual, so with the spoken word. The modern conference speech unconsciously echoes the advertising copywriter's style of the 1980s. Advertising has moved on since then, the industry accepting that consumers can tackle sentences with quite complex structures; but to the politicians of the Nineties, the Eighties are still the latest thing.

It is time, then, for an all-purpose framework for the podium politician who wishes to impress. I have taken as my theme nuts, but for 'nuts' you can substitute almost anything . . .

(*Party leader runs on, to disco fanfare, eyes burning*)

'As I look about me, as I look around. Ahead.

'Forward.

'I see a vision.

'Let me tell you what I mean.

'I mean nuts.

'True nuts.

'New nuts.

'Not yesterday's nuts. No going back to the old nuts. No return.

'Instead, nut reborn.

'Young nut, shared nut, growing nut.

'Nurtured nut. Nuts fulfilled.

'Cherished.

'Nourished.

'Undiminished.

'Nuts new dawn.

'Let me explain.

'Big nut.

'Not small nut.

'Huge nut.

'British nut.
'Yes, British.
'Strong.
'Tough.
'Tough nut.
'Not Brussels nut.
'Oh no.
'Caring, committed, community nut.
'Nut with values.
'Firm nut.
'Focused nut.
'Single nut.
'But never isolated.
'Oh no.
'Upright nut.
'Proud nut.
'Confident nut.
'Not timid.
'No bad nuts. Rotten. Soft.
'But firm. Uncracked. Unyielding.
'But we must have safeguards!
'My priorities – passion if you like – nut, nut and nut.
'Roasted nut.
'Nuts in every classroom.
'Nut superhighway.
'Trained nut.
'Reskilled nut.
'Educated nut.
'Modern nut.
'Flexible, mobile dynamic nut.
'Nut for the 21st century.
'A thousand nuts for a thousand years.
'A nut on every street corner.
'Nut on the beat.
'Neighbourhood nut.
'Responsible nut.
'Decent nut.
'Principled.
'Three nuts and you're out!

'One nut: bold, courageous, firm.

'Tough on blight, tough on the causes of blight.

'No more lost nuts, spoilt nuts.

'Undervalued. Underfunded. Undermined.

'Seventeen wasted years!

'Integrated nut. Strategic. Global. Galactic.

'Proactive. Not reactive. Not negative.

'Positive.

'Open nut. Not closed. Honest nut.

'No sleazy nuts.

'I tell you this.

'Choice of nut.

'Real choice.

'Excellence.

'Honour.

'Excellence and choice.

'Choice and excellence.

'Diversity and choice.

'Diversity, excellence, choice, nuts, and honour.

'Opportunity nut. Fair, reasonable, reaching out.

'Nut 2000.

'Nut mission.

'Nuts for all.

'All our people.

'New solutions.

'No false promises. No betrayals.

'No lies.

'No letdowns.

'No more.

'No.

'I see aspiration. I see hope.

'Hopeful nuts, high-wage nuts. Skilled, sophisticated.

'Future nuts: limitless, optimistic and empowered.

'Stakeholding nuts, investing in nuts, partnership of nuts, nut
potential, nuts anew.

'A force for good, for nuts unborn. So many nuts!

'A need for change.

'A fresh start.

'And let us now redouble. Let us now commit. Reach out, I say.

'Reach up.
'Down.
'Forward.
'A nutty covenant. I tell you. A nutty vow!'
(*Spouse of party Leader runs on to stage and embraces Leader passionately. Crowd goes wild. Press goes wild.*)

Breakfast with Bottomley

15.10.96

'I'm only too easy to meet,' cried Virginia Bottomley to a crowd of startled MPs, regathered after the summer recess yesterday, 'in any number of settings!'

What could the fragrant Mrs Bottomley mean? What settings did she have in mind? Parascending? Boating on the Serpentine? Call me uninventive, but a cup of tea in her office would surely do.

The Heritage Secretary had been goaded into this surprising offer by her Labour Shadow, Jack Cunningham. At Questions yesterday, he asked her to confirm that for £500 one could have joined Mrs Bottomley at breakfast during her party's conference last week at Bournemouth. 'Is that proper?' In fact, Dr Cunningham was taking something of a liberty with these reports.

It seems Tories with funds to spare were being invited to sponsor the breakfast, but those with no more than loose change to offer were still permitted to approach the great lady at the muesli bar. Still, Cunningham decided to take a crack; and who can blame him?

Unable to decide whether to be indignant or dismissive, Mrs B decided to be coquettish. So cheery a picture did she paint of her approachability at breakfast, at tea-time or at any other time, that one wondered where she finds any time at all to be Heritage Secretary. This merry informality she contrasted with the '£1,000 Labour charge for nosh-ups with Tony Blair in Park Lane'.

And there was more. 'I am available at virtually every major tourist event.'

Really? The Changing of the Guards *and* Mrs Bottomley? Bottomley at Stonehenge? Bottomley among the Crown Jewels? Bottomley at the Zoo? At your picnic at Henley? Leading the donkey rides at

Cleethorpes? There can only be one logical conclusion to Mrs Bottomley's dash for crowd appeal. Can Mystic Meg's contract with the BBC be safe for much longer?

Who Bores Wins

16.10.96

Holy smokes! Have we waited all summer for this? At their first Prime Minister's Questions since July, John Major and Tony Blair bored the pants off us.

'A thousand days to prepare for a thousand years!' the Labour leader had been crying, by the seashore, a fortnight earlier. That thousand days begins now. One had hoped Mr Blair might have marked the event by kicking off his final stint crying in the Westminster wilderness dressed for the part. 'His raiment was made from camels' hair and a leathern girdle about his loins,' says the Good Book 'and his meat was locusts and wild honey'. But Mr Blair's raiment was made from Armani and a silken necktie about his collar. Upon the dispatch box, no stone platter, no locusts, no honey. No beard, either. His hair was by Michaeljohn (£60).

'A buccaneering spirit,' Mr Major had promised us not a week ago, at Bournemouth, 'gritty resolve'. 'I'll be out there among you!' How then would he greet the start of *his* last stint before the prize fight? Would he come swaggering on wrapped in a hooded dressing gown, hair tousled, shadow boxing? No. *His* raiment was made from wool worsted (Austin Reed) and a nicely pressed white shirt about his breast. Mr Major's hair was by Trumpers (£19.50 with shampoo). So the signs were not good. Still, we thought, perhaps the fireworks will be verbal.

The first question was from Labour's roguishly likeable Ronnie Campbell (Blyth Valley), the only MP known to have a tattoo. 'As a working-class warrior myself,' he began – then made as to remove his jacket: 'I'll take my coat off,' he nodded to the Prime Minister. A good start, but his question was routine, about Major's children's private education. Mr Major's answer was routine, too – about Blair's child's private education. Things were going downhill.

Up got Tony Blair. *Countdown: 5-4-3-2-1 . . . start of the Thousand Days*. Total letdown. The Labour leader bleated away about the failings of the internal market in the health service – words such as 'disgrace', 'crisis' and 'fundamental damage' thudding harmlessly into the leather seatbacks.

Up got Mr Major. *Countdown: 5-4-3-2-1 . . . start of the fabled Tory Fightback.* Total letdown. The Prime Minister droned on interminably about expenditure, waiting lists and numbers of staff – meaningless statistics ricocheting emptily around the Chamber's walls.

'The Rt Hon Gentleman is *quite* wrong . . .' (Major); 'I really do not know how he can *dare* mention dentistry . . .' (Blair). To MPs without number is granted the gift of boring us at length and for hours. Only to a rare few is granted the gift of boring us briefly and at once. Blair and Major are among them.

They were joined yesterday in this Mission to Bore by Paddy Ashdown. Mr Ashdown, after years of crack training in the Special Boat Squadron, can bore at a single glance.

Hats Off to a Dying Era

24.10.96

MPs assembled at the Commons yesterday for the State Opening. H.G. Wells, writing 85 years ago, caught the spirit of the occasion. 'A memory hangs about me of the House in the early afternoon, an inhumane desolation inhabited almost entirely by silk hats.'

The hats have changed, but the desolation yesterday seemed, if anything, more intense.

Silk was no longer the order of the day, except for Bernie Grant. Returning to his roots, the Labour MP for Tottenham swept into the chamber swathed in yards of pale blue silk, robed about him in the style of a West African chief, plus a blue silk hat.

Beside him, the Commons chaplain, who had turned up for prayers in a modest little outfit of crimson and gold, looked positively dowdy. He didn't even have a hat.

Elizabeth Peacock did. The Conservative MP for Batley & Spen wore, above a scarlet suit, a bowler-like creation swathed in what appeared to be black mosquito-netting. In royal blue, Marion Roe (C) was crowned by a big black hat pierced at the front by two enormous crossed arrows – our first fear being that, en route from her constituency of Broxbourne, Mrs Roe had been ambushed by a company of archers.

It was melancholy to watch them. Perhaps this was the last State Opening of an era. For Peter Shore (Lab, Bethnal Green & Stepney) it undoubtedly was; the brave and independent-minded former Cabinet minister is not standing again. His lonely stand on defence was immensely controversial within Labour, before a modernised party adopted it as their own.

Unrobed, unthanked and without a hat, Mr Shore arrived early yesterday, watching the young pups with mild and detached gaze. Opposite him, Douglas Hurd, also departing, seemed alone; not long ago colleagues and whips would have been tugging his sleeve for a word on this or that, and every journalist's eye would have been upon him.

How suddenly do fires which seemed to blaze steadily for years fade! All at once, people who seemed to be part of every story are part of none.

Sketchwriting for the *Morning Chronicle* 160 years ago, Charles Dickens describes an early incarnation of such men: 'There he stands, leaning on his stick; looking at the throng of Exquisites around him with most profound contempt, and conjuring up, before his mind's eye, the scenes he beheld in the old House, in days gone by, when his own feelings were fresher and brighter, and when, as he imagines, wit, talent, and patriotism flourished more brightly too.'

One day, men who are young now will misremember yesterday's mean-spirited and fractious Commons, met this week for one last mean-spirited and fractious gasp, as some kind of a golden age. It is as well to remind ourselves that it was not.

Clapham Passengers Know Best

29.10.96

While Michael Howard, the Home Secretary, and Jack Straw, his Labour Shadow, yelled at each other for more than an hour yesterday, excited backbenchers squawking, snarling or squeaking their contributions, I calculated that omnibuses of the numbers 3, 11, 12, 24, 29, 53 and (on their way to Clapham) 77 and 88 would have passed the House, most of them full.

Had the passengers and crew of any one of those buses been invited to alight at Westminster, toss a coin, divide themselves into two teams, 'Government' and 'Opposition', then occupy the Commons Chamber; and had the MPs taken these passengers' places on the bus; then two things would have been certain. First, a more sensible debate on guns, combat knives and stalkers would have taken place in the Commons. Second, there would have been a riot on the bus.

Irresistible Force – Immovable Object

31.10.96

Good Commons speeches are like buses. None turn up for ages then two turn up at the same time. Just when you despaired of witnessing any Commons performance of any stature between now and the next election, two barnstorming orations remind you that good debaters still exist at Westminster.

First over the hill in the Economy debate yesterday afternoon was Gordon Brown. We could almost hear the hooves thundering as he approached. The moment he rose, the Shadow Chancellor was on a roll. Buoyed by the Chancellor's embarrassment over interest rates, Mr Brown took his speech at a furious gallop, and was never unhorsed. Critics scoff (Clarke did) that this was the speech Brown always makes. So it was, but you might just as well complain that Pavarotti always sings *Nessun dorma*. So he does, the important question being whether he belts it out in better or worse throat than before. I have never heard Mr Brown belting out his familiar personal solo of dire economic news in more confident voice.

Like an Old Testament Jeremiah, and in his peculiar thunderous growl, Brown bashed the table and hammered home all the old Family Favourites from the *Shadow Chancellor's Songbook*. Britain was being overtaken in 'the world economic league'; Britain was high on the European inflation league and low on the European investment league. The OECD, VAT, the EU and CGT were flung around the Chamber, as acronyms, quotations and statistics bounced from the rafters and clattered to the floor.

While Brown stormed on, knocking interruptors aside, this sketch was able to identify the key to his idiosyncratic speaking style. The first part of a sentence is delivered normally, but, a few words from the end, Brown suddenly comes down hard on each successive word, hitting each singly, stopping, then hitting the next – the final word being roared at the lowest key with a dreadful finality. It is like a plane coming in to land, smacking the runway, bouncing, and coming to a shuddering halt. Thus: 'They're near the bottom of every. One. Of. These. **Leagues**.' Or: 'The truth about the economy is that they are economical. With. The. **Truth**.' The effect is awesome. Brown sat down to a heartening cheer.

Kenneth Clarke rose to reply. He had just had to raise interest rates – and now witnessed a revitalised Opposition. Anyone of less Tiggerish buoyancy would have been disheartened, but not our Ken. Within seconds, he, too, was up to speed, throwing out statistics of his own, ridiculing Brown's gloom.

'Best inflation for 50 years!' 'Unemployment at its lowest level for five and a half years!' Clarke soon had the Tories laughing and cheering behind him. 'The only people who don't believe the strength of the economy are either mad, dead, or sitting on the benches opposite!' he cried, starting the sentence with insufficient puff and ending it in that strangulated squawk he has made his own. Clarke began to irk Brown, who interrupted him. The Chancellor reacted by goading him more, and by the end the Shadow Chancellor had bounced up seven times to protest or question.

It is said that little divides these two men ideologically. Certainly they were unconsciously aping each other's style: trading statistical missiles, parrying with scornful laughter, resting elbows on the dispatch box, or placing one hand on hip and sweeping the air with the other. Two political heavyweights, in every sense. Irresistible force met immovable object yesterday, and, for one glorious hour, the Commons floor shook.

It Isn't Clever and It Isn't Funny   *6.11.96*

Nobody likes a tell-tale. With every parliamentary session, Madam Speaker grows more to resemble a kindergarten teacher driven to her wits' end. Now, to her despair, the kiddies have taken to telling on each other.

On a Monday, one of them tells Miss that someone else has been using Commons notepaper for unofficial business. On a Tuesday, another tells her that someone has used OHMS envelopes for party correspondence. Betty Boothroyd's patience grows more thin.

'Miss! *Miss!*' said Labour's Jim Dowd (Lewisham W) yesterday. (Well, that's what young Jim meant: what he said was, 'On a point of order, Madam Speaker'.) He complained that Tory ministers visited his constituency without telling him.

Wearily, Miss Boothroyd reminded MPs that it is a convention at Westminster that MPs inform each other when visiting each other's constituencies. Miss! Miss! *Miss!* . . . this time it was the Tories' Graham Riddick (Colne Valley). The gangly child told Miss Boothroyd that it was Labour MPs who failed to notify others of their visits. He accused Labour's leader and deputy leader of this. Madam Speaker kicked at her footstool with elegant shoe.

Miss! Who was this ginger-mopped infant on the Tory benches? It was Ian Bruce (Dorset S). And what did little Ian want? To be excused? To complain that an older girl next to him, Elaine (Dame Kellett-Bowman, 72), had shoved him with her elbow? No. Ian wanted Miss to know that Tony Blair (43) was talking too much. 'He used 342 words in his questions to the Prime Minister last Tuesday, and 380 words on Thursday,' whined Ian. 'After 150 words, could you cut him off before his third question?'

Barely controlling her temper, Miss told Ian that she was perfectly able to find out for herself how much Tony was talking, and besides it wasn't just Tony. *All* the boys and girls talked too much. John Major then accused Tony Blair of 'kindergarten soundbites'.

As a kindergarten soundbite, this soundbite was a good deal more effective than Mr Blair's own kindergarten soundbite. Mr Major is creating a vigorous secondary market in soundbite derivatives: soundbites attacking other people's use of soundbites. He sat down to an enormous cheer.

14.11.96   # Such Lovely Feet

Betty Boothroyd has beautiful feet. I can reveal this, having spent a fascinating half-hour studying her right foot.

In two centuries of *The Times*'s publication, no description of a Speaker's foot has ever appeared in this newspaper. Probably no Press Gallery reporter has ever seen a Speaker's foot. There is no mention of it in Dicey's *The Law and the Constitution*. Extended glimpses afforded to this Sketch must be unprecedented over six centuries.

The unshoeing of Madam Speaker occurred yesterday afternoon at 3.05. But first, a word of explanation.

An unusually boring session of Questions to Education and Employment ministers was testing the patience of even the parliamentary clerks, one of whom was scratching under his wig.

Barry Sheerman (Lab, Huddersfield) was determined to be cross. Describing an answer from the junior Education Minister Eric Forth as 'pathetically inadequate', he met clucks of irritation from the government benches. 'We have to say "pathetic" all the time this afternoon,' he protested. He did not say why. The Tories were equally cross. They faced another debate on BSE in which Labour's Robin Cook was to taunt the Government with a wit which had even civil servants, in their box, trying not to giggle.

Tory ill-humour had reached its nadir when, after a fair question about education from Labour's new recruit (the former Tory Alan Howarth), a young toff called Henry Bellingham (C, Norfolk NW) had risen. 'If,' he sneered, 'the Hon Gentleman had had a more fulfilling education himself, he might not have experienced the mid-life crisis he had this year.'

That raised eyebrows even among Tories. Bustling hotly to her feet, Madam Speaker protested that this was hardly the sort of thing Hon Members cared to hear. Miss Boothroyd was educated at Dewsbury College of Commerce and Art. Mr Bellingham is an old Etonian. Readers may conclude that the score so far was Dewsbury 1, Eton 0.

But the strain on the Dewsbury old girl was intense. It must be hot in those tights. The gown, though becoming, is a nuisance. And the shoes (Miss Boothroyd designed them herself: black patent leather with enormous brooches) appear to pinch.

Add to that the frustration a Speaker must feel as MPs squabble away the afternoon in pointless debate, and those shoes must pinch all the harder. Miss Boothroyd had placed both feet on the little footstool before the Speaker's chair. She was restless, fidgety. Slowly, the right shoe slipped its heel from under her own and slid forward until it lay beneath her instep, her regal toes slipped loosely in, only their tips sheathed. I held my breath. Would she?

She grew bolder. Withdrawing the foot completely, she brushed the shoe from the footstool.

Now exposed, Madam Speaker's foot lay delicately on the green leather, perfectly naked beneath the television lights, hidden from the House but visible to a sketchwriter perched above.

It was a fine foot, about size 4. Some women in their middle years suffer from corns or the deformation caused by ill-fitting shoes, but not Miss Boothroyd. At Ipanema beach I have seen worse feet on women half her age. Each toe was perfect.

Your sketchwriter became quite transfixed, his vision focused downward, the rest of the chamber and its graceless company fading into no more than a rude background to this elegant foreground: Madam Speaker's footstool, Madam Speaker's foot.

24.11.96   # Going Out in Style

Kenneth Clarke's last budget.

As Kenneth Clarke spoke yesterday, uninsured whisky-tippling Scottish dukes driving gas-powered Bentleys, who roll their own cigarettes, whose pay is not profit-related, whose wives do not work and who have a pathological fear of flying, will have raised their glasses in a grateful toast to a generous Chancellor. The rest of us scratched our heads and reached for the pocket calculator.

It was a brazen and stylish performance, containing many good jokes and washed down with nearly half a carafe of whisky and water. It met from an unusually well-armed Tony Blair the most crackling Opposition response in recent memory.

The Budget speech was heard, as ever, by a packed chamber. Standards of exotic garb for the occasion have fallen sadly over the decades and we had to make do with the knobbly knees of Bill Walker (C, Tayside N) in a dowdy kilt.

Mr Clarke was furnished not with the glass of whisky and water a Chancellor traditionally keeps at his elbow, but with a whole carafe. At one point he began refilling his glass at the same time as explaining how he was going to eliminate fraud. Warming to his fiscal theme, the Chancellor forgot his right wrist, still pouring the whisky. He remembered in the nick of time, just as the glass brimmed to overflowing.

Up in the Strangers' Gallery, Mrs Gillian Clarke, her hair in a neat bun, looked on with the resigned despair of one whose husband is forever burning the toast.

As Clarke sat down and the cheers began, I looked up at Mrs Clarke. She had been watching like an anxious mum. As the cheering intensified she relaxed, permitting herself a small, proud smile.

Then Tony Blair rose. Moments before, Peter Mandelson had rushed in with an envelope on which was written the figure 2120. This was handed to Mr Blair. 'Two thousand one hundred and twenty pounds' worth of extra tax for the average family!' declared the Labour Leader, minutes later, with his customary supreme intellectual self-confidence.

Cows Don't Know. Do MPs?   *24.1.97*

People say that you can tell whether it is going to rain by watching the cows. 'Ah, look at those cows lying down. Rain must be imminent: the cows are preparing a dry patch.' But it might just show the cows *think* it is about to rain. They may be wrong. One should not assume that because cows are *in* nature, cows understand nature.

A similar mistake is made by non-political people observing MPs. 'Ah, look at those MPs down there: they are behaving as though there was about to be a general election. It must be imminent.' They think that because MPs are *in* politics, MPs understand politics.

Not so. Most MPs have no idea what is going on. So to report that MPs at Prime Minister's Questions yesterday were behaving as though a general election were imminent does not mean it is. It means MPs *think* it is. They may be wrong.

They were.

Grimsby or Bust for Bum Watcher

4.2.97

A boil on the bum of the millennium. This was the description offered by Austin Mitchell (Lab, Great Grimsby) of the Millennium Dome planned for Greenwich. It contributed little to the millennium debate, but did settle what has been for years an undecided question at Westminster. Is 'bum' a parliamentary expression?

It was open to Madam Speaker yesterday to rule the term unparliamentary, and to tell Mr Mitchell to withdraw it. She did not. MPs should note that henceforward and until the dissolution of Parliament, bums are in order. It was not only Mr Mitchell's language that was exotic. He sported an enormous tie featuring colourful pictures of some of the stars of *Baywatch*, dominated by Pamela Anderson in a red swimsuit. Even in a marginal constituency like Grimsby, there should surely be limits to the lengths to which intending parliamentary candidates should go to catch the voter's eye?

The London MP, Toby Jessel (C, Twickenham) has been developing quite a line in startling arguments which nobody had thought of before, clinching the debate. Last week he disposed of the Royal Yacht controversy after a back-of-the-envelope calculation that it would cost us all less than £1 each, and £1 was really very cheap for a large yacht.

Yesterday, he confounded us with an unanswerable case for celebrating millennia in style: people were, he said, 'absolutely astonished and utterly amazed' at opposition to the plans, because 'you only get a millennium once in a thousand years'.

There was a stunned silence. MPs had not thought of this. It was all so obvious. This was our last millennium until the next one! Opposition to the cost just fell away. Shocked, himself, by the simplicity of his argument, Mr Jessel sat down.

She Won't Dance – Don't Ask Her

11.2.97

'As my noble friend well knows, it takes *two* to . . .' Baroness Chalker of Wallasey paused, tantalisingly. Could she, would she, dare she, say 'tango'? With Lady Chalker it might take two to tango, but it would take four to clear the wreckage from the dance floor. A substantial baroness in a substantial green plaid two-piece suit of car-rug design, Lady Chalker occupied a place on the government front bench in the Lords yesterday a yard from Baroness Trumpington – an older baroness built on similarly monumental lines.

Lady Chalker, Minister for Overseas Development, is known in her department as 'the African Queen' and revered among the tribes of the Great Lakes as a great white benefactress and semi-deity. Lady Trumpington, beside whom the late Margaret Rutherford appeared wimpish, is affectionately known by fellow-whips as Trumpers. Two big ladies. The thought of them tangoing with each other was distracting, the thought of either tangoing with anyone else, terrible.

'. . . to organise a cease fire.' Our faces fell. The lady was not for tangoing.

Tory Goes Soft

28.2.97

Is Michael Brown (C, Brigg & Cleethorpes) losing his bottle? Once in tune with the splendidly robust mood of today's Tory party, Mr Brown has gone all wishy-washy and sentimental. Hard-nosed Home Secretary Michael Howard heard Brown complain to the Prime Minister yesterday about 'stowaways, who have been arriving, unfortunately, dead, in small ships, at Felixstowe'. They had travelled 'in dreadful conditions. Though they *are* illegal immigrants they are arriving, as I say, dead, and something ought to be done about it.'

'Unfortunately' dead, Mr Brown? Illegal immigrants *unfortunately* dead? Get a grip on yourself, man. Have a drink with Michael Howard. He'll sort you out.

The Cyber-beasties Advance

7.3.97

It's not that Labour's arguments are stronger than the Tories'. It is more that creeping feeling that nothing is to any avail. Over tea after Prime Minister's Questions yesterday I discussed with a former sketchwriter, Andrew Rawnsley, his reverie in which Mr Major is playing a children's computer game. An army of grotesque red cyber-beasties is advancing towards the Tory player, munching their way through walls, parachuting from the air and hang-gliding from cliffs.

For the Major player there are means of counter-attack – exploding tax-bombshells, whammies, double-whammies and killer-rebuttals – but these are in limited supply. Time, too, is running out. And still the Blairite cyber-beasties advance. *Munch-munch-munch* – here they come. They are through the battlements and waiting to storm the fortress.

Munch-munch . . . the beastie onslaught went into overdrive at Prime Minister's Questions yesterday afternoon. The cyber-assailants ambushed John Major over *E.coli* and a review of hygiene in slaughterhouses. Beastie Leader, Tony Blair, let fly a string of missiles concerning documents, civil servants and recommendations. Whether there was anything in these missiles was unclear, but Mr Blair munched his way forward with such confidence that the effect was to beleaguer the Prime Minister.

John Major appears to have become a Buddhist. In recent days he has faced attack with a Zen-like detachment, reciting his responses in a kind of trance, relaxed as you please. It would not have been out of place if someone were to have lit a joss-stick, or tinkled a little bell, in the breaks during his increasingly prolix replies. By the end of Prime Minister's Questions, Major's nerve remained steady, but the cyber-beasties and their Leader were swarming closer.

Back on His Box

18.3.97

Major's final débâcle begins.

After tea with the Queen it must have made quite a contrast. In Luton town centre yesterday John Major pitched himself into a walkabout which teetered perilously close to mayhem as a band of hardcore Militant-style mobsters teamed up with the usual spotty student-demo brigade – 'grants suck' – to offer the Prime Minister and the electorate a nostalgic reminder of the way we were 18 years ago. 'How much did Major pay these people?' I heard a BBC reporter asking colleagues.

There was something sweetly amateurish about the whole thing. To the trilling of a mobile phone and the heckles of beer-swilling English youths, an 18th-century kind of electioneering met a 20th-century election, perhaps our last.

As news of Mr Major's swoop on Middle England spread, more than a thousand had gathered. Leaping from his green Jaguar near a shop called Going Places, the Prime Minister was quickly engulfed in an extraordinary scratch-team of Tory ladies, gamely cheering 'Hurrah!', thin-faced yobs with shoulder bags, a posse from the Referendum Party – elderly women with sour lips – and a gathering mass of inquisitive shoppers.

Mr Major did what he always does in moments of tension. He started patting people. After a few introductory pats he stormed into a bank, inspected the cash machine and a share shop, and re-emerged, patting left and right.

This was 1990s Britain indeed. Along the first floor of the Woolwich, counter clerks gawped as Mr Major plunged past a baked potato stall, patting.

He then pushed hastily on towards Harveys solicitors, still patting, to a scattered cry of 'Five more years' and another of 'Give oop, John'. A tiny boy shinned right up a 'no-parking' sign as the Prime Minister struggled through to a terrazzo by a Burger King.

'You're out Bright!' shouted a pair of greasy anoraks as the sitting MP, Sir Graham Bright, took the microphone and declared 'Luton is now a prosperous town'. But the loudspeakers were faulty and most of the speech sank beneath the loyal cheers of Tory ladies and a chant of 'What do we want? More money for students!' Then the Prime Minister mounted his famous soapbox. There was a shout of 'ten more years', another of 'boring' and then a sort of hush. Mr Major began to speak. 'They won't stop the Conservative Party,' he declared.

'You're lying!' shouted a Geordie. Then he revised his heckle. 'You've got a nerve – but you're lying.' It was in some ways the most eloquent tribute of the afternoon.

Some of Mr Major's speech was audible. He looked at times rattled but always determined. As he made his way towards the waiting cars, the police appeared to lose control and he was almost pinned against the Alliance & Leicester Building Society. 'More uniforms!' barked a slightly panicky police voice into a walkie-talkie. 'Eighteen more years!' shouted one brave lady.

Behind the Prime Minister, they retrieved the wooden soapbox which, should he win this fight, will be parcelled up and auctioned in bits as holy relics for centuries to come.

At the bus stop outside the town hall, a little troupe of pensioners awaited their bus. Mr Major came, saw and patted. The crowds came. The police came. And, finally, all departed as the prime ministerial Jaguar sped off up the hill.

Previously engulfed, the bus stop came back into view. The pensioners were still there, waiting.

And Out It All Came

21.3.97

Just when you thought it was safe to return to Westminster . . .

They need to coin a new term for it. 'Mace rage', perhaps. As Parliament rises, the Prime Minister simply explodes like a bank manager driven beyond endurance. John Major flew off the handle during his final Prime Minister's Questions yesterday, lashing out in all directions. If it was less than statesmanlike; it was more than lively; it was awesome.

Major started hitting people almost before anyone had uttered. He took a swipe at Dennis Skinner, challenging him to quit. He landed a punch on John Prescott (who had not even spoken) accusing him of being in hock to the railway unions. And he accused Paddy Ashdown of finishing the session as he had started it, awash in piety and pomposity.

But it was Tony Blair who caught the full force. Needled by the Labour leader's accusation that he was conspiring to suppress a Commons watchdog report on alleged sleaze, the Prime Minister began a bombardment which threatened to keep Parliament sitting until Sunday.

It was like one of those domestic scenes in which some small but ill-judged remark sets a spark to the blue touchpaper – and *bang*.

Everything Mr Major hates about Mr Blair came pouring out. Accused of sweeping corruption under the carpet, the Prime Minister angrily retorted that this was pretty rich, coming from a man who 'sells policy to the trade unions for cash'.

A sharp riposte. But getting it off his chest just seemed to get him going. Blair was someone who 'refuses to comply with the code of practice on party funding, who calls for party openness but won't publish the secret funds of his own office . . .'

It all came pouring out. It was as though, having been the butt of personal remarks for more than two years of Tony Blair's opposition leadership, and having, night after night, lain in bed repeating and repeating, *sotto voce*, all the things he *might* have replied but had always thought better of before, he now let fly.

On and on he went: '. . . who attacks share options but takes money from millionaires for his own party; and attacks businessmen; and asks them to fund things for him; who flew Concorde and failed to declare it . . .'

Was there no end to this?

'. . . who has a Deputy Leader [John Prescott] who spends a weekend at a five-star hotel and doesn't declare it and who flies to the other side of the world to do newspaper deals and never admits to them . . .'

Finally, shortage of breath, if not material, brought his tirade to an end. But not before one last outburst: 'If there's any double standards, they sit *there*, on the opposition benches!' he yelled. The Prime Minister sat down to perhaps the loudest Tory cheers he has received all this session. Minutes later, he left to renewed cheers, as many government backbenchers stood in the aisles, waving their order papers.

Edwina's Last Stand

8.4.97

The 1997 general election begins.

The shock on Edwina Currie's face was apparent in the butcher's, but she said not a word. Mrs Currie was at the Allenton shopping centre outside Derby. Between her and the butcher lay a counter of raw and cooked meats, side by side.

A former Health Minister needed no reminding what had caused the

E.coli outbreak in Scotland, but this was no time to make enemies: the Tory candidate for South Derbyshire is facing an uphill battle in a constituency to which unhelpful new bits have been added.

This shopping centre was one of those bits and her mission was to conquer. Outside, a busy ring-road set in rows of thirties semis with the occasional monkey puzzle tree could almost have been Hendon – until you saw the load of hay passing by. A mixed-up, scrappy place, South Derbyshire – not really a place at all. Just like middle England. Cat flap country.

With her was the Tory candidate for Derby South, Javed Arain. A Jewish lady towing an Asian gentleman behind her. He was ambitious but nervous: a learner driver out for a practice spin with a grand prix champion. Mr Arain bumped into an old trade union official. Mrs Currie tut-tutted. 'One of the things I've got to teach Javed,' said our Damon Hill of the political circuit, 'is that you don't argue with Labour voters.'

Rumours of her visit had not reached the Pearts bakery when I arrived. Was she around? I asked.

'No. I think we'd know,' replied the shop assistant. 'She usually has gateaux.' Moments later Mrs Currie sailed in, in pale lilac.

'You do look nice,' said the assistant, as groupies crowded round. One small terrified lady customer with a Kwiksave bag tried to extract 12 white baps from the maelstrom. Mrs Currie cornered a lad in a Nottingham Refrigeration boiler suit. 'Are you one of mine?'

'No. We've come to fix the fridge.'

'Where are you from?' she said to a man in the Autoparts Superstore. 'Pentagon Vauxhall,' he said.

'Where do *you* live?' she said to a startled lady with wet hair, pinned over the basin in a hairdresser's. She couldn't speak.

'You're mine, aren't you?' she chirped at an old fellow in Blades barbers, a hairclipper poised inches from his left ear. He mumbled.

'Sitting there like captives,' she chuckled to us outside, 'Ha!'

Next, the lilac tornado hit Green's Footwear. By now we were getting the hang of her technique. Here were people with one shoe off, who could not run. But she saw a sign 'Sunbeds upstairs' and stormed up to interrogate a bewildered youth, waiting for his tanning girlfriend.

'I don't vote,' he stammered.

'You should. Where are you from?'

'Belper.'

Belper is not in Mrs Currie's constituency. She swung away to confront a woman just emerged, flushed pink, from a stripped pine cubicle. Whatever it was this woman had expected to see after her brief exposure to the ultra-violet, it was not a lilac Mrs Currie. She looked frightened and disorientated. 'Where are you from?'

Then off Mrs Currie went down the pavement, Javed struggling to keep up.

Everyone recognised her. Most people liked her. Many seemed quite excited to meet her. But some stubbornly refused to vote for her.

'I met this woman,' one of her supporters told me, 'who, when I asked her if she'd vote Conservative, said "No, I don't hold with all these political parties. I'm voting for that Mrs Currie off the telly".'

The anecdote was recounted as being encouraging to South Derbyshire Tories, and in a way it is. But things have come to quite a pass when a struggling candidate takes comfort from the fact that voters may forget she's a Tory.

'Who's that?' a little girl asked her grandad outside the Rose and Crown in Chellaston, whither Edwina Currie had repaired for a Diet Coke. 'That's our MP,' he said, proudly. 'Edwina Hotpot.' He posed for a photograph with her.

Hurricane Hughes Hits Hospital   *11.4.97*

Half propped-up on her pillows in the Cotton Ward of the Royal London Hospital at Whitechapel, Florence Warden lay with her head slumped forward. Was she conscious? It was hard to tell.

Sitting by her bed, a thin, middle-aged man with a tattoo on his arm held her hand. Silent, motionless and blank with worry, he stared into space. Neither knew – neither would have cared – that Simon Hughes, the Liberal Democrat health spokesman and candidate for Southwark North & Bermondsey, was on his way.

Unusually, Mr Hughes is not so enveloped in the self-importance a politician carries with him as to forget the world he is in. His entourage entered Cotton Ward like a tropical cyclone. But at the eye of the cyclone – Mr Hughes himself – was a calm and kindness which, even in the few minutes he spent with each patient, communicated itself.

Politicians and hospitals hardly mix. The scene teetered between tragedy and farce as Mr Hughes knelt before an old chap with respiratory problems, wheezing through a high-tech elephant mask. Mr Hughes, in smart Commons suit but afforded, now, the captive audience that the Commons has never granted him, made a short speech on the evils of smoking. The old boy in blue pyjamas was in no position to argue. Mr Hughes wheeled round to Professor Robert Davies, who was accompanying us. 'Well, will there be a cure for asthma?' He stopped short of adding, 'Yes or No?' The professor looked taken aback.

'Hello my dear!' called Mr Hughes gaily as he passed women in various states of insensibility or distress. 'Now, what seems to be the problem?' he said, approaching the bed of Betty Weemes, lying provocatively across one pillow.

'The winders need cleanin,' said Mrs Weemes, who had donned earrings for the occasion and looked rather smart. Alice Peeke, lying in the next bed, waved.

Mr Hughes had put them at their ease. He then attempted a serious talk with them about the structure and funding of the NHS. By now his aide was getting impatient. 'Come on Simon,' he implored, with a weariness born of long practice, but Hurricane Simon could not leave without talking to all the patients he had left out. As we moved down the corridor, we realised we had lost him again. 'He's popped into another ward to hug everybody,' said an experienced Hughes-watcher.

We hurried past an Accident and Emergency room where a fellow, blood pouring from one eye and his shirt soaked, scarcely moved his head as the hurricane passed.

There are moments during political campaigns when the backdrop looks like precisely that: pictures – harrowing, exotic or bizarre – projected as arresting scenery before which the candidates strike a pose, wait for the camera-flash, then pass on. In the campaigns of the next century it may prove unnecessary for politicians to leave their party HQs. Fishing, farming, shopping or hospital images will be recreated around them by hologram. But every now and again, Mr Hughes spoilt the perfect artificiality of the occasion by getting genuinely stuck into a human problem which had brushed his elbow.

He became caught up in an inquiry as to what had started a fire in which a mother of two children had been burnt. Unlikely to solve this, Mr Hughes was finally pulled away, begging the children to look after their mum.

Hurricane Simon hit the 'air-ambulance' helipad. The chopper was summoned as we watched. As men in orange boiler-suits leapt into the roaring, LibDem-yellow machine, which took to the skies in a rush of wind, you could see the envy in his eyes. Why, with this machine he could descend from above in a big noise, dispensing mercy and Liberal Democracy.

The visit over, politicians, aides, reporters and photographers left the hospital. Up in the Cotton Ward, the man with the tattoo was still holding Florence's hand: still silent, still motionless, still blank with worry. Her head was still bowed.

For Simon Hughes another hospital, another election, another whirlwind tour. For Florence Warden, the strangest of dreams.

Maggie Runs Out of Credit   *19.4.97*

For the Baroness Thatcher, another Friday, another walkabout. For Shirley Taylor, Tesco till-operator, a nightmare. Lady Thatcher had no cheque guarantee card.

All had gone so swimmingly well. It was British Week at Tesco's in Maldon, Essex, and Union Jacks decorated the merchandise. The baroness, in stunning blue with a gold English rose brooch, swept in from her blue Daimler. She looked a million dollars. Senior staff stood in line, as if for inspection. Several Tory women swooned, one so excited that her knees gave way.

The former Prime Minister surveyed the huge store. 'It makes shopping so much easier,' she breathed. Her hair was perfect. 'How *are* you dear?' she gushed to randomly selected cheese operatives and shelf-packers. 'One does have to be careful one doesn't spend too much,' she confided in a female fan. 'I named my Dobermann Margaret, after her,' the fan later told me.

A shopper asked, nervously: 'You are going to support Mr Major, aren't you, Lady Thatcher?'

'Of course, dear.' And she began to shop. After a nasty brush with a French apple at the fresh produce counter, her eye lighted on a massive carrot. '*British* carrots?' she inquired, with bayonet glance. 'From Norfolk, Lady Thatcher.' Phew.

'Is Friday your busy day?' she demanded of a dumbstruck young member of Tesco's staff called Gareth. 'No, I expect it's Saturday.'

'Good thing I'm here on Friday, then.' Gareth was quite overcome.

Pausing for a terrifying instant by the Danish Speckle Bread, she plunged on towards the Selected Crusty White. Bakery staff hovered. 'In my day,' she told them, 'bread grew hard on the shelf.'

Lady Thatcher was hitting her stride. She had bought an orange and two lemons and made for the cheese and pâté counter. Eyeing the full fat soft French brie as though the cat had just been sick, she lighted on the England's Choice selection, and selected. A journalist recommended the Brussels Pâté. 'I can't stand garlic,' she snorted, and selected a chicken, mushroom and white wine cream pâté – British.

We made for the beef. 'I bought this,' she declared, brandishing a bloody piece of Scottish rump, 'because it's £1.50 off.' A tub of Tesco's own-brand strawberry yoghurt was chosen. Cress and Essex lettuce were tossed into the basket. Battered cod was rejected in favour of Tesco's own-brand British bacon, as the baroness made for the checkout counter, to ripples of applause and admiration.

Lady Thatcher took this as a call for an encore. Breaking from her arranged plan, she decided to do a reprise shop: a quick twirl through the fruit and vegetables again for tomatoes and conference pears. Then she was headed off by the soft toiletries and diverted to counter 19.

Ah, fateful day for Shirley Taylor! Looking only slightly tense, the operative at counter 19 did everything right. Each purchase was rung on the till, and Shirley remembered to offer her Special Customer a Tesco Clubcard, which the baroness, unconvinced, signed and popped into her handbag. Then she took out her Midland chequebook. The till said £21.44, a sum Shirley Taylor will never forget.

'And your cheque guarantee card?' she asked the baroness pleasantly.

Lady Thatcher looked blank. Panic entered the eyes of her staff. Lady Thatcher, suddenly shaky, offered Shirley the Clubcard she had just been given.

'No, a cheque guarantee card,' said Shirley, firmly but politely. 'It's an awful nuisance, but it's the rules. I can't put it through without it.' Disbelieve me if you like, but it looked as though Lady Thatcher did not know what a cheque guarantee card was. Plastic has not entered this baroness's life. A minder said, desperately, to Shirley, 'I promise you there won't be any problems,' but Shirley knew the rules.

'Well, I'll have to go round putting everything back,' said Lady Thatcher. Tesco executives groaned inwardly. Then, recovering herself, and in Lady Bracknell tones, the baroness declared: 'Something will have to be done!'

But what? Ah, cash! She opened a purse. It contained £25 and no cards. Shirley Taylor's relief was palpable. Panic over. They presented Lady Thatcher with flowers. She presented her shopping to a minder, and swept away, to applause.

Tony Walks on Water – Diane Docks

24.4.97

Labour minders had hidden Diane Abbott from the press after she sneered, 'Tony walks on water'.

'Diane Abbott? She will be here tomorrow, but we don't know exactly where.'

I had difficulty in tracking down the Hackney North & Stoke Newington Constituency Labour Party, who are not in the phone book, and now it seemed that they had difficulty tracking down their candidate.

They promised to ring back. They never did. So I rang them again yesterday morning. 'Her schedule does not allow anyone into her constituency today,' they said, then hung up. So I asked *The Times* to ring. 'She is not in the constituency, but may be later,' the enquirer was told.

So I turned up at the door of her Stoke Newington office yesterday morning. Two party workers behind the counter looked sheepish. They paused. I thought I saw someone move behind a screen. 'Yes, she's here,' one worker said, hesitantly.

Diane Abbott stepped forward.

I should explain that she and I are on good terms and she cannot have regarded me as hostile. She is known for her forthright left-wing views and occasional eccentricity ('I don't even know Tony Blair; never had a conversation with him,' she said last year) but I am less likely than most to mock. She looked deeply embarrassed. 'Sorry,' she said, 'you can't write about me today. I am off to help Alan Simpson, the Labour candidate in Nottingham South.'

Could *The Times* photographer take a picture of us? 'Sorry, no photographs.'

This was becoming unreal. I phoned Mr Simpson's office. 'No, she is not coming here today. She's arriving tomorrow on the 11.45 train.'

I do not see myself as a doorstepping journalist or wish to become a nuisance, least of all to Miss Abbott, whom I used to respect. But now the photographer and I had the bit between our teeth so, after checking there was no other exit, he stood opposite the door to the Labour offices and waited. I tucked myself away with a mobile phone. An hour later he was still waiting.

I could see her behind the counter. 'She came to a Charter 88 meeting,' a Liberal Democrat told me, 'but when we asked her views, she said, "All I have to say is that Tony Blair walks on water."'

Four hours later, she was still hiding. They sent out an Abbott-lookalike decoy who hopped into a minicab, but we were not fooled. They sent a spy to the pub where I had started writing this, but I hid. Soon I must go home. The photographer is still there. So is she. And Tony Blair walks on water.

1.5.97

Journey's End

Eve of poll.

'Never say die' would have conceded too much – that he knew everything was slipping away. Unspoken, it was John Major's quote for this concluding day.

'You've had it, haven't you!' said a journalist, with all the delicacy of a television professional to the Prime Minister.

'No.'

But the fizz was gone. We had started yesterday milling around in Smith Square where the Prime Minister was preparing for the final press conference of his campaign.

'If you can keep your head when all around you . . .' Lesser spirits would have been lowered, but if his were low, he barely let it show. Chin up, calmly defiant, with a brave smile and a friendly word for those he met, Mr Major threw himself into one last dispiriting day's campaigning as though there was everything still to play for. 'You've got to admire him,' was a phrase on the lips even of hardened journalists.

The first question at the press conference came from ITN's Michael Brunson. Had Mr Major read an article written by his older sister: 'I hate seeing my little brother looking so tired and knowing it's his own side that have done this to him.' Everyone laughed because we knew it was true. Mr Major's grin said one thing – and his voice another, he praised his MPs for their support. Anyway (he said to Mr Brunson), 'have *you* got a big sister?'

Determinedly undownhearted, he even pretended to take seriously a question on the composition of his next Cabinet. That this press conference could change nothing, rendered all the more noteworthy the poise, civility and good grace with which the Prime Minister conducted it. He did so with real stature, and with class.

Neither had deserted Mr Major by the time he reached Wembley Stadium for a tour of an exhibition there, before the World Cup qualifying match to be played last night. One of the stands was giving away free miniature bouncy footballs and Britain's Prime Minister arrived to find a crowd of political journalists bouncing tiny black-and-white balls off the floor, a memorably surreal moment from an often surreal election campaign. With Norma by his side ('Come on, Normie,' he called), he plunged into the crowd, smiling and shaking hands.

Near me was a stall promoting football for FA Cup followers with learning disabilities. Mr Major entered the stall, chatted, inquired and expressed surprise and admiration at their efforts ('just fantastic!') before moving on. One can observe, without belittling the importance of such efforts, that this must have been very difficult for a man at the end of his premiership and on the brink of defeat to do. 'Nice bloke,' I heard someone say, *sotto voce*.

They handed him a football. 'Go on! Lift it up!' the photographers and TV cameramen began to yell. Mr Major declined. 'It's your last day, for heaven's sake!' shouted someone. Mr Major smiled. As he smiled (I was now quite close) I noticed for the first time that he was absolutely exhausted.

'A message for London voters Prime Minister?' called a journalist. Mr Major paused, shut his eyes and shook his head, chin dropped, with a momentarily exasperated smile that said 'Oh, sod it.'

Sure You've Switched Off?

The new Commons assembles.

As MPs crowded into the Chamber, the first rogue mobile phone went off. A portent of things to come? It was billed as the Election of the Speaker, but there was no election. It felt more like a Happy Ending, with a surprise last-minute appearance of a spectre at the feast. Another portent?

MPs gathered early for the ceremony. The spectacle seemed unreal. All the wrong faces in all the wrong places – and hundreds of the faces airbrushed from the scene. From a little bunker between the Government and the Opposition side, white-suited Martin Bell peered out, waiting for the shelling.

Has the chamber ever been so packed? On the Government side, new MPs crowded the doors and overflowed into the galleries upstairs. And what a sight the Labour benches made! Scores more women than have been seen there before gave an aspect almost of fiesta – many dressing in the tutti-frutti colours of Labour's election-poster campaign. Where Ted Heath brooded for 18 years, Dennis Skinner now occupied the front bench below the gangway. Those behind looked too young to be MPs.

One sat with Tony Benn. Had Peter Mandelson not warned him not to talk to strange men? Ben Bradshaw, victor of a battle in Exeter with a Tory who dubbed him 'bent Ben', kept a precautionary arm around Gwyneth Dunwoody (Crewe & Nantwich).

On the Opposition side, gingerly testing their new benches, sat the remnants of Margaret Thatcher's once-proud parliamentary army. Virginia Bottomley, equally reckless in choice of companion, sat beside Alan Clark.

When Tony Blair arrived the government benches began to clap – there being as yet no Speaker to admonish them for this unparliamentary display. As John Major approached an empty front bench, a whip moved quickly to his side, for company. But who was this at the clerks' table below the Chair? The Father of the House, Sir Edward Heath, in morning suit, was there to preside in the absence of a Speaker. He looked like a vast black beetle. The beetle called Mrs Dunwoody to propose a Speaker. In royal blue, Betty Boothroyd sat serenely among the Government, as though unaware how short her stay was to be.

Mrs Dunwoody (feisty, right-wing old Labour) made a fine, funny, moving speech without notes. The veteran John MacGregor (C, Norfolk S) seconded her. Next, Miss Boothroyd was to indicate her gracious acceptance of the Chair.

Then Tony Benn (Chesterfield) rose. Sir Edward looked startled, John Prescott scowled. The Prime Minister's grin froze. Not (he announced) 'since August 1, 1951' had he spoken from the government backbenches. Then a Labour government had controlled the destinies of hundreds of millions of colonial subjects abroad. 'We even controlled the Bank of England.' Prescott's scowl deepened. Benn reminded his new colleagues that 'believe it or not, we are free men and women'. Prescott's face was thunder.

Accepting the honour, Madam Speaker recalled the Maastricht Bill, which 'had to be debated in this Chamber, as it was a constitutional issue'. There was, as she intended, a gasp. The government are toying with the idea of removing their constitutional debates from the floor of the House.

Mr Blair spoke lightly, and well. Mr Major spoke with poise and good humour. But into a sunny afternoon at Westminster Mr Benn and Miss Boothroyd had cast two small shadows. Perhaps this Parliament will amount to more than a collection of mobile phones.

It didn't.

Such Joy! So Much Hairspray!   *8.5.97*

So many purple suits! So much hairspray! The mood teetered between a fashionable charity premiere of a star-studded new show and the headmaster's First Day address to new boys and girls.

Or should we say new girls and boys? The pastel and primary colours of the hundred-odd women present turned their male counterparts into backdrop.

'You are all ambassadors!' declared Tony Blair. Four hundred eager faces, gathered for this first prime ministerial address to the new Labour MPs, looked up in rapture. *All* ambassadors? Not in their wildest dreams had they thought Cabinet patronage extended this far.

The occasion was staged at Church House whose circular hall

permits journalists to peer over the rim, as into a goldfish bowl. In the bowl, 400 new MPs had milled around, waiting. Cries of 'darling!', 'well *done*!' and 'I just can't *believe* it!' surfaced through the hubbub. Grunts and snuffles of a thousand little hugs and *mwah! mwah!* kisses rose ceilingwards.

Somewhat removed from all this, Tony Benn sat near the back, sucking his cheeks. Dennis Skinner strode in, a man unchanged. In the same jacket, the same tie and the same jaundiced expression he always wears, Skinner looked adrift: a castaway on a sea of bright eyes, expensive haircuts, southern accents and soft suiting.

He marched up to the new Cabinet. He began shaking their hands. Had the Beast of Bolsover been tamed?

He had not. Skinner sat down in the seat kept empty for the Chancellor and stayed there, beaming. Everyone looked embarrassed. Jack Straw looked terrified. A hatchet-faced apparatchik herded him away to an outer circle, not far from Barbara Follett, power-dressed creator of New Labour Woman. The irony was delicious.

Peter Mandelson, Minister without Portfolio (did ever so vacant a title belie so occupied a plot?) ambled palely down the aisle. When Mr Mandelson appears, something is about to happen. It was. John Prescott was about to happen. Unable to suppress glee, the Deputy Prime Minister belted out his curtain-raiser for the Real Thing. 'I don't want to say some of the surprising constituencies we won in!' roared the great butcher of Tory Government, and English prose.

The doors opened and in strode the Prime Minister, to roars of applause. Two door-keepers must have been ready behind the doors, one assigned to each, to open both in a synchronised movement.

Blair looked relaxed. He stared around the hall. What a spectacle! The scene resembled a high-school dance. Most of the girls sat together in clumps. The boys laughed extra loud, to show how confident they were. The Prime Minister spoke like a headmaster exhorting new pupils to uphold the highest standards – and never to eat on buses, in uniform.

Around the ceiling a huge, devotional frieze proclaimed in gold leaf 'Holy is the true light and passing wonderful, lending radiance to them that endured in the heat of conflict . . .' His conflict over, Mr Blair looked radiant. The Parliamentary Labour Party looked passing wonderful. I glanced around Church House. '. . . wherein they rejoice with gladness, evermore.'

No mistaking the gladness and rejoicing. Evermore? Time will tell.

Dances With Wolves

Count Dracula, hearing wolves howl, remarked 'Listen to the creatures of the night. What music they make!' To witness Donald Dewar and Michael Howard – dark and unsmiling – circling each other with bared teeth and duelling with stealth and eloquence, was to experience in all its mystery the noise of the creatures of the night.

Is there a subliminal message behind the pronunciation Miss Boothroyd has adopted for the Scottish Secretary's name? Yesterday she called him 'Mr Dour'. Truly there is nobody more dour on the Labour front bench. Tall, stooped, hand-wringing, gloomy of countenance and mordant of wit, Donald Dewar contrives a blend of anxiety and solemnity, like a funeral director on the verge of bankruptcy.

In his sombre way he also possesses an acid brilliance as a Commons speaker. Yesterday the Scottish Secretary offered a display of his mastery at the dispatch box, in combat with the Tory leadership contender, Michael Howard. There is, as has been observed, something of the night about Mr Howard.

This, then, was a minuet of ghouls. The spat was important for both. Dewar's referendums on devolution depend on the 'guillotine' motion he moved. Howard's prospects depend on his performance in the days left before his party's leadership contest: he was auditioning for Leader of the Opposition.

Donald Dewar's spoken English is a pleasure to encounter and must be a joy for *Hansard* writers to take down. Without notes he delivers the polished construction that would be other people's third drafts.

To write, in measured prose, 'there has been an organised attempt – perfectly legitimately undertaken but equally legitimately met – to obstruct . . .' might not be exceptional. But to *talk* like that off the cuff, as Dewar did, impresses.

Ready on the front bench, Michael Howard does not sit, he crouches, waiting to spring. His text was carefully drafted and neatly typed. Comparing the Prime Minister to the young Robespierre ('who also had a fondness for the guillotine') he accused the Government of 'contempt for decency, for debate, for Parliament itself'. Mr Howard speaks silkily and with great poise, but there is something in the catlike pleasure he takes in debate that even in moments of tension and anger hints at the game. Mr Howard's speech was immaculate in everything but its ability to convince us that he would not, himself, try the same tricks as those of which he was accusing Labour.

Dewar went on to become Scotland's First Minister, then died suddenly.

22.5.97 **Enter the First Poodles**

Boring. That was the verdict after the new, improved, extra-length, super-constructive Prime Minister's Questions, unveiled amidst much excitement yesterday. Within days, Tony Blair has experienced a sensation it took Margaret Thatcher years to organise: scores of little wet backbench tongues caressing the prime ministerial boot; a sea of moist, adoring eyes around him; and the sound of orchestrated panting from those desirous of office.

Reporters' pencils dropped on to empty notepads. Tories stared at the rafters. Even Labour backbenchers yawned. One Liberal Democrat left almost before his leader had finished speaking, *two* questions from Paddy Ashdown being more than he could bear. In short, Tony Blair's reform was a complete success for him. Interest leaked away from the session as fast as water from Thames Water's pipes.

The new Prime Minister managed his first 30-minute interrogation with ease. Mr Blair was not so much grilled as gently burnished over a warm flame, as with a marshmallow. Claims that the reforms to PM's Questions will offer an opportunity for holding the Premier to account, came to nothing. Instead, a troupe of backbench poodles came prancing in, on cue, with an array of patsy questions, choreographed by whips.

Labour poodles are not the same as Tory poodles. Tories would ask their Prime Minister to remind us how dreadful the Opposition were. Labour backbenchers ask Mr Blair to remind us how wonderful he is. Thus, yesterday, Jean Corston (Lab, Bristol E) asked the Prime Minister to tell us of his determination to prevent crime. Stephen Twigg (Lab, Enfield Southgate) begged him to expand on his plans to create a 'Drugs Czar'. Lorna Fitzsimons (Lab, Rochdale) longed for good news about crackdowns on antisocial behaviour. All were rewarded with a biscuit.

Eric Illsley (Barnsley Central) requested (and – abracadabra! –

received) a mini-announcement on plans to restrict landmines. And Stuart Bell (Lab, Middlesbrough) told his Leader that his conduct had been so splendid that all we could ask was what Mr Blair might do for an encore?

By now Mr Blair's boot had been licked until soggy. But Maria Fyfe (Lab, Glasgow Maryhill) was anxious for a lick, too.

Ms Fyfe's voice reaches a pitch audible only to bats, but some words of her question did dip to human frequency. They included 'congratulate', 'My Rt Hon Friend the Prime Minister' and 'new questions session'.

And still the extended tongues dangled, hopeful. But it was 3.30. In half an hour Mr Blair had had time to be told how marvellous he was almost a dozen times. No wonder he prefers these new, longer sessions!

New Labour – Old Routine   *15.5.97*

Labour's first Queen's Speech.

New Britain? Pull the other. The same Queen in the same old House of Lords went through the same old rituals. In the Commons, two Labour backbenchers attacked the Labour front bench, and attacked each other. So what was new? John Major then attacked the Labour Party. So what was new?

Tony Blair attacked 'the Government'. So what was new? Paddy Ashdown called Mr Major 'the Prime Minister', attacked both sides and promised to be constructive. So what was new?

Then John Redwood made another bid for the leadership of his party. So what was new?

One thing, at least, was new: the MPs. Gentlemen readers of *The Times* will be familiar with the sensation of male awkwardness as one walks into a ladies' hairdressing salon. One feels like an imposter. Sprays and lotions scent the room . . .

An air of expectancy fell upon the assembly as Black Rod approached. If he hammered on the door, we did not hear it. Marching up, he declared 'The Queen commands that Honourable Members . . .'

'*Requests*' came the correction of an unidentified republican voice on the Labour side.

' . . . *commands* that Honourable Members . . .' continued Black Rod. '*Requests!*' insisted the republican '. . . to attend Her Majesty in the House of Peers.' 'They ought ter borrer a few seats,' growled Skinner.

After lunch, the debate on the Queen's speech began, Peter Mandelson crouching on the step at the Speaker's feet like a hired hitman awaiting instructions. He grinned wickedly when Gerald Kaufman (Lab, Manchester, Gorton), moving the motion as by custom a senior government backbencher should, declared himself 'a total sycophant' to Tony Blair. 'In Mr Mandelson's opinion,' added the mordant Kaufman, 'total sycophancy must be regarded as a suspiciously lukewarm form of support.'

Kaufman's was a brilliant speech. He gently mocked his own leader, then mocked the 'old' Labour manifesto of 1983, and brought laughter to both sides when he referred to 'those increasingly far-off days when Finchley was a Conservative constituency.'

It was safe to laugh at this last joke. But we noted the doubtful expression on many new Labour faces at Kaufman's jokes about his own side. Were they allowed to laugh? Would Mr Mandelson punish them?

A right-winger, Kaufman was followed by left-winger Chris Mullin (Lab, Sunderland S). His mention of socialism ('the word didn't do me any harm') and his witty, biting attacks on *The Sun* provoked the same unsure looks on young colleagues' faces.

John Major seemed unchanged. He spoke with poise and good humour. But when he began the attack on the new Government's polices, we saw the wisdom of his decision not to delay his departure. The speech was cogent, but MPs' attention wandered. Why listen? What was the *next* leader's line? This was what interested them.

In reply, Tony Blair kept forgetting he was Prime Minister. He attacked the Government's record on health, education and employment. For just a little longer, perhaps, he can do this. 'Enjoy it,' one thought, 'while you may.'

The Parties Go On

The Tories begin the election of a new leader.

'This means more parties, that's the important thing,' gurgled an excited Tory MP, Peter Luff (Mid-Worcestershire), passing the journalistic pack outside Committee Room.

Five parties the night before had not been enough for him.

For just an instant after the result was announced there had been complete silence. Then uproar. Mobile phones and bleepers joined an atonal crescendo as reporters scrambled for interviews with MPs, candidates, and each other. 'What does this mean?' was the question on everyone's lips. Nobody knew, of course.

The tension had been gripping. Twenty minutes after the last vote was in, still no signal had come from the committee room, its oak door slammed shut.

What was the delay? 'How long does it take a Tory MP to count to 164' became the joke of the hour.

For journalists this had been a long day, the champagne brought by Michael Colvin MP being to revive scrutineers only.

First among the candidates to vote had been Peter Lilley and John Redwood, their arrival coinciding unfortunately with the declaration of constituency results by Sir Archie Hamilton, chairman of the backbench 1922 Committee, showing both men near the bottom of the heap. Smiles froze, teeth clenched and spinners spun.

Peter Lilley looked (in Noel Coward's description of a much-facelifted actress), 'a very *old* thirteen.' John Redwood, who does not age as humans do, looked wired. At 10.53 William Hague arrived, looking svelte. Then came Michael Howard, looking *soigné*. Finally Kenneth Clarke bowled along, looking fat.

There had been (according to those within) a flurry of Tory MPs 'showing' voting slips as they voted. No Tory completely trusts another. 'Even if I had voted for someone else I wouldn't tell you,' said Geoffrey Clinton-Brown, one of Kenneth Clarke's campaign team, delphically. Emerging from the room just before the ballot closed, one MP was asked how he had voted. 'I'll tell you in 15 minutes,' he replied. Sir Edward Heath sailed up the corridor just in time. 'I was the first Leader to come through by vote,' he said. 'Of course there was none of this nonsense we've had for the last six weeks. *We* didn't take anyone out for drinks or lunch.'

Nobody was rude enough to suggest a reason why Sir Edward's campaign managers might have steered him away from this tactic. If the aim were to win a chap over, taking him out for a drink or lunch might backfire for Sir Edward.

19.6.97   # Maggie's Blessing

William Hague finds a big backer.

'Now *have* you got that? *Hague.* Would you like to hear the name again? William *Hague.*'

She stood at the St Stephen's entrance to the Commons, the only non-royal woman in Britain whom it is unnecessary to name: it is sufficient to mention the blue suit, the coiffure and the handbag.

'Move to your left, Lady Thatcher!' Alarm melted as she recognised this as a camera-call, not a political instruction. Beside her stood a colleague with blonder hair but less of it, and no handbag.

'Move a little closer to him, Lady Thatcher!' For a woman who had moved within days from spurning William Hague's leadership campaign to joining it, she had moved far and fast enough already. Wisps of Mr Hague's remaining hair were lifted by a mischievous breeze: a fleeting impression of moulting cockatoo.

They stood there together for five minutes – mostly in silence – as cameras snapped and crowds pressed the barriers. MPs supporting Hague stood near by, unnoticed. All eyes were on her. She persists as a living symbol: a portable totem, no longer required to speak, her presence alone conferring ideological benediction.

Tories used to say Margaret Thatcher kept the Ark of the Covenant. These days, she *is* the Ark of the Covenant. The Ark sailed off to the Commons tea room.

But Mr Hague wanted us to know she was his. At a rally beforehand at the Atrium restaurant, a journalist asked him why she had been won so late to his charms. Hague looked indignant. 'Lady Thatcher has known me for *twenty years*,' he complained. 'Her statement today is a warm endorsement of me.' Norman Lamont peeped, badger-like from the foliage of a false fig tree.

Another tormentor quoted Teresa Gorman: 'Nice boy but not a big hitter.'

'I *am* a big hitter,' protested young William, his voice, mercifully, not breaking on the '*am*'. 'Ken is a big hitter. I'm a big hitter, too.'

'I have the broadest base!' he declared. We called to mind Kenneth Clarke's base and wondered.

These occasions are undignified, but Hague showed poise and humour. He mocked the unusual marriage of Kenneth Clarke and John Redwood, without personal spite.

He had arrived to a shaky start, hovering at the door with Michael Howard, then thinking better of it and making his entrance later. Just like old times.

The Atrium was packed. At the door lounged a muscular hunk in shorts – neither a bouncer nor a skeleton in any of the campaign teams' closets, but a fascinated member of the nearby gym.

Around the door waited a cluster of young Haguesters. This is a new politico-social grouping, a sub-Blairite phenomenon of which we may be seeing more.

They are under 25, exceptionally fresh and clean, with bright eyes and soft, manageable hair. They might seek employment as models for deodorant or hair-conditioning products. They do not (as the young Thatcherites did) look mad; but vulnerable. They blush easily.

Mr Hague's lectern read 'the Natural Coalition' while his backdrop was adorned with posters saying 'Fresh Start'. An impression grew that we were attending the launch of a facial scrub. Archie Norman MP, the young whiz-kid who rescued Asda, strode on in shirtsleeves and declared 'Hague! The man who can and will.' The Haguesters whooped.

Can and will what? Echoing through the Atrium came the Haguesters' musical choice: the haunting theme tune from *1492 – Conquest of Paradise*. The music was stirring.

But Christopher Columbus never got to where he meant to go. He got somewhere, but it didn't turn out to be what he thought, at all.

Are You William the Conqueror?

20.6.97

What were you doing at the moment William Hague was elected Tory leader? Lobby correspondents, already drained by the ebbs and flows of two previous ballots and five weeks of being sleeve-tugged and lied to by Tory MPs, huddled – emotional husks – in the corridor.

Three times a hush descended on massed reporters, awaiting the result. The first two proved false alarms. What was the delay? Rumours circulated of confusion at the count in Committee Room 13. It was said that a couple of the more impressionable new Tory MPs had voted for Margaret Thatcher as leader, after her tea room visit yesterday. Another rumour was that scrutineers were unable to decide whether to credit John Major's ballot paper, spoilt with the words 'sod off Redwood', to William Hague.

And then the result. Hague 92, Clarke 70.

'*Yes!*' squealed a claque of teenage Haguettes. One TV anchorman, reporting live, had launched into a script beginning 'What Julian Lewis MP thinks . . .' to be interrupted by Lewis himself who happened to be passing.

'That's not what I think at all,' said Lewis, striding into camera shot.

Journalists stampeded for the next Hague-opportunity: the St Stephen's entrance, where he was to appear. 'What's going to happen?' I whispered to a hardened hack who joined me there.

'Hague will come out. Then Clarke will come out. Hague will be happy, then call for unity. Clarke will be sad, then call for unity. Later, supporters of each will start bad-mouthing the other.'

'No bellyaching!' was Mr Hague's rallying call. He left to rafter-raising applause. His bellyaching begins this weekend.

No Froth But Plenty Of Kick

26.6.97

William Hague leapt like a tiger at his first chance to intervene at Prime Minister's Questions yesterday. As a novice bungee jumper pushes to the front, to get it over with, Mr Hague's anxious lunge at the dispatch box suggested not so much an impatience for the fun as an ache to have done with it.

Yards to his left and impassive as an elderly basking seal, Sir Edward Heath watched the fourteenth new Leader of the Opposition tackle a Prime Minister since, as a young MP, he watched Winston Churchill tackle Clement Attlee half a century ago. John Major watched from the back benches. This was William Hague's debut. The political world was watching. No doubt his mother was watching. Maybe his girlfriend was watching. From the crowded Peers' Gallery in the Commons, half the House of Lords seemed to be watching. Some of his friends were watching. All his enemies were watching. He made a good start.

At first very nervous and fiddling, with notes covered in inky scrawl, he was on the edge of his seat before Tony Blair had even risen for his first question. This came in the Black Country accents of Dennis Turner (Lab, Wolverhampton South East). The Prime Minister was ready for a dozen great issues of our time. What would Mr Turner ask? Hague was agog.

'I wonder whether my Right Honourable Friend has had time to study my Weights & Measures (Beer & Cider) Bill? A full pint with the froth on top!' urged Turner. It was a pity Hague could not keep still and was already straining for the dispatch box. To shrieks of 'No froth on top! Ha, ha, ha!', Labour fingers pointed at his head, but the Prime Minister steered clear of baldist controversy and spoke of his commitment to a full pint. Too wound up to notice the joke, Hague shot to his feet. His voice was uncertain. Betty Boothroyd had to silence Labour backbenchers, still cackling 'No froth on top'. But when he was heard, it was Blair's turn to tense up. Five times the new Tory leader put it to him that one of his Welsh backbenchers was complaining that he had been threatened by the Welsh Secretary with expulsion from the party, unless he toed the line on devolution. And Hague alleged that local councillors had tried to intimidate their MP.

Blair flatly denied both charges. The Welsh Secretary (he said) had assured him that the first was untrue; and Blair had ordered an investigation into the second, which showed that to be a fiction too. Allegation and denial shot back and forth like a Wimbledon rally. Hague's supporters roared; Blair's roared. You could take your choice which to believe.

11.6.97   # The Reviews Begin

Truly it has been said that this Government has hit the ground reviewing. A written answer in the Lords this week is mind-boggling. Lord McIntosh of Harringay listed 38 reviews announced since May 1.

There are Huge Reviews of Absolutely Everything. 'A comprehensive spending review' on every aspect of spending. 'A strategic defence review' covers all aspects of defence. All aspects of transport are covered in 'a fundamental review of transport policy'; aid strategy is to be reconsidered *in toto* in a review of international development; 'a review of the tax benefits system' is wide-ranging, 'a review of the Post Office' rules nothing out – like 'a review of the economic regeneration of Wales'.

But most all-embracing of all is the White Paper 'on better government'.

For those who like their reviews more sharply focused, however, the Government offers a review 'of the law relating to silicone breast implants'. There are also reviews on surrogacy, 'the bureaucratic burden on teachers', and 'the breast cancer screening service in Devon'.

Admission charging by national museums forms the subject of its own review; indeed, nothing is too specific – neither the Skye Bridge tolling arrangements, the National Lottery, the London health services nor 'the arrangements for celebrating the Millennium' have escaped the roving gaze of Mr Blair's review-hunters. Perhaps the motto of new Labour should be 'seek out and review' (in the Latin *'Quaerere et inspicere'*; or, to adapt Che Guevara's *'La lucha continua'* (the struggle goes on), can I propose *'La revisión continua'*?

La revisión includes 'a bus review', 'Scottish enterprise review', and review of 'film policy'. Reviewing film policy, Mr Blair's team must not be distracted by a review of the Scottish roads programme, Crown Prosecution Service, 'private finance machinery', 'arrangements for enforcing the rules on the welfare of animals exported live to the Continent', and 'a review of steps to strengthen the democratic control of the three public water authorities in Scotland'.

Puzzling to the army of review-spotters now gathering with their thermos flasks in corridors at Westminster is the emergence of the 'fundamental review'. How is a fundamental review distinguished? How about the 'strategic review' (of roads, for instance), the 'special review' (of Social Fund appeals), the 'careful review', the 'thorough review', or the 'continuing review'? Then there are the 'task forces' (like the one on youth justice). Are these reviews?

I mentioned a few of the 38 reviews Lord McIntosh admits to. But I have done my own research. He seems to have omitted reviews announced in the Commons into: educational SSAs, energy saving, eye tests, VED, petrol prices, Scottish homes, hens, immigration policy, 'internal migration', unemployment figures, 'the system of justice', mental health, Northern Ireland, shops, pesticides, pensions, pilotage, departmental publications, parliamentary privilege, policing objectives, quangos, Service properties, student benefits, asylum, water abstraction licensing, water charging and smoking in the House of Commons.

So it is with amazement that we observe minister Mark Fisher kicking the habit in just one case. 'The government has no plans to review the concessionary television licence fee regulations.' What went wrong?

Later they did review the concessionary TV licence regulations.

Okapi Dobson Scents Extinction   *17.6.97*

Alongside chips with mayonnaise, an unexpected pleasure of Belgium as a tourist destination is Antwerp Zoo. Situated near the station in a drizzly region of Flanders, this boasts one of the world's finest collections of central African fauna. At its centre is a small herd of okapi.

The okapi is growing rare. With the markings of a faded zebra, the body of a stunted giraffe and the long tongue of an anteater, the beast is perfectly adapted to lick termites off high branches in the Congo rainforest. Sadly it is not equipped for much else. Its coat is no camouflage outside the sun-dappled forest floor, and hunted almost to extinction by pygmies, the okapi is – frankly – on a one-way ticket to nowhere.

Except Antwerp. Here many of history's last okapi huddle in the Belgian mist, an expression of infinite pathos betraying some half-sensed animal intimation that they are at a Darwinian dead-end.

They are okapi and they are not ashamed. They could and would not be anything else. But they know that being an okapi is no longer where it's at, and that soon there may be no okapi at all. Railway trains shunt and whistle in the distance, mayonnaise-flecked school parties giggle and goggle through the wire, and the okapi of Antwerp peer into the drizzle, remember a happier epoch when there were trees and sunshine and termites, and brace themselves for extinction.

Watching Frank Dobson at the Commons yesterday, I was carried mentally to Antwerp Zoo. The Secretary of State for Health is a socialist and he is not ashamed. He cannot and would not be anything else. But he knows that being a socialist is not where it's at in Tony Blair's new Labour Cabinet, and that soon there may be no socialists at all.

Hunted almost to extinction by the tabloid newspapers, his ideological markings no longer any camouflage, even in Camden, he knows his career is on a one-way ticket to nowhere.

Tories giggle and journalists goggle and Mr Dobson shakes his beard and rises at the dispatch box, his gritty gaze betraying some half-sensed animal intimation that he and his kind are at a Darwinian dead-end.

He remembers a happier epoch when there was Clause Four and the GLC, and the red flag flew over Camden Town Hall . . . And braces himself for extinction. But not quite yet.

Dobson knows the knives are out for him but he is damned if he is going to give the Cabinet butchers the excuse to sack him. Yesterday he had come to the Commons to explain his plans to unpick the 'two-tier' system by which GP fundholders secure advantages for their patients. Mr Dobson had not, however, come to abolish GP fundholding itself. But of course 'old' Labour was against GP fundholding altogether. He could tell from the cheers and jeers behind him that many Labour backbenchers still hold that view, and believe he shares it.

You could sense from Dobson's body language that he is anything but an enthusiast for fundholding. He described Tory NHS reforms as having been based 'largely on the advice of a heroin addict and fraudster'. Backbenchers begged him not to stop here, but to abolish fundholding completely. But he dared not encourage them . They were off-message – and Peter Mandelson wields a mean blowpipe. Mr Dobson sticks doggedly to his brief. While there were termites left, even in this barren new Labour terrain, he would lick them. And when the pygmies come for him, as he knows they will, he will go with dignity into extinction.

They did, and he did.

Bald Eagle Loses to Sheriff Tony

24.7.97

Tourists in the new towns of the American Midwest used to witness a touching sight: Red Indian chiefs, wandering the sidewalks in their feathers, unrevered in an alien world. Down on the reservation they were masters of all they surveyed. But here feathers drooped and bearing faltered. The contrast between scenes was poignant.

Journalists yesterday witnessed both. We saw Big Chief Bald Eagle, the young warrior recently annointed leader of the Tory tribe down on the reservation at Smith Square, spiritual homeland of his people. Here a tent filled with warriors and elders was held spellbound, the womenfolk ululating, the senior members of the tribe growling '*hyah-ya-ya-yah*' in the traditional manner.

And we saw him in the big new settlement of the Palefaces, known as Fort Blair or 'the Houses of Parliament': lands seized from his tribe, where his writ no longer runs. He tried to speak; he made a powerful case: but Sheriff Blair kicked dust in his face, the Palefaces laughed, and few of the journalists bothered to write any of it down. His tribesmen, gathered behind, raised a plucky whoop, but they were hopelessly out-numbered. At Central Office William Hague had made a substantial speech outlining his plans for a reorganisation of the tribe. He argued these with intelligence and conviction.

The spin doctors' press release accompanying Hague's new photo-portrait promises a man 'looking serious but with a smile playing around his mouth and eyes'. Wondering where else a smile might play, we heard some common sense delivered with humour in that pleasant but determined tone which is becoming his hallmark.

Tories must start to listen, he said. *He* would. He would be listening all summer long. Members, too, must listen. Listen at work, listen at play, listen at home, listen on land and at sea, listen down the pit and in the leafy lanes. The rhetoric began to go rather to his head. The list of places where Tories must listen lengthened. A nightmare vision grew of a Britain in which wherever we go we find Tories – in the hedgerow, behind the soft-toiletries or under the bed – listening.

After a standing ovation, the new party chairman thanked him. Lord Parkinson is looked quite rejuvenated now he is in charge. Both chiefs were cheered a second time.

So it was sad to see Bald Eagle in the Commons chamber. Here he wanted to know why the Prime Minister had said last week that a Welsh assembly would control the police, and this week that it would not. Sheriff Blair speak with forked tongue, and four times failed to answer Hague's question – but nobody seemed to notice.

Then Barry Jones (Lab, Alyn & Deeside) asked for an assurance on the Future Large Aircraft, and received one on Airbus – but nobody seemed to notice. This Commons is becoming an Orwellian world in which answers do not relate to questions, but nobody says so, and everyone wonders whether he is mad, or everyone else is. A smile played around Tony Blair's lips, but not his eyes.

Better Luck This Time

31.7.97

He didn't like it. The expression on Tony Blair's face as William Hague tackled him at his last Prime Minister's Questions before the summer recess will have sent Mr Hague's diminished troops home for their holidays with a spring in their step.

That Mr Hague was thrashing astonishing horsepower from a Robin Reliant of a scandal seemed to increase the Prime Minister's fury. Mr Hague's confident delivery, and the glum and irritable expressions on the faces of Labour backbenchers behind Blair, suddenly had the game going the Opposition's way; and Blair, magnificent advancing but ragged in retreat, spent as wretched a six minutes as any since this new Parliament sat.

Five times Mr Hague asked Mr Blair about the shareholding of Lord Simon of Highbury, Minister for Trade and Competitiveness in Europe, in BP. Five times Mr Blair railed at Hague for insinuating that this was improper, his fury increasing each time. But Mr Hague got vocal support from the Opposition benches. Mr Blair was rattled. Perhaps because of their public-school backgrounds, Tories are better than Labour at general growling, hooting and yobbery. Madam Speaker was reduced to barking *'you'll* be out n'all' to Tory brandy-louts.

But Tories surpass Labour backbenchers, too, in their ability to grunt. The Commons grunt, a sound much like a teddy bear being turned upside down, is a noise emitted more from the gut than the larynx. Like those classroom noises which Teacher cannot pin on any particular boy, the grunt foxes the Chair. The sound can be supportive or sceptical, depending on the precise pitching of the tone. Women, genetically programmed for noises of reproach, cannot grunt at all in the right frequencies; so Labour is at a disadvantage here. Tories are expert grunters. They boosted their man's morale with strategically placed volleys of constructive grunting during his questions; and knocked Mr Blair off his stride by lobbing hostile grunts his way at critical moments.

During the unusually long summer recess, Labour personnel managers should consider arranging grunting weekends at grunt-training camps for their male backbenchers.

Hughes's Attention-seeking Goes Aquatic

23.9.97

The 1997 conference season begins.

For the political sketchwriter returning to Britain from abroad, it is at first a struggle to get things back out of proportion. Nothing achieves this faster than attendance at a Liberal Democrat conference.

Here in Eastbourne, the trivial becomes grave, the laughable is greeted with a straight face and the obvious studiously ignored. It is a dream world in which little can astonish.

Nobody raised an eyebrow when the opening debate yesterday afternoon on 'Safety in public transport', coming as it did within days of a terrible train crash, focused on the need to provide adequate lighting on station platforms and to guard female passengers against sex pests.

All Liberals can recognise a light switch. Some know about sex pests. Few understand signalling circuitry. So the focus was natural.

But even I was unprepared to encounter an MP in orange boxer-shorts holding a length of flexible blue plastic piping between his legs, up to his neck in a swimming pool and dancing to a tango played on a poolside ghetto-blaster, with press photographers in attendance and two journalists taking notes.

Simon Hughes (Southwark North & Bermondsey) is a good-hearted and hard-working MP with an eye for publicity. Few who witnessed it can forget his appearance at a Bournemouth conference dressed in green Lycra cycling shorts, to publicise bicycle lanes and himself. Hardened photographers are haunted by the memory of Mr Hughes at the Glasgow conference last year, rolling down the steps of the office of a French cultural attaché, dressed in a black bin-liner and wearing a skull mask to draw attention to French nuclear tests in the Pacific, and himself.

So maybe we should have anticipated his arrival at an event listed in the conference guide as 'Chartered Society of Physiotherapy: *Who can hydrotherapy help?* Visit and learn more – or bring your gear and take part. Swimming pool, the Grand Hotel.' Delegates of all shapes and sizes joined a Gadarene rush into the pool to dance.

They were instructed by a shapely aquatic physiotherapist to twirl around, hold hands in a ring and bob up and down to a taped rumba, to torpedo from the waves like porpoises and then to 'march' through the water in an exaggerated stride. 'March! March!' she trilled. 'Left, right, left, right.' Liberal Democrats practised this with vigour: the closest some are likely to come to a military display, but rendered acceptable on account of being performed underwater.

Late as ever, Simon Hughes arrived. The trunks were Day-Glo and labelled 'Speedo', and he was holding in his tum.

Hughes entered the pool for one-to-one tuition, executing a stately breaststroke. The instructress held him while he performed a frog motion with his legs. A portable cassette-player thumped out some Latin rhythms.

Then an attendant threw in a section of thick blue plastic tube, a few feet long, for exercises. Perhaps misunderstanding his instructions, Mr Hughes pulled it between his thighs, creating a strange effect. His researcher rushed anxiously to the poolside to advise against this manoeuvre. The photographers closed in.

Some days ago your sketchwriter was swinging from a length of monkey-rope in the Amazon and wondering how to readjust to the normality of British politics as a working journalist. I now realise this will not be necessary.

Memories Of Steel

30.9.97

Labour's first party conference in government begins.

Abiding in the mind after Brighton this week will be the memory of steel: steel railings everywhere, steel in the Prime Minister's smile, steel in Labour's grip, steel in the eyes of the evangelists of 'new politics' as they pump your hand and scrutinise your security pass.

Long before you arrive the steel security fences start. To these the party has pinned two posters in equal numbers. One, red on a white background, declares 'New Labour New Britain'. The other is white on a red background. It says 'New Labour New Britain'. On the approach to the promenade this message is repeated 81 times. Turn to confront the security zone itself, guarded against attack from the ocean by more steel. Upon it appears the message 'New Labour New Britain', 215 times.

In the middle stands the conference centre. Its facade is decked, to the left, by a huge banner hanging vertically. It bears the message 'New Labour New Britain'. To the right hangs another banner. It says the same. Between the vertical banners is a horizontal one: 'Brighton & Hove welcome New Labour' – an audacious departure from the standard text which, it is to be hoped, will not confuse delegates, or over-tax intellects. From the beach comes the lament of a trombone solo played by a man complaining about sick pay. Few notice.

To enter the hall you must first enter a long tunnel. In this the visitor passes the message 'New Labour New Britain' 42 more times. Frisked at a security check, visitors can read 'New Labour New Britain' four times more on the walls above the X-ray machines. In the final section of tunnel the thought 'New Labour New Britain' appears seven times, and 'Group 4 – Have you got your pass?' once.

I joined delegates crowding in to hear John Prescott and looked down at the conference floor. Virtually everybody was white. But in a small reserved area behind me most seemed black or brown.

'Gosh,' I thought, but without surprise, 'they've put the coloured people in a separate pen, away from the cameras.' In fact, this was the international visitors' section. Outside, beyond the steel, one could hear the wailing of dissident demonstrators borne on the wind, but very faint.

Robin Cook showed delegates a video of Tony Blair on a walkabout, Tony Blair in a helicopter, in a coach, at a school, in a car, in a field and hugging some children, all to the accompaniment of happy music.

John Prescott introduced a woman who showed slides to assist delegates' understanding. There were graphics of three stick-figure men, the third engulfed in light and bearing the logo 'new', to illustrate Labour's new support. Near the end of her show came a slide saying: '1997: Labour's Best Election Ever', then another saying 'Thank You'. Wisely, the final slide did not say 'Now Go Away'. Best not to spell it out.

Later, Gordon Brown spoke with authority, and the pallor of the undead. Were one to glance down and notice that a junior minister had talons where fingernails should be, it would hardly have seemed worth mentioning.

I had woken in the night in my conference hotel, disturbed by the deep bark of a big dog somewhere outside in the dark where guards patrol; then by the sound of a crowd-barrier being dragged across asphalt.

Then a scream, twice repeated. Then silence. A detainee, off-message and suspected of unmodern thoughts, under interrogation by Mr Mandelson's mind-police? Or just a seagull on the early tide? Strange thoughts crowd the brain at this surreal celebration, with something acrid in the air. Beneath the applause there is a grinding of teeth.

Wrapped in the Altar-cloth of National Redemption

1.10.97

He has even renamed the country. 'There is a place for all the people in New Britain!' he cried.

Old Britain is used to political texts which are socialist, capitalist, traditionalist or even anarchist. But yesterday we heard a speech which can only be called salvationist. The Prime Minister wrapped himself not so much in the Union Jack as in the altar-cloth of national redemption.

The audience here at Brighton were by turns bewitched and bemused by Mr Blair's weird, redemptive fervour. Time and again his text would drift off toward a new Jerusalem. I had the impression of an addict wrestling with an abstract noun habit.

The Prime Minister would drag himself through the cold turkey of a passage on nursery vouchers, Welfare to Work and water prices, then,

'I could sense confidence returning to the British people, compassion to the British soul, unity to the British nation . . .' and off he went.

Hauled back to the small matter of policy, Mr Blair explained plans for expanding literacy . . . but it was no good. 'I tell you, we need to bring a change to the way we treat each other.'

'Uh-oh,' I thought, 'here we go.'

'We are a giving people,' he cried, in language redolent of Diana, Princess of Wales. 'Make this a giving age . . . believe in us as much as we believe in you.' Taking an expansive view of his role in history, the Prime Minister concluded that at the last election 'fear itself was defeated. Did I not say it would be a battle of hope against fear? On May 1, 1997, fear lost. Hope won.' And off he went, hooked on renewal. Is there no way of gently steering this man clear of visionary nouns lest he start shooting up again, and damage himself?

Prescott Leaves Track   *2.10.97*

'Fifteen years ago I swam up the Thames,' bellowed John Prescott at a stunned conference, putting paid to theories that the Deputy Prime Minister arrived on an asteroid or was discovered in a swamp. That Mr Prescott could be some sort of amphibian may explain his speech. Under water it might have made sense.

Prescott had to persuade delegates that a motion on railway nationalisation should not be voted on. He succeeded magnificently. After hearing him, none doubted that the matter needed further thought.

Veteran Prescott-watchers know that once a Prescott speech begins, nobody – least of all Mr Prescott – can be sure where it will end or where it may go on the way. Nothing is certain except that sooner or later the wheels will come off, and the crowd will love it, and love him.

Yesterday the wheels came off early. This was Prescott the Secretary of State rather than Prescott the conference rabble-rouser, the difference being that he did have a text. So he ignored it. Or, rather, he adopted the technique of glaring periodically down at his notes and selecting a word, a phrase, an idea, at random. These were flung into the stream-of-consciousness flow of his speech like leaves into a torrent, bobbing up and down hopelessly for a moment before sinking in the flood.

'We're advancing the decentralisation!' he cried, promising English agencies 'modelled on their successful Scotch and Welsh counterparts'. This must be the first time in half a century a government minister has used the word 'Scotch', other than to order a drink. It is possible that his hotel room service menu had become muddled with his speech notes.

Next came an unusual concept: 'public expanditure'. It is true that high office has done nothing to trim Mr Prescott's girth, but it is more likely that here he was slipping in a covert reference to enlarging the state sector – which ministers are forbidden by the Chancellor from mentioning.

'I opposed the Tory raily sell-off,' he cried, 'with every fibre of my being.' In the International Visitor's pen, dozens of puzzled little foreign faces furrowed. Pity the Romanian attaché, under orders from Bucharest to fax a summary of the Deputy Prime Minister's key arguments. Telegrams sing through the diplomatic wires: '*Explain reference to raily. Daily? Gaily? Clarify.*'

'I give that promise how to integrate a public accountable railway!' The mysterious vow was heard in silence. 'To produce a report to be the best way . . . four billion pounds at the first priority.' The international visitors laid down their pens in despair.

'I'll let you into a secret. Last night . . .' Delegates sat up; a public confession? 'Er . . . last month, I nationalised the Docklands Right Railway.' Little prospect, then, of privatising the Loyal Maily?

'Any modern railway system has been doing it for years, and that's why they're modern . . . Transport and railways are at the heart of our feeling.' Perhaps stirred by his reference to internal organs, Mr Prescott then mentioned the Transplant and General Workers' Union. Has organised labour now reached the operating theatre?

Nice Mr Maples and Nasty Mr Duncan Smith

10.10.97

Yesterday Conservatives ventured into daytime-TV territory. Roving microphones moved among the faithful as Tory conference-goers thrilled to an audience-participation chat.

Oprah Winfrey it was not. Her job is safe from challengers like the session's chairman, Graham Park.

'These are the mechanics . . .' began Mr Park, explaining to a full house that the two gentlemen on what appeared to be bar stools in front of him were John Maples MP and Iain Duncan Smith MP, spokesmen respectively on health and social security. Tory representatives were invited to pose their queries to either gentleman.

Mr Maples and Mr Duncan Smith bore more than a passing resemblance to Mr Nice and Mr Nasty, or the Mutt and Jeff of a hard-cop/soft-cop interrogation team. Soft-suited, soft-spoken, soft-coiffed Maples would make a perfect customer-care manager for a large chain of private clinics. He was the embodiment of tact.

Duncan Smith, with his high forehead, shark-like smile, deep-set eyes and penetrating stare, could be mistaken for a superintendent (special investigations) in the Stepney & Shoreditch police. A rising star on the Tory right, Duncan Smith, like the former MP for Chingford whom he replaced, relies on a sub-Tebbit snarl, a populist turn of phrase, and a very good brain.

We started with Mr Nice. A fellow called Guy, from Birmingham, invited Maples to agree that there was no need for a royal commission on euthanasia. Mr Nice agreed that this was a very difficult question. He hugely understood the feelings on both sides. He doubted whether any decision at all was called for. He told a man concerned that too little is spent on rural health that country people tended to think too much was spent on the towns, whereas town people tended to think the opposite.

Christine from Hackney asked about alleged 'corruption' in Labour councils. Would Tory spokesmen please expose such evils? This brought Mr Nasty hissing to his feet. 'Just you try and stop me!' he snapped! 'The rug must be lifted,' continued Duncan Smith, on 'rotten, rotten' Labour administrations. 'Corrupt, always with a hand in the till.

'And who swallows it? You don't. They do,' he gargled, gesturing up to where journalists sit. 'The media.' The audience peered up and began to boo. I fingered my notebook nervously.

Then a lady from Kensington asked Maples about vitamin B supplements. Mr Nice explained that it was all very difficult, adding, kindly, that there was a Committee on Safety in Medicines. There was now a danger that others might chip in with their ailments and the whole thing turn into a mass-participation doctor's surgery.

The event was unfortunately staged. Directly behind Nasty and Nice, the chairman was on a higher bar stool. As Maples and Duncan Smith alternated their replies, Mr Park beamed and scowled behind, centre-stage, his facial expressions – caring or angry – more watchable than the presenters.

I fear I did not stay. Passing a party stand near the exit, I saw 130 photographs of William and Ffion, arrayed on a desk. Tory hallgoers had been offered the chance to pose between them for a personal portrait, one at a time, as the happy couple peered cheesily and wearily into the camera. In some snaps, William had his mouth open while Ffion had hers closed. In others it was the other way round. In a few, both mouths were open or shut. I pointed out this interesting fact to the man behind the stall.

'I'm not going to say anything in case you write it down,' he wailed.

He Said Banana

29.10.97

Yesterday Tony Blair said 'banana' in the Commons.

It sounded odd from this Prime Minister: somehow beneath his dignity. The leader's Brighton speech had been a triumph. 'Vision . . . passion . . . the British soul . . . beacon to the world . . .' had echoed round the hall. 'Fear lost. Hope won. The giving age began!' he had cried. 'Britain! A young country!'

Now here he was, looking tired, minus yet more tufts of hair, and saying 'banana'. Not the giving banana, the young banana or the beacon banana. Just banana.

The occasion was a statement to the Commons on the conclusion of the Commonwealth Heads of Government Meeting. Mr Blair began gurgling away in grand style: 'Delighted to welcome Commonwealth Heads . . . my thanks to the people of Scotland . . .' he gushed.

'Warmth of Her Majesty's reception . . . Economic Declarations on "Promoting Shared Prosperity" . . . Harare Declaration of 1991', the Prime Minister rumbled, as the capital letters rolled. 'Arrangements for African, Caribbean and Pacific . . .'

But *oops!* What was this? We sensed a tiny frisson of alarm ruffle Mr Blair's composure as his eye caught the next word. He almost gulped.

'. . . banana exporters.' He said 'banana' very quickly and rather quietly, anxious to move on. Mr Blair soon recovered his dignity and his capital letters. 'Code of Good Practice . . . South Asia Regional Fund . . . every Highly Indebted Poor Country . . .' But once you have heard a person say 'banana', a sliver of the awe in which you had held them is lost, never to be recovered. Something similar happened when John Gummer said 'porpoise' at the dispatch box, twice, in 1993.

And there was more to come. Perhaps in some schoolboy pact to make Blair say 'banana' as often as possible, Tory backbenchers kept asking him about the Caribbean. John Wilkinson (C, Ruislip Northwood) demanded to know how the Prime Minister would 'safeguard the banana regime'. Blair refused to say 'banana regime' but could not avoid saying 'banana' once again in his reply.

Bowen Wells (C, Hertford and Stortford) leapt up. Did he understand the importance of this fruit to Commonwealth nations? 'Economies,' said Blair, pained, 'that are completely dependent on, *er*, one particular, *er*, form of produce . . .'

To tell when the Prime Minister is under pressure, note the frequency with which he stammers 'I mean' and 'y'know'. William Hague challenged him on claims that his press officers had been rude to Commonwealth heads. Blair was exasperated. 'Frankly, y'know, *er*, these sort of press stories, we should brush them off.'

On greenhouse gases: 'It wasn't the role of the Commonwealth Heads of Government to come to some sort of, y'know, declared view.' To Tam Dalyell, on Lockerbie: 'I mean, there's nothing I can really add, I mean, frankly.'

Labour's George Galloway (Glasgow Kelvin) asked why the Commonwealth was rejecting membership applications from Yemen and Palestine. Blair looked cross. 'I mean, we didn't reject them, we said we'd keep them under review,' he complained.

A Tory wanted Nigeria's expulsion; Blair spluttered 'in relation to what happens in the Commonwealth, vis-à-vis *them*, I mean they *are* out'.

Nobody mentioned bananas again. I mean, frankly, it would have been, y'know, the last, *er*, straw. I mean.

6.11.97   # Dr Jekyll and Mr Snide

A creepy story is emerging between the lines of Wednesday's Commons Questions: the tale of Prime Minister Jekyll and Tony Hyde. Prime Minister Jekyll is a fair-minded fellow with a ready ear for the other chap's point of view. Generous in debate and civil in manner, his whole wish is to lift the argument to a higher plane.

Whatever your opinion, magnanimous Prime Minister Jekyll can find something with which to agree. Relaxed, high-toned and tolerant, he yearns for an end to the petty point-scoring which poisons our politics. Prizing country above party, he invites all who care about Britain to join him in prayerful contemplation of the national good.

How sharp is the contrast with a very different fellow! Tony Hyde is vituperative and sly. Ever-vigilant for a means of wrong-footing opponents, his instinct is to avoid the argument and kick them in the nuts. Tony Hyde is uncompromisingly partisan, quick to sneer, to mock and – in victory – to crow.

Both these gentlemen appear at the dispatch box on Wednesdays, Prime Minister Jekyll and the Rt Hon Tony Hyde being wont to take turns in answering backbenchers. Thus it was that at 3pm yesterday it was Tony Hyde who took the first question, which was by chance from a Tory, Nigel Evans (Ribble Valley). Evans was worried about the EU budget. 'I don't think I've ever heard such nonsense,' sneered Hyde. Then (though nobody had raised this) he began to attack the 'negative, foolish' attitude of the previous Government. Next, a Labour back-bencher, Helen Jones (Warrington N) asked about the International Development White Paper. By chance it was the Prime Minister who took this one.

Genially he agreed with her, and offered a thoughtful disquisition on overseas aid. But it was Tony Hyde who took the question which followed, from Opposition Leader William Hague. Hyde simply refused to answer Hague's question about new EU proposals to regulate small business. Instead he just kept shuffling his notes and attacking the previous Government. Pressed repeatedly by Hague, Hyde grew angrier and more mocking. Finally, he began shouting 'business prefers *this* side's position!' and turning round, grinning, to his friends for endorse-ment, like a playground bully.

It was a relief, then, to find Prime Minister Jekyll on his feet next, to answer a Labour backbencher, Peter Pike (Burnley), on the wind-chill factor. 'My honourable friend is absolutely right,' he agreed, caringly.

Labour backbencher Claire Ward (Watford) asked about threats to the Lottery. Jekyll was genial: 'My honourable friend is absolutely right.' 'My honourable friend is absolutely right,' he smiled to Oona King (Lab, Bethnal Green & Bow) who wanted a fitting memorial for the civilian war-dead. 'My honourable friend is absolutely right,' was his answer to the Labour backbencher who wanted new powers to supervise sex-offenders.

To Charles Clarke (Lab, Norwich S): 'My honourable friend is absolutely right.' And his reaction to the thoughts of Labour's Austin Mitchell (Grimsby) on international debt relief? 'My honourable friend is absolutely right.' How unlucky that this Prime Minister was never on hand when an Opposition member rose. To these Tony Hyde, instead, offered a string of gibes, taunts and sneaky references to their own problems.

We cannot guess by what rule of thumb Prime Minister Jekyll and Tony Hyde decided to divide the questions between them. We merely note that they seem to have formed a useful working arrangement. Could they by any chance be related?

The Woman Who Won't Give In   *7.11.97*

Christine Hamilton wore a scarlet jacket with wide white collars. She has lost weight. She looked elegant, if tense and rather pale. Under a huge, striped golfing umbrella she was sheltering herself outside the St Stephen's entrance to the Commons, leaving a small space under the canopy for her husband, Neil. His hands shook with nerves.

Ten yards away, separated by a crash barrier from a horde of newsmen, was Martin Bell, the independent MP for Tatton who ousted Hamilton last May. The Hamiltons loitered in the drizzle. Christine was indignant.

'Go on, dear, put him on the spot.'

'How do you mean?'

'Oh go on, dear: just go.'

'D'you think I should?'

'If you don't go, I will, and you know what I'll say.'

'Well . . .'

But Mrs Hamilton made the decision for him, stepping half a pace away and withdrawing the shelter of her umbrella. Like a small bird prodded from the nest by its mother, he must now fly. Without her. 'If *I* go anywhere near that man I shall just explode,' she hissed.

Neil Hamilton hovered over to the scrum, and stood hesitantly behind it, hanging back. In the end it was the photographers who pushed him forward to 'encounter' Martin Bell; but neither had much to say to the other.

Half an hour before, Neil Hamilton had called his own press conference in the Jubilee Room at Westminster. The event turned into something of a circus in which poor Hamilton played the role both of ringmaster and clown. The room was full. Journalists attending Hamilton press conferences these days go in the faintly ghoulish mood of those who flock to road accidents.

Silence was broken by a dispute between press photographers and a TV cameraman whose lights spoilt their capture of the moment, when a helmeted policeman checking the room loomed behind Mrs Hamilton as though about to make an arrest.

Silence fell again. Hamilton called for a glass of water. Was this a last request, or would he now ask for a cigarette – or even a priest? Then he spoke, launching into an angry and at times disjointed rant against his critics and inquisitors. Mohamed Al Fayed had lied, he claimed. The Select Committee on Standards and Privileges had slipped up. Sir Gordon Downey (the Parliamentary Commissioner for Standards) was slovenly and unjust. The press had unfairly persecuted him.

He had been tried by a Court of Star Chamber, he went on. This was the 'hoax of the century'. Fayed was 'a modern Titus Oates'. He and Christine would fight on. All the while, Hamilton's hands were shaking. His voice shook, too, as he lost his place in his notes. He is plainly under intense strain. You could say he sounded dotty. He was certainly obsessive, and anyone with experience in public life knows the symptoms. Had Hamilton's case been conveyed by letter it would have been in green ink, with a copy sent to the Queen.

But anyone with experience in public life also knows the shudder as you brush away some dotty-sounding plea. Might there be something in it? A huge grievance does turn sane people dotty.

When once I asked David Mellor why he had never challenged the fabrications about his 'Chelsea strip', he replied, 'Who's interested in a verdict of only two-thirds guilty?' In essence that is what Hamilton was asking for – and nobody was interested. Few if any in the Jubilee Room yesterday gained the impression he had been blameless. Some of us, however, left feeling vaguely uneasy about the process by which he had been blamed.

Bad Fairy Casts Spell On Dome   *11.11.97*

Was that a smell of sulphur in the air? It was like the moment when the Bad Fairy stalks on to the pantomime stage. Fear, loathing and fascination hung in the atmosphere in equal proportions. One MP even hissed.

Peter Mandelson had finally been brought to the dispatch box. There he was – living, breathing – in immaculate grey suit, white shirt and turquoise silk tie. His hair, held in place by perhaps the lightest application of spray, was perfect. And he would speak! What was his voice like? Darth Vader? A whole new generation of MPs and cub reporters have never heard Mr Mandelson speak in the chamber.

He would answer for five minutes. So after six months on the salary of a Minister of State we can fix his estimated value as a Commons speaker at about £247 per second. What could Mandelson be about to say to justify this rate of pay?

As the elusive minister sat in silence, tense but poised, awaiting his moment, the preceding Questions to the Culture Secretary Chris Smith seemed an eternity. Besides, there were no interesting questions for Mr Smith.

A ludicrous feature of the Commons Questions procedure is that these are notified in writing a fortnight before the afternoon on which they are to be asked. Two weeks ago nobody was talking about donations to the Labour Party from the moguls of motor racing; no one had suggested squeezing a quart of British opera into the pint pot of Covent Garden.

There were, therefore, no questions on the only topical subjects in Smith's portfolio.

Light relief was provided by Sports Minister Tony Banks, who is still finding it hard to shake off the habits of an Opposition backbencher, and yesterday (if I heard aright) took to heckling his own fellow-ministers. Junior minister Mark Fisher was being harried by MPs concerned that there were too many children's cartoons on television. Defending the BBC, the minister protested that children would search in vain for a silly cartoon on the BBC.

'They can come 'ere then,' crackled a voice which seemed to come from the minister sitting next to Mr Fisher. Banks adopted his innocent, 'not me, guv' expression, and I may stand corrected.

At 3.11pm, a whole minute late, Mandelson rose, pale as Banquo's ghost, in complete silence. MPs had 300 seconds to interrogate him. They never got past the first question on the Order Paper.

This was from Phyllis Starkey (Lab, Milton Keynes SW) and lacked the monumental quality the moment seemed to demand. She asked about 'provision of an adequate transport infrastructure' for the Dome. Mr Mandelson sounded nervous. He would not say 'Dome'. He kept talking about the 'Millennium Experience'. He spent his entire five minutes babbling about it.

Unless Tony Blair rescues him at a Cabinet reshuffle the poor man's whole career is now trapped for the rest of the century by this infernal Dome.

There would be masses of 'exciting and enjoyable things to do' at the Experience, he prattled. There would be 'a new Millennium pier' from which to take a boat there. Or you could 'park 'n sail', he trilled.

'Park 'n sail' was the message of the day, repeated twice. Like 'wash 'n hold', 'spray 'n stay', 'smash 'n grab' or indeed (as Mandelson doubtless hopes at the next reshuffle) 'cut 'n run', the phrase is memorable and may come to be permanently associated with his name. Peter 'park 'n sail' Mandelson.

Too bad that, as he spoke, a judge in Boston was stealing the limelight. It is just possible that Park 'n Sail will not grace the front page headline in this newspaper.

Louise Woodward did. Park 'n Sail never materialised.

Britain's Bosses Go To The Wall For Blair

12.11.97

In Birmingham, Tony Blair addresses the CBI – sort of.

It is a fact of no great consequence, yet indicative of something so remarkable about our present condition that the ordinary journalistic rules of simple sentence construction fail me, that at 12.20pm on a clear-skied autumn Tuesday, in a year almost within sobbing distance of the end of the 20th century, 500 richly suited men and women, individuals at the very top of their chosen business professions, busy people, people of singular intellect and judgment who between them hold the levers of power across a great swath of British commerce and industry, hastened by aeroplane, taxi, train, Rover, Jaguar, Rolls-Royce and Mercedes-Benz from the four corners of the United Kingdom and gathered in a darkened hall in a conference centre in Birmingham and sat together waiting in an excited, expectant and expensive hush, for the transmission upon a large rectangular cloth screen of a moving picture of the features of Anthony Charles Lynton Blair, and for the sound of his voice. The performance is now available on tape. How expensive this was to produce we cannot say, but it must have been one of the most costly to watch in the history of broadcasting.

I, too, hastened to the CBI conference, choosing the front row.

As a talk from a real headmistress neared its end, excitement mounted at the prospect of a talk from a virtual Prime Minister. The chairman, Sir Colin Marshall, indicating the screen above his head, warned his audience: 'There is a danger that at some point the Prime Minister may appear up there.'

He did. 'I now have a cue that tells me we have to conclude,' Sir Colin blushed – and there Blair was, larger than life, on the wall. The gap between his eyes was nearly two feet across. 'Tony Blair is moving to us through cyber technology,' Sir Colin gasped as, through the ether, an image of Mr Blair's dreadful tie, orange with black polka dots, was beamed to Birmingham, six feet long. The Head was frowning and nodding.

'Education is your undoubted passion,' Sir Colin warbled to the Tie, 'we await your words with great anticipation.' Might he be about to prostrate himself in front of the screen?

Mr Blair said nothing much and said it for about 20 minutes. His eyeballs were the size of tennis balls and kept flicking, so you knew he was reading a script. 'Let me set out the basic principles of a modern economic policy.' The Eyeballs flicked. Five hundred eager little faces gazed up at the screen as Mr Blair expanded.

'There is a new sense of national purpose!' exclaimed the Mouth. 'Together, let us get on and do it!' The Eyeballs were still. A thousand plump little hands applauded the wall.

'You have kindly agreed to respond to a couple of questions,' Sir Colin said to the Eyeballs. The huge Head nodded. Odd that although hanging in the air were a number of doubts on a variety of newsworthy controversies, Sir Colin asked the Tie to lay our fears to rest over trade union legislation and to enlarge a little on 'the challenging global targets that you, Prime Minister, have made a centrepiece of your political agenda.' The Mouth knew all about global targets.

'Thank you,' Sir Colin breathed, 'for such a detailed explanation.' The Eyeballs blinked. 'We hope next year we'll have the privilege of your company in *person*.' A very slight frown flickered between the Eyeballs. 'And that,' Sir Colin gushed, 'rounds off our conference extremely well and on a very positive note indeed.'

The slightest inclination of the Head acknowledged the tribute. Then they turned him off.

17.11.97   # The Honeymoon Fades

Blair's first summer recess ends . . . with the Ecclestone affair.

This Prime Minister has never looked so downright cross. His frustration argued at the same time for innocence, yet loss of control. The sweaty lip, the flowering eyeballs, the worn, strained and scratchy look, and the impression of a touch too much make-up, may stay in viewers' minds long after the arguments are over.

A relaxed John Humphrys, fingering his chin coolly, caused the Prime Minister to appear rattled and angry, and say nothing very much. The credit Mr Blair had bought by volunteering this interview he spent through an appearance of being cornered. Within months, few outside the world of political journalism will remember much of what

Humphrys asked or Blair replied. Instead, they will remember the look and sound of an embattled Prime Minister; they will remember the way his eyes seemed to bulge angrily, just as Margaret Thatcher's used to; they may remember noticing face powder for the first time; and they may remember a moment when the Prime Minister seemed close to losing his rag as he told Humphrys, with the implied menace of an over-weaning head prefect, to 'spit it out' and stop hiding his own opinions behind those of others.

I felt some sympathy for Mr Blair. Time and again politicians are reminded (John Major often was – to no effect) that however peeved you feel, it never helps to sound peeved. Blair looked and sounded utterly exasperated. It could be righteous indignation that makes him so, but the impression was of impotent fury – a loss of control of events. In a Prime Minister this does not do, and in Tony Blair we have hardly seen it before.

'Do you regret that?' asked Humphrys. 'I *explain* it,' shot Blair, with an air of irritated rationality. 'But you're still not saying, "I got things wrong"?' The Prime Minister's face looked like thunder. Under pressure, Mr Blair sends confusing signals. His performance remains fairly controlled. It was notable that at awkward moments he was struggling with a desire to look down at the table rather than up at his interviewer, but determined to gaze Humphrys in the eye at key points, which he did in an almost studied way. One was reminded of a drama school graduate or a Dale Carnegie course in making friends and influencing people.

Yet, despite iron self-possession and a beautiful suit, an impression persists of Mr Blair's being in some way adrift, awaiting instructions. Here was a Bertie Wooster, seriously in the soup, screaming silently for his Jeeves. As we watched Mr Blair before Sunday lunch, and recalled Rory Bremner's caricature the evening before of a cocky and over-wired marionette, Bremner never looked crueller. The Prime Minister's penultimate line rang true for me. He would never, he said, do anything he believed wrong for the country. Watching him as he spoke, few will have felt they were looking at a crook.

But his final line was less convincing. 'The country's got to look at me and, in a sense, got to decide whether the person they believed in is the same person they've got now.' It was unwise to ask viewers to make that comparison. Even his supporters may have felt they had just watched a man different in many ways from the Tony Blair who first took over the Labour Party. He seemed to have lost authority. His plea that we trust him carried the echo of a husband accused of infidelity, assuring his wife she is looking at the same man as the one who proposed to her and carried her over the threshold; nothing has changed. But of course, everything has. These melancholy exchanges do take place, once the honeymoon is over.

18.11.97 New Labour's Working – *Ting*

Harriet Harman, Social Security Secretary, and her deputy, Frank Field, do not seem to see eye to eye.

Madam Speaker, cried Simon Hughes, MP, yesterday, opening a Liberal Democrat-inspired debate on something or other. 'We are the people's *constructive* Opposition.'

MPs headed in droves for the gangways and exits in a kind of panic; journalists followed. If there is one thing worse than name-calling and vulgar abuse (which of course all MPs deplore) it is constructive opposition. All of us are in favour of reasonable debate, so long as we do not have to listen to it; and to voice the word 'reasonable' in the Commons chamber produces a similar effect to shouting 'fire' in a crowded theatre.

Happily for this sketch, the session preceding Mr Hughes's debate positively bristled with anger, ambush, fear and loathing – and that was just between social security ministers in the same Government. Principal protagonists in this puff-adders' nest are Harriet Harman, Secretary of State, and Frank Field, her Minister of State.

Miss Harman stayed cool, but something about the Social Security Secretary's karma whispers terror beneath the Clinique. One way the merciless Mr Field likes to terrorise his prey is to copy the technique of snake stalking bird. Yesterday he never uttered, nor moved, until more than halfway through the session. He scarcely seemed to breathe, but stared immobile and unblinking at her.

Once, after about half an hour of this war of nerves, Mr Field suddenly did move. I saw Miss Harman flinch. But he was bluffing. He moved only to fetch himself a glass of water; then returned to his noiseless, serpentine vigil.

As a bird can be petrified by this icy aggression, so Miss Harman seemed somewhat hypnotised, trance-like, as she spoke. Yesterday, with Mr Field eyeballing remorselessly, her chirrup took a desperate edge. This may explain why she began intoning, like an Eastern mantra, the same eight words. Over and over again, in a sort of chant, she droned, 'Reforming-the-welfare-state-around-the-work-ethic'.

We began waiting for the little *ting* on a bell, employed by adherents of the Shinto religion, to bring the thing they chant for.

Richard Spring (C, Suffolk West) asked about help for the disabled. '. . . reforming-the-welfare-state-around-the-work-ethic' chanted Miss Harman. *Ting* we thought. Dennis Skinner (Lab, Bolsover) called Labour's promise to stick to Tory spending plans a kind of 'two-year quarantine' for socialism. '. . . reforming-the-welfare-state-around-the-work-ethic', chanted Miss Harman. *Ting*.

Christopher Chope (C, Christchurch) mentioned single mothers. '. . . reforming-the-welfare-state-around-the-work-ethic,' chanted Miss Harman. *Ting*.

Maybe the Government has embraced Shintoism, believing that to achieve their heart's desire all they need do is announce a review, then start chanting the appropriate eight or nine-word mantra over and over again – until the thing just happens, of its own accord.

The Lords Debate Tarts   *19.11.97*

In the Lords yesterday attention turned to the rude cards by which prostitutes advertise in London phone boxes. Their Lordships proved quite knowledgeable on the subject. The Baroness Trumpington heaved so massively with laughter as to arouse fears for the structure of this 19th-century building.

But the question had to await the investiture of new life peers, accompanied by the usual procession of beribboned flunkeys dressed in carpets and people wearing Cornish pasties on their heads, prancing around according to what we call 'tradition' in this gilt, paste and plasterboard apology for a senate. The fake antiquity dates from 1958, when life peers were invented.

I looked down at their assembled Lordships. I have never – no, not even in a provincial American television studio – seen so much hair dye.

Black Rod, who may not be wearing a toupee, strutted about in a frock coat and black leather gloves like a poncified cat-burglar.

Lingering doubts fled. It is definitely not cool in 1997 to be a Lord.

We moved to tarts. Not that the Earl of Bradford, whose question on 'unauthorised advertising in London phone boxes' trod delicately, mentioned these women.

For the Government, Lord Haskel, who looks like a high-class haberdasher, did. Advertising cards placed by prostitutes, he said (*cries of 'aah!'*) were 'deterring people from using phone boxes' (*cries of 'oh!'*). BT was barring calls to these numbers.

Why did Lord Bradford then affect such gratitude that someone else had dared say 'prostitute'? This is not, after all, a shy peer. *Who's Who* suggests that his Lordship, who has a beard and lives in Weston-under-Lizard, has published a book called *My Private Parts and the Stuffed Parrot*. Even the steamiest of the cards that peers were complaining about yesterday draw the line at that sort of thing.

The minister went on to explain that legal action to ban these cards had been blocked by lawyers acting for the London Collective of Call Girls. At this point Lady Trumpington began shaking in a helpless fit of giggles. We imagined the card which this former Tory whip might (heaven forbid) place in a BT kiosk . . .

'Substantial Lady offers discipline for the mature gentleman. "Naughty boys must pull their socks up." Phone Trumpers on Westminster too-too-too – Oh! Oh! Oh!'

Lord Annan rose. 'In recent years,' he said, a 'disastrous' legal judgement had deemed the *Ladies' Directory* (a discreet catalogue of prostitutes' services) a 'conspiracy against public morals'. But surely there had to be ways these women could advertise?

Indeed. One merely notes that this case (Shaw vs the DPP) was decided in 1961. Only in the Lords is 36 years ago 'recent'.

Lord Campbell of Alloway wondered 'what on earth was the use' of blocking telephones 'when the girls can get another – perhaps using the name Mimi instead of Fifi'. This revealed as much about Lord Campbell's interior life as about telecommunications.

Lord Palmer – to cries of Oh! – thought the call-cards were good for the tourist trade. This Lord Palmer is the Palmer of Huntley & Palmer's biscuits. He may not know that, according to a new book about the work of the Wolfenden Committee (which in the 1950s examined the law on homosexuality and prostitution) members declared in their private deliberations from using the h or p words. They bantered instead about 'huntleys' and 'palmers'.

Lord Palmer may not care to be linked with palmers – but at least nobody has ever called him a huntley.

An Old-Age Traveller   *25.11.97*

Peter Temple-Morris crosses the floor.

It was John Wilkinson (C, Ruislip Northwood) who began the trail which led to the arrival in the chamber of Peter Temple-Morris (Leominster) – who sat down on the wrong side. Mr Temple-Morris has left the Tory party and yesterday crossed the floor.

Labour staged the event magnificently.

Mr Wilkinson's question was about refugees. Laurence Robertson (C, Tewkesbury) wanted to put ministers straight: we were not talking 'about New Age travellers, but old-age travellers'.

At the word 'new', Dennis Skinner jerked upright. The unreconstructed Labour MP for Bolsover is everything new Labour hates, and the feeling is mutual. 'New Labour, new traveller,' he spat. A bearded wraith of a junior minister, George Howarth, spat back: he trusted 'old-age traveller' did not mean Skinner.

Hardly. Three months short of his 60th birthday, Peter Temple-Morris, his hair soft and snowy-white as a goose's breast, travelled south across the bar of the House, then travelled west, on to the Labour benches.

A Prime Ministerial Statement had just begun. Drowned by cheers from behind him, Blair grinned maddeningly.

The interruption was no accident. Rumours of the moment at which he would arrive had been circulating for hours. Temple-Morris knew exactly where to go. As if by miracle, a solid phalanx of Labour MPs opened like the Red Sea to swallow the newcomer into a Temple-Morris-sized gap between Dale Campbell-Savours (Lab, Workington) and Harry Barnes (Lab, Derbys NE).

The cheers, and Mr Blair's merry grin, continued.

Shaking hands, Temple-Morris became instantly engrossed in friendly conversation: a chat for which Campbell-Savours seemed prodigiously prepared and from which neither flagged. The launch of Mr Temple-Morris into his new pond helped the PM off to a fine start.

Blair was reporting on an EU 'Jobs Summit' triumph in Luxembourg. He wore for the occasion a tie decorated like a peacock's tail.

The design was auspicious. When sure of his ground, Tony Blair is now an almost ostentatiously assured performer. Undented by a well-crafted attack from William Hague, Blair handled yesterday's statement with real poise, batting every objection airily and fluently aside. His timbre, hand-movements – his whole bearing – reek of power. His voice breathes command. Only that grin still lets him down.

Rereading J.M. Barrie's *Peter Pan* recently, I was struck by the parallels between Tony Blair and Peter Pan, and between the British public and Peter's number one fan: Wendy. It was Wendy who made a young man of Peter by attaching him to his own shadow . . .

'. . . *and now he was jumping about in the wildest glee. Alas, he had already forgotten that he owed his bliss to Wendy . . .* 'How clever I am,' *he crowed rapturously,* 'oh, the cleverness of me!'

It is humiliating to have to confess that this conceit of Peter was one of his most fascinating qualities. To put it with brutal frankness, there never was a cockier boy.

But for the moment, Wendy was shocked . . .

'*Wendy,*' *he said,* '*don't withdraw. I can't help crowing when I'm pleased with myself.*'

With Temple-Morris comfy behind him, his backbenchers cheering him, the Tories scowling and the press writing it down, our modern Peter Pan couldn't help crowing.

His Tinker Bell, the Minister without Portfolio, was nowhere to be seen: Mr Mandelson had flown away to scatter magic dust over crowds of journalists.

26.11.97   # Brown Baffles Bunnies

As Gordon Brown spoke yesterday, the Tory benches stared at him as if mesmerised. These were not the massed ranks of a well-armed Opposition spoiling for the fight. They were more like a bunch of rabbits, frozen in the headlights of an oncoming political juggernaut.

That the Chancellor appeared to have nothing of importance to say –
or that the Shadow Chancellor, Peter Lilley, brought a prickly little list
of questions to which Mr Brown seemed to have few answers – hardly
mattered. What mattered was command. Brown had command. The
Tories have lost it. When the Chancellor spoke his own side cheered –
and the Opposition fell silent. When Lilley spoke Labour just laughed.

Gordon Brown's presentational skills have been transformed over the
past year. He used to be boring *and* deafening; now he is just boring. He
used to thunder; now he just rumbles. He used to sound positively
suicidal; now he just sounds faintly grumpy. He used to seem gripped
by some black and fathomless internal rage; now he just looks cross.

Joking apart, the Chancellor's delivery is more deft than once it was.
He has learnt a lighter touch and stopped thumping the table. Most
important, he sounds confident and sure of his ground.

He sounded so yesterday. Mr Brown has his favourite phrases, and
they were brandished with aplomb. 'Boom and bust,' was repeated
three times, with a sort of presbyterian foreboding, hitting the boom
with resonance and the bust with relish. Another favourite – 'when it is
prudent to do so' – was delivered in the oak-lined, copper-bottomed
tones of a Scottish mutual society's senior fund-manager, though the
effect here was somewhat marred by Mr Brown's placing one hand on
his rump, elbow out, in the 'I'm-a-little-teapot' pose he has an unwitting
habit of adopting.

But, like some latter-day emperor, the effect of Mr Brown is to stun
us all into silence – and if he seems to have no clothes, we are not so
impertinent as to mention it. How else could the Chancellor have got
away yesterday with taunting Lilley over his party's defeat at the
Winchester by-election last week? 'From two, to minus 22,000,' he
jeered – of the Tories' lost majority. Labour fell about. The Opposition
fell silent.

But (as Malcolm Bruce timidly reminded us some time later) it was
to the Liberal Democrats that the Tories lost. Labour's vote fell from six
thousand to nine hundred, their lowest share of the vote since the War.
Not that this bothered Brown. 'They are not fit to make their presence
felt in this House . . .' he boomed at cowering Liberals, 'they should go
back to their constituencies and prepare to adapt to reality.'

That (to Labour cheers) Gordon Brown could trumpet the Winchester
result at the Tories without a squeak of protest, then tear a strip off the
party which actually won Winchester, is a measure both of his

command, and Opposition demoralisation. As Brown swung his beam off the benches opposite and swept from the chamber, fifty rabbits scuttled for the hedgerows.

Vulcan Redwood Fluffs Earthling Test

27.11.97

Amid generous surroundings at the Savoy Hotel in London yesterday, MPs and journalists gathered to dine, and merrily to toast the winners of the Parliamentarian of the Year awards, hosted by the *Spectator* and Highland Park whisky.

I was one of the judges.

Gordon Brown, Parliamentarian of the Year, took the occasion in his stride, aware, no doubt, why it was given. When the Chancellor stood up at the dispatch box a month ago, Labour were in trouble over the single currency. By the time he sat down it was the Tories who were on the run.

They still are. If you want to know why, you could have done worse than listen to their Industry spokesman, John Redwood, receive his award yesterday. Chosen for his frontbench questioning, he had stood out (we all agreed) for his dogged pursuit of a minister, Lord Simon, over his shareholdings, and the President of the Board of Trade, Margaret Beckett, over what Tories consider her parliamentary truancy.

I do not know whether his criticisms have been fair, but politics is a rough old game, and Redwood has proved an energetic shin-kicker.

But yesterday was an occasion for generosity. He had, after all, *won*. He had forced Lord Simon to relinquish his shareholdings early; he has embarrassed Mrs Beckett; and now he was being recognised for his efforts.

Mr Redwood chose the occasion to make another rather personal attack on Lord Simon, a respected man – and then to take a swipe at Mrs Beckett.

It is hard to explain why this was so inappropriate, but if you had been there, you too would have felt it. You, reader, if you had been at the Savoy, would have understood.

Mr Redwood did not. This was an occasion to say thank you, raise a glass or two of Highland Park, and perhaps to make clear that his campaigns were not intended personally. That too he missed.

In a room containing more than its complement of conservative-minded men and women, this Tory jarred horribly. He just didn't get it. He didn't even know he hadn't got it. We actually began to feel sorry for him.

This was a failure not of reason, but of grace. The occasion provided a metaphor for the state the Conservative Party is now in.

Rogue Prescott Lost in Thicket   *3.12.97*

Questioning Ann Taylor, the Leader of the House, on prospects for the Wild Mammals Bill (which outlaws hunting with dogs) the Liberal Democrats' David Chidgey (Eastleigh) got into a muddle and called the proposed legislation the Wild Members Bill.

He spoke truer than he knew. For what was the distant trumpeting? John Prescott was smashing his way up through the forest, brandishing in his trunk a fat sheaf of papers: his local government financial settlement. Announcing (to all intents and purposes) the likely level of future council tax increases, John Prescott promised MPs 'a plain English guide' to local government finance. With due respect to Mr Prescott, a plain English guide to Mr Prescott is even more urgently needed.

It was one of the longest statements anyone in the Press Gallery can remember a minister making. It was also one of the most technical. Mr Prescott's civil servants must have been desperately keen that this rogue elephant of the grammatical jungle stick to his text. He tried, Heaven knows he tried.

But an annual local government financial settlement is a thicket of verbal briars, and Mr Prescott's speechwriter had laid terrible traps for him. Journalists had the benefit of a printed text.

We held our breaths as the minister approached sentences like '*we expect to see a reduction in the net costs of outstanding debt,*' but Mr Prescott waved his trunk and crashed straight through. Then, on page five, as the Wild Member gathered speed, thundered past Standard

Spending Assessments, took a tight corner at Elderly Residential Social Services and came stomping through Local Authority Debt, we leapt for cover as he hooted and bellowed his way into New Capital Expenditure. We could see trouble ahead: an exceptionally nasty little thorn bush composed of this deceptively simple sentence: '*I am proposing to put right that wrong.*'

It was tragic that a man who could galumph his way through acres of dense gibberish like '*altogether we have made extra provision of one thousand and sixty million pounds (£1.06 billion), or 5.7 per cent, to go into English schools in 1998–99 than* [sic] *this year,*' should come a cropper on so small a piece of gorse. But Prescott became horribly snagged.

'I am proposing to put right that right wrong!' he trumpeted. The Deputy Prime Minister sensed immediately that he had blundered, but became confused as to how. He tried to reverse out of the bush. 'For the record,' he roared, 'I'm putting that wrong right!'

For the record, he wasn't. His text said he was putting right that wrong. But he was nearly there, and much closer than putting right that right wrong. Mr Prescott disentangled himself from the paragraph and stomped off into Area Cost Adjustment.

10.12.97　　# Tebbit Meets His Match

There is an old *Punch* joke about a sign at a zoo: 'WARNING: if attacked this animal defends itself.' Over in that noble zoo they call the House of Lords, this should hang from the bars of Lord Williams of Mostyn's cage – as Lord Tebbit found to his cost yesterday.

Admire or detest him (this sketch admires), Norman Tebbit is one of the wryest and most mordant men in British politics. And there is something wonderfully destructive in his soul.

It is said of Tebbit's first lessons in game-shooting that the instructor would shout 'Fire!' but the young Norman kept missing the bird. But when they tried shouting 'Kill!', Tebbit bagged the bird first time.

Yesterday in the Lords, he had Lord Williams in his sights.

A small, mild-mannered peer, Williams of Mostyn is nevertheless a shrewd and senior Labour spokesman: so senior that one Fleet Street gossip column mentioned his name in connection with the Lord Chancellor's job, should there be an unexpected vacancy. But Lord Irvine of Lairg shows no signs of going, so Lord Tebbit began his question to Lord Williams yesterday with sarcastic felicitations to Williams (whose 'charm' he praised) on the rumoured good news, which he said he hoped was true. Mostyn remained impassive.

Then Tebbit went on to the attack. He had asked the Government about the 'scope' of 'the work of the Ministerial Group on the Family'. 'In these days, when the Government is going to have no more secrets,' he sneered, 'why, despite a number of written questions, are they unable to explain their definition of the family?'

Tebbit's purpose was clear; he has been a persistent critic of progressive notions in a sexually permissive age. He had come to the House of Lords to torment the Labour front bench on the subject.

Lord Williams began with a straight bat. The Government, he said, did not 'seek to prescribe how people live their lives'.

He was critical of those he had heard aptly described in a quote he had read: people 'who cannot imagine that what does not accord with their own ephemeral prejudice could be popular or morally defensible'.

Lord Williams paused. That quote, he said, came from a book by Lord Tebbit. He had bought it in a second-hand bookshop in Moreton-in-Marsh. The book was priced at £13.99 – *UK only* – 'that's to stop those nasty foreign people reading it'. Their lordships began to giggle.

But Lord Williams had not finished. The book had been repriced, he revealed, 'at £3.50'. Then it had been reduced to £2. The final reduction was to £1. 'I bought it for 50 pence.'

The biter bit, Lord Tebbit did not come back for a second bite.

Lord Williams became Leader of the Lords in 2001.

It's Tony Poppins – But Medicine Won't Go Down
11.12.97

As the Government's plans for single parents hit trouble, Diane Abbott gets her revenge.

'The nation's First Nanny,' Crispin Blunt (C, Reigate) called Tony Blair. This chapter in the Tony Poppins Annual is headed *The Medicine Fails To Go Down*. Clare Short's face said it all. 'Fed up' understates. As Mr Blair's thunder turned to bluster, to rant, to bleat, she sat beside him, tapping her fingers on her notepad.

The hush as Diane Abbott rose to tell her Leader softly that he was wrong was as unforgettable as the noisy energy with which Blair beat the air and by turns hectored and rebuked. This was Blair's bloodiest half-hour.

William Hague had been insistent; but cutting single parents' benefits is a Tory idea, so the hour was not his. He attacked on a narrow front, alleging that Mr Blair was 'not straight' with the voters in proposing what before the election he had criticised.

The Prime Minister struggled to deny this. Under pressure he began taking refuge in the time-honoured response of a nanny with a pushchairful of trouble: You're wrong. Why? Because.

He told Hague, 'Sorry, but that is simply not correct,' and, 'Sorry: just to repeat again . . .' To Paddy Ashdown he said 'That is simply *incorrect*,' and, again, 'That is simply not right.' To Phil Willis (Lib-Dem, Harrogate & Knaresborough): 'That is just *nonsense*.' To Laurence Robinson (C, Tewkesbury): 'We have kept every single promise. *Yes* we have.' And to John Townend (C, E Yorks): 'On the *facts* he is *wrong*.'

Ms Abbott was devastating: a sweet moment for a woman humiliated by Labour orders that she avoid all contact with the press during the general election campaign. 'How does he justify . . .?' Abbott began, almost whispering. Ms Abbott's voice has never been quieter nor reached so far.

By now Mr Blair was rattled. His answers became longer and looser. He looked exasperated. Paddy Ashdown twisted the knife, reopening another wound. How about closing tax loopholes like off-shore trusts, he asked, using the proceeds to rescue benefits? 'Why ask the poor to pay for the poor?'

'That is simply not right,' bleated the Prime Minister, above the hubbub.

Ministerial resignations followed.

Tidings of Discomfort and a
Seasonal Stocking
22.12.97

It would take (to misquote Dr Johnson) a surgical operation to get tidings of comfort and joy into the understanding of a Member of Parliament. MPs gathered yesterday for their last day's proceedings before Christmas, to question the Home Secretary, Jack Straw, and to remind each other, and Britain, what a wicked old world this is.

The closest anyone came to seasonal jollity was when Bob Laxton (Lab, Derby N) presented Madam Speaker with a single, rather manky-looking, Christmas stocking. It was empty. Apparently it had come from his constituents, David and Mary, in Derby. Mr Laxton held up this questionable offering, dangling limply from one hand, as Betty Boothroyd did her best to fix her features into that 'just what I always wanted' expression.

Invited to join this first gesture of new Labour's Giving Age, the pleasantly understated junior minister Alun Michael looked doubtful and glanced nervously at Miss Boothroyd. 'As there is only one stocking, Madam Speaker, and as it is empty, I assume it is to be filled by Father Christmas, and not by Madam Speaker's leg . . .' He trailed off.

Miss Boothroyd looked tolerant, but faintly unamused. It is really not done to mention Madam Speaker's legs, either of them, in the chamber. The only part of Madam Speaker we may mention with impunity is her eye, which members strive assiduously to catch.

MPs went on to discuss crime, murder, road accidents, corruption, electronic tagging and identity cards.

As this sketch departed the joyless scene for its own Christmas break, the House was awaiting the arrival of a statement on mad cow disease, held up by computer failure.

Our much-vaunted Year of Change, which had begun with statements from ministers on the continuing problems of BSE, ended in the same way.

Superbloke Takes Wings

13.1.98

This sketch has seriously undervalued Kenneth Clarke. I have suggested that the former Chancellor's ordinary blokeishness was an act. The untucked shirts, the self-drive van to remove belongings from 11 Downing Street, the stay at a £25-a-night Blackpool bed & breakfast establishment during the last Tory conference . . . all, I have implied, were just calculated media stunts.

On Boxing Day your sketchwriter, bound for Eritrea, boarded an Ethiopian Airlines flight to Addis Ababa. In the crush for economy seats, I seemed to recognise a chubby figure accompanied by a lady with her hair in a bun. It was Kenneth and Gillian Clarke, with friends, going to Uganda on a birdwatching holiday.

At the transit lounge in Addis Ababa, the former Chancellor walked straight past the inviting doors of the Golden Lion VIP Room and was to be seen at the public bar, quaffing Ethiopian beer from a bottle, among a crush of ordinary Ethiopian blokes. And whom should we spot, a fortnight later, on the flight back to London last Friday? Still travelling (with his friends) in the economy class – and by now tanned and tieless – Mr Clarke was doing his best to get some sleep in a cramped seat surrounded by noisy passengers and their babies, none of whom seemed to recognise him.

My last sighting of this impressive bird (after an 11-hour flight) was outside Terminal 1 at Heathrow, where the crumpled MP for Rushcliffe could be observed wheeling his luggage wearily around the pavements, disconsolately seeking the friend who was to collect him.

So Mr Clarke really is an unpretentious man. I am sorry I ever implied otherwise.

Another tanned political figure took the chair as the Commons reassembled yesterday for the new year. Betty Boothroyd's gorgeously golden-brown skin testified to a very sunny Christmas in West Bromwich this winter.

Theatre of the Absurd

The Commons reassembles.

The Prime Minister has now dropped every pretence of giving answers. Anything awkward he just ignores. This is so successful it is surprising nobody has tried it before. His reply makes no logical link with the inquiry which prompted it; a sort of Dadaesqe dialogue reminiscent of the Theatre of the Absurd.

For William Hague this was infuriating. Despite the rabble on the Tory benches around him, the Conservative leader remains lucid. He repeated what should have been a devastating quote from one Social Security Minister (Frank Field) directly contradicting another (Harriet Harman). Mr Field had said means-testing would 'penalise work, tax savings and place a premium on dishonesty'. His boss had said she planned to extend it.

How would Tony Blair answer? Simple. He just told Mr Hague it was important to reform the welfare system. Hague tried drawing Blair back to the quote itself, then gave up and said the Tories might support welfare reform if the Government would explain what they were doing and why.

Mr Blair said that there would have been no need for reform if the Tories had not left a mess. Mr Hague then observed that the blue of a butterfly's wings was quite extraordinarily intense in early summer . . .

Well, no: actually he did not; but few eyebrows would have been raised if he had. There was a surreal sense that we were all incarcerated in some sort of Kafka madhouse.

A couple of idiotic Tories (too dim to understand that the one thing which could still sink Robin Cook would be a public nudge and wink from sympathetic Tory chaps) tried to censure the Foreign Secretary's sexual adventuring.

The Prime Minister could have ignored these tilts. Instead he snapped at John Bercow (C, Buckingham) that he reminded him of a former MP, David Shaw 'whose hallmark was to be nasty and ineffectual in equal quantity'.

Like St Paul, Mr Blair is prey to those sudden rushes of venom which choke the personally virtuous. He lashes out. Sometimes he draws blood. But does it befit a Prime Minister? Just before Christmas he made a sneering comparison between the Liberal Democrats' mild-mannered Treasury spokesman, Malcolm Bruce, and Tinky Winky. Everybody laughed, but . . .

A year ago he called John Major 'knee-deep in dishonour'. Major winced but . . .

This sketch remembers when nice, bumbling Robert Adley MP (not long, as it turned out, for this world), asked Neil Kinnock whether there was anything he had not changed his mind about, and Mr Kinnock said yes, he had formed the opinion early that Adley was a jerk, and stuck to it. The remark seemed clever for half an hour.

Soames Loses Dignity in Underpants

20.1.98

Poor Nicholas Soames hardly deserved it, especially from one of Her Majesty's ministers. The Tory MP for Sussex Mid was in full flood yesterday, telling Peter Mandelson of his concern about what was to be put in the Millennium Dome. Soames is a vast man.

'*You* could have an exhibition inside your own underpants!' shouted somone. The accent was cockney. I looked down to see where it came from. Some backbench Labour wag, no doubt: it's easy to be a cheeky chappie when you have no ministerial dignity to maintain.

It was the Minister for Sport. Tony Banks is fast becoming a national treasure. And the idea of Mr Soames's massive Y-fronts being converted into some sort of millennial tent was priceless. Soames took it with his usual good humour but the important points he was making about a lack of accounting transparency over the developing dome were fatally undermined.

22.1.98 # Body Language Says it All

Have you seen that television advertisement for a small car, whose message is that in dangerous situations we make ourselves small? Children are shown instinctively shielding themselves, crouched and clenching the whole body, hugging arms across chest for protection.

If Gordon Brown's body language at Prime Minister's Questions yesterday had been an amateur performance by an actor in a village-hall whodunnit, playing a Chancellor of the Exchequer driven to the verge of homicide by suspicion of his Prime Minister, then the theatricality would have made you wince. He would have been hamming.

Mr Brown sat with Tony Blair to his right. Mr Blair looked relaxed in the 'imperial' haircut first modelled by Sir Derek Jacobi in the role of *I Claudius*. But Brown had drawn his left shoulder away as though shrinking from a nameless horror. His right arm was swung diagonally across the chest, gripping his left shoulder. His bent knees were pressed tightly together, like the mummified child victim of a human sacrifice. Even his head tilted slightly away, in a sort of frozen jerk.

Real Nobility Does Not Need Dignity

28.1.98

The gilded splendour of the Lords made an odd setting. 'I like pigs. As a child, I grew up with them on a smallholding. Not the mass-production variety, but three sows who slept in deep beds of straw of their own construction, foraged in the orchard and reared their piglets without sow-crates or tail-docking or, indeed, antibiotics. They were Socialist pigs because they came originally from a herd owned by Nye Bevan. I clearly remember lying in the straw with an arm around a large recumbent sow while she listened with every appearance of intelligence and sympathy as I told her my childhood problems, to which she responded with reassuring grunts.'

The Baroness Mallalieu, QC, was speaking in Monday night's debate on the Welfare of Pigs. Imagine a Commons frontbencher admitting in debate to cuddling pigs and telling them personal problems! Before we pull our Second Chamber apart, is it not worth appreciating the special strengths of a legislature in which nobody cares if they sound silly?

You Can't Lose in Ulster

30.1.98

Blair speaks on Northern Ireland.

T.E. Utley was right: 'Those who plunge deeply into the Irish bog are revered for their courage and commonly exonerated from their ineptitude.'

Perennial amongst the cant spouted by political wiseacres is that Northern Ireland is a bed of nails for British ministers. 'Ah, Ireland,' they nod sagely, 'graveyard of political reputations.'

Nonsense. Northern Ireland is a bed of nails for the Northern Irish. For London politicians who avoid being blown up, the graveyards of Ulster are a bed of roses.

To my recollection, no Cabinet minister has ever left the post of Northern Ireland Secretary with personal reputation lowered. And no Prime Minister ever damaged his standing on the mainland by venturing into peacemaking in the Province. Even at the trough of John Major's approval-ratings you could always raise a cheer for him by commending his brave and patient efforts to build peace in Northern Ireland.

The reason is simple. Expectations among the English are zero. We do expect the Government to mend the roads, so we grumble when they fail. But who expects Ulstermen to love each other?

Both sides there being widely regarded here as mad, it is impossible to disappoint us by failing to reconcile them: we just sympathise with anyone who tries. Against the discordant background noise emanating from the Province itself, our politicians find it easy to make their music sound harmonious.

Yesterday at Westminster, Tony Blair picked up his fiddle and played as sweetly as any before him.

Tell Blair He's in Charge

5.2.98

Tony Blair delayed his departure to Washington long enough to look in at Westminster and treat his party in the Commons like some sort of doggie. In America they have drum majorettes. In Britain we have new

Labour backbenchers. Panting poodles sat up and begged; each was awarded with his or her biscuit.

The Prime Minister escaped serious questioning even from the Leader of the Opposition. William Hague, perhaps stung by accusations that his pursuit of Robin Cook's private arrangements sounded undignified last week, opted now to play the statesman instead. He offered Mr Blair Tory support in standing up to Saddam Hussein.

Those of us who, last week, deplored Hague the scandalmonger were forced to admit yesterday that there are also problems with the alternative. It's hard to be gritty and Churchillian when you're only 36 and not in charge. Still, Hague sounded composed – if not stately. He came back later with a plea for farmers, which will have pleased farmers.

Oddly enough, Tony Blair's performance as world statesman also needs more work. His problem is the opposite of Hague's. Blair *is* in charge – but cannot help slipping into the role of playground nose-thumber. Though Prime Minister for some time now, his attacks on the Conservative Government continue unabated. It is as though, uncertain what else he can say which will be greeted with any warmth by those behind him, he yells yah-boo-sucks at Tories and Iraqis, confident that that at least will please.

Yesterday the Prime Minister called Saddam a liar – twice. He called the Tories hypocrites and opportunists once, 'appalling' hypocrites and opportunists once, and 'opportunists, with not a single constructive thing to say' once. 'That's why *they're* in opposition and *we're* in government!' he screamed. 'What a load of rubbish!'

What's eating the guy? You don't have to say this kind of thing when you're Prime Minister. People know you're boss. But Blair sat behind his dispatch box while Hague was complaining about farm incomes yesterday, with his jaw working, his eyebrows tugging skywards and the expression of a chap fighting the temptation to flick blotting-paper pellets at the Opposition Leader.

Both men were spared the Commons scenes during the stupid debate that morning on Robin Cook's diary secretary. A deputy Speaker, Michael Martin, appeared helpless or supine as government back-benchers mounted one of the ugliest displays of Commons barracking observers had seen in years.

That Deputy Speaker became Speaker in 2001.

Only The P-word Describes It

6.2.98

Lord Irvine of Lairg fiddled with his wig. He was bored. 'There was this old lady,' Lord Stoddart of Swindon told the House, 'who asked at her local shop for a pound of potatoes. And the shopkeeper said: "They're *kilos* now, madam." "Very well, then," she said. "I'll have a pound of kilos." '

The rumble and titter of what passes for laughter among titled persons ricocheted around the gilded chamber. You get it all, over in their lordships' House: jokes, anecdotes, a philosophy lesson, a thundering sermon . . .

And Lord Irvine of Lairg. He sat, later yesterday evening, upon the Woolsack, studying his nails. Brushing aside the tails of his wig for a better view, his lordship tried spreading his fingers out, palm facing away, to examine the ends of each finger, and the overall picture.

Then he turned each hand over and leant a little forward to observe each palm, half-clenched, the fingers curled over to display the nails side by side.

He seemed to approve. From time to time he would look up (the Earl Russell was in the middle of a rather brilliant, offbeat speech about the history of religious exemptions), but finding the other people's speeches less interesting than his nails, would resume the inspection.

Is the Pope Catholic? Is Lord Irvine pompous? How shall we describe the Lord Chancellor without being unoriginal?

Sketchwriters hate the obvious, but if you want a word picture of Sir Cyril Smith and rule out 'fat', you will struggle. In a thumbnail sketch of William Hague, how do you avoid the word 'bald'? What was Tom Thumb, if not small? Pinnochio, if not a liar?

And ransack the thesaurus though you will, no expression better captures the essential Irvine than pompous.

After Lord Russell had sat down and a couple more peers had earnestly tried to explain their doubts (the subject was the application of the Human Rights Bill to religious institutions), the Lord Chancellor himself spoke.

Again, I tried to avoid that word. But spend just a moment listening to the bewigged oracle, and 'pompous' leaps at you from behind every bush. Probably witnesses have been applying the description to Lord Irvine since he first threw his rattle out of his pram (probably it was *in* his pram that the infant Derry first began insisting on the full-bottomed wig), but there is just no avoiding the word. Eventually even the doughtiest sketchwriter stops trying to dodge this overused adjective, sighs, and writes it down. POMPOUS, POMPOUS, POMPOUS.

As Lord Irvine warbles and stammers relentlessly on in that faintly sneering tone – a creature of exasperated rationality confronted by a pack of half-wits – you begin to doodle. *Puffed-up. Inflated. Swelling. Arrogant. Lofty. High-falutin. Grand* . . .

And yet, if you listen and follow his argument, you have to add to these words another one: *clever.* The intellect is unmistakeable. This is the tone and manner of a very superior mind, obstinately unwilling to consider wherein it might be mistaken. No speaker in their lordships' House so unfailingly conveys the subliminal message that it's all terribly obvious, he is immensely clever, and the rest of us are just appallingly dim.

I do not know if Lord Irvine has ever asked for a pound of potatoes and been told that it's kilos now. But if any shopkeeper was so foolish, he would have his reply double-quick: 'So give me 0.4536 kilograms of potatoes.' Lord Irvine could think that up in less time than it takes to examine a fingernail.

Mr Mandelson Defends His Body

17.2.98

Is Peter Mandelson the Angel of the North?

'Nice little pelvic bulge, and even though it's a bit of a strange shape, there's no question it's a man,' said the sculptor. His description of the Angel does seem to fit. So when Mr Mandelson (Lab, Hartlepool) boasted yesterday that the Angel comes from Hartlepool, the implication was not lost on us.

Moments later, the snake-hipped Dome supremo offered the nation a tour of his body. Sadly for Britain, this was not the lean, oiled, coiled, sleek, smooth, rippling, eel-like torso of the Minister without Portfolio himself. That remains forbidden fruit.

It was the other body in which Mr Mandelson takes a proprietorial interest that he thought we might care to visit. Tory spokesman Richard

Spring called it 'a giant-sized reclining statue'. It will grace the Millennium Dome. We shall be able to visit its internal organs.

Mr Spring asked whether the body is 'male, female or gender-neutral?' Mandelson invited us to see for ourselves. Visitors to the Dome 'will be able to travel round the body'. He was sure they would find it instructive. What could he mean?

I was left to dream the impossible dream: that the Angel of the South reclining in the Dome, might, even at this late stage, be redesigned – and modelled on Peter Mandelson's own body.

Imagine the internal tour (through what portals, heaven preserve us even from speculating): *'And this vast cavern is the spleen. Huge, isn't it?*

'Next on our itinerary are the cavernous bile ducts – watch it, madam, that greeny-black liquid is corrosive! That shrivelled nodule we just passed? That was the heart.

'Hurry along, now – hear the echo? this neck's made of brass – to the cranium: there's room for everyone in the frontal lobe reserved for fiendishly complicated plots – quite right, sir, the eyes in the back of the head are a most unusual feature . . .'

Only a daydream. I awoke just in time to see Mr Mandelson slide, hissing, from the chamber.

27.2.98   # Gloriana and Pooh

Gwyneth Dunwoody (Lab, Crewe & Nantwich) was looking fabulous yesterday. Generous of mind, gracious of manner, graceful of form and richly robed in autumnal colours, this paragon of every parliamentary virtue, half woman and half goddess, tossed a noble head of golden curls and spoke wisdom and truth to MPs. Members were struck dumb by the majesty of her words, the power of her argument and the splendour of her bearing.

Among many she is known as Gloriana. Sweet as any nightingale, her song did not disappoint.

'If anybody outside is to know what is happening in this House . . .' they should not have to rely (my italics) *'on a series of very cheerfully written and wholly inaccurate reports which relate only to the individual idiosyncrasies of MPs.'* Sketchwriters reeled, cut to the quick. MPs looked up at us in the Press Gallery and pointed. It was us she was talking about!

Wholly inaccurate? Dwelling on personal idiosyncrasies? This was cruel and unfair. We *never* exaggerate. If anything we understate. Poetic licence has no place in the sketchwriter's trade. We describe only what we see. We are scrupulously honest.

The very thought that we might trivialise, or do anything to under-mine the dignified efforts of members – anything to attract attention to the individual rather than the argument – repels us. We see Parliament as a noble forum for the debate of great national questions, not vulgar posturing.

Let me offer an example of our refusal to stoop. Taking advantage of the Prime Minister's important visit to America a fortnight ago, a backbench MP recently elbowed her way into all the newspapers (and television too) by means of a publicity stunt. Raising what was called 'the Poohgate scandal,' she tabled Questions demanding the return from a New York public library of stuffed toys representing Winnie-the-Pooh, Eeyore, Tigger, Piglet and Kanga.

'*MP Demands Freedom For The Pooh Five*' said the British headlines. '*Pooh On You!*' cried the *New York Post*. The American President was asked to comment. The story began encroaching on the serious coverage the press would normally give a prime ministerial visit to Washington.

Then she gave it another stir. In a full-page article in the *Daily Mail*, the MP was quoted as saying: 'Just like the Greeks want their Elgin Marbles back, so we want our Pooh back – along with his splendid friends.'

Of course, it was tempting for parliamentary sketchwriters to get in on this act. But – without wanting to sound too high-minded – we felt that bids for personal publicity like this were beneath us. Mrs Dunwoody's posturing on behalf of the Pooh Five did not make it into our sketches. We might have been accused of personalising, or producing cheerfully written trash.

Neither this Wallpaper, Nor He, Goes

3.3.98

Lord Irvine's redecorated apartment draws criticism.

The Lord Chancellor yesterday unveiled the most expensive crockery in the history of English porcelain. The affair of the refurbishment of his Lords apartment, he told MPs, was 'a storm in a teacup'. £650,000! Some teacup.

The venue for the teacup's press launch was a place of splendour almost rivalling Lord Irvine's own pad. The carved oak doors of Committee Room 8 at the Palace of Westminster had opened to admit a scrum of journalists to a room carpeted in Puginesque designs of red, blue and green, and exquisite wallpaper (ah, wallpaper!) in red and silver. Here the Commons Select Committee on Public Administration was to question the Lord Irvine of Lairg.

Question him on what? Who cares! Journalists just wanted to see him carpeted. Opportunities to question a figure of such majesty are rare – you do not bump into Lord Irvine on buses – and we suspected that, though the committee's inquiry was actually into information and human rights legislation, ingenious MPs would find a way to bring the conversation round to wallpaper. Wallpaper was the story.

So imagine the disappointment when the chairman, Rhodri Morgan (Lab, Cardiff W) asked about privacy laws instead. The normally grand Lord Irvine had listened to spin-doctors. 'Don't blurt things out,' they had advised. 'Be 'umble; promise to write to them.'

He was unbelievably 'umble. He really didn't know a lot about this, he told MPs; he wasn't the minister in charge.

It was the turn of the resentful-seeming Melanie Johnson (Lab, Welwyn Hatfield) to question. Wallpaper, surely? Spirits sank as she began an interminable string of questions about judicial appointments. Even more 'umble, he promised to write to her on this and that. Was she, he asked, ever so 'umbly, 'hospitable to my idea?'

Richard Shepherd (C, Aldridge-Brownhills) came next, grinning sardonically. Did he have a wallpaper question up his sleeve? No. Clever questions, cleverly asked, elicited a series of 'umble replies. Lord Irvine would write to Mr Shepherd, too.

Still no wallpaper. We despaired. Then the chairman called David

Ruffley (Bury St Edmunds), a Tory with an instinct for the jugular. We sat up. If the Government were so keen on freedom of information, sneered Ruffley, why was it so hard to drag the truth from the Lord Chancellor about his refurbishment plans?

Blue touch-paper: Irvine went for it. 'Umility was cast aside. Interrupting the MP ('this is a speech, Mr Ruffley') he started to declaim . . . about wallpaper! Hoorah! Facts and opinions, complaints, dates, justifications and protests came pouring out. At last! Something Lord Irvine was passionate about. It was he who had volunteered the subject. 'I want to seize the wallpaper charge straight on the chin,' he cried, eyes blazing.

'But we are here to talk about freedom of information,' whimpered Mike Hancock (Lib Dem, Portsmouth S).

'This is *quality* wallpaper,' cried the Lord Chancellor. 'Not something from a DIY store which may collapse after a year or two.'

The idea of one's wallpaper falling down surprised Mike Hancock, who said B&Q could do better. Lord Irvine looked baffled. A colleague whispered to him – probably telling him what B&Q was. He resumed his disquisition on interior decoration.

'When they said this would be about the pattern book,' complained Rhodri Morgan. 'I thought they were referring to the writings of the former Governor of Hong Kong.'

It was the shrewd-seeming Andrew Tyrie (C, Chichester) who asked whether Irvine had foreseen the fuss. 'A remarkable storm in a teacup,' said Lord Irvine, beginning to calm down. The storm had abated.

But the teacup will be all over today's newspapers.

Lucy Licks Mr Mandelson – Official

27.3.98

The most interesting thing about the statement Frank Field made in his welfare Green Paper was the progress of the head of David Blunkett's guide-dog Lucy up Peter Mandelson's lap while he made it.

Lucy is a black, curly-coated retriever of placid but whimsical disposition. One of her whimsies came over her as Mr Field rose nervily to say the unsayable. We fast realised that the unsayable was unsayable only because it contained so many abstract nouns that the absence of linking action-words turned the statement into something which would only work in Gregorian plainsong. Mr Field's upturned eyes and meek tenor would have suited plainsong, were incense permitted in the chamber.

Eyes wandered to Lucy. She was licking Mr Mandelson's hand.

To be loved let alone licked by any warm-blooded creature is an unusual experience for the Minister without Portfolio, who looked edgy. But to be seen on television repelling innocent affection from an animal could lose an election. With clenched jaw he put up with it.

Mr Field moved from 'rooting out fraud and abuse' to 'the creation of a decent society'. Lucy was frankly bored. Peter was frankly nervous. Lucy moved her head from his hand to his inside-knee. Frank moved to 'encouraging greater self-provision'.

Lucy explored a little further up Peter's elegantly flannelled leg. Frank explored 'a single work-focused gateway into the benefits system'. Peter looked seriously worried.

'Now I wish to turn to pensions,' declared Frank, tremulously. Lucy turned to Peter's inner thigh, resting her dark, silky curls lightly there. Peter seemed to relax in the face of the inevitable. '. . . the support they need to lead a fulfilling life with dignity,' trilled Frank. Lucy finds her life entirely fulfilling and cares nothing for dignity.

Her wet nose explored a little further. 'We will legislate for new gateways,' promised Frank. The warm muzzle, cosily cradled, had found gateway enough.

Frank started to talk excitedly, about 'action zones'. Mercifully, Lucy did not respond, her intentions being pacific. This was fortunate for Peter. Mr Mandelson was responsible for having the testicles of a dog called Fitz removed from pictures advertising Labour before the last election. Lucy was perfectly situated for canine revenge.

But Peter trusted her. What passes for a smile flickered across those guarded lips. Frank spoke of 'opportunities to develop our talents' within 'a framework of guidance'. He asked everyone to help him 'create a better world'. And sat down. But for Lucy the small world within the framework provided by Peter's right and left legs was all she wanted. Gingerly, Peter stroked her ear. Frank was now calling for a 'Third Way'.

Odd Song From the Valleys

23.4.98

Praise be! Something interesting has occurred during Questions to the Welsh Secretary. Halfway through a session tedious even by the standards of Welsh Questions, a Labour MP's mobile phone went off yesterday.

MPs' attention (and the Commons cameras) had been on the front bench, when there came a sudden, high-pitched trill.

Madam Speaker shot into the air. Nothing more enrages her. As she has explained in a Statement, she is reconciled to silent vibrations in Honourable Members' pockets, *never* to trilling noises, particularly loud ones. '*Whose* telephone is that?' she shrieked. Hundreds of eyes moved to one end of the chamber in the right-hand corner, near the exit to the Aye lobby at the back.

Too late! All that could be seen was an empty stretch of green bench and a swinging door. The culprit had scarpered. So fast had he dived that escape was complete before heads could swivel. The hastily deserted bench now contained only smug colleagues whose wide-eyed gaze said 'Not *me* guv'.

A scattering of turned heads could have led an expert at spot-the-ball competitions to the exact point where the guilty MP had sat, but then we would have needed video-footage of the whole chamber prior to the escape – and there is no CCTV at Westminster.

Had Miss Boothroyd thought fast she could have ordered her bewigged flunkeys to rush to the doors and lock the Aye lobby, imprisoning the miscreant. But by the time thoughts turned to means of capture, he had slipped from the lobby by a side door, by-passing the chamber. Betty was foiled!

Yet at least a dozen Labour MPs, in the vicinity of the crime, must have known the identity of the colleague so recently with them. Might the Chair do as schoolteachers sometimes do, and keep the whole class back until somebody grassed on their Honourable Friend wot dunnit? She let it pass.

Words Speak Louder Than Actions

28.4.98

Imagine a Commons gathered for a Cabinet minister's statement. None of the details of what, when, why or by whom matters. The time – indeed the century – is immaterial. So is the identity of the minister and the subject of the statement.

Forget such irrelevancies; study instead the wording; guess the mood. Is it optimistic? Does the minister understand the problem? Is anything serious about to be done? Is this the *vocabulary* of one who knows what to do?

The minister rises. 'Madam Speaker . . . pleased to lay before the House the Government's White Paper, *Tackling xxxx to Build a Better Britain* . . . strategy for the next ten years . . . strategy . . . effective action a priority . . . distinctive strategies . . . important step forward . . . fresh long-term approach . . . galvanise efforts . . . new energy and action . . . tackle these challenges.

'Responsibility for action . . . partnership essential . . . consistent in our messages . . . communities . . . range of problems . . . communities . . . more strategic response . . . considerable expertise . . . effective and consistent . . . intensive review . . . new strategy . . . rigorous assessment . . . real impact . . . new strategy . . . clear, consistent and rigorous targets, early priorities . . . clear baselines for targets.

'Action comprehensive . . . wide-reaching programme . . . focus as necessary . . . tackle . . . focus . . . impact . . . programme of action . . . programmes for young people . . . action . . . action . . . enhanced effort . . . focus . . . tackle . . . a detailed resource framework building the strategy . . . clear commitment . . . objectives . . . aims to tackle . . . tackling problems . . . only a beginning . . . action and achievement . . .

'Co-ordinating role . . . work together to tackle . . . strategy on the ground . . . relevant and effective . . . strategy ambitious but realistic . . . clear and challenging . . . new objective . . . partnership and common purpose . . . commitment, effort and energy . . . real progress . . . I commend it to the House.'

In political discourse, a reliable general rule is that the sincerity with which a lofty term is used varies in inverse proportion to the frequency with which it is invoked. To put it as Emerson did: 'The louder he talked of his honour, the faster we counted our spoons.' Shakespeare captured the same thought in 'The lady doth protest too much, methinks'.

Key words in the discourse extracted above are 'action' and 'effort'. We may conclude that both are despaired of. Another is 'tackle'. We may conclude that no serious attempt to tackle anything is envisaged. Also recurring often are 'strategy', 'focus', 'clear' and 'co-ordinate'. We may conclude that the approach is unfocused, unclear and unco-ordinated, lacking strategy. The appearance twice of an unusual word, 'rigour', suggests that there can be none.

'New' keeps coming up. Conclusion? There is nothing new. So does 'commitment': it must be lacking. But the giveaway is the repetition of the words 'real' and 'realistic'. We may conclude that the plans announced are unreal and unrealistic.

When I tell you that some 23 government backbenchers bothered to attend, their numbers swelled by 16 opposition MPs, you surely guess that yesterday Ann Taylor, the Leader of the Commons, was unveiling a national strategy to tackle drugs. She promised a clear, focused, ambitious, energetic, galvanised, rigorous, co-ordinated strategy of action to tackle the problem.

There was a thin cheer. You may conclude that the Government has more or less given up.

Top Hat Defends Garter *1.5.98*

In Commons bars, MPs may discuss skirt. In the Other Place yesterday, peers discussed garter.

Or Garter. For it emerged that Garter is a sort of nickname given to the Garter King of Arms, the chap who, dressed in a gaudy hearthrug, prances about at Ceremonies of Introduction when new peers take their places. His name is Peter Gwynn-Jones. In other workplaces, pals might call him Pete. But peers call him Garter.

Odd, to name a bloke after an item of lingerie. Might peers start addressing each other as Panties, Jockstrap or Special Cleavage Bra? To summon Lord Mowbray, do mates shout 'Oi, Eyepatch!' Is Lady Trumpington code-named 42-DD?

The subject of the debate was a select committee's proposals for reform of the Ceremony of Introduction, removing much of the kowtowing, writing Garter out of the script, and modernising to no obvious purpose beyond enabling new Labour to press release news that Cool Britannia now extends to Wicked Ermine and Bad Woolsack.

Peers were reconciled to reduced flummery but lamented the loss of Garter.

This was not Lord Richard's view. The Leader of the House, who gargles on vintage port and might better be dubbed Cigar, acknowledged work done 'behind the scenes' by Garter but wondered if we needed to see him.

The ceremony would still provide 'a good day out for family and friends'. Relieved bishops learnt that they could still wear their robes. Reform, said Cigar, was 'a very small but perhaps important piece of history'.

Carpet-Slippers disagreed. Some may know this decent Tory former knight, who slightly fails to set the pulse racing, as Lord Dean of Harptree. He breathes calm and carpet-slippers, Carpet-Slippers saw a role for Garter.

So did Plumed Hat: Lord Waddington, lately Governor of Bermuda, thought this move, after only 377 years, 'indecent haste'. But String Vest (plain-speaking Lord Elis-Thomas, a former Plaid Cymru MP) had found his own introduction 'degrading and objectionable'. Specs (the Archbishop of Canterbury) slid out. Slip-on Shoes thought the compromise reasonable.

Lord Rodgers of Quarry Bank (Bill, a former SDP type) is a bit of a smoothie, somewhere between typewriter mechanic and lounge lizard. He thought that hats worn at Introductions so obscured faces that new peers might never be recognised.

Next on her feet was Beads. The Baroness Lockwood, in mauve jacket and orange necklace, defended reform. The toothbrush-moustached Duke of Norfolk (Tache) defended Garter. Red Socks (Lord Cranborne) listened attentively, but Silk Dressing-Gown was absent – sadly, for Lord St John of Fawsley loves this sort of thing. Hair Oil was there: Lord (Kenneth) Baker of Dorking looked, as ever, amused.

I left after the Bishop of Norwich had spoken. Dog Collar, reviewing the theory that the three bows in the ceremony represented the Trinity, canvassed the suggestion that ten more might honour the Ten Commandments too. Lord Bradwell (Tom Driberg) has passed away, I mused. Y-Fronts, who made a pass at anything in trousers *except* men with beards (the reason many Labour MPs grew beards) could have added seven further bows: one for each Deadly Sin.

Dog Collar said that he and Top Hat (Earl Ferrers) had recently communicated by telephone from respective hospital beds. 'I assured him of my prayers. He sent me champagne. It seemed to me a model of what a good relationship between Church and State should be.'

MP Brings Icing to PM's Cake   7.5.98

Call me a feminist, but I do think it degrades women to expect a grown-up lady to dress as a birthday cake to wish the Prime Minister a happy birthday.

You knew as soon as you saw Jean Corston's pink outfit that this was going to be somebody's big day. Hers. The Labour backbencher fluttered into the chamber yesterday in extraordinarily shiny pink silk, secured at the front with a row of dozens of little pink buttons. The effect was spoilt by the omission of plumes and a drum. Her question was second in the list. One's heart sank.

There followed an interlude in which William Hague, who has been warned by pollsters not to rain on Tony Blair's Ulster Parade, chose to drizzle on it instead.

In one of those 'while I would be the first to applaud . . .' homilies – an ill-intentioned shove masquerading as an arm on the shoulder – we watched what Tories presumably think demonstrates that no fuzzy-brained dream-merchant can pull wool over the eyes of this tough-minded Tory anti-terrorist. Hague wants to ride two horses: public approval of the agreement and the hostility of the Orange-tinged Tory Right. We sigh and look away.

Our eyes return to find the pink tunic on her feet. No need to read the Order Paper: a glance tells you which of today's new Labour backbench women plan to star at PM's Questions. They are all dressed up.

Jean Corston was all dressed up but sadly had nowhere to go. She wanted to wish Tony Blair happy birthday and regret that he was *so* busy leading the nation that he would have no time to spend this special day with his family. But *Tories*, she ventured, did have time to spend with their families – they'd been chucked out by the electorate! Boom-

boom. After her *bon mot*, Ms Corston looked around to await the delighted laughter of her friends.

The next Labour backbencher on his feet, Barry Jones, who is 60 next month, proved that age is no barrier to sycophancy. Old poodles never die. The MP for Alyn & Deeside, sidling a little stiffly to his hoop, jumped gamely through. Did the Prime Minister agree that playgroups made a fine contribution to British society? Mr Blair shocked MPs by agreeing and – surprise, surprise – happened to have a handy factoid about a new grant with which to delight us.

Old poodle was followed by Young Pup. Ian Pearson (Lab, Dudley S) had the grace to look shamefaced before asking Blair to confirm 'three incontrovertible facts' – all three of which celebrated Labour's very excellent record in education.

All in all it was a happy day for the Prime Minister. Such was the joy that when Anne Campbell (Lab, Cambridge) rose, looking radiant, one half expected her to break into a birthday poem:

Now you've got to 45,
Vibrant, tough and full of drive,
Backbench fans can all declare
Happy Birthday Mr Blair!
But she attacked the Tories and the Liberal Democrats instead.

Poodles Caught During Hoop-training

22.5.98

It hardly seemed worth looking in on Treasury Questions yesterday – for why see the film when you have read the book? Friends in an opposition party had handed me the script in advance: they had found a spare copy lying around in Westminster.

The document was headed *Treasury Questions – 21 May – interventions on Sterling*. A glance made plain its purpose. These were 'planted' questions for use by pliant new Labour backbenchers, in support of their government front bench. Whips had guessed that the Chancellor would come under pressure from opposition MPs about the strength of sterling and the damage this threatens to manufacturing exports. They wanted loyal backbenchers to be ready to chip in on his side.

That is where the lucky recipients of this script came in.

They were to learn by heart (MPs are not allowed to read out) the following: '*Is my Right Honourable Friend aware that what manufacturing wants is stability, and will he join me in congratulating the engineering industry for an increase of output of over 3 per cent in the last year?*'

MPs are no longer considered capable of thinking up questions like this on their own. Even the Right Honourable Friend was spelt out for them.

The next question runs: '*Would my Right Honourable Friend agree with me what manufacturers most worry about is a return to Tory boom and bust? And has he seen the latest survey which suggests there will continue to be expansion in manufacturing employment and investment over the coming months?*'

The next inquiry repeats, word for word, the 'Tory boom and bust' mantra, then has the questioner ask: '*Could I take this opportunity to remind the Chancellor that exports of British manufacturers have actually increased by over 7 per cent in the last year?*' Gordon Brown, via his lackeys, is arranging *to ask himself* whether he may remind *himself* that manufacturers' exports have grown by 7 per cent.

Spoilsports might suggest that what the Prime Minister likes to call hoo-ha could be saved if Mr Brown skips Treasury questions, lies quietly in a darkened room and reminds himself of what he already knows.

But that misses the point: it gives the backbenchers something to do.

All that flummery and swank, all those wimps. It seems an expensive and cumbersome way of getting bad prose drafted by deadbeat propagandists to be printed in *Hansard*.

Finally the poodles are advised to yap: '*Could I ask my Right Honourable Friend to put to one side the negativity of the party opposite and consider the fact that there are actually 5,000 more jobs in manufacturing now than there were a year ago?*'

I refuse to tell you who asked which question yesterday. It may help their careers.

Matron Flies in

3.6.98

A new Tory destroyer, HMS *Anne Widdecombe*, was launched yesterday at 14.33 hours. She blew her whistle and ploughed straight into HMS *Frank Dobson*, a middle-aged corvette of considerable firepower. Both sustained superficial damage but neither sank.

Arms akimbo and glowering at the Secretary of State, the formidable hulk of the Tories' new chief health spokesman presents a fearsome sight to the Government benches. Beside her, a slim and agitated new sidekick, Alan Duncan, completed this Hattie Jacques & Charles Hawtrey of a duo.

And what a carry-on! From the look in Widdecombe's eye, Frank Dobson must have been grateful for the interposition of the dispatch box, for she looked ready to lumber on to the table and come at him from on top with her big black handbag. Spokesmen normally stay seated, confident that a nod in the Speaker's direction will get them called: but Widdecombe leapt up and down like an eager backbencher.

An opening salvo came from Alan Duncan, whom the Speaker called Ian. What a start! On your first day the Speaker forgets your name. But Duncan was not deterred. Mr Duncan declaims as from a balcony. He must be daunting over the cornflakes. Then Miss Widdecombe lunged at the dispatch box and started slugging it out with Mr Dobson – also on the subject of waiting lists. She was not subtle. He was not nimble. Neither was brief. The result was much banging about, punctuated by the rattle of statistics and the thud of hyperbole. Nobody won.

Frank Dobson resembled a teddy bear with attitude: Ann Widdecombe illustrates beautifully the use of 'bosom' as a collective noun. The two of them (neither, as Dobson reminded us, at the fashionable end of their parties) swung at each other like the survivors of a long and acrimonious marriage, familiar with the argument, hating each other's guts, and staying together for the sake of the health service.

Mount Mackinlay Rises Proud   *4.6.98*

If there is anything you could call a hill in Thurrock, it should be named Mount Mackinlay tomorrow. In decades to come, the young of Thurrock will tug their dads' sleeves and ask if they remember where they were on the afternoon of June 3, 1998, when Andrew Mackinlay (Lab, Thurrock) took on the might of his own party machine.

I was there. At Prime Minister's Questions I witnessed an act of unbelievable bravery.

A Labour MP stood up and twitted Tony Blair – to his face!

Humble little Mr Mackinlay, with his crumpled suit and dropped aitches, took a sling and let fly at a massively armoured Prime Minister and his fearsome Chief Whip. Mr Mackinlay told Mr Blair to stop scaring his MPs off their duty to hold the Government to account.

The chippy, chirpy, middle-aged Mr Mackinlay cannot stand an inch above 5ft 6in. Since winning Thurrock for Labour in 1992 he has inhabited the front bench below the gangway – home of Dennis Skinner and a small gang of professional hecklers. Noisy as the rest, Mr Mackinlay is distinguished by his likeability, humour and opinions more populist than ideological. A minor hammer of the Tories, he has never looked like a whips' poodle – but nor has he given his own front bench any serious trouble.

Until yesterday. His question to the Prime Minister had been selected by ballot as the first of the afternoon. He was first to be called – and will have known this for some time beforehand. Unless you know the pressures this puts upon a government MP, you will not appreciate Mr Mackinlay's courage. The moment the list was published, a Blair lieutenant will have been on the phone. 'You're first up for Wednesday. Your question's in the post.'

'I'll ask my own question, thanks.' Angry silence. Phone rings again. 'Well at least tell us what you plan to ask.' 'What I choose.' Another angry silence.

Another phone call. 'The PM would be *enormously* obliged if you'd give him a vague idea of your concern – so he can prepare a really helpful reply.'

'Sorry.'

Then the taps on the shoulder in the tea room; the approaches via friends; the quiet aside in the Members' Bar; the threatening glance in the gents . . . all these, brave Mr Mackinlay will have resisted.

Yesterday he rose in his place at 3.30pm. Mr Blair looked up edgily. Mr Mackinlay began diplomatically. He remembered the craven way *Tories* used to question their government, he said, 'The fawning, obsequious, soft-ball, planted questions . . .' All sides began to laugh. The reference was to this Prime Minister. Sitting with Mr Blair, the Chief Whip studied his fingernails. Will you *'discourage* such a practice,' he said to Mr Blair, 'and encourage, rather than discourage, loyal Labour MPs who seek to provide scrutiny and accountability?'

There followed the loudest cheer heard this year in the Commons. The Prime Minister tried to grin. 'I fully respect your independence of mind,' he replied – then, with infinite menace: 'and I'll do my very best to see you retain it.' Meaning 'and while I live and breathe, a backbencher you'll stay'.

'Ooh!' squealed the mob.

The next question was from John Hutton (Lab, Barrow & Furness). To call it toadying would be to invite a libel action from toads.

MPs and journalists roared with laughter. The Chief Whip winced. A whole row of robots had been pre-programmed. It was too late to de-program them. You cannot just switch these people off. Yet.

Mr Hutton was later made a minister.

9.6.98 # So She Was Only Pretending!

Yesterday at questions to the Social Security Secretary we saw Ms Harman in a new light. A feature in the *Daily Telegraph* had gushed; 'Harriet Harman admits that sometimes she pretends to be stupid.'

A mystery is solved! A generation of bewildered Commons-watchers have wondered how anybody could be so dim. Why does she never engage with the question, never see the joke? Why does she answer by parroting single, simple phrases, repeated in a passionless monotone? Now we know. *She is only pretending to be stupid.*

Sometimes (she reveals in the article) she pretends never to have heard of the question. Asked once about nuclear emissions, 'I didn't know what the line was'. Afraid 'people listening might think "Bloody hell, what an airhead!", I kind of felt myself choosing to sound completely ignorant.'

It was fascinating yesterday to watch Ms Harman employing this technique in her job as Secretary of State. 'Most women are somebody's daughter,' she announced to astonished MPs: a thought which had occurred to few.

Helen Jackson (Lab, Sheffield Hillsborough) asked a more pointed question about helping women to combine family with work, but Ms Harman did not take us much further. She told Mrs Jackson that 'parents need time with their children'. She offered an example: 'Around the time of birth.' On this Ms Harman must be right. She might have added that it is common for parents to be present at the conception too.

Ms Harman returned to the dispatch box, still pretending to be stupid. She read out her answer to her backbench colleague Tony McNulty (Harrow E) in the flat, inflexionless drone of a difficult schoolgirl forced to read aloud as punishment. 'We've had to phase the roll-out and do it slowly and at a measured pace,' she droned. Having long ceased to understand ministers' answers, one begins to lose confidence they understand them themselves.

'We were in story-limitation mode,' Ms Harman wittered in that *Telegraph* interview, 'so I went round every economic forum and made myself look an airhead.'

Ms Harman was succeeding yesterday beyond her wildest dreams. She's pretending, of course. But how will we know when she isn't?'

Was It All Worth It? 10.6.98

Join our sketch on a magic carpet ride (with a stop or two) back over the decades. For the first leg of our flight we hop nearly a quarter century to 1974.

A young MP of 34, described in Roth's *Parliamentary Profiles* as 'dark, handsome, trendy-looking, idealistic, full mop of curly black hair' has just made a stunning leap, early in his career, to ministerial office. The youthful new junior minister at Agriculture (who only three years earlier voted against Britain's membership of the Common Market) is to introduce a Bill providing a minimum wage for farmhands. To have come so far, so fast, gives promise of a meteoric political career. 'Watch this space,' say all the wise heads of political commentary.

We note the opinion and reboard our flying carpet, this time for a much shorter hop: back to 1971.

London is abuzz with rumour. Is the actress who took the female lead in Ken Russell's outrageous new film about Tchaikovsky, *The Music Lovers*, to get an Oscar for her stunning performance as the composer's disappointed bride? London dinner parties crackle with controversy over whether she was well-advised to appear naked in that now-notorious railway-carriage honeymoon scene. But nobody questions her talent.

Did she get the Oscar? Yes. We take note, hopping on to our time machine: a leap back six more years to 1965.

A new research fellow in gerontology has just been appointed in the Sociology Department of the University of Essex. He is only 26: obviously a brilliant academic. 'Looks like a schoolboy storybook hero,' writes the journalist Colin Welch. 'Tall, dark, lean and earnest,' say others.

Already fascinated by politics, he is on the intellectual Left and a member of the Fabian Society. The young research fellow is soon to contest Colchester in a by-election for Labour.

Did he win? No. We record the attempt, and move on for our shortest hop, just two years this time, but we are now 35 years back from today. It is 1963.

The room is swaying – for we are at sea. Who is the burly young steward bearing down on us, sweating under the weight of that tray of minestrone? He is 25. He looks confident. Already active in his seaman's union, his wider ambitions (if he has any) are known only to himself.

Yesterday in Parliament, the Deputy Prime Minister and Secretary of State for the Environment, Transport and the Regions, John Prescott, 60, was a little burlier, no less sweaty, and as confident as ever. The man they call Two-Jags brushed aside a scattering of Tory jeers about his non-appearance at the parliamentary cycle ride that morning. 'I welcome National Bicycle Week,' he roared. How far away now, that minestrone?

Beside him sat his junior ministers. Bespectacled Michael Meacher, 58, earnest as ever and still lean, was tackling an inquiry about the environmental impact of water prices. What price now that fellowship in gerontology? And where are those revolutionary dreams?

Gavin Strang's tousled, romantic black locks are greying a little at 54. Trendy would be the wrong word and idealism, if still there, is concealed. He never quite made it to the top but, well, Transport matters, doesn't it?

'It is the responsibility of the Lancashire County Council to decide how they will prioritise funds for the road for which they have responsibility.' Glenda Jackson, she declared, summoning what theatricality the lines will bear. Twenty eight years on and still sticking to her script. No Oscar for this, we fear. But at least she no longer has to take her clothes off.

An Angel Passes Over Three Graves

11.6.98

A bad day for Jack Cunningham. He scores a big European victory on BSE – and the Prime Minister struggles to avoid congratulating him in the Commons. This bodes ill in the Cabinet reshuffle, and government backbenchers should beware. Simply to praise *any* Cabinet minister is no longer enough: at the cutting edge of sycophancy, you must know which.

Lawrie Quinn (Lab, Scarborough & Whitby) thought he was on to a winner. Rising at PM's Questions he tripped over himself in his enthusiasm to hail the progress on BSE made yesterday in Brussels, applauding the 'political diplomacy' of Dr Cunningham, then squeaking ' . . . and, er, really all credit should be done, er, and given, to Jack Cunningham!'

The Tories jeered. But where was Mr Blair? Replying, the Prime Minister did not mention Cunningham's personal achievement, remarking only that there was far to go.

A few fools had made the same mistake at Questions to David Clark, who as Chancellor of the Duchy of Lancaster is in charge of freedom of information.

Used singly the two words 'freedom' and 'information' are suspect enough to those on-message. Conjoined they bring Mandelsonians out in hives. Dr Clark is supposed to deliver on Labour's manifesto promise to rip down the curtains of bureaucratic secrecy. The very thought! A couple of ill-briefed government backbenchers were unwise enough to encourage him in this task. You could sense their electronic message-pagers vibrating. '*Return-to-base, return-to-base . . .*' Slogging his way miserably through his replies, all poor Dr Clark could do was insist that proposals *must* be prepared for consideration.

On open government, sensible government backbenchers belt up. To creep is wise, but the intelligent creep does not creep indiscriminately.

On yesterday's evidence, they should think twice before yapping in Robin Cook's support, too. Mr Blair was tackled hard by William Hague on the Sandline affair, and the latest row over when Foreign Office ministers were briefed. Blair defended his colleagues, of course, but . . . maybe the Prime Minister was just tired. Energy and emphasis, not to say coherence, appeared to flag.

It meant little – just one of Mr Blair's off-days – but the Prime Minister did seem beset on all sides by minor difficulties. Each, alone, was no more than irritating; and it may be that Mr Blair does not care, or need to, how his weekly half hour in the Commons goes. But there were moments yesterday when he almost seemed to be losing the plot.

William Hague, whose weekly bleat of a sort of shopping-list of everything he thinks is wrong with the Government is becoming stilted, may feel he is making no headway. But older readers will remember Winston Churchill's unexpected choice of a poem by a Christian Socialist, Arthur Clough, to rally morale:

For while the tired waves, vainly breaking,
Seem here no painful inch to gain,
Far back, through creeks and inlets making
Comes silent, flooding in, the main . . .'

So far it is hardly a flood, just a sort of sloshing sound down among the rocks.

Still, one intervention did cheer Blair. A new MP, Roger Casale (Lab, Wimbledon) told him that 'all the children in Wimbledon are already wired up to computers'. An astonishing success for Labour's command-and-control strategy! The Prime Minister was overcome by a fit of the giggles.

Blair did for all three, Cunningham, Clark and Cook, in the end.

Widders' Outleak Anything But Blook

17.6.98

A vicious rumour about Anne Widdecombe was fuelled yesterday: she's looking good. To suggest that the defiantly unfashion-conscious new Shadow Health Secretary might give a moment's thought to her appearance will be regarded by her as the wildest slur – I risk a libel action – but the allegation must be made. She was almost chic.

For her debut speech in yesterday's health debate Miss Widdecombe chose – if not a little black dress – then at least a *medium*-sized black dress. And beyond appearance there was substance.

The House heard an exceptionally well-written and passably well-delivered speech which, as the fearsome Miss Widdecombe got into her stride, had the handful of Labour backbenchers present looking cowed, if not convinced: if not defeated, scared.

With her sharp-beaked new pet, junior spokesman Alan Duncan, at her side – a hawk light enough to rest on her wrist were she to wear a leather falconer's gauntlet – she rose to a good cheer and an expression of implacable mirth on the bearded countenance of her foe, the Health Secretary Frank Dobson. As she plunged on he found the mirth hard to sustain.

I wonder whether, buried deep in that formidable bosom, there resides a secret hope of the highest office? Her debating style is not unlike Margaret Thatcher's, but, if anything, more engaged. Her tactic is to hurl facts and accusations until the enemy squeal – then shout them down as they do so. When combat threatens to become technical she reaches for the vocabulary of the classroom or kitchen.

'Always somebody else's fault!' she yelled, like a teacher refusing to take further excuses, when Mr Dobson tried to blame his altered timetables on Tory statistics. 'In a *minute!*' she barked, as a Labour backbencher rose to interrupt with a question: then, when she was ready to hear him, '*Yes!*'. If yesterday she did not quite snap 'next!' at an interruptor she was ready to take, then she will. How long before she chants: 'Come on if yer hard enough!'?

She roared halfway into an arresting phrase, 'In Oxfordshire the outleak is especially blook', before realising she meant the outlook was especially bleak, and took a second run at it.

When Miss Widdecombe works up momentum she threatens to come right off the road.

And she yodels! Perhaps it is the excitement, but the Shadow Health Secretary's voice keeps breaking on unexpected words – and leaping an octave up, for just a syllable.

Thus, yesterday, 'the entire STRUCture of Labour's health reforms.'

Or, even more surprisingly, the final digit in a list: 'the thirtieth of June, nineteen ninety-NINE'.

By the time she sat down Mr Dobson was rattled. So rattled that when Mr Duncan asked him 'what was "early" about Labour's early pledge' to cut waiting lists, Mr Dobson floundered: 'It was certainly early, and we *are* doing something about it.'

Audio-Lego Piloted at Westminster

26.6.98

Londoners will be familiar with our infuriating new experiment on the Tube for the Circle and District lines. Tube bosses are testing a pre-recorded in-car public address system, telling passengers where they are.

The messages for each station have not been recorded separately, but constructed from the building blocks of individual words or phrases. A simpering 'classless' female voice has been used, the poor woman having been required to say into a microphone 'the', 'next', 'line', 'lines', 'Embankment', 'Circle', 'station', 'stations', 'change here for', 'this is the' . . . and many more.

Using computers, London Transport managers have assembled a suitable message for each station, built from the appropriate parts, assembled in the right order. The Tube driver presses the buttons.

The result is horrendous. Intonation is haywire, words not elided properly, and there are stupid pauses – the voice rising, falling and halting meaninglessly. The effect is Orwellian. Passengers grind their teeth as this dreadful, sinister, robotic, singsong whine invades their calm. A huge anger builds until one is hard-put not to vandalise London Underground property. I hope the lady who provided the voice was well paid, for she must now be susceptible to assault by anyone who ever hears it again.

'This is the – Circle – Line. The – next – station – is – Embankment. Change – here – for – the – Northern – and – Bakerloo – Lines.' Whoever hatched this customer-relations disaster ought to be shot.

Watching Treasury ministers at Questions yesterday, a revealing oddity struck me. In two separate answers, far apart in time, ministers used *exactly* the same verbal formula: 'the Comprehensive Spending Review which will be published shortly.' Not a word altered, though so many other ways of saying something similar are available: 'which will be/should be/is to be published/concluded/released . . . soon/before long/before the summer/in due course . . .' No word varied. Order unchanged. Too uniform for coincidence.

And it dawned on me. Ministers' answers are being assembled by new Labour on the same audio-Lego principle as the London Underground's. Millbank Tower has collected approved 'on-message' expressions, supplying these to ministers. The minister presses the appropriate mental buttons, stringing together a word-perfect but gruesomely hollow answer. The advantage for the co-ordinators of Labour's 'strategic message' is that nothing untoward can ever be said. There are no words to say it.

Master of this art in the Treasury team is the flesh-creepingly smooth Alistair Darling, Chief Secretary. Listening to Darling yesterday we could identify the on-message phrasal building blocks. These included 'a prudent level', 'fabric of society' and 'the stop-go policies of the last government'. Also recurring were 'the fact is', '£2 million extra for the Health Service', 'a bit rich from the Tories', 'a sustainable base for the future', and, of course, 'the Comprehensive Spending Review which will be published shortly'.

Could Mr Darling himself, along with his utterances, be an assemblage of approved parts – a New Britain Action Man, or Alistair-doll – rather than a man? Slim, tallish, impeccably-suited with white shirt and sober but cheery tie, Darling (though young) has beautiful, soft, white nylon-like hair and a classless accent with just the faintest hint (very new Labour) of Educated Scot.

'As-we-move-into-the-next-millennium . . .' purred Darling – another approved phrasal block. More mannequin than man, one suspects that to avoid embarrassment to shoppers during window-dressing, the ordinary bits beneath Mr Darling's trousers may have been replaced by the smooth bulge which is also to grace the private parts of the giant humanoid in the Millennium Dome.

'Explosion of Women' Shock

7.7.98

The sparky Lorna Fitzsimons (Lab, Rochdale) revealed such a shocker yesterday that we wondered why she chose a routine question to social security ministers instead of demanding an emergency debate. Under new Labour, apparently, women are exploding.

Ms Fitzsimons brought the dramatic news to a fellow-woman, Joan Ruddock, a minister who oversees women's issues. 'We see,' Fitzsimons told her (and aghast MPs), 'the explosion of women in part-time work.' Do we? Where? What a prospect.

Looking round the chamber at some substantial lady Members best not named, one trembles at the likely damage. There would be shrapnel everywhere . . . gold buttons, flying handbags, shattered earrings and yards of heavy fabric. Innocent bystanders could be strangled by catapulting lingerie. Twanging elastic can inflict a bad burn.

Fitzsimons herself, hugely ambitious for ministerial office, sees a backbench job as only part-employing her potential. What if La Fitzsimons explodes? Image those hold-ups as projectiles, those Cool-Britannia specs hurtling, missile-like, as all the accoutrements of power-dressing fly outwards: shoe buckles, Cuban heels, Gucci logos, sharp elbows and bits of spiky brooch . . . lethal.

Frank Field, the minister for Welfare Reform, did not explode. He has never yet exploded. But he looks as though he may.

Mr Field is at the smouldering-fuse stage of his career. If, after the coming reshuffle, this Minister of State sits where he sits now, and his boss, Harriet Harman stays where she is, I predict Field will explode by Christmas. Yesterday, as Ms Harman wittered her way through answers of a vacuity which would shame a budgerigar, her smouldering sidekick looked fit to detonate at any moment. A new junior Tory spokesman, John Whittingdale, asked a straightforward but technical question about the treatment of dividend tax credit, which he said was robbing elderly savers. Harman replied that what Britain needed was 'a thriving, skilled economy'.

Quentin Davies, another Tory spokesman, invited her to answer his colleague – or to answer him: why were local DHS offices sending circulars which frightened pensioners into moving to cheaper homes, destroying their peace of mind?

Harman's answer? 'This Government is very concerned about health and social services for older people.'

Mr Field's lip was buttoned tight. The fuse spluttered.

Tony McNulty (Lab, Harrow East) gets our Crawler of the Day award. 'Would she agree,' he asked Harman, 'that this new Labour Government had done more in a year than the previous Conservative Government ever did, and *they* caused abject poverty and should hang their heads in shame?'

'I welcome the points my Honourable Friend has said,' replied Harman.

Field did not say any points. The more fed up he looks, the less he says. When one of his own backbenchers, Jonathan Shaw (Chatham & Aylesford), asked a long and worthy question about disability living allowance, Field replied 'Yes'. Again Mr Shaw rose, with an even longer question, divided into three. Field rose, looking testy.

'Yes, yes and yes.'

The session over, Ms Harman stayed to deliver a lengthy statement on the Child Support Agency. 'Work for those who can, security for those who can't!' she cried. I would like to say I saw a thin smile play upon Mr Field's lips, but not yet the explosion. If the Prime Minister is wise, he should get bomb-disposal experts working urgently.

In the end, Mr Field did explode. Ms Harman imploded.

Integrated Transport Panacea   *8.7.98*

Stephen Timms (Lab, Planet Zog, also East Ham) raised with environment ministers yesterday the problem of the Thames gateway – whatever that is. He was almost the only MP not to be told that the solution was the integrated transport strategy . . . *coming soon!* In modern ministerial discourse the integrated transport strategy resembles the philosopher's stone of old: a mysterious object which, once unveiled, will turn everything to gold.

What is the integrated transport strategy? Animal mineral or vegetable? Is it a bird or a plane; an argument, a plan or an invention? All we know is that, whatever it may be, the Government is convinced we need one; ministers have promised to produce one; and, once produced, the integrated transport strategy will prove the answer to a thousand problems. One only hopes they patent it.

Is parking a difficulty for you? The integrated transport strategy will solve it. Is your bus difficult of access? Are the kerbs too high for your pram? Is the M25 jammed at rush-hour? Is Derby bus station a mile's walk from Derby railway station? Fear not. Soon we shall have an integrated transport strategy, and all will be well.

Jeff Ennis (Lab, Barnsley East & Mexborough) was concerned that traffic fumes are hastening death. Michael Meacher, the Environment Minister, reminded us that an integrated transport strategy was on its way. Norman Baker (Lib Dem, Lewes) was worried about ozone levels . . . ah, this, said Mr Meacher 'is one of the reasons we need an integrated transport strategy'.

Fiona Mactaggart (Lab, Slough) called for an annual roadworthiness test for vehicles. 'The integrated transport White Paper comes out soon,' trilled the Transport Minister, Gavin Strang.

He did not tell us anything about it. Does *he* know what's in it? If so he is guarding the surprise. So fixated on this mystery were ministers that they found it hard to concentrate on anything else.

'The minister did not mention natural gas in his reply,' complained an aggrieved Gordon Prentice (Lab, Pendle) – as though every minister should. 'I'm sorry I failed to mention gas,' stammered Meacher. Gas may be *part* of the integrated transport strategy.

Jacqui Lait (C, Beckenham) wondered when we could expect the roads review. Around the same time as the integrated transport strategy, it seems, when 'all her questions will be answered'. Gillian Shephard, chief Opposition transport spokesman, wanted to know about widening the M25. You can guess the reply.

Jonathan Shaw (Lab, Chatham & Aylesford) was concerned about public transport. The junior minister, Glenda Jackson, comforted him: 'The integrated transport policy White Paper will be out soon. Integrated *public* transport will be a key element.'

'Our integrated transport policy White Paper will be the first for 20 years!' she cried to Gerald Howarth (C, Aldershot). When Christopher Leslie (Lab, Shipley) asked for news of the Bingley relief road, he was told to await . . . well, you got there ahead of me.

Suspicious about this highly unspecific solution to every woe, we turned to the Tories: had they had a more concrete proposal? They sure had. Anne Winterton (Congleton) was certain how to reduce toxic vehicle-emissions. These, she advised, came mostly from 'older engines owned by the less well off.' Solution? Why, simple! The Government should 'encourage them to buy new cars'. Silly really that the poor hadn't thought of that before. Come back, Marie Antoinette.

Small Blockage Removed – Hague Lets Rip

9.7.98

Mr Hague returns from minor surgery.

How did he look, after his op? From my gallery seat only William Hague's bald patch was visible. I studied it before he spoke for indications of his mental state. It looked pale and stressed. Who would have guessed that an assault of such ferocity was about to be launched on the Prime Minister? If this is what a small operation on his sinuses does for Mr Hague, then he should check into the Darlington Memorial Hospital for another before every High Noon with Tony Blair.

Hague was magnificent yesterday; agile, scornful, impassioned, canting, deeply unjust – everything an Opposition Leader should be. He left Blair bleating in the dust. By the time Hague stalked from the chamber he had roused the benches behind him to a storm of synthetic indignation such as has not been seen at Westminster since . . .

. . . Well, since Tony Blair did the same when *he* was Leader of the Opposition.

Hague had also kicked a new buzzword into the political arena. 'Kicked' understates. He picked it up, socked it in, socked it in a second time, picked it up again, whacked it through the goalposts three or four more times, threw it in the air and smashed it yet again into the net.

This, shouted a furious Hague at Blair, was 'the culture of *cronyism*'. The Prime Minister was being brought into ridicule by 'the *cronies* he has surrounded himself with'. These were 'money-grubbing *cronies*', they were 'pocket-lining, feather-bedding, money-grubbing *cronies*.'

And these were just his first questions. Hague was soon on his feet again. The wife of a Labour pollster had been proposed for a top job at the BBC. What was this which ('even with *my* sinuses') he smelt? It was the stench of *cronyism*. This was 'Government For Sale'. It was . . .

. . . *candidates are invited to supply the missing word (eight letters, beginning with c and ending with ism)*. According to a newspaper interview, Mr Hague puts many of his past problems down to a 'post-nasal drip'; a graceless and impertinent way of thanking the majestic Sir Patrick Cormack, his Deputy Shadow House Leader. He can afford to be more generous now, for nothing could stop him yesterday. Blair, at bay and having a thin time, stumbled into a universal condemnation of *all* the *Observer*'s charges, and kept repeating in aggrieved tones that the Opposition Leader was making generalised accusations because he knew of no specific wrong.

Again Hague leapt to his feet. This was 'a defining moment'. It was now clear that Blair's crowd had 'too many *cronies* and too few principles'. Having exhausted the six questions an Opposition Leader is allowed, exhausted the Prime Minister, exhausted all of us and exhausted the possibilities of arranging the word crony and its derivatives in as many different sentences as can be divided in ten minutes (seven times), Mr Hague called it a day.

16.7.98   Mandelson Lifts a Trouser-leg

In the minutes before Tony Blair arrived at the Commons for questions yesterday, I saw a horrid thing. Sitting half-obscured in a corner at the end of the front bench, Peter Mandelson decided to check that his left sock had not fallen down.

To do so, the Minister without Portfolio pulled his left trouser halfway up the leg. We were afforded a full view of the leg. The sock *extended all the way up to the knee.* No flesh was visible, just sleek, discreetly bulging, thin grey cotton, elegantly sheathing ankle and calf. Another couple of inches and the sock could have been suspended from above the knee. There was something prewar-Berlin about the hosiery. If Marlene Dietrich had sat beside him she would not have looked out of place.

Wherever They Lay Their Hats   *28.7.98*

Wherever he lays his hat, that's his Dome. 'Without Portfolio' no longer, Peter Mandelson stalked in at seven minutes past three to no sound beyond the prickling of hair on the backs of 100 MPs' necks.

Dome Questions were scheduled for 3.10 and Mr Mandelson, repositioned as Secretary of State for Trade and Industry, has taken his Dome there with him, rather in the way that a hermit crab carries its adopted carapace wherever it goes.

Wherever he lays his hat, that's his bunker, too, for Mr Mandelson takes not just his Dome but his enemies in tow. If Mandelson had thought that at the Ministry without Portfolio it was the office rather than the occupant whom Gordon Prentice (Lab, Pendle) detested, his very first question as Secretary for Trade and Industry ended those hopes. It was from Mr Prentice.

The crisp bitter-lemon-voiced Scottish leftwinger launched into his most insolent attack yet on Mandelson. Asking about the use of lobbyists to promote and secure funding for the Millennium Dome (and receiving no answer), Prentice complained sarcastically that he had 'expected a more illuminating answer from the minister who casts such a long shadow'. He refused even to call Mandelson 'my Rt Hon Friend'.

A long shadow indeed. Wherever he lays his hat, there's his shadow. Clare Short's 'creature in the dark' irks many in his party. When one Labour backbencher praised the Millennium Experience as 'symbolising something' about the way Britain was going, Diane Abbott (Lab, Hackney N), another left-wing critic, nodded in contemptuous irony.

It was a Commons Cabinet debut over which Mr Mandelson will take perverse pleasure. He relishes the role of stage villain. His very first questioner, *on his own side*, having omitted to congratulate him, he received from the Opposition front bench the rudest of congratulations. For the Tories, Peter Ainsworth told the new Trade and Industry Secretary that he certainly knows a great deal about trade.

To all this loathing, Mandelson seemed impervious. He had, after all, moved into one of the top jobs in Government.

For lesser ministers, mere survival was relief enough.

'I'm still here!' squawked a delighted Tony Banks to startled MPs yesterday.

'Hanging on in there! Holed up in the Department for Culture, Media and Sport, with a *"come in and get me, copper"* notice posted on the door . . .'

Mr Banks glanced up at the Press Gallery, anxious that we notice. The Minister for Sport may be reckoning without the possibility that he is (as he put it) 'still there' only because the Prime Minister has forgotten he exists.

Banks's boss, Chris Smith, still Secretary of State, was hiding the unspoken 'phew!' more diplomatically.

The threat had passed. Wherever he had laid his hat this morning that is *still* his home.

30.7.98

Why, Tony?

Every now and again this Prime Minister, in many ways one of the most assured performers Downing Street has seen in decades, misjudges. Usually the misjudgement arises from a very slight panic about his own authority. He slips into the nervy dignity of a head prefect scared of mutiny in the Lower Sixth – and over-compensates. The misjudgement can be startling. Yesterday was such a day.

It had been, for a croaky-voiced Blair, a shaky half hour of PM's Questions – at the hands of a fluently contemptuous William Hague. Now Frank Field was about to make a personal statement on his resignation as Minister for Welfare Reform.

Should Blair stay or go?

There are arguments for going. Prime Ministers cannot attend every dog-hanging. Field was not in the Cabinet. The precedent might prove awkward. Some will have wanted Field cut down to size. Serve him right, pious little squirt.

Yet to leave would look bad. Blair might seem insolent – or frit. Thatcher sat through Geoffrey Howe's personal statement. Major had the grace to endure Norman Lamont's barbs. There was also the matter of courtesy toward a man whom Mr Blair might be thought to owe some regard.

On paper the argument looks evenly balanced. In the event there was no contest. He should have stayed, listened quietly, and left immediately afterwards. For Mr Field was on his feet within seconds of Mr Blair's sitting down. There was no way the Prime Minister could get out of the Chamber without causing a stir.

And it looked dreadful. The Opposition Front Bench began shouting angrily as the Government Front Bench made (metaphorically) for the emergency exits.

There were two reasons for his ill-grace, I believe. One is the head-prefect syndrome. His authority had been tweaked. People might giggle. Short of demanding that the whole Commons stay behind until the gigglers owned up, it was safest to absent himself.

The other is image-management, to whose demands Blair is super-sensitive. He remembers pictures of Thatcher's face as Howe plunged the knife. An image can brand a career.

He has resolved that media picture-libraries should never contain any such of him.

Fair enough, but now a different image enters the half-remembered mental archive of those present: the Prime Minister of the United Kingdom and his Chancellor of the Exchequer scuttling for the door, as a small, pale and anguished-looking individual whose goodwill nobody doubts, rose to explain the end of his career.

Lib Dem Ripples At Metaphorical Coal Face
24.9.98

The conference season begins.

A nervous young delegate began his speech. 'Good morning,' he ventured – then hesitated. 'Or good day.' It is politically incorrect to make assumptions here at the Liberal Democrats' Brighton conference.

'Complacency is not an option!' gasped another braveheart. Delegates were debating education, and the metaphor was churning. 'As Liberal Democrats,' cried a defiant blonde lady, 'we want to make a ripple!' There was applause. 'But will it work, down at the coal face?'

Jackie Ballard MP, Liberal Democracy's answer to Jo Brand, lunged for the rostrum in turquoise and purple. The loud, funny, large and bouncy lady who represents Taunton was limbering up for the lunchtime fringe.

'I have a dream!' she bellowed – adding, as an afterthought, 'don't clap too often.' Would her dream make a ripple at the coalface, or would complacency prove an option? Metaphor-mix was near overload.

Circuits cooled as Robert Maclennan MP, the departing party President, rose to anoint and introduce his successor, the Baroness Maddock. Mr Maclennan is about as messianic as a village curate and delivered his come-on-down-Diana! fanfare with all the raw energy of a particularly decorous Japanese tea ceremony.

Diana Maddock is a nice, sensible-sounding woman in spectacles, her hair neatly chiselled in grey waves. She should marry Jack Straw. Their children would be born in specs with breeze-proof wavy grey hair. From the cradle, the little Maddock-Straws would be nice and sensible, eschewing soft toys and placing their rattles neatly beside their cots.

Lady Maddock came across like the personnel manager of a large branch of Marks & Spencer, addressing staff on a bonding weekend. But her task was to uplift, so she chose Everest as her theme, drawing her metaphor from mountaineering. 'To make our mark on history,' she observed, 'we have to plant our flag at the very top.'

'We're going to have a mountain to climb – an Everest. But think of the views from the top! . . . You – our sherpas – are willing and able. Our route to the top is bathed in sunlight.'

It was not easy to imagine Lady Maddock in goggles and crampons, nor to picture the delegates, kindly people in sensible shoes, deserting their tea and biscuits for the Himalayas. All that Gore-Tex! It became no easier when their President's metaphor made a sudden detour into the circus ring. 'For you, Paddy,' she announced to Mr Ashdown, 'we would jump through hoops of fire.' Lady Maddock should not jump through a hoop of any kind, let alone a hoop of fire. Her perm would catch light.

Still on the slopes of Everest, Lady Maddock commended something called 'Do It 2000' and 'gender-zipping', presumably not a reference to Bill Clinton. What did this mean? 'We were all disappointed when at the 1997 election we found only three of our MPs to be women,' she announced, mysteriously.

How was this discovery made? Was there some kind of a check? Had Gore-Tex disguised the essentials? Was gender-zipping the problem – or the solution? Complacency was not, of course, an option, but, bathed in sunlight and badly singed after jumping through the hoops of fire, how is a girl to make a ripple at the coal face and still, specs frosted in ice, plant her pole on the summit of Everest by teatime – or even Do It 2000?

For Jackie Ballard this may be a dream. It sounds more like a nightmare.

The Other Side of Jenkins
25.9.98

Roy Jenkins's recommendations to the government on proportional representation are anxiously awaited.

'When I first met Paddy,' trilled Diana Maddock, 'he was dressed as a frogman.' Diana Maddock puzzled delegates. The Liberal Democrat's newly crowned President was acting as warm-up artiste, introducing Paddy Ashdown's end-of-conference speech.

A frogman? Had she found him on a lily-pad? Had she kissed him? Diana never did explain. The rest of her introduction deepened the mystery. 'Since then I've got to know him *much* better.' There were titters from the press benches. 'And he pinched a member of my staff.'

Your sketchwriter spluttered. Rude thoughts were not dispelled when Baroness Maddock thanked the police, on behalf of the leadership, 'for their discretion'.

A burst of disco music filled the hall. Startlingly for Liberal Democrats, for whom acceptable technology is pedal-powered, all the big yellow screens forming the backdrop to the Brighton stage-set swivelled violently on their vertical axes, almost batting Mr Ashdown off the platform in mid-entrance. The screen which had said 'MOVING FORWARD' flipped to reveal its reverse side – which was blank. What could this mean? Moving backward? Sideways?

Mr Ashdown did his best. He even told a joke about a Labour MP who had set fire to another Labour MP. But nobody could set this conference alight. How *do* you warm up an event which knows it is itself only a warm-up to a main event?

'The other side of Jenkins,' the Liberal Democrat leader has been telling interviewers, 'is another country.' On *Channel 4 News* he told Jon Snow that the other side of Jenkins was 'another planet'.

Why is Roy so blocking the view? Lord Jenkins of Hillhead is a big man but it should be possible to walk round him in an afternoon. Shortly to unveil his new map for electoral reform, he has turned the Liberal Democrat conference into an anxious pause.

Still, all joined the cheering, Simon Hughes MP running forward with such violence on to the rostrum steps to lead it that poor Charles Kennedy, who has been putting himself about mightily in Brighton this week, was left behind, grinding his teeth.

Both clapped vigorously – but, oh, the hatred in that applause! All around Paddy there has been a sudden rush of unswerving loyalty. They are lining up for the kill.

28.9.98

Debates R Us

Labour's stage-set for Blackpool this year must have designed by the Early Learning Centre. Debates R Us. Everything's in cubes, big letters and pretty colours. On jaunty, angular shapes distributed bewilderingly across a soft-lit back-drop suffused in purple, happy or uplifting thoughts are recommended: A NEW DEAL FOR THE YOUNG, each word a different colour to catch the kiddies' attention. It is becoming hard to convey the essence of new Labour in a newspaper that prints words in black and white only. A horizontal strap of little squares in cheery colours, such as might tile the floor of a disabled lavatory, leads to a big square, subdivided into 16 small squares.

These keep changing colour, melding softly from magenta, through burnt lime, to yellow and pink.

Modern conference sets are devised to 'say' something. This one says 'do stop crying children and look at these pretty shapes. Daddy is doing his best.' But the children are tetchy. They are refusing to wear their special Somerfields necklaces, on which identity passes swing. Trade unions selling red ones for Old Labour rebels are doing a roaring trade. Some MPs are sporting these. So is Neil Kinnock.

Whenever delegates meet, eyes sneak downward to the necklace – discreet signal of one's on-message-ness or otherwise. In protest against falling farm incomes, your sketchwriter is using Derbyshire bailing twine.

With her fluid name, against a backdrop of changing coloured squares, Ms Mowlam's mumsy tones are well-suited. 'Prime Minister, Leader of our Party, and good friend,' soothed Mo.

Up strode Tony. The Prime Minister began a string of jokes. By degrees chummy, glib, and frankly pretty fed up, Mr Blair faced a dismaying series of rude questions. Adopting by turns his 'I feel your pain', his 'I tell you straigh' this ain' gonna be easy' and his 'ge' real or getoutamylife modes, Blair retreated in a hail of glottal stops. People should stop carping and support 'the Labour Government you got!'.

Winding up, Mr Blair became so exasperated that, getting it all off his chest, he got into a sort of loop, ranting away at an audience that had begun to thin. He seemed unable to muster his argument into a conclusion.

There's a lot of weasel here to go pop.

His Smile Was Global   *29.9.98*

'I'm not another statistic, I'm David.' David Obaje was shrewdly chosen as warm-up for Gordon Brown in Blackpool.

Young David was so grateful for what Gordon had done for him. Black, well-dressed, with pony-tail (but neat: a *My-Little-Pony* tail) David had come to tell us how Gordon rescued him from a life of 'breaking concrete'.

'I can't *tell* you how important it is to me to get on in life!' David was what the cool call a New Dealer: a lost youth nudged by the New Deal into the arms of capitalism. 'Thanks to the support Rathbone CI gave me,' David was saved.

'Rathbone CI gave me a new outlook on life, gave me a chance . . . New Deal works. So do I!' He departed to wild applause.

David reminded me of those reformed sinners exhibited at evangelical rallies. The subtext was salvation. I watched Mr Blair. Every so often a politician lets real feelings show. Tony Blair was in rapture. His face lit with pleasure as David told of rescue by training charity Rathbone CI. He clapped fit to burst. The trappings of office, officialdom, bickering unions momentarily faded as Blair embraced what he was in all this *for*.

'I want to start,' began Gordon Brown, cannily, 'by paying tribute to David Obaje.' A Brown speech is always a journey. Where will he go? What passion will be thrown into the sightseeing? This was a calculated itinerary taken at measured pace. Not yet the moon-probe.

The speech visited Tony Blair four times, in a respectful if routine way – the phrase 'under the leadership of Tony Blair' inserted politely into anything misinterpretable as a boast. Mr Brown visited Peter Mandelson only once, in a sub-clause.

Then the Chancellor went global.

He went global whenever economic worries required mention. If there is a recession, it will be *global*. If competition threatens British jobs, blame the *global* market. Mr Brown went global 23 times yesterday, mostly to explain problems. Successes were home-made.

An early port of call was unemployment. Ah, but not British unemployment – 'the battle against unemployment in Europe'. Next came recession. In Japan. Along with Japan, 'one quarter of the world' was in recession.

We visited 'the world's financial system' – which turns out to be the problem: 'overexposed' and 'under-performing'. To understand job losses in Britain we toured 'global technological change', 'international competition', 'the world economy' and 'global economy'.

Mr Brown then revisited 'global markets', before a scary outing to 'a world of instability'. World instability recurred four times. Scores are: *global 8; world 5; international 2; Europe 2; France 1; Germany 1; America 1; British downturn 0.*

Globe-trotting over, it was time for a journey into the interior. Of Mr Brown. 'The next stage of our long journey of high ideals' (which turned out to be shared with Tony Blair – phew!) was in Mr Brown's case *not*, he insisted, 'the ambitions of office'.

High priests of media commentary, to whose attention this passage had been drawn by mysterious processes to which you and I are not privy, noted it, and had underlined it on their preview texts. Blair and Brown are pals again, and I'm Napoleon.

Mr Brown ended his speech with a pledge to 'the next generation'. After lunch Peter Mandelson, the Industry Secretary, adorned *his* speech with a pledge to 'the third generation'. Of mobile phones. As applause for Mr Mandelson died rather early, Mr Brown smiled, as a pal might. His smile was global.

Two Cheers for Cheerlessness

30.9.98

It sounded awful '. . . exhausted bodies lying on sofas, carpets strewn with drafts and redrafts; at 4.30 in the morning, standing with his back to the door saying "you're not going till we've sorted this".'

And that was just the preparation of Tony Blair's conference speech, though he had used the word-picture to describe his Good Friday talks on Northern Ireland.

It rang as true of speechwriting. Imagine the scene: 4am yesterday. Blair glances around wearily. Stale sandwiches, crumpled jackets . . . This speech was supposed to uplift – but how do you say 'quit whining and prepare for some bumps' for 20 pages – and still uplift?

'I know,' exclaims Mr Blair. 'Remember that conference in the early Eighties when Margaret Thatcher was a couple of years into government . . . (at Thatcher's name, Blair's courtiers bow, knowing this will please their master) . . . and everything seemed to be going wrong. She made this . . . *defiant* . . . speech. Soundbites Mr Average could connect with. 'The lady's not for turning' wasn't it? Can't we say something like that? How about "the Tony's not for turning *either*"?'

Thoughtful silence from team.

'When the going gets tough, Tony gets going?' suggests a junior. Blair scowls. Ambiguous. Others chip in.

'Grit, not frit?'

'Guts, not gits?'

'Spine, not spin?'

'Or,' ventures his chief press secretary, 'backbone not backdown?'

Blair hesitates. 'OK, let's go with that. Thanks, Alastair.'

But that was not the only sticky patch in this oddly aggrieved and defensive speech. Another had come as Mr Blair wrestled with a draft passage warning Labour they might get unpopular . . .

'Isn't there something in the Bible, Ali?' Alastair looks at sea. 'Like, y'know "blessed are ye when other guys knock you . . ." or some such?'

A Gideon's Bible is produced. St Matthew: *Blessed are ye when men shall revile you, and persecute you, and shall say all manner of evil against you falsely, for my sake. Rejoice and be exceeding glad: for great is your reward in Heaven.*

'Spot on. Take this down,' says Blair, dictating; 'For let me warn you. When you make reform, people will oppose you. They will stand up at public meetings and be applauded for attacking you . . .

'There will be attacks to the left of you, attacks to the right of you, attacks from behind and in front, for my name's sake; but blessed are ye, for yours is the Kingdom of Heaven . . .'

'Er, Tony . . . that's great until the bit about 'for my name's sake' and Heaven. Don't you think that ending might seem – to your critics – a bit, well, *preachy*?'

Anger flashes momentarily in Blair's eyes. He suppresses it. 'Mm, OK, tone it down. After '. . . attacks from behind and in front say, er, "success in life never comes without a struggle." How about that?'

'Fantastic, Tony.'

And so it came to pass that, lit in white, decked in purple tie, against a backdrop of purple cubes, he delivered his updated version of the Beatitudes. Big suit. Big cuffs. Little promises. This was a grim, scolding speech: an exasperated prophet, railing against the frailties of his tribe.

The message was simple: 'Fasten your safety-belts and blame the global market, and the Tories. Get real and stay cool, O ye of little faith – but it took an hour. Still, though the setting was purple, the prose was the least purple we have ever heard from Mr Blair. For that, two cheers.

The Rt Hon Darth Vader is Watching

2.10.98

One image dominates this Labour conference at Blackpool: one face, one figure, one looming presence. If Tony Blair has not won universal love, he commands at least his party's complete attention. Mr Blair does not need Darth Vader's black hood and rasping breath. His arrival into any gathering distracts and transfixes without stage effects.

Even when, as debate proceeds, he slips in at the back of the rostrum of the huge Empress Ballroom, eyes among the audience are dragged involuntarily towards him. The speaker's neck-hairs prickle. Blair sits down behind, watching, breathing. Blair is there.

So it was in the first debate yesterday, on 'democracy and citizenship'. Speakers trooped up to the sci-fi glass lectern to attack proportional representation and (implicitly) complain about collusion with Paddy Ashdown. They felt safe to have their little moan. Blair was not there.

Ron Davies, the Welsh Secretary, made a workmanlike speech about devolution but the atmosphere was flat, inattentive. A text which includes the sentence 'Cardiff is one of Europe's most vibrant and cosmopolitan cities' is probably not going anywhere – and a speaker's in trouble when even an attack on John Redwood gets only feeble applause. But why should delegates pretend to like Davies? Blair was not there.

A lady delegate lapsed in mid-speech into Welsh. Few even noticed. That the sign-language lady's arms dropped limply to her sides, like a puppet whose strings had been cut, was the only signal of this switch from babble in a language we understood, to babble in a strange tongue. And nothing mattered. Blair was not there.

'Be quiet or go away,' said Margaret Beckett, chairing, to chatterers at the back. The remark could serve as the unofficial motto of this whole conference. Or does the AUEW'S Ken Jackson win the prize: 'We're not 'ere just to give the Prime Minister a standin' ovation once a year, we're 'ere to give 'im support for 365 days a year.'

Such loyalty – and Blair not even there to hear him! But he slipped in during Donald Dewar's speech.

The Scottish Secretary had kicked off dutifully and ground on, few listening, when a tall figure appeared at the back, and slid towards a seat. That dark, expensive suit! Those elfin ears! The air crackled. The Presence sat, alert, head cocked, listening. Suddenly Mr Dewar seemed interesting. He must be, of course – for Blair was there.

When Dewar had finished, Blair rose and walked, catlike, towards the exit. But at that moment the next speaker, a woman of no importance, said 'as Tony said on Tuesday . . .' Darth Blair froze, and looked at her, and left. He may just have caught her next remark – 'As Tony reminded us . . .' – as he stole down whatever dark tunnel forms his corridor to and from the light.

IKEA Shows Tories the Way   *7.10.98*

The stage for the Tory conference at Bournemouth has been furnished by IKEA. Pointless little tables and pink, green and blue armchairs dot the platform. Distinguished figures stare out as if beamed up from a VIP lounge, unsure why they are here, but hopeful of catching a waiter's eye. Vast, translucent shapes on the wall form themselves into an arrow, pointing at the exit sign.

Poor William Hague. A leadership bid on his first day! True, Ann Widdecombe spoke only on health; but when, to screams of ecstasy, this remarkable woman, this inevitable gay icon, roused Tories to their feet with a passionate call for the return of the hospital matron, there could be no doubt. The Tories' own Hattie Jacques was pitching for the top job: Matron to the Nation.

Abandoning not just lectern but script too, Miss Widdecombe strode back and forth in *front* of the podium, driving cameramen to despair, flapping her arms, waving an accusatory finger and haranguing an adoring crowd like a strutting lay preacher. Breast heaved, larynx wobbled and her voice began yodelling up an octave with excitement. One sentence lasted four minutes.

Widdecombe earned an unstoppable standing ovation. On it went, throwing the timing out; finally emptying the hall as overwhelmed representatives staggered off for a quiet lie-down, to dream of an enema from Matron; and depriving poor Cecil Parkinson, outgoing party chairman, of half the audience for his emotional farewell.

By contrast, Hague was heard with sympathy and affection, and an ovation that owed more to duty than to rapture.

Lone and dreary,
Faint and weary,
Through the desert thou didst go.

Joining us in the opening hymn, Hague had looked careworn, almost bleak. It must be hard to sing '*Yet possessing every blessing*' when the front of that morning's *Sun* portrays you as a dead parrot.

On the Bournemouth platform, Hague kept up the refrain: 'time to move on'. The phrase was shrewd, for 'time to change the subject' lacks bite. But, ringed by IKEA chairs, Hague had the air of an exasperated hostess whose argumentative guests simply wouldn't shut up.

He should have read his IKEA catalogue. Your sketchwriter has brought a copy to Bournemouth. The chairs in his grandees' corner are from the Tullsta range, with Maltebo fixed cotton covers and 'loose-back lumbar cushion for extra comfort'. So far so good. But the occupants of these chairs are less easily arranged. They're human. If only Mr Hague had read on to page 51, he could have designed the perfect Tory stage-set:

'*Create a corner with a lot of cuddly little friends! All IKEA soft toys*

*are filled with non-allergenic polyester fibres and washable at 40°C.
Safe to bite and soft to play with, they make very good listeners, too!'*

Hague Utters Victory Growl   *9.10.98*

Was it a footpath? Was it a sexual position? Was it a way to fry your eggs? Was it an avenue in Milton Keynes? All we knew was that whatever the British Way might be, it was the way William Hague was going. The phrase appeared 19 times in yesterday's interminable harangue to the Tory conference in Bournemouth. The words Britain or British made a stunning 74 appearances.

'The way to keep government in its proper place' was the British Way. 'The way to safeguard independent institutions' was the British Way. The NHS was also 'part of the British Way'. The British Way was about creativity, about 'doing what has to be done'.

There is a British Way to be in Europe and a British Way to 'nurture freedom and responsibility'. There is almost certainly a British Way to wipe your nose, but Mr Hague did not set this out.

Lest we became confused, Mr Hague explained further. 'Our way is not the First Way, or the Second Way, or the Third Way. It is the only way for us. It is the British Way.' It also turned out to be the Conservative way.

This was clearly a leader trained in the marketing-speak of product differentiation. Fed up with the Third Way? Try the British Way. As an exercise in sounding decisive without committing oneself to anything at all, the tactic succeeded magnificently.

It must be some kind of a feat to lecture more than a thousand people for an hour or more, drive broadcasting schedulers crazy, and knock Channel 4's *Countdown* off its 4.30pm perch without mentioning a single policy. The closest Hague came to any sort of announcement was a promise to consider an English parliament. This actually ran counter to the British Way.

Dead parrot? This bird squawked at us continuously for 31 pages. Like a Yorkshire housewife slamming her husband's cold dinner on the pub counter, Hague ranted away at Tony Blair, Gordon Brown, everyone else in the Government, Paddy Ashdown, constitutional reformers, all Liberal Democrats, Alex Salmond, the SNP, Plaid Cymru, court delays, the IRA, Harriet Harman, offshore trusts . . . None of these people or institutions, it seemed, understood the British Way.

On and on it went. If Hague did not actually say 'and another thing . . .' his body language did. It is lucky he did not even start with a teleprompter machine; had he done so he would undoubtedly have rooted up the electronic lectern, thrown it into the audience and ploughed on.

And lo! Behind him, an enormous pink egg hung seemingly in space, softly glowing. The arrival of other leaders has been marked by a fire in a bush or a star in the East; but the British Way appeared to be an egg in the sky.

There was another novelty in evidence yesterday. Mr Hague has started to accompany his jokes with a little dry gargling noise in his throat. This comes at the end of any comic passage, rather like a boom-boom, marking it as humorous. The sound is somewhere between the nicotine rasp of The Simpsons' Marge and the contented growl of an elderly cat.

'When we listen to Britain,' Hague cried, 'we are listening to the friends of tradition and continuity.'

We were also, it emerged, listening to the defenders of liberty and freedom, the upholders of moral and social responsibility, patriots, true internationalists, a vigorous, courageous and independent people.

Well, if you say so, William. But when Britain listens to *you*, what do we hear? On yesterday's showing, a sort of *gnrrgh*.

Lilley – You're No Nellie

10.10.98

There are occasions when the humorist's pen drops useless to the desk. No wit of his can make the scene he describes funnier than it already is. The joke writes itself. The rest of us are reduced to reporting it. Yesterday at Bournemouth, the Rt Hon Peter Lilley MP, former Chief Secretary to the Treasury, former Secretary of State for Social Security, former Shadow Chancellor, and now the Deputy Leader of the Conservative Party, began to sing.

To the horror of the entire press corps, the alarm of his colleagues on the platform, and the utter astonishment of more than a thousand Tory delegates, this slight, nervy, cerebral, primly self-deprecating man – this Niles Crane of modern British politics – steadied himself at the speaker's lectern where he was delivering his end-of-conference address to departing delegates, and launched, in none-too-steady baritone, into a rendering of a lampoon version of *Land of Hope and Glory* – the words rewritten in comic pastiche by himself.

It was dire. It was gruesome. Cynical, battle-hardened journalists – men who have sat through policy-lectures by John Redwood and survived; women who have been handbagged by Baroness Thatcher and never flinched – cringed, covered their ears, hid their eyes and winced in embarrassment and sympathy, as the Tories' answer to Jussi Björling began (and, we fancy, ended) his career in light opera.

After an eternity, Mr Lilley's song ended. Tory delegates – the *fools* – cheered and stamped their feet – please God, ironically. This had a disastrous effect. Like an over-enthusiastic uncle at a family Christmas who mistakes sympathy for encouragement, Mr Lilley drew a deep breath and sang again. This time it was his parody of *Rule Britannia*. *Rule Britannia*, never an easy song even from the bosom of Dame Nellie Melba, quickly defeated Mr Lilley's sense of pitch.

Lilly, I've heard Nellie, and Lilley you're no Nellie.

He did have other songs, he told us, but they were not fit for public performance. Not, we thought, that this had deterred him from singing the first two. Above the head of every journalist in the room hung a THINKS bubble in which Peter Mandelson was even now rushing an early copy of the Lilley video to a Millbank edit-suite. Already, mocking Social Security Secretary Alistair Darling's timidity over welfare reform, Mr Lilley had cried 'not tonight, Darling!' Labour's next party political broadcast has just made itself.

Lilley's diva-diversion did have one saving grace. It was, in a grisly way, entertaining, as public executions are entertaining.

His speech had not at first promised much. An oration which begins 'haven't we all had a fantastic week!' fills the heart with gloom. 'Growth is down/Under Gordon Brown,' he chanted. Nobody whose name rhymes with silly, frilly, chilly and willy should make poems out of his adversaries' names. The outlook was bleak.

'In Canada, the Ontario Conservatives . . .' began Lilley. The outlook bleakened further. 'The major theme has to be extending . . .'

Ladders? We thought – but no, Lilley wanted to extend freedoms.

'Labour's reform hearse – er, horse – fell at the first fence,' he burbled. He then got halfway through saying 'Labour is trying to seal our tongs' when he realised he meant steal our songs.

Then he sang. They won't steal that one.

10.10.98   # Portillo's False Start Habit

From the Sun: *Michael Portillo, out of parliament, books a theatre for a conference speech.*

Michael Portillo is one of the dozen most interesting and important politicians of our age.

No matter that he is currently without a seat in Parliament. These things can be arranged and, mark my words, will be.

No matter that, after a glittering start in the last Conservative government, he cocked a few things up, got too big for his boots, unwisely revealed his ambitions for the leadership of his party, made a silly speech as Defence Secretary to a Tory Conference, peaked too early, made enemies, and ended up with too few friends.

Portillo acknowledges all these mistakes, and has learned from them.

His recent television series, Portillo's Progress, revealed a man able to listen, change his mind, and begin again.

None of this surprised me. Though I have never been a close friend, I have known Michael for more than 20 years. I like and admire him. He and I worked for the Tory Party together in our twenties – before Margaret Thatcher won power.

The young man I remember then is not very different from the man I see now – super-intelligent, thoughtful, *un*-dogmatic, *un*-ideological, sensitive, highly principled, insanely ambitious . . .

And impatient.

That was always Michael's biggest problem. This man wants the boss's job, he just can't hide it – and he just can't wait. It plagued him then, it damaged him when he served in John Major's Cabinet, and it damages him now.

It damaged him again this week in Bournemouth.

Portillo wants to be – and could be – Prime Minister within a decade. But he's got to get from here to there.

'Here' is all-too plain. The former MP for Enfield lost his seat at the last election. He holds no office in his party and is in no position to bid for the Tory leadership.

The Tories have a leader already. William Hague faces an uphill struggle, but he's a fighter, a good man, and his party will back him.

They have never ditched a leader without giving him the chance to fight at least one general election.

They will not do so now. If Hague loses the next election, he's in trouble. If he loses badly, he's finished. This side of that test William Hague is – short of being found in bed with an under-aged sheep – untouchable.

So how should Portillo play it? You and I can see straight away. Play it long. I'll tell you what I would have done. I'd have come to the Bournemouth conference, but I would have shunned the limelight. I would have been a guest at a fringe event, made sure it was in a SMALL room and watched with pleasure as crowds fought for the privilege of getting in.

The media would all have been there. Friends would have begged me to speak. At first I would have refused. Under pressure, I would have been dragged, protesting, to the floor to make a short speech, a passionate, unscripted endorsement of William Hague's leadership, and a plea for party unity.

Then I would have gone home, feted by party loyalists as a loyalist, feted by rebels as a king-in-waiting – but one who plays by the rules.

Did Mr Portillo take this advice? On the contrary.

He hired a THEATRE seating some 1,500 people only hours before Mr Hague was due to speak on Thursday. Tory delegates did not know what to make of this, whether Portillo's intentions were hostile or whether to come.

I went. The place was only two-thirds full. The atmosphere was flat. Portillo made a thoughtful speech but not a barnstorming one.

And the whole thing went off half-cock. The suspicions of loyalists were obviously aroused. Portillo's relationship with Hague was, surely, poisoned. And his own keenest supporters were left unsure whether they had heard the starting pistol or witnessed a false start.

Michael's a brilliant man, but under the family crest should appear the motto 'Small misjudgements a speciality'.

Do you remember that Waterboys hit from the Eighties, *The Whole Of The Moon*? Mike Scott's lyrics were brilliant.

You came like a comet Blazing your trail . . . A torch in your pocket, The wind on your heels, You climbed on the ladder, You know how it feels To go too high, Too far, Too soon. I saw the crescent, You saw the whole of the moon.

Portillo got off lightly this time. Attention had switched to Hague's own speech and his difficulties with his Euro-MPs.

It was a lucky escape. Unlike in the early Nineties, when he seemed about to challenge Major, then seemed to lose his nerve, last week's little picnic for Portillo's ambitions in Bournemouth escaped much comment.

But friends and enemies will be watching him from now on. The way forward is clear, Michael: Loyalty, loyalty, loyalty.

Your party knows you're there. If anything happens to Mr Hague then, believe me, they'll be in touch.

Until then, chill out. Not yet the whole of the moon.

What, Us, Unrepresentative?

15.10.98

What justification could there be, cried Lady Jay, Leader of the Lords, yesterday, for selecting Members of the Upper Chamber according to 'an accident of birth'?

The Baroness Jay of Paddington, Margaret (née Callaghan) to her friends, is a forceful, clever and good-humoured person and a coming political star. On any test her merits justify her elevation.

But it is just possible to wonder whether these merits might have been noticed as they have been had she not been the daughter of the last Labour Prime Minister.

'Seventy-seven per cent of hereditary peers were educated at Oxbridge,' scolded Lady Jay, questioning how representative such people could be. But Lady Jay was educated at Somerville College, Oxford – as, moments later, she had the grace to acknowledge.

The debate on Lords reform had been preceded by the introduction of two new life peers. Amid much cap-doffing, flummery and declamation, two men – Margaret Thatcher's top spin-doctor, Tim Bell, and Tony Blair's best practitioner of the black arts of backstage party management, Tom Sawyer – found the highest favour Her Majesty can bestow.

'Most trusty and beloved subjects,' intoned the Reading Clerk, as the Baroness Thatcher (in big hair) presented the Baron Bell of Belgravia (no joke); while the Lord Levy (tennis partner of the Prime Minister and caretaker of Mr Blair's blind trust) presented the Lord Sawyer, in a Number Two haircut and designer stubble.

Answering questions before the debate began was another newish peer and Industry Minister, Lord Simon, a Labour sympathiser who was plucked from the board of BP. Capable, useful – yes – but *representative*? Opposite sat a range of Tory life peers, more than a few of whom I recognised as having been generous to their party in their day. Good men, every one, but . . .

As I left, Lord Phillips of Sudbury was making his maiden speech. Lord Phillips was Paddy Ashdown's solicitor.

Real Men Wear Frocks   *16.10.98*

Unlike some people, explained the Bishop of Winchester to assembled peers yesterday afternoon, 'bishops have commitments in the *real* world.'

He wore for this pronouncement an ankle-length white nightie gathered and rucked at the wrists, beneath a black, loose-fitting, over-the-shoulder garment reaching down to the knee; and an enormous silver necklace. How real can a guy get?

As real, at least, as the tenth Lord Walpole, 60, his white hair gathered in an extravagant ponytail for yesterday's debate on Lords reform.

The debate was almost derailed in the opening moments when a rogue hearing aid went haywire and began screaming inside one of their lordships' ears. Audible through the whole great, gilded chamber, it must have been hell for the unfortunate old codger who owned the ear. He tore wildly at his head to get the device out.

As normal service resumed and what bishops are pleased to call the real world reasserted itself, attention was distracted again, this time by a small but intense traffic jam caused when a wheelchair-propelled peer tried to exit in what looked like a panic and became jammed in a passageway between two barons and a viscount's knees. A couple of peers zapped into action and freed the conveyance. When it comes to dealing with wheelchair gridlock, earpiece dysfunction or walking-stick retrieval, their lordships spring to the rescue like the SAS.

The People's Darling

20.10.98

Maybe it's something about the surname Darling. Maybe being called darling by everyone, all the time, ever since you were in nappies – being your teacher's darling, your wife's darling, your constituency's darling, the whips' darling, Gordon Brown's darling and now Tony Blair's darling – finally penetrates your soul until, in the words of the 17th-century mystic, Thomas Traherne: '*You are clothed with the heavens and crowned with the stars: and perceive yourself to be the sole heir of the whole world.*' Whatever the cause, Alistair Darling, former Chief Secretary, and newly promoted Social Security Secretary, strode yesterday into the Chamber to reopen the batting for Labour after the summer, betraying by the faintest of smiles that he knows he is a Darling: everybody's darling, the People's Darling.

His hair looked as though his Mum had wet it down with spit before giving him his sandwiches and his apple for the teacher. His tie, horizontally striped in pastel shades like a souvenir of the sands from Alum Bay on the Isle of Wight, offered a discreet hint of gaiety amid the quietly expensive folds of a very good suit. Nothing fazes a Darling.

Mr Darling did well at the dispatch box, which is to say he uttered nothing remotely interesting to anyone, even himself, leaving us unaroused except by the mystery of this 44-year-old's silver-white hair and jet-black eyebrows. In that *almost* smug way with that *almost* smirk, his mind as quick as his tongue was guarded, he anticipated every trap his interrogators laid for him and sidled good-temperedly around it.

The closest approach we are likely to make to anything like fun with this department, now that Harriet Harman is no longer the Secretary of

State, may (if we are lucky) come from the new junior minister, Stephen Timms, an amiable and clever alien from the Planet Zog.

You know how you get a feeling about people? Mr Timms strikes me as slightly goofy but fair, and fundamentally straight. If so, he is doomed.

Mr McShane and Mr Purchase Cuddle

28.10.98

A modern whip's duties do not exclude helping the Home Secretary to dress. As Jack Straw slid along the front bench to take up his place for yesterday's debate, he brushed past the whip-on-duty, Jane Kennedy. She noticed he was not wearing an Armistice Day poppy. With feminine deftness she removed her own poppy and attached it to his lapel as he passed – scarcely delaying him.

Ten years ago this would not have been necessary. Now, with a television camera pointing straight at it, that patch of green leather in front of the dispatch box must never be occupied at this time of year by a minister not in possession of the requisite poppy. Ms Kennedy saved Mr Straw from a minor gaffe.

Poppies were not the only symbols on display for the cameras yesterday. I spotted one red Aids ribbon, two green ribbons whose significance escaped me, and innumerable pink ribbons, highlighting the fight against breast cancer.

Depending on the time of year, MPs come out in pink Alexandra Day roses, red St George's Day roses, St Patrick's Day shamrocks and St David's Day daffodils. The day approaches when an MP will be regarded as a vacant display-space, on which to pin any number of television advertisements for the cause of the hour.

And none, yesterday, showed a keener sense of the presence of those cameras than Denis MacShane (Lab, Rotherham), a busy, cheeky MP with a roguish sense of humour and an all-consuming desire to be – if not loved – noticed. Mr MacShane did not speak, but by Jiminy he appeared.

Let me explain. If you, reader, were to find yourself alone on a long bench with space for five or six – and then joined by someone who, though neither a lover nor a close relation, chose to sit so close against you that the two of you were all but cuddling – so close that a railway ticket could not be placed between you – you'd think it odd, wouldn't you?

And this was what befell Ken Purchase (Lab, Wolverhampton NE). All at once, Mr MacShane started to cuddle him.

There was a reason. Mr Purchase was sitting directly behind the Foreign Secretary, Robin Cook, who was due to answer a question on the arrest of General Pinochet. Everybody knew that, of all the proceedings of the House yesterday, this was the occasion most likely to be reported on the evening's television news.

And whom would viewers see behind Mr Cook? The portly frame of Mr Purchase.

There was only one way for MacShane to get in on the picture. He had to snuggle up close to Purchase, even edging him a bit to one side. The result was a view from the Press Gallery which television viewers will not have seen within their small frame. A television audience will have seen what looked like a packed chamber – MacShane and Purchase squashed up behind him. But your sketchwriter saw two middle-aged gentlemen, one fat and the other thin, pressed together like limpets – plenty of space to each side of them.

They looked like Laurel and Hardy. Throughout the session it was easy to tell, even without looking at the minister taking the question, whether this was the Foreign Secretary or one of his juniors. When it was the Foreign Secretary, Denis pressed up hard against Ken. As soon as a minister of no interest to the cameras took the floor, Denis relaxed and bottoms shifted a little to allow Ken his personal space back.

I am pleased to report that both wore poppies.

30.10.98   # Lord Jenkins Lost in Dessert

Addressing the nation's press in the plush surroundings of the Institute of Directors yesterday, Lord Jenkins of Hillhead told us that the overriding aim of his proposed change to the voting system, was to 'avoid the electoral desert'. The trouble with desert imagery is that with Roy Jenkins it sounds as though he means dessert.

Lord Jenkins has seen many desserts. But he has surely never seen a desert. All that aridity! No limpid pools, no baskets of fruit, no bathing nymphs! Were the great man to be conveyed, perforce, through a desert it would be necessary to pull down the blinds in his carriage, lest the sight of a landscape devoid of everything lush offend him.

He appeared yesterday (in a phrase once used by my *Guardian* colleague, Simon Hoggart) to be cupping the breasts of an invisible peasant girl as he spoke. Avoiding the desert, he sounded more like a maitre d'hotel warning guests off a dodgy poires belle Hélène.

Accused by a journalist of collusion with Tony Blair and Paddy Ashdown, Lord Jenkins allowed that he had never even spoken to William Hague. Ever. 'I do not know Mr Hague,' he protested. He had never met him. They had not been introduced. 'I would have wegarded it as impertinent to wing him up and say "I'm coming to see you about electowal weform."'

Dear me. A moment's thought made that obvious. How could anyone expect so distinguished a personage as Lord Jenkins to make the first move towards acquaintance with a young man who had not even been Prime Minister, let alone master of an Oxford college. The very thought. The fate of our constitution may hinge upon the failure of mutual friends to effect an introduction between Lord Jenkins and young William.

'It is always difficult to predict the future until it has happened.' Small grunts of delight from guests who grasped Jenkins's little jokes punctuated the discourse. From the assembled company – journalists, politicians, academics, acolytes – came appreciative laughter and intelligent chuckles at each of his lordship's amusing remarks or wise saws.

Turbo-charged by self-belief, Roy Jenkins exemplifies more strikingly than any contemporary in public life an individual's ability to be taken at his own estimation of himself – the confidence he exudes being complete. This was not so much a press conference by Lord Jenkins; it was an audience with Lord Jenkins. We felt honoured.

If we could not, at first reading, actually understand his new voting system, then it can be a matter only for shame that the nation could fail to rise to Lord Jenkins's hopes. His plans are not on trial. We are.

We failed. His plans were not embraced.

Davies Falls on Sword

3.11.98

The Welsh Secretary resigns after an unexplained outing on Clapham Common.

Like some latter-day Caesar, the Prime Minister was away receiving the tributes of a foreign tribal chief when it fell to his ruined Governor of Wales, Ron Davies, to bring down the curtain on a career at court.

A personal statement from a warrior whose reputation has just been wrecked is perhaps the closest we come in modern times to a public execution. An audience of the ghoulish, the sympathetic and the simply curious can be expected to pack the stadium.

Mr Davies had to sit through a tedious three-quarter hour of fractious exchanges on the G7 Rescue Package. He knew that eyes were on him throughout. Thumbing and rethumbing palely through his speech-notes, he looked in need of a rescue package of his own.

As tradition dictates, he was flanked by two fellow officers in Caesar's army. These serve as friends and are allowed to do so without any suspicion falling upon them of implication in the condemned man's offence.

They are there to keep him company before the sacrifice. Colin Pickthall (a backbench centurion from Lancashire) and Wyn Griffiths (who mans Labour's fort in Bridgend) offered comforting pats on the shoulder. Afterwards they would leave him to his fate.

Mr Davies rose to complete silence. Often a 'hear-hear' greets the victim's introduction, but this former commander was met by blank or sympathetic faces, but no sound. He spoke to a hushed background, receiving no indication of his audience's reaction. For an ebullient MP accustomed to noise and knockabout, it will have been deeply unnerving.

It would have been easier for him if someone had at least jeered . . . but nothing: just dropped jaws and silence, as the man who, until days ago, ruled a principality, assumed the manner of a patient racked by intense personal strain, baring his soul on a psychiatrist's couch.

For Caesar himself, Mr Davies had thanks for 'the Prime Minister's solicitude'.

Some condemned men insist on their innocence, railing against accusers. Others try to explain. Some confess and apologise. Mr Davies offered a weird testimony, part plea-in-mitigation; part gratitude to family and friends; part lashing-out against the messenger-media; and all wrapped in an appeal for tolerance with no indication (beyond a hint) of what we were to tolerate.

He sat to a few pats from a few around him. There was a general 'hear-hear', subdued from his own side, a little more sympathetic from the Tories. But then they should know.

And that was it. There was a warm hug from a rival in Wales, Rhodri Morgan, then an arm on the shoulder from the Tories' Peter Bottomley, who had crossed the floor. And a few more handshakes.

A little later, once nobody could accuse him of lacking the guts to stay, Mr Davies slipped out, into oblivion.

What Prime Ministers Hear   *3.11.98*

The new German Chancellor calls on Mr Blair.

Journalists summoned to the Durbar Court at the Foreign Office yesterday witnessed a graphic Anglo-German demonstration of the fact that adoration knows no language-barriers.

Tony Blair spoke English. Gerhard Schröder spoke German. When the Prime Minister talked, the German Chancellor watched and listened in a sort of uncomprehending awe. When Mr Schröder spoke, Mr Blair did not so much listen as pose – in a manner almost statuesque: as though receiving a citation.

Blair addressed Schröder with the air of a man expecting more to be marvelled at than understood, naming him only once: as plain 'Gert'. But the German Chancellor, speaking German, peppered his conversation with his British counterpart's name. It was not clear whether Mr Blair was following the German or the translation – but when he heard the words 'Tony Blair' the Prime Minister's lips pursed with recognition.

The contrast between the two men was striking. Mr Blair's command, his poise, his ease of manner, his choice of words – at the same time assured yet circumspect – was impressive: well-suited to the dignified vacuum the Foreign Office specialises in contriving. In more than half an hour the Prime Minister said absolutely nothing (I noted the sentence 'a dynamic economy within a society with high levels of social inclusion') yet accomplished this with grace and good humour.

The shorter of the two, Mr Schröder stared up at Herr Blair, High Priest of the Third Way, almost reverently, occasionally licking his lips. Several times, when Blair had spoken, he said: 'I have nothing to add to that.' Once he alluded (in my translation) to 'the extremely clever approach of the Blair Government'. 'I feel the same way,' was another response. 'I've never been to Tuscany,' he said when Italy was discussed. 'At least you've visited.'

After some crack by Blair, Schröder said: 'Now I've got to think of something.' Often stumped, he showed it. His apparent directness and occasional stumble were rather likeable; of the two, Mr Blair was the more *Volks*-Chancellor-ish; Mr Schröder the self-deprecating Englishman.

A famous two-frame cartoon illustrates *What People Say, and What Dogs Hear*. In the first frame a man is saying: 'Good boy, Rover, come here, Rover boy.' In the second frame the dog hears: 'Blah blah, Rover, blah blah, Rover blah.'

Had we illustrated *What German Chancellors Say and What Prime Ministers Hear*, the latter frame would have been captioned: 'Blah blah, Tony Blair, blah blah, Tony blah.'

Two Splits on View

4.11.98

It's a social embarrassment men do face. A tap on the shoulder even as you notice the breeze on your thigh. Your trousers have split. Your boxer shorts are showing.

Yesterday afternoon at the Commons, two famous men experienced such mortification – and one had come to watch the other. Up in the Peers' Gallery overlooking the Chamber, a former Chancellor, Lord Lamont of Lerwick, revealed a massive patch of white underpant as the side-seam on the right side of his dark trousers opened up for the amusement of any MP who cared to glance heavenward. New Tory Split! Lucky it was on the Right.

Down on the Floor, Gordon Brown did his best to cover an embarrassing hole in government finances. With government spending pulling one way and the national debt pulling the other, it was no wonder: given Gordon's tight fiscal stance, something was bound to rip.

The Gordon Gap was an intellectual breach; the Lamont Split was visual. Horrified journalists stared at the Peers' Gallery, uncertain whether his lordship was aware of the scale of the problem. If a patch of blue in the sky no bigger than a man's hand suggests clear skies ahead, what does a patch of white, half the size of a former Chancellor's underpants, teach us about the economic outlook? We did learn that the Lamont undergarment is massive, and dazzlingly white.

Gordon Brown's announcements dazzled less, but he scored one success: 'No denial of short-term difficulties!' he cried.

What sleight of hand. Consider the genesis of that phrase 'no denial of short-term difficulties'. You start with 'difficulties' – those being the only fact we have. Then you re-express the difficulties as 'short-term' – the qualification being an expression of hope, not fact. But to cry 'short-term difficulties' still sounds off-message, defensive: new Labour should always assert. Something positive to be proud of is required. So let the Chancellor claim credit for not hiding the difficulties. That there is no way a Chancellor could conceal such things is irrelevant: he is not concealing them.

Thus did an admission that there are problems become, in Mr Brown's script, a boast about his candour. Truly the workings of a spin-doctor's mind are a marvellous thing.

Kippers Will Come Home to Roost

10.11.98

Ironic is not quite the right word for the Secretary of State for Trade and Industry, Peter Mandelson; but he speaks as though his remarks are not be taken on the obvious level; as though nothing is what it may seem. His trademark is the wink. He performs with the showily conspiratorial aplomb of a stage magician. You can almost smell the smoke.

Thus when Mr Mandelson told the Tories yesterday that their failure to share his enthusiasm for the Millennium Dome was due to a lack of *patriotism* (he emphasised the word) it would be tempting to treat this as an outrageous slur; tempting but wrong. Mandelson knew very well the charge was outrageous, did not really mean it, and takes pleasure in shocking us by making it. There is something pantomime about Mr Mandelson: 'Ooh you are awful, Peter – but we like you.'

One of the traps of political life is that in time a politician comes to believe his own propaganda: Baroness Thatcher finally succumbed to hers. Tony Blair has to his. But Peter Mandelson shows absolutely no inclination to believe a word. He positively delights in the absurdity of the poses he strikes. Consciously or otherwise, the attempt is to separate the politician and the man.

The Industry Secretary was appearing yesterday wearing his Millennium Experience cap. One by one, backbenchers tilted at the elegantly tailored windmill. Michael Fabricant (C, Lichfield) asked a shrewd question about the contractual terms (or lack of them) upon which private companies sponsor the Dome; Mandelson gave the shrewd answer: a string of wry vacuities.

An eloquently scornful Austin Mitchell (Lab, Grimsby) complained that what had been billed as a celebration of British history had degenerated into 'a mammoth piece of commercial hucksterism'.

Totally ignoring Mr Mitchell's question, Mandelson offered so shamelessly wide-eyed an encomium to the Millennium Experience's 'Children's Promise' pledge scheme – involving '*seven* children's charities' – that the implicit parody of the US tele-evangelist will have left TV viewers searching their screens for a telephone number for credit-card pledges. Blair would have meant it; Mandelson was sniggering *at himself*.

Lawrie Quinn (Lab, Scarborough & Whitby) put in a millennial plug for a Whitby brewery and Whitby kippers. So 'magnificent' were the products of Whitby, warbled Mandelson, almost rolling his eyes, that he wished he could move the whole of Whitby into the Dome. Another Mandelson classic: its distinguishing characteristic being that the reference could be sold to two different markets in two different wrappers. For the provincial market (and *Whitby Gazette*) this was 'Dome Minister praises Whitby'. For the illuminati of our Westminster political class, however, the headline was 'Peter sneers at Whitby'.

It was a polished performance. If Mr Mandelson did not, before leaving the chamber, twirl a moustache or execute a stylish bow – if we did not quite catch a flash of scarlet in the lining of his cloak – then he invited us to imagine it.

Once, John Biffen and the late Nicholas Budgen used the implicit wink to keep our respect and their sanity. But the most accomplished practitioner was Harold Macmillan. 'Supermac,' however, never let on: never let the horny-handed sons of toil guess at another version. Mandelson's hubris is in the mockery. We loved the joke about Whitby kippers, but how long can you keep the joke from Whitby? Mandelson risks the fury, scorned, of that kipper-producing part of Britain which would not know the meaning of *classe politique*.

Girls Need Fathers   *18.11.98*

Help! Dad! I'm in trouble! Quick!

If the cry comes from a favourite daughter, what father could resist? When, as I watched yesterday's Lords debate on the European Elections Bill, I saw Lord Callaghan of Cardiff rise to speak, I ran to watch. It was Daddy to the rescue.

This must be a crisis. Jim Callaghan, Britain's last Labour Prime Minister before Tony Blair, speaks rarely in the Upper Chamber. When he does, he speaks well. When he does, it matters. His eldest daughter, Margaret, Baroness Jay of Paddington, Leader of the House of Lords, calls upon her father rarely in the House they share. When she does, she's in serious trouble.

And so it proved. I have seldom seen Lord Callaghan speak more angrily or eloquently. At times he was shouting. In language almost never heard in the genteel place, he described Tory troublemakers as the 'hooligan tendency'. Adapting a remark of Balfour's he declared: 'I'd as soon consult my valet as consult the Earl of Onslow about political tactics.'

Lord Onslow, an amiable but maverick fellow, proud to be a hooligan on this Bill, will have glowed with surprised pride. You need some sense of the courtesy and mutual regard which normally prevail among peers to appreciate the passion that insult was meant to convey, and did. This, declared Callaghan, his voice rising, was a 'second-level issue' – no occasion for constitutional impasse. On the front bench his daughter nodded in anxious approval.

'Call off your troops!' he shouted at the Tory Chief Whip, Lord Strathclyde. It had the ring of desperation. The crossbenchers – nervous, principled creatures – flinched. What were they about to do? Join a Tory conspiracy? Were they right to do it? The closest thing the Opposition could find to a Callaghan checkmate rose. Lord Tebbit angrily defended Lord Onslow. Was his friend supposed to send his valet, then, to speak?

Lord McNally, once a Labour MP, now a Liberal Democrat peer, repeated the determined but defensive arguments his party has used for supporting a government measure they do not like. He sounded rattled. He called Callaghan 'my noble friend' though they are of different parties. Aah! shouted the Tories, regarding this as a Lib-Lab giveaway. 'If you don't know that he'll always be my noble friend, then you don't know me,' shouted McNally, abandoning the traditional indirect speech in his fury.

I have seldom seen both sides more a-quiver. Both conveyed a sense of knowing they were on the brink of something from which it would be hard to retreat. Just as Lord Williams of Mostyn (also pale and quiet with emotion) was about to sum up for the Government, one of the bishops rose.

Bishops are the unguided missiles of the Upper Chamber – unguided by human agency, anyway: you can never know what a bishop is about to say because all too often he does not know himself.

Bishops do not quite quake as Quakers quake when inhabited by the inner light, but they convey a trembling innocence which suggests both naivety and authority: the holy fools of their Lordships' House. This Bishop (of Hereford), protesting his dissociation from every group – the Opposition, the hooligan tendency, the Eurosceptics, the anti-PR peers – insisted that he was still 'deeply unhappy' about the Bill. He would vote against it.

So it was God versus Daddy. God won. But Daddy will be back.

20.11.98   # Lords Rise as Commons Sits

A doomed upper chamber throws out a bill.

Does anyone know the Old French for 'Whatever happened to that one, then?'

We ask, because at the Prorogation of Parliament which occurred yesterday in the Lords, a list of the Acts which Parliament has passed in the session now closing is read out. But where the devil was the

European Elections Act?

After each Act's declaration, a behosed flunkey turns solemnly from the Throne and declares '*La Reyne le veult!*' which means 'The Queen wants it'.

Thus, yesterday: 'Waste Minimisation Act.'

'*La Reyne le veult!*'

'Registration of Political Parties Act.'

'*La Reyne le veult!*'

One by one, the Bills which had gone forward from both Houses of Parliament were listed as Acts. But one key bill, promised by Her Majesty herself in that very chamber in the last Queen's Speech, was missing. Should these mysteries not enjoy an archaic reportage of their own? In *The Times*'s Revised Lords Procedure, it might go like this:

(*Reader:*) 'European Elections Act.'

(*Flunkey:*) '*Ou est-il?*'

(*All peers:*) '*Tory faux pas!*'

Instead, the errant Act was notable yesterday only by a silence – and a curiously agitated air among the Lords and Ladies themselves. They just couldn't sit still. Not within living memory had their doings occupied the front pages of all the tabloid newspapers together. Good heavens! They actually mattered.

In a Question before Prorogation, about the dispensing of aspirins by pharmacists, Lord Stewartby, 63, had begun: 'My Lords, as one of those who does take a junior aspirin every morning in hopes of avoiding a heart-attack . . .' (sympathetic nods) 'as a result of excitement in your lordships' House . . .'

They were almost rolling in the aisles. One bishop, slumped so deep in prayer that it was possible to mistake his meditation for slumber, sat bolt upright, electrified.

Even the Queen's Speech (read out on Prorogation by the Lord Chancellor) seemed to have woken up. Out goes the dull and dignified language in which draftsmen used to frame the Queen's Government's account of its own doings in the session being closed; and in comes the jauntily tabloid language of new Labour's rebranded Britain.

Her Majesty's Speech stated conventionally enough ('We remember with pleasure our visit to Canada in June,' she lied) but all at once snapped to attention: 'The education of young people has been my Government's TOP priority!'

Can you honestly imagine Her Majesty saying that? As well suppose she might start her day by summoning a footman: 'After breakfast, a brisk walk with the corgies is my TOP priority. Then we'll go walkabout in Windsor, shaking hands with the many, not the few . . .'

Her speech to the Lords and Commons (MPs standing crowded at the Bar by the chamber's entrance) droned on for ages, strolling boastfully through the achievements of the past 18 months. If the Queen did not quite declare 'no return to Tory boom and bust!' then we must assume that someone at the Palace had drawn the line at Alastair Campbell's first draft. But Downing Street did appear to have got the Government's 'vision' for the future past the Royal censors.

At last it was over, MPs were dismissed. Madam Speaker and her cohorts – dowdy in the presence of all this finery – bowed and left, MPs following. We could hear the hubbub of a departing crowd of elected politicians, echoing down the corridor like the sound of a farmyard, fading as the beasts lumbered back to home pasture.

The lords, hereditaries and all, were left in silence, all gilt and ermine and scarlet, staring into an abyss.

Why isn't William Working?

26.11.98

'Parliamentarian of the Year' is quite an accolade. The *Spectator/* Highland Park trophy was presented to William Hague yesterday at a grand luncheon at the Savoy. The award suggests a politician who has swept all before him.

But Hague hasn't. The Tory leader has had a wretched year in which, despite the bull's-eye presented by a curiously unlikeable Government, he has seldom seemed to score. So can William Hague be called a big parliamentary striker?

I was one of the *Spectator's* judges: a group of commentators drawn from across the political spectrum, from the *Guardian* to the *Telegraph*. The others will not mind my remarking that, despairing at the way the Commons has been elbowed to the political sidelines, we agreed that on those sidelines Hague's performance had been notable.

At Questions, the Boy William can usually fight a Goliath of a Prime Minister to a draw, always stings, and quite often wins. No other has been so consistently strong.

Yet the Commons chamber has not seemed to matter in 1998. So should we reward someone who has mattered within it? I am sure we were right to stick to our remit: Hague has proved an able parliamentarian, and yesterday we said so.

But is anyone listening? Why does the Hague Experience impress at Westminster, yet fail to register outside those neo-Gothic walls? Struck down by flu, I missed the awards lunch yesterday. Unusually, this week I have been watching William Hague and Tony Blair through the small screen rather than live on the big Commons stage.

And for the first time I understand why non-political friends raise eyebrows when I protest that the Tory leader is a good Commons performer, and Tony Blair often a ragged parliamentary act. For that's not how it looks on television.

On screen, Blair is animated; Hague looks stiff, wooden. Blair has a flexible tenor: light and shade and varied pace. Hague sounds grinding, gravelly. His humorous eyes seem deadened by the camera.

The television gap with Blair is at its cruellest in Commons 'feed'. The chamber's cameras being fixed and the rules conservative, there is no scope for imaginative camerawork. Viewers get an unremitting view of that head in all its Mekon-like intensity.

Hague reminds us of those 'It's your shout' programmes in which viewers can enter a curtained box and deliver themselves of their views, on automatic camera, for three minutes. Hague is lucky to get thirty seconds.

And the voice, still adjusted to 'declamatory' mode for Oxford Union debates, grates on the small screen. Hague's *forte* (there is no *piano*) is the ringing denunciation, the 'J'accuse', punctuated by withering and funny asides.

In the chamber – a small, feisty figure, a raised fist in a grand auditorium – this works well. Snipped into a soundbite and squashed into a 2ft-square frame, it looks forced.

Westminster boffins must accept that, like a wine that does not travel, the parliamentary talent that was celebrated at the Savoy yesterday perishes somewhere in the ether between the camera lens and your rooftop aerial.

Even The Heckling's Cribbed

2.12.98

'The Clerk will now proceed to read the orders of the day.'

As the late Tom Driberg MP once remarked, once you realise that this daily proclamation from the Chair can be sung to the tune of *John Brown's body lies a-mouldering in his grave*, it becomes impossible to take it seriously.

Yesterday the reduction of Parliament to kindergarten singsong took another gruesome step. Labour whips had prepared for a Tory onslaught in a debate on the economy by circulating crib-notes with 'impromptu' interruptions among the MPs sitting behind ministers. These 'Suggested Interventions' listed killer-questions, numbered one to ten, with which eager new Labour jellybabies were to interrupt the Tory Shadow Chancellor, Francis Maude.

Armed with scripts, Labour backbenchers filed obediently in, and sat there rehearsing silently, the smarter ones managing the read-through without moving their lips. But – catastrophe. Someone had left, and a Tory had found, a copy of this cribsheet on a Westminster photocopier.

The Tory had circulated copies. Now all his side had the list too. On Tory copies the informant had scrawled: *'Recovered from a photocopier. Tee-Hee!'*

Tee-Hee!! was about the level of it. Tory kiddies were cock-a-hoop, Labour kiddies all but sucking their thumbs in a sulk.

Minutes into Francis Maude's speech, one of his own side, Howard Flight (S Downs) leapt up. Revealing how he had come by his question, Mr Flight told Maude he planned to save Labour backbenchers trouble by asking it for them: 'Question 2: Can the Shadow Chancellor tell this House why he is opposing the extra £40 billion for our public services that this Government is investing?' Armed with the list, Maude had his answer ready. Labour should have cut their losses but the command on their pagers came too late to abort an attack by Geraint Davies (Lab, Croydon Central). Would the Conservatives scrap Bank of England independence – yes or no?

'Question ten! Ten!' squealed delighted Tories.

Fools rush in. Dale Campbell-Savours (Lab, Workington) asked Maude about Tory policy on the minimum wage. 'Eight! Eight!' the Opposition chorused. By the time Maude sat down, supplies of the list had reached the Press Gallery too. I was able to tick off questions one, two, six, eight and ten, all asked.

And Madam Speaker was handed the list. We followed Miss Boothroyd's amused smiles as she followed Government backbenchers following their own scripts.

This sketch has a modest proposal to make. Modernised Commons procedure, widely applauded, has long removed the need for back-benchers to read out their questions already pre-notified to ministers, and listed on the Order Paper. They just call out the number.

So why not do the same with interruptions, too? And heckles? In fact, why not number the responses as well, and call out numbers in place of answers?

Instead of a Tory shouting 'When are you going to get waiting lists down?'; Dennis Skinner heckling ''Ow many of you lot are on BUPA then?'; the minister replying 'I'll take no lessons from a party who, for 18 years . . .' (etc) – and Miss Boothroyd telling them all to shut up – it would go like this . . .

Tory: 7

Mr Skinner: 16! (*laughter*)

Minister: 2! (*hon Members*: hear, hear)

Madam Speaker: Order! 1! I said 1!

And in place of this sketch's well-worn denunciation of the MPs' poodle-parlour, *The Times* could just print: Commons sketch 22.

Bleak On-message Message for Geoffrey Robinson
11.12.98

It must be a scary feeling. The snipers circle. The glass shields protecting you slide noiselessly back. You look around for comfort – but your friends have slipped away.

In panic you stab at your mobile phone . . . no reply, just a recorded message: 'Alastair Campbell is busy right now; have a nice day.'

Such was the lonely figure sitting on the Treasury Front Bench for Questions to the Chancellor of the Exchequer yesterday. Geoffrey Robinson is on the political equivalent of death row. Nobody said so. As is the convention, nobody on your own side mentions it.

Nobody turns against you in public – they just stop supporting you.

Privately the whispers grow: 'Oh, done for, of course, Lost No 10's support. Tony won't carry him. Gordon has been forced to let him go.'

The most chilling moment for the Paymaster General yesterday was not when, with a dismissive wave, the Tory Shadow Chancellor, Francis Maude, derided his 'swansong' at Treasury Questions. 'When,' asked Mr Maude, would the Government 'abandon the search for a face-saving exit, and sack him?' But Maude has been predicting Robinson's demise for months.

No, sideswipes from declared enemies you can bear, and Robinson did. The Paymaster General maintained the air of chubby geniality which (in this sketch's view) has rather likeably distinguished him this year. It was when Stephen Byers rose to support him that his heart must have sunk. The Tories had impugned the Paymaster's honour. Byers did not *quite* defend it.

The Chief Secretary was standing in for their boss, Gordon Brown, whose father has just died. Called upon to defend his fellow minister, he attacked the Tories instead. He deplored their decision to make 'a deliberate personal attack'. Robinson was an 'effective' minister, he said.

Some defence! The Tories and the newspapers call you a tax-avoiding, high-living, corner-cutting, millionaire Maxwell-crony, and the best your mates can say in reply is that you're 'effective'.

But Byers had not finished. 'And I look forward to working with him – for . . .' he continued. At last the vote of confidence! Look forward to working with him for what? Years to come? Future years? For a long time yet? Many years to come?

'. . . for many months to come,' said Byers. There was an intake of breath on both sides. We noted the remark as significant, but entered a reservation: ministers are not textbooks; sometimes the wrong words slip out in error. Maybe Byers hadn't meant it like that?

The Chief Secretary resumed his attack on the Tories. They would regret their remarks about his colleague, he said. 'I look forward to working with him . . .'

Ah. He was about to correct that verbal slip . . .

'. . . for many months to come.'

So there we have it. The authorised version. Twice. Either Mr Robinson is gravely ill, or he's for the chop. The cautious, greying Chief Secretary is not one to ad lib. A man who, at different times and in response to different questions, said 'steering a course of stability in an uncertain world' *five times* yesterday, knows something about staying on-message. For Robinson, the message is bleak.

He did not last long.

Frank Puzzles Alice   *15.12.98*

Into the looking-glass world of Commons politics wandered Alice last Thursday. I took her to the Press Gallery to see Frank Dobson railing with such violence against tobacco that the bearded Health Secretary looked like doing himself an injury.

'Smoking kills! . . . it is a deadly habit . . . it is the principal avoidable cause of premature death . . . it harms people who do not smoke . . . it harms babies in the womb . . . it causes not just lung cancer but cancer of the mouth, the larynx, the oesophagus, the bladder, the kidneys, the stomach and the pancreas . . .'

Alice turned pale. 'That man who looks like Father Christmas thinks smoking is very, very bad, doesn't he?' she whispered. The attendant glared, for you are not supposed to talk. Alice fell silent.

'Smoking causes one in seven deaths from heart disease!' cried the bearded one. 'Tobacco companies . . . recruit new smokers to make up for their loyal customers whom they kill off every year . . .'

'What can Mr Dobson do to stop this terrible habit?' whispered Alice urgently. A *Hansard* reporter fixed her with a stern gaze. She blushed.

The beard soon answered this question. 'To reduce tobacco consumption the Government raised tobacco duties . . . last year and again this year . . . Everyone who cares about the health of the nation should . . . support this strategy.' All the MPs cheered. Alice and I left. We had heard enough. Nobody could doubt what the Government thinks of smoking or how it plans to stop it.

Alice spent the weekend in Vienna, arriving just in time for the final day of the European heads of government summit. She was a bit surprised that nobody mentioned smoking, as the bearded man at Westminster had left her with the distinct impression that everyone in Europe was as upset about it as he.

She had been really scared to hear that a million people in Britain die every ten years because of smoking, and expected the Prime Minister to say a great deal on the subject to his fellow Heads of Government. But at Vienna the subject hardly seemed to come up. She wondered if Mr Dobson and Mr Blair spoke to each other much.

Alice returned to the Commons yesterday, at my invitation, to hear Tony Blair make a statement about the conference to his fellow MPs. She and I sat together and watched Mr Blair stride in, looking very confident in a fetching royal blue shirt and a purple tie. Alice was impressed. She was expecting the Prime Minister to say more about smoking.

He did. In a proud voice he crowed that he had had considerable success persuading other countries not to abolish duty-free shopping. When he said this, the same MPs cheered as had cheered Mr Dobson.

'But aren't cigarettes one of the main things they sell duty-free?' whispered Alice.

'Shh!' I hissed.

'But . . .'

'Shh!' I insisted, 'you must leave the Gallery if you cannot contain yourself.' Blushing again, Alice left. But she is an irrepressible child, and at once telephoned the Duty Free Confederation. They were very pleased about Mr Blair's announcement because – as they told Alice – a quarter of a billion pounds is spent every year on duty-free tobacco in Britain.

I left Alice while she was still trying to contact the bearded Mr Dobson to warn him about all the people who may be killed by Mr Blair's decision. Naive child.

Come Again, William?

17.12.98

Halfway through a bewildering exchange between William Hague and Tony Blair yesterday, something dawned on me which explained everything. The Prime Minister hadn't the least idea what Mr Hague was talking about.

Once you understood this, it became clear. There was no longer any need to try to make sense of the failure of Mr Blair's answers to mesh with the Opposition leader's questions. For all the difference it made, William might as well have consulted Ffion and asked his question in Welsh.

Hague chose as his subject a topic on which Paddy Ashdown has already tackled Blair: the proposed removal of tax credit on share dividends from pensioners too poor to pay tax.

This is now to go ahead. When the Liberal Democrat leader raised the problem last week, he had asked the Prime Minister for a final decision. In reply Mr Blair had promised it would be announced 'as soon as possible'. He had said nothing about the issue itself. In retrospect it looks likely that this was because he did not know what Mr Ashdown meant.

For when Hague asked about it yesterday, Blair seemed to flounder. The Prime Minister began recommending the new 'second pension' announced by the Social Security Secretary the previous afternoon. Interesting, but hardly germane. At the Opposition dispatch box Hague persisted, but from over the way came something redolent of the *Marie Celeste*: lights on, nobody at home. 'Lots of people', said Blair, were going to get the chance of a good pension scheme.

No doubt – but what of Hague's question, which was not about pension schemes at all? We had heard 'no rational justification' from the Prime Minister for removing dividend tax credits, complained Hague. But in fact it was worse than that: we had heard nothing about dividend tax credits at all.

It was then it struck me that this could be because Mr Blair did not know what dividend tax credits were. The impression grew as, brow furrowed, Blair launched into a prepared précis of yesterday's statement on pensions. Again Hague complained he had heard no answer on dividend credits: 'Why not think again?' Blair replied that 'our proposals are better' than Tory ideas. Then he launched into an attack on the mis-selling of pensions under the last Government. Labour cheered nervously.

Blair was simply expanding on every topic he knew with the word 'pensions' in the title. Even Prime Ministers are caught short, sometimes.

The Guts to Say 'Stop'

18.12.98

The PM defends bombing Iraqis.

If you seek an argument against that most fashionable of political virtues, consensus, you would have found it yesterday at the Commons as the Prime Minister enlisted the whole House's support for the Government's policy of bombing Iraq.

For once, all parties were on-message, 'constructive'. All you could hear was the ominous noise of a huge assemblage of politicians charging in the same direction. There being no anti-war party, the ruling passions within each party were deferred to. MPs on both sides vied only to find more felicitous ways of expressing the accepted wisdom. Scarcely another opinion was heard. Few unkind questions were asked. Half an hour's exchanges could have been summarised thus:

Prime Minister: 'Let's bomb Baghdad, boys!'

MPs: 'Hooray!'

PM: 'Not that we do this lightly; but with heavy hearts.'

MPs: 'Hear, hear!'

Solitary Leftie: 'This is a blunder.'

MPs: 'Shame! Resign! Saddam's lackey! Speak for England . . .' etc.

Regardless what view one takes of the wisdom of the bombing, it was dismaying to see so momentous a decision endorsed so lightly by MPs, or with so little reflection of the range of opinions which exists privately among them.

George Galloway (Lab, Glasgow Kelvin), a convinced opponent of Operation Desert Fox, was almost lynched when he spoke. There were cries of 'Disgraceful!' from his own side.

Much was said by people in Gucci shoes about courage in battle, but it did not take guts to cheer for the war party at Westminster yesterday: it took guts to do anything else.

They're All the Same

*Mandelson falls, over his house-purchase loan from Geoffrey
Robinson.*

Yesterday morning I heard the first cuckoo of the political season. The
song seems set to swell, and new Labour might as well get used to it:
'They're all the same.'

'They're all the same,' said my minicab driver en route for Euston
station, before 10am, before Peter Mandelson had even resigned.

'They're all the same,' said the florist at Euston.

I boarded the train and was met by a friend at Northampton. 'It's
getting to feel like the last days of the Tories,' said my friend. 'You
know what people will say, don't you? "They're all the same".'

We drove up to Derbyshire. I visited Bakewell, passed a friend in the
street. 'Politicians – they're all the same,' he said, 'in it for themselves."

And so the cry goes up. Has ever a corporate identity so assiduously
assembled by so many at Millbank for so long been ruined so fast? Has
ever a more earnest and relentless campaign to educate the public into
distinguishing one political product from another been so cruelly
detonated? New Labour's City of Dreams has been more compre-
hensively wrecked in two nights of media bombing than anything Tony
Blair could organise for Baghdad. And all with one easy, lazy, little
sentiment, 'they're all the same': a lethal weapon, worse than anthrax.

But of course they are not all the same. The voice of the mob is very
strong in politics and the mob wants to believe – has always wanted to
believe – that the powers-that-be are lining their own pockets,
'feathering their own nests', 'in it for themselves'.

It isn't true. Consider the celebrated resignations of recent years.
Almost every one has been about foolishness, lapse of judgement,
arrogance: almost none has been about real corruption. How common is
it in our national politics that a senior politician tries to enrich himself
at the citizen's expense? How common is it that decisions of national
importance have been skewed by sex or money?

It almost never happens. Almost always we indict our politicians for
the *appearance* of being compromised; how rarely do we find they did
act corruptly. Once we have tipped the entire vocabulary of horror and
disapproval on Mandelson's head, it's worth reflecting that nobody has
suggested that he ever took any departmental decision on any basis

other than the national interest, or would dream of doing so. His sins were much, much smaller.

But they were so easy to understand. We know about mortgages. We know what houses cost. We understand personal loans. Mandelson was therefore dislodged within hours of his critics' first attack. Geoffrey Robinson took nearly a year to go – yet he was the more dispensable of the two and the charges against him include far more serious criticisms than can be levelled at Mandelson. But they were complicated. Start talking about the accounting arrangements of Maxwell subsidiaries, tax avoidance through discretionary offshore trusts – and my minicab driver, my friends in Bakewell, I too, begin to flounder.

We understand adultery. Parkinson had to go. We enjoyed the stories about David Mellor. Tim Yeo had an illegitimate child. But we never got to the bottom of Maxwell's corruption – in truth, we hardly tried – and he escaped.

Mandelson, whose public-spiritedness I think few would question, fell easily because his jury have themselves applied for mortgages. Nobody who knows him really thinks he acted wickedly. The more serious the indictment, the harder it can be to make it stick. They are not all the same, but some of the more trivial are a lot easier to understand.

Thing Gives Gomez Blair a Hand

20.1.99

Aficionados of the Addams Family movies will be familiar with a creature called Thing. It is a disembodied hand. It scuttles around the Addams' creepy mansion doing the family's dirty work. Need a tap fixing, a corpse burying, a mess shovelling under the carpet or a cat throttling in the night? Thing will fix it.

Big-suited Gomez Addams, the head of the household, relies implicitly on the Hand. So does his wife, the palely cadaverous Morticia. How Gomez reminds me of Tony Blair.

At Foreign Office Questions yesterday, a hand appeared, a man's hand, just before the first question on Europe. This sketchwriter could not say whether the Hand was unattached because, were there a body in tow, its owner had placed himself in the least visible spot in the chamber.

Let me explain. The press sits in a balcony over one end of the chamber, arranged like a shallow dress circle above the Speaker's chair. Only the tops of the heads of MPs at this end are visible. The chair is crowned with a huge canopy, blocking views of the benches beneath and creating a blind spot on one bench on the government side. Its occupant is invisible to almost all the press; invisible to me.

But I could see a Hand. A right Hand. Visible only from the wrist, like Thing.

The Hand appeared some way into questions yesterday, and settled, fingers fanned, on the edge of the seat. Horrified, I watched it. It seemed to be intently following ministers' answers: tensing, fidgeting, relaxing . . . depending on what they said. No name, no face, but a weird sense of responsibility, control. We have heard of the Minister without Portfolio (one such, with his Dome, was famous), but now, fretting here on the green leather, seemed to be a Portfolio without Minister.

And it was with European policy that the Hand looked most concerned. It missed the exchanges on St Helena, ignored Kosovo, and arrived just in time to hear Norman Godman (Lab, Greenock & Inverclyde) ask about the enlargement of the European Union.

The Hand looked relaxed about a careful reply from the minister, Joyce Quin. But when a leftwinger, Jeremy Corbyn (Lab, Islington N) rose, it scratched angrily at the seat panel. Dennis Skinner (Lab, Bolsover) shouted 'When does Albania get in?' The Hand scratched harder.

Andrew Mackinlay (Lab, Thurrock) complained that too few members of the Government were visiting the aspirant members of the EU. Fingers on the Hand quivered. Would it like to visit them, representing the Prime Minister?

The Tories' Michael Howard asked a muscular question about joining the euro. The Hand scrabbled impatiently on the bench.

Discussion moved to India and Kashmir. The Hand stretched lazily, fingers outstretched and at rest. When immigration, Iraq and the Middle East were raised, the Hand became bored, drumming fingers. When questions turned to 'ethics' in foreign policy the Hand lost interest and curled up.

I glanced at my order paper: Burma, Basra, Nigeria . . . no more questions on Europe seemed likely to be reached. Perhaps the Hand had made a similar calculation. It rose into the air above the bench. Then, hovering left towards the door, moved from my vision, hidden by the canopy over the Speaker's chair.

I leapt up. Dashing to a corner from which the Hand's exit might be visible, I strained to see.

Someone was hurrying out. It was Peter Mandelson, pale and tense. The Hand was with him.

The Unexpected Proceeds Routinely

21.1.99

Paddy Ashdown is to retire.

It was a typically decent performance from Paddy Ashdown at Prime Minister's Questions yesterday. He had kept the secret well. Almost nobody in the chamber, and nobody in the press, knew.

All we knew was what was routine. The Liberal Democrat leader gets two questions to the PM every Wednesday; yesterday was Wednesday; and Paddy Ashdown was Liberal Democrat leader – had been for as long as young Liberal Democrats could remember, and would be, surely, for years to come. This was routine.

William Hague and Tony Blair pecked piously at each other for five minutes on Northern Ireland. Mr Ashdown rose. Everyone groaned. This too was routine.

MPs from other parties always groan when Paddy stands. Last week (and for the first time) he responded to a particularly loud groan by smiling 'and a happy new year to you too!' Even enemies chuckled. It was gracefully done. None of us guessed the poignancy.

Yesterday the groan was only an average groan. Ashdown took no notice and asked about the Balkans.

That, too, was routine.

He usually does. It is common to accuse Liberal Democrats of shameless populism but there are no British votes in the Balkans and even Ashdown's own parliamentary party have wearied of his dogged concern for this faraway place of which we know little. Mr Ashdown sticks to his guns on Bosnia, Kosovo, Serbia, for one reason only: he believes it matters. Rather as with those One-World obsessives who bang on about over-population in Africa, who you know are right but to whom you cannot quite make yourself listen, Ashdown's fate is to be right before anyone's interested.

Among Liberal Democrats, this too is routine.

Yesterday he got further than usual with Tony Blair, persuading the Prime Minister to say that the use of ground troops by Nato in Kosovo was not ruled out. Ashdown made no pretence of attacking the Government, and Blair made no pretence of attacking back: he answered generously.

Perhaps it was a sort of farewell. Mr Blair was strangely muted for the whole session. He couldn't even rouse himself to shout at the Tories much. He sounded bleak. He knew that a soul-mate was about to jump ship.

An hour later the news broke and the Press Gallery went wild. We who have for the most part disparaged, belittled or laughed at Paddy Ashdown, gossiped, speculated – and turned our minds to finding something nice to say, since he's bowing out.

This too is routine.

Now the war-dance starts among his senior colleagues in the Commons. Men and women who for many months have been whispering of their despair at his closeness to Blair, complaining that he is shackling their party to an unattractive Government, and dreaming aloud about a challenge to his leadership . . . these people are now his friends again.

From yesterday onward, no ill will be spoken of Paddy, especially by those who used to be critical. All at once he will bask in the uncomplicated affection of an entire party. The backslaps, the 'won't you think again?', the 'there's nobody who could take Paddy's place' will swell to a chorus among those who seek to take Paddy's place.

The race is between Simon Hughes, Charles Kennedy and Nick Harvey. The young curate-*manqué*, permanently scarred by cycle-clips; the ginger Tom who got the cream; and the encyclopaedia-salesman with eyes of the undead, suspected of strangling old ladies . . . all have been careful to be loyal, recently.

That, too, is routine.

22.1.99

A Self-wipe Minister

Britain's new Trade and Industry supremo has an amazing ability. Stephen Byers is the talking equivalent of invisible ink. Within seconds of his speaking you cannot recall a word he has said: he simply wipes himself from your consciousness.

I was at Westminster early yesterday for Questions to the Secretary of State for Trade and Industry. It was the dispatch box debut of Peter Mandelson's replacement. I needed to note Mr Byers's answers. It was spooky. I couldn't. Time and again I tried to write down what Byers was saying or had just said. Time and again, all recollection fled.

Byers rose. My mind began to wander. I pinched myself and gripped a pen, forcing myself to listen. 'I would like to thank my Hon Friend,' droned Byers to Stephen Ladyman (Lab, S Thanet) 'for his warm words of welcome . . .'

Attention began to slip. I wrestled with oblivion but an unseen force was loosening pen from fingers. I wrenched attention back. '. . . We can do more . .' – and my mind blanked. Short-term memory was wiped.

So total is Stephen Byers's self-wipe function that it may be some form of hypnosis, a horrifying new technique in mind-control now learnt by new Labour. The fellow speaks and – *ffst!* – it's gone, snatched from recollection by some mysterious force.

And new Labour ministers can now do this. They leave no mental trace. Stephen Byers is the typewriter with no ribbon, the leadless pencil, the printer without ink. 'External financing limit . . . regime in place . . . high quality service at affordable prices . . .' Byers bleated – and I blanked. The rest escapes me.

Byers is neither big nor small. His hair was grey. His accent was neutral. His suit was grey. His *tie* was grey. He looks like the assistant accountant to a large dental practice in Northampton. He was wearing glasses – or was he? Dammit, that's gone too.

When I managed to re-engage consciousness, he was speaking again, to George Turner (Lab, NW Norfolk). 'Steps have been taken . . . I've no doubt at all . . . steps have been taken . . . no conflict . . . no doubt . . . no conflict . . .' only fragments survive, shards of cliché.

But Byers's was not the only debut at Industry Questions. Michael Wills, the new Minister for Small Business, was at the dispatch box for the first time. He will go far. Mr Wills takes self-wipe to new levels. I cannot even remember seeing him in the chamber before.

And *Hansard's* computer memory is susceptible to his magnetic powers of erasure: Wills seems to have wiped most of his previous interventions from the record, which notes only eight utterances in twenty months.

On yesterday's showing these are the very models of a modern Labour minister. Replying to a question about abolishing red tape from Brian Cotter (Lib Dem, Weston-super-Mare), Mr . . . er . . . crikey, something is trying to pluck the name from my memory . . . replied 'Madam Speaker, this Government is committed, we are committed, we are indeed committed . . .' What devilish cunning. We remember that they are committed, very committed indeed – but to what? Ah, that we cannot quite recall.

Answering, minutes later on the Millennium Experience, the Minister Janet Anderson unwittingly hinted at a chilling comparison with the New Labour Experience. In the 'Mind' zone of the Dome she said, 'the public will be able to interact with advanced, intelligent robots'.

To interact with Mr Byers is to do likewise.

Amy's Strange Adventure   *11.2.99*

How did it look to Amy? Tony Blair was observed yesterday at Prime Minister's Questions by a special guest. Amy, 14, from Hertfordshire, had phoned in while Mr Blair was appearing on *This Morning* with Richard and Judy last week to tell us all about his wife's swimsuits and Glenn Hoddle. Blair's propagandists, their eye on the main chance, arranged for Amy to be carted in to Westminster to watch the PM joust.

Poor girl. She could have been listening to Cleopatra CDs on her Walkman. Instead she chose a crowd of jeering middle-aged men with soup-stained ties. The child is unhinged.

When first she entered the Strangers' Gallery, ushered in by inexplicable men in black tights, the hall she saw was half empty. A grey-haired lady with the air of a head teacher was sitting in a sort of ornamental bus-shelter at one end, keeping discipline.

A crowd arrived – and in walked Amy's new friend, the Prime

Minister, wearing his 'lucky' tie (silver, with green blobs) and an inane grin. For no apparent reason a man began to rant about land reform in the Highlands while Blair tried not to look bored. What did Amy make of this?

'William Hague!' announced the lady in the bus-shelter. A youngish man, almost completely bald, with a Yorkshire accent, got up. Something seemed to have upset him. He started shouting about the Foreign Office being an old banger. Mr Baldy was plainly deranged.

But now Mr Lucky Tie came over all queer. He ummed and ah'd and looked sick as a parrot. Baldy shouted even louder – about customs raids. Lucky Tie's grin fixed, then faded, as Baldy went ballistic, hurling abuse, questions and sneering jokes, while those behind him screamed 'hear hear!' and 'ha ha!' and those behind Blair shouted 'Rubbish!' and 'No!' and the bus-shelter lady screamed 'Order!'

All at once, Baldy subsided. A man from Cheshire told Lucky Tie something about the millennium bug that he seemed to know already.

A tall Scout-leader type asked two questions, about arms exports and Africa. Lucky Tie seemed unwilling to answer them, so he answered a different question. 'Bye-bye Paddy!' shouted an elderly man, in a rude way. What was Amy making of this?

A gangling fellow with swivelling eyes boomed out something complicated about illegitimacy and marriage. The man's friends, sitting around him, looked embarrassed. Lucky Tie did not seem to want to answer this either. Everyone started shouting.

From her bus-shelter the lady in buckled shoes and tights flew into a rage and began to scream and shout. This may have startled Amy, but in the chamber they behaved as though it was completely normal.

Then Baldy leapt up again and yelled something about tax. Lucky Tie got crosser and crosser but avoided the question. Baldy shouted that he knew the answer anyway – and gave it. Amy will have wondered why, in that case, he had asked the question. Enraged, Lucky Tie worked himself up into a cry of 'Tory boom and bust!' – at which those behind him gave a terrific cheer.

Baldy subsided again. An elderly gentleman from Totnes invited Lucky Tie to accompany him mackerel fishing, adding that they wouldn't catch any. Lucky Tie said 'Thanks' but he was getting tired of invitations from this fellow. And, within minutes, they had all rushed out of the chamber.

Amy will have departed too. On Monday she told the Prime Minister that she was interested in politics. If she is still interested in politics, she needs her head seeing to.

Bayoneting Lord Boston   *18.2.99*

If any bovver-boy really seeks to win his political spurs, I challenge him to start a fight successfully with Lord Boston of Faversham. It is simply not possible. Easier to win a fight with Baroness Thatcher than pick one with Lord Boston.

You might as well try to provoke St Francis of Assisi into fisticuffs. Lord Boston is so insistently, emphatically, ineffably polite that it amounts almost to an act of aggression: a raised, silk-gloved fist in the face of a coarse world.

As Chairman of Committees in the Upper Chamber, his lordship, who turns 70 next year, has to field those tiresome queries about fabric and facilities which, in a public school, would fall to the bursar. The row last year about the Lord Chancellor's wallpaper would have finished a brittler chap off, but Boston is of more pliable stuff.

Yesterday it fell to this acme of amiability, this summit of civility, this paragon of *politesse*, to answer the grumbles of the disabled over facilities in the Palace of Westminster for blind or partially sighted peers. Of course for Lord Boston, after the steeplechase of Lord Irvine of Lairg's fixtures and fittings, this was a gentle afternoon trot. He excels in what might be called Exemplar Lordspeak: a language in which every hard object or decision crumbles, like a dunked biscuit, into a loose flotilla of limp subordinate clauses linked by extravagant courtesies.

'Your lordships may be so good as to call to mind what, in my noble friend's inimitable and luminous way, he has been kind enough to describe as the special expertise of your lordships' House . . .' This barrage of cordiality is proof even against a Tebbit; against a grunting little posse of partially-sighted peers, it proved invincible. Boston burbled respectfully away about 21 lifts, new handrails, 'tactile floor covering', innumerable ramps and 'a guide dog exercise ground'. There were audio recordings of proceedings, too. His lordship said he would be 'happy to consider' any further suggestions, but said it not in the perfunctory way most people do: he convinced us that he would be really, *really* happy – that his heart would sing – if anyone had a suggestion. After this, nobody had it in them to be cross. Lord Morris of Manchester (who had asked the original question) melted, but mentioned that the RNIB could advise. Oh, trilled Lord B, he would be '*very* happy to receive representations from the RNIB'. Then, with a beatific smile, he asked if he might congratulate Lord Morris on being invited by Rehabilitation International to chair their World Planning Group. Morris beamed. Everyone rumbled '*Hear, hear!*'

Lord Longford, 93, made a valiant bid to mix it with Boston. Some peers, he complained, 'can't get the help they need. Can't we do more? They're stuck. *Stuck.*'

Longford might as well have bayoneted a blancmange. It takes two to quarrel, and Boston was not playing. When Lord Ashley of Stoke, who has been cured of profound deafness, tried to raise the stakes and discuss other disabilities, Boston was all smiles. Sadly, he simply *mustn't* stray from the terms of the question, 'but we're all very pleased with the enormous progress Lord Ashley has made himself – and has endeavoured to pass on to others'. *Hear, hear* took on a special piquancy.

Lord Boston is an example to us all. Why, in that case, does one have to suppress a sneaking desire to watch him and Norman Tebbit wrestling in mud?

Three Strive to be Greyest

26.2.99

Three men awoke early. For each, yesterday was a big day. Stephen Byers, Trade and Industry Secretary, knew he must perform at questions.

Alun Michael knew that when he opened the debate on Wales, later, the speech would strike the keynote for his newly confirmed leadership of the Welsh Labour Party.

And for Richard Livsey, Liberal Democrat spokesman on Wales, his own speech mattered hugely. This was the last St David's Day debate before the Welsh assembly elections. His party have high hopes.

Three men with different purposes. But one goal they shared. To win the title Most Boring MP in Britain. Each was in hot contention; they are this sketch's finalists. Thursday offered each a chance to shine – at being outstandingly dull.

'Mirror, mirror, on the wall, who is the dullest of us all?' muttered Mr Byers as he shaved, taking care not to cut himself lest colour pierce the grey. He slicked his hair into shape, not a grey strand out of place.

Shirt? Plain white. Mr Byers surveyed a range of two-piece suits, well-cut but not ostentatiously so. Briefly he considered a charcoal flannel. No, too dark a grey. A dove-grey pinstripe? Too light a grey. He chose a mid-grey suit: Third Way grey.

Tie? Grey of course, but silk or wool? He chose grey silk, setting off suit, hair and disposition beautifully. A grey government limo had arrived with his red (ugh!) box. He set out for Westminster.

Alun Michael was there already. Forced, against every instinct, to wear a daffodil (in order not to stand out) he had chosen grey suit, mid-blue tie.

Richard Livsey paced his office floor rehearsing his speech. He must iron out any wrinkle of interest – adopt a monotone unrelieved by the least vocal modulation. It was going well. Four pigeons were comatose on the windowsill.

First over the wire was Stephen Byers. Magnificent! He said absolutely nothing, speaking often. But the judges must mark Byers down: he was almost crisp. Vacuity should be limp. 'No comment' raises an eyebrow where a page of pap lowers eyelids – surely the aim.

After noon came Alun Michael. Splendid. He spoke without meaning for nearly an hour, ostensibly on Wales. In the Strangers' Gallery they were keeling over.

Michael was helped by an almost empty chamber (a couple of Tories, eight on his own side, and one Liberal Democrat) but I was ready to cast my vote for him when the Liberal Democrat rose. Richard Livsey gave us a tour de force: this man was not just boringly boring; he was spectacularly boring. People turned to each other in wonder that anyone could be so boring.

'St-David's-day-is-as-we-know-a-special-day-in-the-calendar,' he droned, never, in all that dreadful dirge, raising eyes from text or voice by so much as a semi-tone.

'We-need-vision-and-leadership-and-we-need-it-desperately,' Livsey perorated, a living demonstration of his own contention. Judges were poised between Michael and Livsey. Then Michael clinched it –

for Livsey. For Rhodri Morgan spoke, the man Mr Michael has just beaten in an unfair contest for the leadership in Wales.

Alun Michael didn't even listen.

He chatted to a pal, then walked out – while Morgan was speaking. That isn't boring: it's stunning. Convicted of astonishing discourtesy, Michael loses to the boringly courteous Livsey.

3.3.99   # Just Too Fluent

What is it about Michael Howard? Few of those who regularly write up the performances of the chief Opposition spokesman on foreign affairs do so without a faint sense of guilt.

We rarely praise him; we usually mock him; we draw attention to that 'night creature' quality that Ann Widdecombe once described, that six o'clock shadow made flesh; time and again we say that he lacks credibility, detracts from whatever cause he espouses, or scares the children. All this is fair comment; journalists have not invented the reactions he inspires.

And yet he's so damn good. Few can match the combination of energy, lucidity and intellect that Howard commands. There is no shortage of rent-a-quote Tory spokesmen who make a lot of noise, most of it incoherent; nor any shortage of more retiring people with better minds, like Peter Lilley. But for tireless persistence with a well-marshalled argument, Howard is matchless. He just keeps pushing and he always make his case.

Yesterday he was at it again, obviously with a bad cold, making a fine speech on the Foreign Affairs Select Committee's scathing report on the handling of the Sierra Leone affair. Howard's rhetoric had a sort of relentless logic. He was well-briefed, with facts and judgements at his fingertips. He was clear, he was poised and he was eloquent. He was probably right, for heaven's sake! But he will hardly be credited in this morning's press.

Twenty-one years ago, the executive of the Conservative Association in West Derbyshire, a safe Conservative seat, was interviewing a shortlist of four for the position of prospective parliamentary candidate.

Among those four were Michael Howard, who was then in his 30s, and your sketchwriter. I won. Since that contest three people have told me, on different occasions, that Howard made a better speech than I did – probably the best of all the candidates. Why, then, did he lose? The answer has always been the same. 'He sounded too much like a barrister.' He was so fluent and smooth that his audience began to doubt whether he believed what he was saying.

I now wonder whether this is unfair. I do not know Mr Howard well, but my opinion is changing. I suspect (sometimes fear) that he really does believe what he says. He has rather stronger ideals in public life than most of his colleagues, though he can speak to a brief, like any minister. Friends say Howard is personally committed (to a degree uncommon in politics) to some of the abiding causes in his Commons career.

Many novels and plays have dealt with the theme of inarticulate passion: men and women too uneducated to communicate the depth of their feelings; convinced of some great truth but incapable of arguing it through. And audiences love a rough-hewn diamond. The figure of the noble savage or dumb hero has always captured the popular imagination.

But is there, I wonder, an even more tragic figure than the poor tongue-tied brute who cannot find words to express his conviction? Is it the over-educated, smooth-talking bastard who cannot help sounding like a smooth-talking bastard, even when he really means it? Is this not the ultimate tragedy – an awkward idealist trapped in the body of a svelte Welsh barrister, passion which, finding too fluent expression, is scorned as rhetoric?

And is that tragic figure Michael Howard?

Hague's Quick Homework   *10.3.99*

The 1999 Budget.

William Hague's blue scrawl said it all. To watch the Tory leader furiously reworking his notes as the Chancellor spoke was to watch a desperate rearguard action. Relaxed, almost rakish in a star-spangled tie, Gordon Brown strode through a Budget that sounded more like a prizegiving than an audit.

Hunched beside his Shadow Chancellor, Mr Hague executed a high-speed shuffle through an untidy sheaf bristling with Post-It notes. Every time Brown turned a page, Hague put his pen through another passage. Sometimes he excised whole pages. When not deleting he was scribbling fit to bust.

The Prime Minister seemed bored. Beside his meatloaf of a Chancellor, Tony Blair looked almost fey. As Brown pulled rabbits, tax-cuts, silk handkerchiefs, computers and hospital wards out of his hat – and as excited Labour backbenchers squealed – Mr Blair showed the strain, staring tight-faced at the ceiling.

For this was Brown's afternoon: one of the best he has had. After a slow start he tossed in a goodie here, a pleasant surprise there: then a tax break, a university laboratory or a school computer or two. MPs perked up. But the prizes grew. Tax cuts, a 10p starting rate, a halving of vehicle excise duty . . . Hague was now a whirlwind of insertion and deletion; the benches behind him had fallen silent.

The Chancellor increased stamp duty on house-purchase: '96 per cent of homes are unaffected,' he drawled. Peter Mandelson's head sank in his hands. Ann Widdecombe scribbled on a brown paper bag. Brown quintupled the pensioners' winter bonus. Labour cheered. Hague crossed out a whole page. Brown linked pensioners' minimum income guarantee to earnings. Government backbenchers went wild. Hague scribbled some more.

This was becoming almost festive. It all sounded too good to be true. Cheering grew as Brown promised to reduce the basic rate of income tax from 23 to 22 per cent. The sharp-minded noticed that he did not mention he was removing the 20 per cent band.

Was it, then, done with mirrors? Amid the balloons and whizzbangs, an air of unreality grew. This, the Chancellor had said, was 'the new economy'. There would be a 'new computer strategy'. 'A million new men and women' would open individual learning accounts.

O brave new world, that hath such creatures in it! Like some latter-day Prospero, Gordon Brown had dispensed with the whisky and water Chancellors used to sip, and armed himself instead with a magician's staff as he unveiled an enchanted island in which things that didn't seem to add up, somehow did.

Call it confidence or bombast, but his speech was heavily punctuated with laudatory references to his own transformation of the economic order. Brown sat down to unmodified rapture all around him.

Now Hague had to speak. In his place I would have dived, sobbing, under the Clerks' Table.

The Opposition Leader's response, launched from a heap of crumpled papers and Post-It notes, was feisty, gutsy, well-briefed and sharp. Those who doubt Hague's resilience should note the way he punched his way out of a corner. Such was the violence and momentum of his counter-attack – stealth-taxes, he called them, in a stealth-Budget – that many who came to cheer the Chancellor stayed to scratch their heads.

Swazis Astonished by Barbarity   *11.3.99*

Asked his view on Western civilisation, Mahatma Ghandi once replied: 'I think it would be a good idea.' The thought may have occurred to King Mswati III of Swaziland as he watched Prime Minister's Questions yesterday – amazed at the savagery.

His Majesty, on a visit to Britain, graced the Distinguished Strangers' Gallery in magnificent scarlet tunic and brocade. Swaziland is a small, safe, stable country in Southern Africa, its constitution a blend of tribal tradition with democracy. Ceremony there is colourful but decorous; nobody is insulted; nobody gets hurt.

How different from our own tribe. The Commons hit new heights of pantomime – or plumbed new depths of barbarism, depending upon whether you view the Chamber as a branch of theatre or of government.

At a luncheon in his honour the previous day at the Mansion House – and to the horror of the Lord Mayor – the King had risen to what sounded like an impromptu tirade in the Siswati language from an unknown guest in a brown leather coat. But this was Swazi etiquette; royal persons should rise to a babble of praise. His Majesty will therefore have been less surprised than many visitors to witness something similar when our Prime Minister rose. Everyone started screaming.

The Swazi King will also have recognised a custom now ritually observed in King Tony's court. Every Labour backbencher asking Blair a question prefaces it with an extravagant verbal grovel. This is getting sillier than the silliest days of the premiership of the Great She-Elephant (the *Indlovukazi* title which the Swazis accord to their Queen Mother and Sir Julian Critchley once borrowed for his own Leader).

'Can I say how welcome is the boost for business . . .' began Jonathan Shaw (Lab, Chatham & Aylesford). Could Phil Woolas (Lab) welcome the £15 million for schools in his constituency of Oldham E & Saddleworth? He could.

Was Blair 'aware how warmly welcome in Scotland' was this week's Budget? He was, after Jim Murphy (Lab, Eastwood) had told him. Labour's Gareth Thomas ('while welcoming . . .' etc) had the cheek to mention a massive oil spill off his constituency of Clwyd W. Off-message, Gareth: King Tony does not wish to receive bad news.

But these primitive traditions were routine by comparison with the War Dance. William Hague rose to wild ululation behind him. In a ritual chant he then asked the same question five times: would the Prime Minister say 'what is the total tax rise, in pounds . . .' this Government have overseen? To an answering cacophony from the Labour side, King Tony insisted, five times, that there was no rise but a fall.

King Mswati looked astonished.

19.3.99   Lucy Offers an Opinion

Lucy was sick on the Commons floor last Thursday morning. I now know why. Yesterday David Blunkett's guide dog was missing from Education Questions, answered before lunch. I sympathise.

Unkind tongues had suggested it was a speech by David Willetts, Mr Blunkett's Tory shadow, which had caused Lucy to take ill last time. Maybe; but something will have triggered the nausea. Watching MPs and ministers discussing education and employment yesterday, led by a dogless Secretary of State, we guessed the trigger. It's the appalling jargon.

Three sketchwriters were almost sick. Education has been hijacked by the educationists. Ministers' discourse has left this planet and spins towards a vortex of techno-babble. It started the moment Estelle Morris, a junior minister, rose. She started talking about phonics – and then 'synthetic phonics'.

The question was about learning to read. Or so I thought. But Ms

Morris explained that reading meant 'accessing the curriculum' and what was needed was a 'value-added baseline assessment'. She added: 'What we now have under this Government to which we can definitely take credit for.' Morris should access a grammar textbook; her phonics had gone awry. Andrew Smith, another minister, told us about 'a comprehensive programme-two evaluation' of 'core performance indicators'. Mostly, Mr Smith was talking about New Deal (the definite article is omitted by the on-message) and New Deal triggers Gateways. Gateways, now 'rolled out', are 'up-and-running'.

'Gateway has been an outstanding success-feature,' wittered Smith. MPs should compare areas 'where pathfinder areas were up-and running with areas before New Deal was up-and-running'. Backbencher David Lock (Lab, Wyre Forest) agreed (I think). 'Gateway phase is absolutely vital to train people into being job-ready'. Not every back-bencher was enthralled. Syd Rapson (Lab, Portsmouth N) confessed to being 'an old sceptic' on 'personal job accounts' which Smith said would be 'up-and-running' next year (not yet rolled out, you see); but Syd's scepticism still looked up-and-running. I doubt he's job-ready. Margaret Hodge, a minister who wanted 'employment-focused action plans', told MPs that a 'client-focused service' could 'access' an 'extensive range' of something or other. Lucy would have been accessing her sickbag.

But back to education, where we were told that 'individual learning accounts' would act as 'catalysts'. This is not even good chemistry, let along plain English. When Mrs Hodge was asked about playschools we nursed the hope she might talk about toys and crayons. Some hope. 'Diversity of provision,' she burbled, meant that 'choice should not be decided by a producer-led interest.' Poor Lucy. This was a world away from 'sit!', 'heel!' and 'good dog!'. Another minister commended 'nationwide access to interactive learning technology'.

Even the normally plain-speaking Mr Blunkett, lacking Lucy's critical reaction, strayed. Talking of 'basic skills needs' in individual learning accounts, he thought that 'many account-holders will want to access advice and information.' A Liberal Democrat, Phil Willis (Harrogate & Knaresborough) thanked him for 'rolling out the issue of tax relief'.

But Blunkett retains a sense of humour. When new Labour says (as Smith did yesterday) that a programme has made 'an encouraging start' you know it's in deep trouble, but Blunkett wanted to assure MPs that under New Deal the jobless would be learning useful skills. As an example of a frivolous skill he was unwise to choose deep-sea-diving, our sun-tanned Deputy Prime Minister's latest passion. There were Tory whoops.

'Hoist with my own petard!' laughed Blunkett, who then (interestingly) covered his eyes in shame. What he meant, of course, was that he was upwardly driven by his own catalyst, triggering a rollout of self-focused embarrassment, now up-and-running.

Warlike MPs Airborne and Moralising

26.3.99

Surrender you Serbs, or British MPs will bore you into submission. Yesterday at Westminster our cutting-edge Commons weaponry was unveiled. Tony Benn called it the chair-borne army, and it's lethal. In a display of rhetorical whiz-bang which would have taken pride of place in any arms fair, Johnny Backbencher showed us what he can do.

But first came Robin Cook. Lord knows what a Sidewinder actually is but one imagines the Foreign Secretary to be the human version. For a quarter of an hour we witnessed not so much the thud of heavy artillery as a whistling, hissing, syncopated zigzag through a minefield of cliché and sophistry.

As Mr Cook wove his way across the battlefield, he was interrupted by one of the most awesome pieces of light weaponry known to brushfire war: the ground-launched, vertical take-off, Harrier Hughes.

Simon Hughes directs, at no notice, a stream of sanctimony so noxious that combatants are left writhing on the carpet. He wanted us to know he was agonised by war – but unflinching. He also wanted us to know he was in the running for the Liberal Democrat leadership.

Cook told MPs he must dash – to Brussels – and streaked spluttering over the horizon. In came the Tory Stealth bomber: Michael Howard. The Shadow Foreign Secretary steered with silky poise between supporting the Government and undermining it; fired off a series of pointed and unanswerable questions; and returned to base unscathed.

Then came a para-landing by Menzies Campbell, chief Liberal

Democrat spokesman, in which the normally impressive posh Scot
became surprisingly tangled in his own parachute strings. His canopy
was supposed to be the United Nations, but Campbell got caught in a
twisted rationalisation of Security Council resolutions, and landed
badly.

Then came the Anderson stutter-bomb. Donald Anderson, Labour
Chairman of the Foreign Affairs Select Committee, skidded croaking
through lines of on-the-one-hands and on-the-others, supporting his
front bench but showering them with sparks as he hit every difficulty
and every imponderable implicit in the Nato action.

After Anderson we were treated to a display of gallant horsemanship
by the Tory cavalry, in the shape of former Defence Secretary Tom
King, as doughty a supporter for Nato action as Tony Blair is likely to
find.

Hm. Now why would that be? We soon realised. Mr King said
'overstretch', then 'unsustainable'. He wants more dosh for Defence.
Just minutes into the campaign – and already the Give-us-a-billion
Brigade are saddled up and galloping.

King was followed by the leftwing Harry Barnes (Lab, NE
Derbyshire). For 27 minutes Mr Barnes orated bafflingly. On he droned,
from the history of Yugoslavia to the International Monetary Fund,
Germany, and points between.

'Is he for the Government?' I whispered to a colleague. 'Who can
say?' came the reply. Heads nodded, eyes glazed.

What a weapon a canister of Barnes stun gas would make against
your Slav insurgent. What hill-fighter could maintain fervour in the face
of this choking barrage of non-sequiturs? The effect was rivalled only
by Bowen Wells (C), the High-Calibre UNO-bore Repeater who spoke
next.

After Wells a magnificent display of tracer-fire from an ancient Benn
lit the sky, as angry and frightened Blair babes squeaked 'Sit down, sit
down'.

But I had to go. Sir Patrick 'Ack-ack' Cormack (C) was airborne and
moralising. Horror gripped me: a vision of Sir Patrick astride a cruise
missile heading for the Balkans and perorating at full tilt, as, panic-
stricken, Serb and Albanian alike head screaming for the hills.

Sing, Brother, Sing

God willing, the Earl of Longford turns 94 this year. With his frail body, leathery, elongated face and gravity-defying tuft of hair, he crackles with energy like a mad scientist recently subjected to an electric shock. The spring in his step comes from the incongruous training shoes for which he is famous, for he is now quite lame; but mentally the springiness remains, though you never quite know which way his lordship will bounce.

So this old bird's final song may not be sung for years yet. But still there was a poignancy both for him and for the last Lords chamber of its kind, in a little poem he quoted during yesterday's debate on Lords reform. It was addressed, he said, to a blackbird whose hours were numbered.

If this be the last song that you shall sing,
Sing well, for you may not sing another:
Sing, brother, sing.

Longford's song would be missed. He muses rather than speaks – but a muser aware he has an audience. Like an eccentric and celebrated professor with a packed lecture theatre, he raises to the status of performance art the stream-of-consciousness ramble.

And he has a habit, a little verbal tic. The earl finishes many sentences by repeating the last words: a sort of echo, melancholy, thoughtful.

The previous speaker, Lord Pearson of Rannoch, had called himself a maverick Conservative.

Mused Longford: 'I don't know how many maverick Conservatives there are about today but I was one 70 years ago, 70 years ago.

'My mind goes back . . .'

His mind kept going back. It seemed something of a gamble each time how far back his mind would go – like throwing a stick for a dog to retrieve, and seeing where it lands. 'My mind goes back 50 years when I heard Lord Cranborne's grandfather, grandfather . . .'

Next, Lord Longford's mind went back some 40 years, when Lord Addison, Leader of the Lords for six years after the last war, tugged the jacket of young Pakenham (as he then was) in mid-oration and hissed from behind: 'Sit down now; you have got the House with you. You'll lose it if you go on any longer.'

'My mind goes back 30 years, to when I was Leader of this place, this place.' The earl spoke of the charms of the Upper Chamber and its miscellaneous team. Lord Cranborne's grandfather, Lord Salisbury, said this was primarily a House of Parliament, not a club. But it was a club too, club too. And what a club! 'This has been a useful place and all of us have come to love it, love it.'

Longford was regretful rather than defiant. 'Are we going to throw all that away, letting it disappear without trace, without trace?'

There was, he realised, 'the possibility of the deal, the deal,' but he accepted that something had to give. 'The time may come when this performance will have to come about, come about.' And if it did – well his lordship would bow to the inevitable.

His mind went back. Sensing he had the House with him, which he did, Lord Longford decided to heed the memory of Lord Addison, all those years ago, and sit down before he lost it. Addison's shade tugged at his jacket, brother blackbird's parting note echoed its way into *Hansard*: if the hereditaries were to go, 'I hope it will be done in a humane way . . .

'. . . humane way.'

Lord Longford sat down to study his notes, hunched, with a magnifying glass as big as a saucer.

Lord Longford died two years later.

War Turns Sombre
14.4.99

Glum is the word for MPs yesterday – supporters and opponents of the Balkan war alike. The Commons reassembled after Easter to hear a sombre but resolute statement from the Prime Minister.

Tony Blair's short speech was less theatrical than before, more carefully argued and in tone well judged. Flanked by all the senior figures in his Cabinet (always a sensible precaution), with the mysterious exception of the man who must find the money, Gordon Brown (always a worrying absence), Mr Blair rehearsed the familiar worries, familiar outrage and familiar determination. Beside him, Robin Cook nodded manically, George Robertson maintained a certain reserve, and John Prescott studied his fingernails.

'As I said in my first statement to the House of Commons,' the Prime Minister reminded us, 'this action will take time.'

Unable quite to recall Mr Blair's saying this, I checked the record. He had said the sufferings of the Kosovans would 'not be ended overnight'. Some 30 nights later, this seemed to understate.

Not that the mood was mutinous. 'Grim' describes it better but support for the Government, though it has lost its froth, has consolidated – or that was how it felt. Few had much new to say. Sir Peter Tapsell (C, Louth & Horncastle), whose indignation had been Vesuvial last time, kept silent, perhaps humming 'I told you so'. Tam Dalyell made the mistake of speaking critically of the Kosovo Liberation Army (the KLA have miraculously ceased to be terrorists) and was heckled angrily for suggesting that it might be involved in drug trafficking. Alan Clark (C, Kensington & Chelsea) made the mistake of venturing praise for the Serbian people ('brave Christians') and was howled at for this indiscretion. From now on there are good guys and bad guys and no shades between.

Mr Blair's sobriety impressed but the spectacle of the British Left in bombing mode is scary. There is nothing more belligerent than a reformed pacifist. Clare Short gave the Defence Secretary encouraging pats. In clinging to His Master's Voice, David Winnick (Lab, Walsall N) pleased the Prime Minister by yapping ferociously at the heels of an imagined Milosevic. Mr Winnick is putting the 'creep' into mission-creep.

William Hague sounded sane but his interventions on Kosovo have somehow lacked coherence. One remains unsure what, if anything, he is actually trying to say.

By contrast, Paddy Ashdown was crisp. The Liberal Democrat leader wanted guidance on the meaning of Mr Blair's new phrase: 'permissive environment'.

The phrase replaces Blair's former insistence that Nato troops would have to be invited into Kosovo. But what, asked Ashdown, *is* a permissive environment? We wondered whether it is what a squatter encounters, finding a window open and the householder absent.

But Blair refused to speculate and told Ashdown, in the tone of a pestered parent, that this was 'all being considered', adding: 'This is a situation in which we have considered all the right options.'

'So that's all right then,' spluttered some doubting Thomas. Anyway, said Blair, 'it's a mistake to say Milosevic isn't hurting'. Ashdown had said nothing of the kind. Nobody doubted it was hurting. What some doubted was whether it was working. But only a few had any doubt that Nato should keep trying.

'This is military action for a moral purpose,' declared Blair. The fastidious shuddered at this dangerously close brush with a soundbite but a more downcast kind of rectitude soon reasserted itself.

Nobody at Westminster is crowing, praise be.

Prescott's Longest Half-hour   *15.4.99*

Deputy Prime Minister! One heartbeat from Britain's war leadership! As Mr Blair's second-in-command trudged from the Chamber yesterday, thunder-faced while the Opposition jeered, earnest prayers for the health of our Prime Minister winged skywards.

Commentators ransacked the metaphor of misadventure to convey the scale of his debacle as stand-in for Tony Blair at Prime Minister's Questions. Some called it a humanitarian catastrophe, but we will be sparing. His wheels came off. All of them. Prescott left the road, overturned, demolished a wall, hit several trees and came to rest upturned in the smoking wreckage of his ministerial reputation. We may now never know whether Mr Prescott did know what the 'withholding tax' was.

It all started with Alan Beith. The bland, blinking Beith deputised for the Liberal Democrat Leader as Blair is in Brussels and, when the Chief's away, Parliament stages a Battle of the Pygmies.

To be roughed up by somebody bigger is bad enough, but by Beith! He asked Prescott if it were true that class sizes had risen. Funk number one. Too proud to admit it but too clumsy to duck, he replied that Labour was 'on target' with a manifesto pledge. Reminded mildly that the answer was Yes, he dug deeper: Beith had 'asked if we were on target', he insisted.

'No he didn't,' MPs shouted. 'Well that's the answer he's going to get,' said Prescott.

He lurched moments later into a tangle with Slavic pronunciation, denouncing someone he called 'General Motherditch'. Bouncing off Serbo-Croat he hit international law, referring to 'war crimes and tribunal indicts'.

The Deputy Prime Minister was breaking up, cool gone, spinning out of control. Clare Short tried to comfort him with whispers. He stumbled over the IRA, reminding MPs that, hanging over us, was 'the sceptre of violence'.

Spotting a wounded bull-elephant, Sir Michael Spicer (C, Worcestershire W) took aim. Could Prescott guarantee there would be no withholding tax?

Withholding tax? Panic in his eyes. Colleagues freeze, helpless to rescue. He rises. Must answer. Something with 'tax' in it. He bellows about a tax he does know, the Tory poll tax. He tries a defence of the local government financial settlement.

Stunned silence all around. Have we misunderstood? Then MPs begin to laugh, howl, hoot. He ploughs wretchedly on, Margaret Beckett's face locks in an embarrassed grin. 'More!' they shout as he collapses into his seat. That could have been the end of it but a fuse had now blown in the Prescott brain. To a question about the National Forest, Prescott's answer seemed to be about the railways; everyone barracked; Prescott explained to Madam Speaker that he had thought he was answering a different question. Miss Boothroyd took pity and, meaning to help, told MPs to check Order Papers and see what question they were on. Confused by the laughter, Prescott took this as a reprimand – then apologised to the Chair for his first apology. New questioners arose. He kept losing his place in his notes. Pauses lengthened to eternities.

Everyone but the Deputy Prime Minister was in the Commons Chamber. But Mr Prescott was in a sort of cosmic vortex, his briefing notes blowing about: arguments, Slav names and impossible taxes hurtling at him out of a black void, mocking laughter and Speaker's reprimands echoing from the dark.

We have all been there, my friends. Hilarity turned to embarrassment and one found it hard to look. This, without doubt, was John Prescott's longest half-hour.

Mission Creep and Language Crawl

22.4.99

NATO is dragged deeper into Kosovo.

For the leader of a democracy the dynamics of humanitarian conflict are complex. 'Mission creep' drags him forward just as 'compassion fatigue' pushes him back. Then 'attention drift' kicks in as the 'boredom factor' descends.

And now comes a sideways vector. Yesterday at Prime Minister's Questions, 'language crawl' emerged. Tony Blair snuck in a new word to describe when NATO might invade Kosovo.

Bit by bit the language changes. We have moved from a month ago when an impression was given that ground troops could occupy Kosovo only by agreement. Later, we learnt that tea and cakes were no longer a precondition: but entry must be unopposed.

By last week, the keywords had become 'permissive environment' – a sort of benign trespass. Naturally (we were given to understand) one couldn't rule out the occasional lone Serb sniper but no serious battle could be contemplated.

Yesterday the terms changed again. The new word is 'undegraded'.

It was the Liberal Democrats' Alan Beith (standing in for Paddy Ashdown, escaped to the Balkans) who prised the new word from Mr Blair. Would he confirm, Beith asked, that attitudes to the use of ground troops had changed?

W-e-e-e-ll, implied Blair, troops could *not* go in, so long as the Serbs' military forces were 'undegraded'. MPs and journalists performed several quick mental flip-flops as negatives cancelled each other out. Does 'we can*not* go in if they are *un*degraded' mean we *can* go in if they *are* degraded?

But the Serb machine has indeed been degraded, hasn't it? So we can occupy? There were mutters and mental whirrings as this sunk in. Just as the boredom factor threatened attention drift, while compassion fatigue grew, language crawl has accelerated mission creep . . . all while Paddy was on politician flit. He'll be furious.

Still, Labour's Ben Bradshaw enjoyed it. Mr Bradshaw is Tony Blair's most warlike young fan. Every time Blair says a word like 'bomb' Bradshaw nods his head in theatrical assent, like a back-window nodding-dog on overdrive. Let us hope the PM never says 'bomb', 'kill', 'nuke', 'exterminate' and 'zap' in the same sentence, or Bradshaw's head would nod right off. Though the debonair and floppy-haired young Exeter MP has seen service in the trenches of the BBC studios at White City, it is not immediately clear that the mud and briar of the Albanian mountains would be his natural habitat. Gucci shoes slip in the snow.

Mrs Golding Reels in Babbling Banks

23.4.99

Boy, can that Tony Banks talk! In Room 15 the Culture, Media and Sport Committee was interviewing the Sports Minister.

Can Room 15 have heard anything like it? Yak, yak, yak – on and on he went, till reporters' eyes glazed over, the policeman standing at the door drooped and even the MPs interviewing him slumped back in weary recognition that in Mr Banks they had met their match.

Well chosen was the young cockney councillor, years ago, as Chairman of Transport on the Greater London Council, for Banks talks like a man on a bus. If this MP were to try a walk-on part in *EastEnders* the television critics would slate him for hamming it up.

Banks talks about anything and everything, in his cheeky-chappie 'now-if-you-ask-my-opinion-squire-and-maybe-you-didn't-but-you're-gonna-geddit-anyway' manner: free-flow, stream of consciousness, directed more by whim and word association than logic. He had been invited yesterday to answer inquiries about sport. But he could have switched seamlessly to stucco ceilings, rubbish collection, the poll tax or in-vitro fertilisation.

While he offered his opinions on chess, Wembley, the Commonwealth Games, or anything, it occurred to me to wonder how long it would take, were Banks arbitrarily to move the discussion on to medieval witchcraft, for anyone to notice. Towards the end even his civil servants were staring at the wallpaper in a sort of vacant despair.

He hardly draws breath. The minister has learnt the habit of anticipating the end of one of his sentences before he reaches it. Then, a couple of words before he gets there, interrupting *himself* before anyone else can do so, and launching into another subject. This is a brilliant ruse for repelling verbal boarders, as those desirous of getting a word in edgeways naturally await the end of a sentence. Banks never gives them the end of a sentence. So it was delicious yesterday to witness, just once, the unusual sight of Tony Banks being caught, pinned down and shut up. Credit goes to Llin Golding (Lab, Newcastle-under-Lyme). Her subject was angling. She hooked and landed him.

Mrs Golding's complaint was that the Sports Council refuses to include angling in its category of eligible sports. Available to the minister was a range of five possible answers: (1) the Sports Council were wrong and he would oppose them; (2) they were right and he would support them; (3) he was willing to offer his personal view but could not interfere with their decision; (4) he was not willing to offer a personal view on something beyond his control; or (5) he would look into it.

Mrs Golding fished with flair. She cast, her bait being the opportunity for Banks to talk. He bit before thinking, felt the hook and began to flounder. She gave him more line, another question, and he floundered more wildly. In answering, Banks managed to include elements from all five of the options I list above. Mrs Golding interrupted, repeated her request for a simple answer, and reeled in. Miserably, Banks promised to look into it, then started babbling again. 'No Minister, thank you,' she interrupted, 'that's all I want to know.' *She actually managed to stop him.*

Mrs Golding should display Banks's head, teeth showing, in a glass case.

A Pawn in Tony's Game

29.4.99

Let us be fair to Charlotte Atkins: Prime Minister's Questions always did rollercoaster between the sublime and the ridiculous.

There is nothing new in the sight of MPs clutching their stomachs as the House makes a sickening lurch from a humanitarian catastrophe in Albania to an outbreak of cat flu in Bolton. Members may raise what they please, and do. The result is an eclectic mix of domestic bees in local bonnets, with questions on the destiny of mankind.

So for Ms Atkins it was more bad luck than bad judgement that her question on the status of chess immediately followed an impassioned outburst from the Prime Minister on the horrors of Kosovo.

That Balkan exchange, like those that followed, had been delivered to a resolute House. I reported last week that the Commons barometer had moved to 'unsettled'. Yesterday it inched back towards a stable high pressure. William Hague (poor thing) sounded rather bleak – just going through the motions. Nobody unexpected moved off-message. But Ms Atkins temporarily lost the plot.

The Labour MP for Staffordshire Moorlands is neither an obsessive nor a fool. And there is no reason why she should not raise, at this highest of levels, the grievance of chess players that their game is not recognised as a sport.

Nor could she choose her moment when to speak: MPs who want to intervene have to start leaping up from the very outset, to catch the Chair's attention. Ms Atkins did.

Disaster! She succeeded too early: immediately after Mr Hague had been cross-questioning Tony Blair about the conflict in the Balkans. Mr Blair had worked himself into particular outrage at Serb atrocities. Steam was still coming from his ears.

This was not the moment for chess. But, as Miss Boothroyd called her name, it was too late for Ms Atkins to concoct a new question on the rape of Albania. She ploughed through her protest against the persecution of chess players.

MPs' brows furrowed. People began muttering and shaking their heads. Frontbenchers looked uncomfortable. After too long, Ms Atkins sat down: a loyal new-Labourite who had asked a fair question, but with unlucky timing.

It was instructive to note the ruthlessness with which Mr Blair let her swing. The Labour Whips' Office now tries to select who will intervene, and to orchestrate questions, so this sketch would be surprised if she had given no notice of what she hoped to raise – but it is possible.

In any event, whether or not Mr Blair could have dealt with her question, he chose to make light of it. In mock-exasperation he protested – in effect – that Prime Ministers do get rogue coconuts like this thrown at them, and simply have to duck.

Rather wittily he remarked that he was looking in vain along his front bench for help. Everyone laughed: laughed with him, and at Ms Atkins, who looked a bit wretched.

The effect was to play to the mood of the House, joining others in grinning at the inappropriateness of Ms Atkins's question. Most journalists will admire the skill and light touch with which Mr Blair extracted himself unscathed from a potentially awkward exchange.

But this sketchwriter, who has been a backbencher, felt for Ms Atkins. Somewhere in her half-consciousness a tiny arrow has now lodged. In a phrase of Thornton Wilder's, 'wrapped in layers of forgiveness and understanding, it sank into her heart'.

Reluctant Toff Enters Fray   *3.5.99*

The first elections to the Scottish parliament.

Eat your heart out, Sean Connery. Schwarzenegger's hit Scotland. Or, at least, the Terminator's match.

According to the Tory election leaflet, the party has no doubts: 'I'll be back!' is the headline – 'So said James Douglas-Hamilton at the election count in 1997, echoing the words of Arnold Schwarzenegger'.

I've seen Schwarzenegger – and James, you're no Schwarzenegger. Indeed this Tory's advantage – and difficulty – is that everyone likes him. Lord James is undoubtedly the nicest toff in politics. Toffs on the stump are a rarity in England these days, but Scotland is different. Can it tip the balance this Thursday for James Douglas-Hamilton?

'The last election was a tidal wave, a *tidal wave*,' he says, blinking, shocked at the force of his own language. A lady helper defends him indignantly; 'It was an anti-Tory thing,' she says fiercely, 'not an anti-James thing.'

We can believe it. Lord James is, quite simply, a poppet. When a Westminster MP, he forsook his hereditary peerage to stay in the Commons and save John Major's majority; then lost his seat to the Liberal Democrats. Now a life peer, he seeks election to the Scottish Parliament for his old Edinburgh West constituency.

He ought to be addressed as Lord Selkirk, but everyone calls him James. His gaffes are forgiven. With more affection than censure friends recite the story that, introduced as Housing Minister to the new occupant of a 'shared ownership' scheme home, Lord James asked: 'How many days each year will you be able to live here?' Famous when a minister for holding open the door of his government car for his chauffeuse, his painful courtesy endears him to all.

He was anxious not to overshadow colleagues. Let me introduce you to our council candidate for Davidsons Mains, John Crombie.' I asked Mr Crombie, who had a small moustache, if the campaign was heated. 'Not heated,' interjected Lord James, worried lest Mr Crombie inject a note of unpleasantness into the contest, 'spirited'. Less keen to discuss the ideological struggle than the local zoo ('the most interesting collection of penguins in Europe'), he told me that he was on the fundraising committee. We discussed the character of gentoo penguins. 'Gentoo? Very ill-natured,' I remarked. Lord James's brown furrowed. Mr Crombie saved the occasion. 'Rockhoppers are the rude ones,' he said.

'And have you heard about the lioness?' said Lord James. 'Sadly she has contracted a sort of big cats' BSE. Happily she is not infectious – there's been a top-level investigation by the most advanced vets.' Not to be left out, Mr Crombie chipped in: 'I've sponsored a ring-tailed lemur.'

I followed Lord James to the doorsteps of a prim, tidy estate. A grandee among the pebble-dash, Lord James met such affectionate deference that it was hard to know which householders were actually going to vote for him. To the despair of his supporting canvassers, he was usually too polite to ask.

A lady came to the door in her stockings. Lord James summoned up his courage. 'Can I . . . em . . . put you down as a *supporter?*' He spoke as though this vast impertinence were tantamount to inquiring about her lingerie. The lady said she was still making up her mind. 'Do you support the Union?' he asked, tentatively. She looked flummoxed: 'What union?'

Backing out of a drive he failed to see two pedestrians. 'Stop!' called Mr Crombie urgently. Lord James stamped on the brake, gasping: 'That would have been quite dreadful!' Unlike most modern candidates, he meant dreadful *for them*.

Lucy's Verdict Clear Again   *11.6.99*

Think you were bored by yesterday's European election? Think how much more bored a black retriever bitch would have been. So bored that for a worrying hour in the Commons I thought Lucy, David Blunkett's guide dog, was dead.

Road users will be familiar with the concern aroused by the sight of a dog's inert body stretched out on the verge. Motoring past, one looks anxiously for a twitch, a tail-flick – anything which might show that the creature is only asleep.

So it was with Lucy. Single red lines about three inches wide run the whole length of the carpet, in front of the front benches on both sides. The space between the lines is about as wide as a road and the effect is reminiscent of the no-stopping 'red routes' into cities. The apparent corpse of a dog lying across this line on the government side looked horribly like evidence of a tragic accident. The European election bandwagon had run down one of our four-legged friends.

She lay there while Mr Blunkett swopped Euro-election banter with a man with white, forward-combed hair: Phil Willis (Lib Dem, Harrogate). Black furry legs (Lucy's, not Phil's) were splayed lifeless on the carpet. Her tail had curled underneath itself, its end resting between the hind legs and pointing forward. Her lip had retracted a fraction, showing a flash of tooth, and a slit of the white of one eye was showing. This dog was comatose. This dog was out. This dog was not with us.

Such was the quiescence that Estelle Morris, the Schools Minister, got away with the most outrageous new Labour cheek this sketch has witnessed. Andrew Robathan (C, Blaby) had complained that Margaret Hodge, an Education Minister, was the woman who, as leader of Islington council, had once overseen the collapse of a London borough's entire education system.

Ms Morris's reply? 'Your Government,' she told Robathan, 'did nothing to put that right.' As Mrs Hodge joined her side's hear-hear, Lucy might at least have stirred herself to be sick.

Tony Benn Weeps

Even through the arid canyons of a forbidding intellect, hidden rivers run. Yesterday in the Commons, Tony Benn, lifetime class-warrior, leveller, theoretician, prosecutor of privilege, scourge of self-indulgence and terror of the bourgeoisie, wept with happiness. To see his son succeed at last in a life's ambition was too much for the elderly ideologue.

As Hilary Benn, 45, took the oath at the Commons Table, his father's face just crumpled. Unkind rumours that he was crying because his son is a Blairite are wide of the mark. Blood is thicker than socialism.

How in print shall we distinguish the Messrs Benn? Mr Tony and Mr Hilary serve best, for Benn I and Benn II would be rejected by Mr Tony as too monarchical (and Benn Sr and Benn Jr too American) for this staunchly republican hammer of Yankee imperialism.

Mr Tony had been waiting at the Bar of the House for some time with Mr Hilary for the ceremony to take place. This was to occur after the Foreign Secretary's statement on Kosovo. The statement ran on interminably as Mr Cook had nothing to say, and not answering questions takes time. Some questions he didn't answer for as long as four minutes. Others he managed not to answer in a shorter time.

From the wardrobe of dark wool-worsted suits, white shirts and red ties which has served him throughout his 46 years (so far) in Parliament, Mr Tony had chosen a dark suit, white shirt and red tie. For his own outfit Mr Hilary had selected a dark suit, white shirt and red tie. The two trim figures stood like a couple of Post Office union shop stewards overseeing a work-to-rule.

They seem to get on – though Mr Hilary has made plain his filial rebellion against Dad's left-wingery. Adapting William Hague's 'In Europe but not run by Europe' slogan, Mr Hilary's campaign message has been 'A Benn but not a Bennite': in with father but not run by father. It has served him well enough, and he slipped through at an ill-supported by-election in Leeds Central last Thursday.

'Members desirous of taking their seats!' cried Madam Speaker (the customary phrase) at about quarter past four. Flanked by Mr Tony and Kevin Barron (Lab, Rother Valley), his sponsors, Mr Hilary strode down the aisle towards the Table: a rather ragged quick-march punctuated by ragged bows, as you would expect from non-militarists; Mr Tony had probably been practising to get them raggeder.

While Mr Tony retired to the back benches, Mr Hilary was handed the oath to read. The bit about God one is allowed to omit (as did Mr Hilary, 'affirming' instead) but the bit about Queen Elizabeth one is not (despite Mr Tony's past efforts: he does not want the republican Irish to be barred). Mr Hilary duly swore his loyalty to the Queen.

Tony Benn had been smiling gently. When his son pledged loyalty the smile froze into a sort of grimace. At first we thought it marked annoyance. But then we realised a struggle was going on in which the facial muscles were ceasing to obey. Tony Benn looked away from those around him and stared up, blinking, towards the ceiling. His face was puckering and crumpled. He stayed like that for about ten seconds. Then he regained control.

Tony Benn stood down at the next election.

When Johns Collide   *16.6.99*

Two big Johns met yesterday and jousted in the chamber. Amid much shouting and waving, each lunged at the other – and missed. John Prescott tangled with John Redwood, or tried to. John Redwood took on John Prescott, or tried to. It was like the meeting of a complex piece of electronic circuitry from outer space and the Thing from the Swamp. There were blue sparks, bleeping noises and a great deal of splashing around. Nobody won.

William Hague must have a sense of humour, or why would he have appointed Mr Redwood to Environment, Transport and the Regions as Mr Prescott's Shadow? Physically the pair look like Laurel and Hardy, Prescott weighing in (surely) at twice Redwood's weight. But Mr Redwood has a neck. Then again, he only has one chin.

Prescott led with both his own as he bellowed out a prepared statement on public-private partnership and the future of the London Underground. The Deputy Prime Minister has now completely given up trying to make sense of his ministerial texts and reads them out without spaces between the sentences or any indication of which verbs govern which objects, or which adjectives qualify which nouns.

Technically, however, he does say all the words – plus a gratuitous sprinkling of definite articles in unexpected places, his personal trademark. We learnt that the transport policy is committed to the North London and beyond. Like a heavy-goods train, once Mr Prescott gets going with one of these texts the momentum is scary. Even after application of the emergency brakes he would take about a page to stop, clattering over the points of syntax and screeching round the tighter bends, derailment – and a fearful smash – an ever-present danger. No one could make head or tail of his statement. Except our humanoid circuit-board. Redwood sat on the edge of his seat throughout, single chin jutted forward, raring to go.

And boy did he go! Let nobody gain the impression that this wizard of pure logic contained himself within a dry argument or painstaking analysis. Oh no. Redwood activated his delete thought and find abuse functions, jabbing intermittently at the find joke button and accessing a thesaurus of invective.

A barrage of insult followed. Prescott was 'two-Jags John'; he'd never been on a Tube train except to pose; he had wrecked the Underground; he had achieved the 'impossible treble' of uniting unions, management and bidders against his plans. Between ideas and reality there was a great chasm . . . find joke . . . 'Mind the gap!'.

Redwood fizzed, spluttered and spat his way to a conclusion – and sat down. The Thing from the Swamp arose, chins a-quiver.

We braced ourselves for violence. But no: just as Redwood had attempted music hall, Prescott now had a stab at Senior Common Room, lowering his voice and adopting a donnish air of disappointed intellect. He said kind things about Redwood's predecessor, Gillian Shephard; regretted that Redwood was relying on newspapers; and looked forward to his Shadow's reading himself properly into the job. Every so often the old monster would surface, and Prescott would begin to bellow – then, remembering, turn down the volume, and try another donnish thrust. Mostly they missed.

As these weird creatures jabbed, head-butted and stumbled their way through the prospects for public transport in London, Lord Archer of Weston-super-Mare peered down, pterodactylically alert, from the Lords' Gallery. He hopes to take charge as Mayor. Heavens, what a trio.

Which Tony is Real?

24.6.99

When Shakespeare said 'one man in his time plays many parts', the Bard did not mean within the same half hour. But yesterday at Questions the Prime Minister lurched from lean and slipper'd pantaloon, to swaggering soldier (sudden and quick in quarrel), to donnish Justice (full of wise saws) and back again; all within minutes. Some roles appealed more than others.

Most convincing was the lean and slipper'd pantaloon. Shakepeare's 'spectacles on nose and pouch on side' would not have been out of place as Tony Blair explained with soft intensity why he refused to moralise or posture on arms decommissioning in Northern Ireland.

This was the Prime Minister at his most convincing. The less he swaggers, the more persuasive Mr Blair becomes. With underplayed passion, yet deftly, he rejected William Hague's demand for a new ultimatum to Sinn Fein. Instead, he gave reasons for seeking peace patiently, begging all sides to take the chance.

Blair articulated his case so quietly – almost wearily – that you needed to lean forward to hear; and people did. This Tony made the Tory leader and his noisy backers sound tawdry and opportunistic. Betraying no anger himself, he roused his troops to anger at the Opposition's tactics.

But that was only one of the Tonys on offer. Next came the soldier, 'full of strange oaths . . . jealous in honour . . . seeking the bubble reputation'. This was the braggart who met Mr Hague minutes later in a different confrontation. The Tory leader raised the euro. Now it was Hague's turn to make Blair sound tawdry. Ducking the Tory leader's testing questions on the Government's attitude to currency union, Blair just shouted abuse at the Conservatives.

He was not convincing. Asked by his opposite number to describe his plan to campaign for the euro, Blair bawled, 'To carry on arguing for our point of view, which is a better point of view than yours'. He called the Conservatives hypocrites and Hague a 'monomaniac' who had 'sold his political soul'.

This Tony hints at the shallowness of the school bully. He sneered at a remark by a Tory spokesman (Nick Gibb) who, asked whether party policy might change, had replied that it depended what was best in the circumstances. This luminously rational remark Mr Blair declaimed mockingly, with an unspoken 'boom-boom' to cue a howl of synthetic laughter from the obedient herd behind. He sat down leering.

More attractive was the third Tony on show. Full of wise saws, Blair parried a shrewd question from Michael Fabricant (C, Lichfield) on how *he* would vote in his promised referendum on proportional representation. He would 'listen to the argument', said Blair. Invited by leftwinger Maria Eagle (Lab, Liverpool Garston) to praise the TGWU, he replied: 'I'm delighted to praise the TGWU, of which I'm a member.' Then (to laughter): 'That's as radical as it gets.'

Which Tony is real? I doubt he knows. So how can we?

A Good Passport Crisis For Widders

30.6.99

Never mind the Balkans; Ann Widdecombe is having a good Passport Crisis.

To the horrors of queueing outside the Passport Office in the rain has been added a new terror: a visit by the Tories' new Home Affairs spokesman. Yesterday (she told MPs) she swooped on the drenched queue in Petty France. Poor lambs. First their holidays are wrecked – now this. Crash barriers should be erected to shield frightened passport-seekers.

'Everyone had an urgent case,' she shrieked at Jack Straw, the Home Secretary, in the Commons debate she called later. 'There were mothers with tiny babies!'

'You chained 'em oop,' shouted a Labour heckler, recalling Miss Widdecombe's embarrassment as Prisons Minister when news emerged of pregnant women being shackled.

She ignored him. She was magnificent. As Mr Straw cowered and Labour backbenchers gaped, the Tories' answer to Winnie Mandela literally threw herself at the dispatch box. For the occasion she had chosen a bizarre outfit in black and white diagonal stripes with a great semi-circular sweep underneath the bosom, underlining – as it were – what is already beyond emphasis. The ensemble could have graced the tailfin of a BA jumbo jet. Whenever she emphasised a point, waving both arms, the whole design shook and quivered.

And her rage over passport queues was terrible. She even tore into Straw for apologising. 'First of all he smiles engagingly,' she jeered, 'then he apologises humbly, then he shrugs helplessly.' By now Straw was hunched miserably, beside him his blow-dried junior minister, Mike O'Brien, whispering explanations and trying not to looked scared.

At moments of high emotion, Miss Widdecombe's voice trills out of control in sudden yodels on unexpected words. Shaken by scorn at the Government's plan for expensive new photo-passports for infants, she squeaked that there were '*chil*[trill]-dren' in the queue.

Maria Eagle (Lab, Liverpool Garston) seemed to think it was the previous Government that had engaged the Passport Agency's IT-provider. Wrong. Widdecombe flattened her.

Denis MacShane (Lab, Rotherham) insisted that *he* did not mind buying passports for his children. She told him he was rich enough.

Straw gulped at a glass of water. She started yodelling statistics at him about the million-plus inquirers who had been met with only a recorded message. Elderly Bill O'Brien (Lab, Normanton, 70) tried to interrupt, was told to wait and tried again. Her wrath was palpable.

'The whole House heard me say 'in a minute'. If he didn't hear me then he may not find himself getting given way to at all.' Poor old Bill collapsed back on his bench, winded.

When, finally, Hurricane Ann blew herself out, a seriously rattled Home Secretary rose and began protesting, his voice raised nervily, at the Tory assault. He had hardly started when Widdecombe shot up again and hurled herself at the table with such violence that we feared for the woodwork. She continued to badger him. Straw never quite recovered his poise.

Mayoralty Bad for Dobson's Health

7.7.99

Rumours spread that Blair wants the Health Secretary for Mayor of London.

Who rattled Frank Dobson's cage? The normally jovial Health Secretary was in a foul mood yesterday as he delivered one of those lacklustre preventive healthcare statements that come around in every Parliament and sink without trace. We are enjoined to eat less cheese and finger ourselves for lumps.

Mr Dobson is being fingered where it hurts, by the political columnists. They say Downing Street wants him to run for the mayoralty of London – because streetfighting Dobbo might be able to snatch the nomination from Ken Livingstone. Arms are being twisted. Hard.

But he doesn't want to play. Not for him a political twilight scrapping with the deadbeats and low-grade *mafiosi* who run local government in the boroughs, being vilified in every edition of the London *Evening Standard* for street litter and points failures on the Tube at Epping. Not for him an unseemly battle with that most ruthless of streetfighters, Ken Livingstone. Too old to start new battles, he's already well stuck in with his battle for the NHS. He desperately wants to stay at Health.

And reshuffle looms. So the scene at the dispatch box as a bearded chap reads irritably through a statement he suspects he may never have the chance to follow up, is only one scene in our play. In another, high over London, a jump-suited Dobson, parachute on back, is wrestled by Blair's jackbooted henchmen towards a howling hole in the fuselage's side. Far below the Thames glints silver in the afternoon sun. Dobson does not, repeat not, want to jump.

Back to the dispatch box. He glances down at his text. How hollow, now, those snappy titles dreamt up by the PR johnnies at Richmond House. Dobson eyes this latest. *Saving Lives – Our Healthier Nation.* Harumph. Saving whose life, pray? Not his, not his political life. How the heck is he going to get through this guff, mind elsewhere?

Miserably he begins to read. 'We are aiming to save 300,000 by the year 2010.' 2010 indeed. He'll be 70. Washed up. *Dobson of St Pancras: baron, Frank. As MP (Lab) FD was surprise choice for Health Secretary in Tony Blair's first Government. Began difficult changes to NHS but left before fruits of drive to reduce waiting lists fully realised.*

Oh the nightmare of it. Dobson refocuses on his dreary text. 'Targets backed by action.' Action! How well he knows that First Law of Ministerial Statements: the more frequent the occurrence of 'action' or 'tackle', the less is promised. He reads on.

'Action against smoking, action to improve diet, action to improve treatment . . .' He struggles to sound as if he means it.

'We are going to tackle inequalities in health . . . Government is taking action to tackle them all . . .' He can't even raise head from text.

He ploughs on in monotone, like a schoolboy at remedial reading. 'A-new-hard-hitting-health-development-agency . . . 300,000-lives-saved-300,000-reasons-for-action . . .' Bejesus – who wrote this stuff?

Somehow Dobson made it through, slumping back on the bench. Hardly a cheer. Louder was the roar of aircraft engines, Alastair Campbell's bark – 'jump you bugger, jump' – the hiss of the wind. Liam Fox, the Tories' new Health Shadow leapt up. 'Normally a farewell performance gets a better cheer,' he sneered. Cruel.

He jumped but his parachute failed to open. Mr Dobson lost the mayoral race.

Battle for Control
28.7.99

Air-Liddell came in yesterday to a delayed landing on the legislative runway – and hit the tarmac with a heck of a thump. Poor Helen Liddell.

Sympathy for the hatchet-faced Scottish minister of English transport is an emotion few expected to feel, but you had to admire her pilot's nerve as proposals to privatise the National Air Traffic Service bounced heavily down the landing strip, buffeted by a storm of derision.

New Labour's awkward late conversion to the sell-off of 'NATS' has been in a holding pattern above Westminster, awaiting landing clearance. This has been postponed (by the embarrassment of proposing precisely what in opposition Labour promised never to do) and the project was running out of fuel. The Transport Department was also running out of money: this sell-off promises half a billion.

Chief Pilot Prescott, in overall command, was good enough to sit beside his junior pilot yesterday for her tensest hour.

What made it worse was that an angry Betty Boothroyd sat in the control tower. Overnight it had emerged that new Labour planned to land this privatisation secretly, in the dark, at a little-noticed jungle airstrip called 'Written Questions'. And to do so just before the

Commons rose yesterday for their long summer recess: too late for MPs to make a fuss.

Furious, Betty had insisted that the landing take place in the full glare of the parliamentary landing lights, at Westminster. She had granted the Tories' request that a minister be dragged to the controls to perform the touchdown there at 3.30pm.

And she had further punishment in store.

But first to the landing. Co-pilot Liddell executed a sharp dive through a tersely worded statement – hitting severe turbulence: the jeers of the Tory Party mocking her conversion to privatisation. An eerie silence from her own benches heightened tension.

Then Labour's Flight ATC99 (from Port Marx to Thatcher International, with stop-off at Third Way) hit the ground – or, rather, Bernard Jenkin, Tory spokesman. Mr Jenkin proved a hard landing patch, and Liddell's nosewheel got a good biffing. But she could have expected that.

What was unexpected was the rock on the runway. Controller Boothroyd directed Liddell straight into Gwyneth Dunwoody (Lab, Crewe & Nantwich), whom the Speaker called as first questioner. Mrs Dunwoody gave Liddell a terrific biffing, for 'offering up' air traffic control 'to the profit motive'.

The next pothole (Lib Dem spokesman Tom Brake) was predictable, though his gibe about 'NATS fat cats' was unkind. But as Liddell was recovering, Betty directed her into a question from Gavin Strang. The former Transport Minister, equally hostile, proved a cruel oily patch.

Thus it continued. Loyalist Sandra Osborne (Lab, Ayr) biffed Liddell too.

Then came the burst tyre: the Speaker called Tony Benn, with devastating impact. Benn said Labour's promise to the rich was 'the only pledge that has been kept'. John McDonnell (Lab, Hayes & Harlington) smashed into Liddell's turbines like an errant goose.

Laura Moffatt (Lab, Crawley) and Martin Salter (Lab, Reading W), two big cracks in the asphalt, rocked her. And, to cap it all, Eric Forth (C, Bromley & Chislehurst) fouled her windscreen by reminding the House that Liddell was once Robert Maxwell's stewardess.

Finally Betty took mercy and directed the minister into the docking bay. She had survived. Her project had landed, danger passed.

Members of Parliament themselves now take off for sunnier climes. And happy holidays to them all.

Blair Flops – As Planned

15.9.99

At the Trades Union Congress Conference.

Tony Blair's speech to the TUC yesterday succeeded magnificently. It bombed, just as he wanted. A rip-roaring ovation from the comrades would have alarmed the nation mightily. A poem Tony Blair had penned (a warm-up, he said, for the Poet Laureate who was to versify later) put Congress on notice of what was expected.

The poem owed much in both metre and profundity to those *Daily Express* rhyming doggerel instalments of the adventures of Rupert Bear. One begins to understand the boyhood influences on the Prime Minister's development as a communicator.

In fact, there was no 'row'. The TUC mood was cynical rather than angry as in previous years. In an auditorium with some empty seats and some hearers preferring to read magazines, Blair was heard coolly by an underwhelmed audience, none of whom was so hostile as to boo, but two thirds of whom could not quite get themselves to their feet at the end.

Uneasy, his hands knotting and his jaw working, Blair wore a tactfully jay-blue striped tie and a dark suit of funeral hue: come to bury the brethren, not to praise them. Thoughtful conference organisers had arranged, as a curtain-raiser for their Prime Minister, a short debate on bullying, followed by another on air rage.

On bullying, a woman delegate spoke movingly of the workplace whispers and silences that can oppress an ostracised colleague. She quoted a worker who had cracked: 'I can't cope, I can't cope. My brain just collapsed under the strain.' She described the cruel gibes he endured, behind his back, from bosses: 'floundering', 'not up to the job'. Nobody was unkind enough to mention John Prescott.

On air rage, an unlucky delegate from the British Air Line Pilots' Association, meaning to attack reductions in legroom, declared: 'The thought of six inches being cut off in front of me brings tears to my eyes!' The ensuing laughter seemed to confuse him.

Blair got few laughs. 'It's a real pleasure to be here,' he lied, then ploughed dutifully through a text memorable only for one baffling line. 'An end to Chekhov!' he suddenly cried. Chekhov? Check-off? What could he mean? 'And a beginning to Kafka,' whispered the man next to me.

That day's *Times* had reported a study by a York don, Peter Bull, on the way politicians use applause. Apparently, audiences clap as expected only 61 per cent of occasions. Dr Bull should study this speech. Almost every time his text had been crafted to elicit applause, he met silence. Blair was interrupted by clapping only four times: the first for seven seconds, the second for eight. Both rewarded attacks on the Conservative Party. Blair got the message. Now circling the runway, undercarriage down but in distress as to how to land this oration, he departed from his text and launched into an unscripted, formless and rambling attack on the Tories. Applause: 11 seconds; 12 seconds.

A dawning understanding then guided the Prime Minister into the oddest peroration we have ever heard from him. Blair's final words (I took them down in disbelief) were: 'Despite all the changes and all the interesting people who address the TUC, I think you'd prefer to have us than the others.'

And that was it. The End. So that is what he means! A remark more revealing than Mr Blair can possibly have intended.

21.9.99   # New Lib Dem Leader Awakes

The last party conferences of the millennium begin.

Charles Kennedy stared around him. It was Monday and he doesn't like Mondays. It was 9am and Mr Kennedy is not a morning person. It was Harrogate, and he is not a bath-buns and lace-doilies posh Yorkshire person. And it was raining.

But in one respect the surroundings comforted him. He was at a table, with microphones, in the company of people who seemed to be celebrities. There were spot-lights. And down there on the floor, applauding hesitantly, was what looked like an invited audience – albeit rather ragged.

Kennedy blinked, puffy-eyed. Then smiled. This must be a quiz show! Was it his team's round? He waited for the question. No gags came to mind. Where were the clowns? There ought to be clowns.

His hand reached for the buzzer. No buzzer. No questions. Puzzling. Then the Mayor of Harrogate stood up. And welcomed everyone. Stranger still. And began to patronise him. The local MP, Phil Willis, rose next. Both praised the Liberal Democrats. Nobody mocked. So not

Have I Got News For You? The audience seemed to like the party. Curious.

Then it dawned. He was leader of the Liberal Democrats. And this was their party conference. He was not required to caper, just to be there. People wanted to see and touch. From the front row Simon Hughes glared supportively, eyes narrowed to slits. Wake up Charlie! Quick. Better look interested. We can all remember our first day at school but this was scarier: Kennedy's first day out as Liberal Democrat leader.

He had promised to look in at the Britain In Europe Campaign's fringe meeting. We got there before him.

So had the Baroness Williams of Crosby. Shirley Williams is the cherry on the sundae of any gathering of the Nice and the Good. Beside her sat Lord Jenkins of Hillhead – she the only Shirl in the world and he the only Woy.

Above fluttered the Lib-Dem logo, the party's bird of liberty less like a cannabis spliff than previously, having been fattened up, like their new leader . . . who now entered, after hovering at the back for a sly fag until the cameras were ready.

He spoke well, impromptu, attacking the 'hobgoblin figures' of the Eurosceptical Tory Right, and offering a brave and unhedged commitment to the single currency.

The voice was firm and the words powerful; but the body language, the face, trouble us. Mr Kennedy looks like a duvet. You want to know whether feather or not. If you poked his cheek would the imprint remain? Tell us your tog rating, Charlie.

And maybe he would. Maybe he would see the joke if you asked. For Mr Kennedy seems to be wittily deconstructing his position almost as he takes it up. At a Campaign for Racial Equality meeting he waited awkwardly to pose with pen in hand, explaining: 'You can never do anything as leader until the photographers tell you to.' Is this to be the first Post-Modern party leadership?

I wonder. 'Something's boring me, and I think it's me,' Dylan Thomas once said. To earn his own respect and keep himself awake, Mr Kennedy keeps veering towards honesty. Black people, he told us, should be trying for jobs as MPs, MSPs . . . anything important – 'or if all else fails they can always stand for a council'.

And this to Liberal Democrats, hordes of them councillors. Steady on, Charlie.

Paddy Bows Out

He could have delivered it better if he had not meant it so much. Yesterday in Harrogate, Paddy Ashdown halted his way through a farewell speech to the party he had led for 11 years. It was a goodbye that neither he nor they were sure they wanted.

In a spikily serious speech, sparse humour was seized upon with relief. 'I bet you wouldn't have clapped like that,' he said to laughter, 'if I was staying.'

Repeatedly he was met by a murmur of sympathy so universal yet so slight that, like the faintest breeze, it touched only those who were there, and left no mark. Broadcast transmissions will have missed it, tape will not record it and TV commentators in their glass cells could not hear it.

The rapid blinking I noticed all around me fell short of the sobs which television needs to make its point, and nobody stamped. Some will judge the occasion as light on theatricality as it was short on length: just 20 minutes.

But it was long on sincerity. 'The easy thing,' said Ashdown, speaking quietly and without the rehearsed emphasis which has distorted his set-piece orations, 'would have been one of those sort of end-of-jumble-sale speeches, where you say thank you to everyone and what a success it all was.' Instead, he launched for his swansong into prophecy. Mr Ashdown had not one, but two big new ideas.

'Mutualism!' he cried. The heart sank. Oh dear, Paddy's read another book. Delegates looked resigned. They had come to say goodbye – and now mutualism. But they're used to this sort of thing from him. He might just as well have declared 'frottage!' – and everyone would have nodded, 'yes, of course, Paddy love, frottage. The politics of the new millennium. Most interesting. Now who's going to draw the raffle?'

Boyish in his enthusiasm for ideas, Paddy has led them through all this before. Paddy the nuclear disarmer, Paddy the warrior; Paddy the free-marketeer; Paddy the non-aligned anti-imperialist; Paddy the pacifier of Kosovo . . .

Yesterday it was Paddy the mutualist; and Paddy the global e-Czar. His foray into globalisation and the Internet hardly rose above the sort of thing one hears on a bus; and it cannot be said that he took 'mutualism' much beyond a fuzzy-sounding call for Christian co-operation.

As for his 'hey presto!' solution to that age-old liberal dilemma – the choice between socialist equality of outcome and a free-market equality of opportunity – Paddy's 'equality of access' sounded more like the cry of a frustrated software programmer than a brainwave which had somehow eluded Rousseau.

Easy to mock. And yet I thought: how admirable to be going out, the oldest by far of our party leaders, not in disgrace, not shafted by his own side or trounced by the electorate, not shaking hands and shuffling head-down into retirement, but still searching, still trying to tug his party forward. It was brave to choose Wilberforce's self-obituary: 'We did not march as a marshalled army towards a distant obelisk. We travelled the highways and byways gathering friends and flowers as we went'; and brave to end with the Irish blessing: 'And until we meet again, may God hold you in the hollow of His hand.'

Mr Ashdown, whose voice was close to breaking, seemed almost embarrassed and apologetic to recite these words. He need not have been.

Wetsuits, Coffins, Tony and Roses

27.9.99

A lone windsurfer, dripping, tousled and wet-suited, wandered through the crowd outside Labour's conference at Bournemouth yesterday, utterly bewildered. Before his eyes a range of papier-maché cows danced. Among them, red devils with horns and pitchforks cavorted and prodded. This was or seems to have been an anti-GM protest. 'Something scary in the dairy,' proclaimed the banner on the float in its midst.

Beneath a pantomime cow with rubber udders made from washing up gloves, a protester squatted. The cow glared at the crowd. Her carriage was drawn by a black car adorned with huge white amoebas. A young man by the waterfront, some yards away from this, was being spun until giddy on a fairground machine consisting of a wheel within a wheel, all spinning against each other, just like the Labour Party.

It was bizarre. The squeals of children from the beach mingled with screams of rage from the anti-GM demonstrators. And, in the middle of this Hitchcockian nightmare an old man with white hair was being shepherded to a megaphone by a young man in a blue Lurex blazer. The elderly gent was Tony Benn. 'We are not anti-science,' he cried, 'but big multinational corporations like Monsanto . . .'

'Boo!' screamed the crowd at the very name.

I left these grotesqueries, the young windsurfer still lost among them, and wandered into the conference centre. On the platform a delegate was in mid-flow. 'We must think from the bottom up!' he cried.

The stage-set was extraordinary. It looked like a podium for a rally to celebrate the achievements of Kim Il Sung. The backdrop appeared as an abstract representation of the surface of Planet Earth, cold, purple-grey, over which a new Labour star (or was it a sun?) rose in a dawn sky, fading from red through pink to violet.

The session ended and a spokesman asked us to be patient while the stage was prepared for the Leader. We held our breaths. The star went out. Obviously about to be eclipsed by a bigger star.

Up a shallow ramp three uniformed stewards wheeled a long red box.

What was this? Was it John Prescott's coffin? Was it the Leader's desk? Was it the fabled war chest? Another steward began to nail it down to the floor, lending weight to the war chest theory. A stewardess entered carrying a bunch of red roses which she placed on the box, inclining us back to the Prescott coffin theory.

The star reappeared. 'Colleagues, please may I ask you to welcome . . . Mo Mowlam and Tony Blair!' a functionary cried.

Thin applause. Tony Blair, almost in black, and Mo Mowlam, in a pale blue jacket and ski pants with a badge hanging round her neck, marched up the ramp. They looked like a bus driver and his conductress. But where was the bus?

Mo welcomed us 'to the new Labour family'.

'We are celebrating on a number of different levels,' she said. Mr Blair's lip tightened. He was celebrating on only one level. Top level.

'It's a great pleasure to be here,' he said, fiddling desperately with some wires coming out of his trousers.

The questions came thick and fast. They were not rigged. Blair no longer requires this. He avoids questions so skilfully that their content is immaterial.

To all questions, he replied using a mix-and match combination of four basic answers: 1, Attack the Tories; 2, We can't afford it; 3, It will take time; 4, Let the debate go on!

It did, but little light was shed, except from the star.

Smiling for the Cameras

28.9.99

Gordon Brown soared yesterday. There were moments during the Chancellor's address when his speech really took off. Gone were the pouting, thumping, earth-bound rumbles of former years as Mr Brown found rhythm and passion in words, and the conference cheered.

Old Mr Leadenchops even seemed to be enjoying it: he sort-of-smiled – *twice* – and went as far as to wave.

But first there was Baroness Jay, on women. Margaret Jay on women's issues was to be followed by Gordon Brown on the economy – a word with Mummy about the curtains, before Daddy arrives for a serious chat about the adding up. One pictured Gordon and Margaret: Mr and Mrs Labour and their three children – Prudence, Prudence and Prudence. There's flash Uncle Tony, too – Tony New-Labour – the younger brother who has hyphenated the family name, stolen the inheritance and usurped the house, letting an upstairs flat to Gordon.

But Gordon stays on good terms in hopes of getting the inheritance back. A bad influence has been Tony's friend, wicked Uncle Peter (now banished), of whom we do not speak. Uncle Robin's usually abroad: his embarrassing past is never mentioned in front of the children. Finally there's Mrs Mo, the help: an absolute poppet but terribly disorganised. She keeps losing the dog, Prescott, and forgetting to feed Beckett the cat.

But yesterday was Gordon's day. There had been unpleasant rumours of a rift between Gordon and Tony. Tony knows how popular Gordon is in the street and was anxious to dispel them. So the Prime Minister took his seat early, during the 'women' debate. In walked the Chancellor. The delighted surprise on Tony's face warmed the cockles of our hearts. Grinning from ear to ear, he smiled rapturously at Gordon. Gordon gave a shy grin back. A few press cameras flashed, but amity was not the story the press wanted. Tony leaned over for a friendly word. Gordon nodded and pointed. A few more cameras flashed.

Then, for just a second, Tony looked away. A blinding burst of camera-flashes lit the hall as photographers seized the moment they had orders to capture. 'Damn,' thought Tony, regretting his inattention and resuming his fixed grin. He stared at Gordon, face-muscles frozen in adoration. Near by, but in another world, John Prescott scratched his head, apparently reading something. Possibly he was doing a magazine quiz.

And while all this was going on, a nervous lady delegate was making a speech about women. Blair, who had listened to not a word, applauded warmly. Then, as Brown took the lectern, the Prime Minister clapped with the violence of a man intent on exterminating every one of a passing swarm of gnats.

During Brown's speech, Blair's tender gaze never wavered. Not that his own name came up much. Brown's written text included three mentions of 'Tony Blair' but (doubtless by accident) two were buried by applause for himself. Has the Chancellor read recent reports of a York University study of a politicians' use of applause? This noted how effective it is when a speaker interrupts his own applause by striving to continue his speech *against* it: a demagogue all but overwhelmed by adoration.

It worked well and often for Brown yesterday. Sadly, it drowned the name of Blair. Still, he patted Gordon's shoulder during the wild ovation which followed, as the two rushed at each other in apparent terror lest one be applauded alone. Awkwardly attempting to reciprocate, Gordon patted Tony's thigh.

Pure Billy Graham

29.9.99

Blair struts his stuff in Bournemouth.

You've got to hand it to him. To speak for an hour – 38 pages – as though about to be burned at the stake was some kind of theatrical achievement, whatever its political merits.

The trembling lip, the defiant cry, the confessional appeal, never flagged.

'I tell you: it is the nation's only hope of salvation!' Tony Blair announced at one point. Uh-oh, I thought, it'll be 'And I say unto you' before we're through.

'And I say to you,' he cried, 'I believe in civil liberties, too!' Here we go, I thought, we'll have 'man cannot live by bread alone' next.

'You know,' he declared, 'we don't live by material goods alone.'

This was pure Billy Graham, and you either like it or you don't.

Labour's Bournemouth conference applauded, of course. If this speech did not quite kindle in the hearts of his party the personal warmth that still eludes him, then at least Blair brought more delegates with him this time than he ever has before.

An Oprah Winfrey-style appeal will reach an element in any audience and the Prime Minister's call (which was apparently impromptu, but in fact was scripted) for sympathy for his long nights and the agonies of decision-taking did touch many of his hearers. It certainly seemed to touch him.

And if the aim was to inspire, Mr Blair got some of them going for some of the time. The applause was more than dutiful, less than wild.

Time and again I was struck by how American this all was. Folksy, direct, unreserved in its tug at the heartstrings, unsqueamish in its call upon the repertoire of horror, love and pity – hungry schoolchildren, frightened mums dropping off their schoolchildren into the arms of drug-dealers, pregnant 12-year-olds. He might as well have begun: 'My fellow Americans.'

There was something squelchy, something of the quack, something of the Southern drawl at the heart of it all.

This was compassion for the middle classes, belief as a lifestyle enhancement.

He talked Keir Hardie, but this was Chris de Burgh. He talked *Fidelio* but this was *Les Misérables*. He talked Engels but this was *The Little Book of Calm*. He talked – his phrase – 'eternal values', but this was Feng-Shui.

'My friends! The class war is over!' he announced. Yes, I thought, and the middle class won. You're living proof of that.

The tension between policy famine and rhetorical feast tugged hard at the seams of this address, but nothing quite ripped.

We must master our future, he told the nation. 'The challenge is, how? The answer is people. The future is people.'

Wisely, this passage was well separated from the policy section where it emerged that if the challenge was 'how?' the answer was more dentists.

'To every nation, a purpose! To every party, a cause!' bawled the Prime Minister.

Those who were doubtful whether Mr Blair had mentioned one should recall his promise of smartcards for 16 to 18-year-old students, offering 'cut-price deals'.

'And now, at last, on the eve of the 21st century,' the Prime Minister concluded, 'party and nation joined in the same cause for the same purpose. To set our people free.'

MPs checked their pagers. The hall erupted as planned. John Prescott, who had been glued to his text, checking that Tony didn't stray, was joined on the platform by his wife Pauline, who held hands with Cherie, who held hands with Tony. John Prescott declined to hold hands with anyone, bless him.

You Wouldn't Treat a Dog Like This

30.9.99

Poodles have jumped through hoops since poodles were poodles, and every circus-goer has seen a Pomeranian dog do tricks, but to witness the world's only dancing boxer-dog you have to come to Bournemouth. Here at the Labour conference yesterday John Prescott capered across the podium while his trainer, Tony Blair, watched approvingly.

Some animal-lovers consider such spectacles cruel. This sketch admits to finding something sad in Mr Prescott's fate. But he looks contented and well fed. If what they have done to him is degrading, then it is degradation of the subtlest kind. He has a chauffeur-driven limousine back to his kennel every night. And as for the tail – well, he's probably forgotten he ever had one.

Though not beautiful, and possessed of a ferocious bark and fearfully crumpled face, the crosser he looks the more you want to pet him.

Shout 'Walkies, Prescott!' and pretend to pick up the leash, and he'll scamper to the door even though you've played the trick a hundred times. Master Tony loves doing this, to amuse us.

The Prime Minister grinned from the platform yesterday, giving the long leash a little tug. Cutely, Prescott responded. 'A new style of living – which puts people first – in the concept of the Millennium Village!' he yapped.

Another tug: this was more serious. Prescott, who has been a passionate supporter of nationalised railways, was to show us his new trick, the semi-privatisation of the London Underground. This meant standing on his head, which is extremely hard for a boxer.

Nose down, he tried to waggle his hind legs in the air. 'We are mortgaging the Tube's assets just like you do with a house,' he barked, perilously close to losing his balance in mid-waggle, so dubious was the logic. Master Brown, who must have taught him this one, seems to have been mis-selling financial products to the poor dog.

Somehow Prescott got through the routine. It was not well done (as Dr Johnson once remarked of performing dogs) but it was a wonder it was done at all. Labour delegates, boxer-lovers all, feel for this creature and his fate, and were kind in their applause.

Now came the beast's most astonishing stunt. The flaming hoop.

Prescott would actually jump right through the privatisation of air traffic control. He looked nervous; his droopy boxer eyes watered. He could hear the roll of kettledrums, sniff the smoke. There it was, that hated hoop. From Tony's leash came a sharp tug.

And he jumped. 'It needs over a billion pounds to keep up with growing air movements!' he woofed – and described the sell-off plans. He landed safely. But wasn't that the faintest smell of singed fur?

Scared of getting this bit wrong, he read out each word just as he found it on the page. 'The airlines are satisfied with that. The raff is satisfied with that.' Did he mean RAF – or did he mean *rrruff*.

Master Tony was satisfied anyway. Every trick performed without mishap! There would be a juicy bone in the fireside basket in Tony Blair's elegant study at Number 10.

Or will there? As the performance ended, Prescott showed one tiny flash of disobedience. He cited his own political creed. 'We have a name for it,' he said, 'it's in our constitution . . .' Master Tony looked up sharply; but too late for the cruel yank on the leash. 'We call it "democratic socialism".'

Wild applause. Tony's lip curled. Something nasty on the carpet.

Embattled Tories Reach Blackpool

5.10.99

Blackpool. Monday. Fish-and-chip papers scud along the promenade. In the wintry sunshine pensioners gather, braced against an October wind, peering bleakly into the dirty grey of a restless Irish Sea.

And that's just the Conservative Party. Here in Blackpool stands a once-proud structure broken by storms, part still intact, part submerged, a semi-detached remnant just poking its head above the water. And that's just the North Pier.

It would be wrong to describe the mood as dejected. The mood is defiant. But it is the defiance of the persecuted. No longer the politics of power, this is victim-politics; a gathering for mutual comfort of the outraged and the misunderstood.

On to the Winter Gardens stage, officials heaved two big, shallow, blue coffin-like things with lids. The new seating arrangements for Ted and Margaret? Then another box. John Major's? Would grey fingers appear along the rims, lids be thrown open and three former prime ministers lunge at the platform party screaming 'Wee Willie!' and 'read my memoirs' – wrecking, yet again, William Hague's plans for a fresh start?

But no. We sang the National Anthem and none of the lids moved. There's no way Maggie would have heard that lying down.

One journalist failed to rise, though. Seated at the press table while the hall stood to attention, he felt a sudden blow. An elderly walrus-moustached Tory representative had taken a swing at him with his briefcase. I watched from the gallery as the two men fell into vigorous altercation, those around them still singing.

In its quaint old-fashioned way the Conservative Party still separates religion from politics, leaving churchmen rather than the party leader to introduce Almighty God into the proceedings. The Rev. Michael Fielding read St Paul's letter to the Corinthians better than I have ever heard it read. Huddled before him, Tory representatives knew how the Corinthians felt: a small, lonely church, encircled by the empire of their enemies.

Above the heads of speakers and the Tory top brass float a series of huge blue bubbles – like those *thinks* bubbles in comic strips. One bubble says 'The Conservative Party' and another says 'The Common Sense Revolution' but all the rest are empty. This may be a subliminal invitation to Tory representatives to try to think of some policies to put in the bubbles. Old dears will be dragged up on to the stage, given giant crayons and exhorted to write their ideas into the spaces. *Hang the Kaiser!* or *No more rationing!*

Perhaps this will come later. To start us off, the conference heard the party chairman, Michael Ancram, and Sir George Young discussing devolution. Afternoon of the Decent Coves: both figures are immensely significant on account of their being sane, and still in the Conservative

Party. Like those pit-canaries they used to take down mines to warn of methane by keeling over at the first whiff of poisonous gas, the continuing presence of such men, still conscious, assures the nation of the habitability of the party by human beings.

Mr Ancram harangued the Winter Gardens for some time, mostly on the subject of Tony Blair, in a rather plaintive voice.

Solemnity, however, was undermined by the lectern. This creation, sawn from hardboard and painted blue, perches its deskette on an abstract, freeform structure with odd angles, holes reminiscent of Gruyere cheese, little feet, and two mikes waving from the top like ears. It resembles a Henry Moore rabbit on a bad day, holding a tray.

Have-a-go Ann   *6.10.99*

Few here at Blackpool are bothering with the mega-roller-coaster they call the Pepsi-Max Big One, for the conference yesterday rode the Tory Big One. 'It's Ann Widdecombe on law and order this morning,' I said to a bright-eyed Tory at breakfast.

'I know,' he whispered. 'I'm excited!'

So was she. All through the preceding debate on education, addressed by sensible Theresa May, you could feel the old timbers of the Winter Gardens shake as, somewhere, Miss Widdecombe pounded the floor in her aerobic limber-up routine. Once, Mrs May's speech was interrupted by a mysterious crash. Ann Widdecombe was spitting out a rivet.

Even as Mrs May sat down, the electric cathodes were being clipped to Miss Widdecombe's terminals and massive currents were arcing across.

From the conference loudspeakers came thumping jungle music redolent of the tom-toms. On the conference floor 800 pacemakers raced. And she strode in, wearing an oversize tartan car-rug. The Shadow Home Secretary has revamped her hair in the style of an ink-black crash-helmet: shock-resistent, brutal.

Called to the podium, she gave it a shove, then marched straight past, standing at the front. Two strong men in black T-shirts rushed in.

'They've come to take her away,' whispered my horrified friend – but no, the men unscrewed the podium from the floor and carried that off instead. Had they been given a description of Widdecombe, and misunderstood? By now she was pacing the platform like a caged lion. There was a terrible danger she would fall off. The shape of Miss Widdecombe is inherently unstable – all overhanging balconies, dress-circles and abutting bulges, swaying about and perched on tiny legs – but somehow she stopped herself crashing over the side.

Her speech was magnificent. Some astonishingly liberal ideas were belted out with such belligerent swagger that Tory backwoodsmen – thrilling to her threat to knock a bit of education into prisoners' heads – found themselves applauding an enlightened programme of rehabilitation.

And, as her blood rose, she began to yodel. Her voice kept squeaking up an octave as though she had a private supply of helium tucked somewhere in that vast bosom. She reached, in these yodels, frequencies inaudible to humans. Bats in the rafters began flying into things. After two fearsome squeaks ('a *mi*-no-*rity* of *pol*-ice time') there was a sudden outbreak of mobile phones ringing from the floor – their circuitry haywire.

'I've been inside 135 prisons!' she shrieked, as elderly gentlemen in the audience trembled excitedly. Miss Widdecombe began a strange, mid-air, hand-pulling gesture, halfway between ringing a cathedral bell and milking a cosmic cow. 'There must be a right to self-defence!' yelled have-a-go Widders – Annie get your gun – pawing the ground and without a single note, her delivered speech on no more than nodding terms with the printed text.

Widdecombe's peroration was awesome, and quite sudden. Then she lunged off the rostrum, somehow surviving the step, and threw herself at William Hague. They embraced. She got her arm right round him. He tried manfully to reciprocate, but ran out of arm. To wild applause she took three curtain calls, raising both hands heavenward as the car-rug lifted alarmingly around the midriffs, then tugging it firmly back down again just as we feared all was lost. Tories staggered from the hall towards an afternoon which would pass in a daze, murmuring, one to another, 'how was it for you?'

They Clap Therefore He Is
7.10.99

First among equals? Equals? Those nerds and weirdos they call the Tory party – equals? Pah! Mayor of London might be the next stop but he was headed further. Much further. Headed all the way.

And it could have been a novel. Maybe it was a novel. One of his own novels.

Every month, the odds getting shorter. Every speech, the sentences getting shorter. Much shorter. Much.

There they were, stretched at his feet, the whole damn Tory party, spread out in the Winter Gardens, gawping. Didn't know what to make of him. Never had.

And there they were behind him. Jeffrey swung round and faced the screens. All the Tory top brass. William Hague, cursed among equals, gulping, bald. Michael Ancram – useful tool, damned useful – sweating. Scared of what he might say. But too scared to stop him.

Jellyfish. He'd have them too.

And there she was in front of him. The lady. His heart missed a beat. She had come.

And she was smiling, enraptured: a luminous shaft of royal blue among the grey suits, grey faces, grey hair of the crowd. Blue as stained glass, blue as a hot summer sky, shimmering from the front row.

Margaret had blessed him. How could he fail?

And there was Mary, beside her. Mary, his lifelong love. Mary who had supported him through thick and thin – supported him even when he'd been stupid. Damned stupid. But he would repay her. He'd take her right up there with him. To the top. But first, London. He had made it to candidature; now the ballot box.

And for this he needed them – their cheers, their unbounded energy, their midnight oil and shoe-leather, tramping the streets, manning the offices, stuffing the envelopes. And they had been doubtful about him, Jeffrey was no fool, he knew that. They were applauding as he strode, coolly triumphant, to the rostrum, but there was hesitation in that applause. Campaigner that he was, he sensed it at once. He had to win these people over right now.

He had worked at the speech. It was a mixture of all the bits that had played best before. He began by introducing his staff – a long list of nobodies, but Jeffrey had always been good with names. He knew this party, knew they liked leaders who knife colleagues but are endlessly considerate to their chauffeurs.

Jeffrey's strategy was clear. It never failed. You could express it in three words. Confidence, confidence and confidence. Talk like you're already mayor. Bark out your plans. Believe in yourself and they'll believe in you. This was his first secret.

'On May 5 next year, on the door of the head office of London Underground, there will be a sign saying Under New Management.'

They cheered. Jeffrey belted it out with gusto but his eyes returned repeatedly, urgently, to his text. He was reading word for word. For this was Jeffrey's second secret: his style might be generous, spirited, free, but underneath he was working hard, very hard. He was a plodder. He was proud of that.

And the speech did win them over. He got his applause at last, in spadefuls. He needed it.

For this was Jeffrey's third secret. A novel isn't a novel without a hero, but a hero isn't a hero without a crowd. He was unreal without them. They clapped wildly as he left the stage.

'They clap,' thought Jeffrey, 'therefore I am.'

Blair Tells His First E-fib

26.10.99

Yesterday Tony Blair opened his new Internet chatline. As a critic once remarked, I have seen more excitement at the opening of an umbrella.

It is lucky the Internet was invented after the wireless. Had it been the other way round, anoraks would be gasping at the wonderful new advance which enables us to hear Mr Blair for ourselves at the flick of a switch.

www.bun.com was the handle we were urged to grab. The technology went pear-shaped almost immediately as frustrated Commons journalists struggled to access the website, the screen offering jolly interim thoughts, like 'End Your Debts Now!' Only the *Guardian*'s man made early progress – your sketchwriter skulking near by.

Finally, Blair's smirking chops appeared in a little blue frame, with 'WOW!' superimposed. 'Historic live chat! Simply click on the Tony Blair icon.'

Icon? So early in our Leader's career? The operator clicked. 'The chat is having a brief interruption,' read the screen. 'I'm attempting to reconnect you.' The interview was heralded by a new caption: 'www.bun.com – where it's safe to surf.'

Blair did not so much surf as paddle. Questions had been submitted over the previous week, and, wonder of wonders, they did not seem to include anything rude. We scanned the text for inquiries like 'Isn't it true you hate computers and are just stunting this up for cheap publicity, you grinning imbecile?' but only respectful surfers seemed to get through. The editor reserved the right to omit questions for reasons of space.

Some got through. 'My mother has always been a Labour supporter and her dearest wish has been to meet you someday. Is there any chance you could grant her wish?' asked the improbably named Julie Robertson-Smythe – obviously Peter Mandelson. 'I'm sure we can get her in,' said Blair.

And I do mean 'said'. According to the Prime Minister's press spokesman, Blair had a 'facilitator' at the keyboard. This means 'typist'.

The banality of the questions touched new lows, until you saw the answers. 'Leanne' wanted to know if Mr Blair agreed it was unfair that, for Millennium Eve 'places are charging such a lot'. Blair did agree. 'Ripping the customer off,' he thought. 'They shouldn't.' Sheila Chambers wondered 'if you and Cherie are concerned about what your children can read on the Internet?' Yes, Cherie and Tony were concerned.

So was I. Children should be kept away from this stuff. Five hours of lesbians wrestling in Marmite live on europorn.co.dk would be less likely to deprave young Euan and Nicky's sensibilities than the trite, degrading pap their Dad was spouting on www.bun.com.

At 2.47 Mr Blair told his first Internet lie. Asked about that 'forces of conservatism' outburst, he replied: 'I never meant to insult anyone working in the public services.' Sadly, sharp intakes of breath among Web-surfers do not register on the screen. 'At the moment the Government's view is that it's safe to eat food,' he told another astonished surfer. 'I'm a fairly bouncy sort of a character,' Blair advised someone who wondered what depressed him: 'one of life's optimists.'

'What I'd say, Jack,' (life's bouncy optimist told a depressed pensioner) was that 'concessionary bus fares will be rolled out over the country in time'.

Then came the shock. Just when we thought the Internet was safe for prime ministers, someone asked Blair's opinion on the future of the monarchy. He did not seem to have one. 'It's a decision people have got to make.' *Blair Announces Royal Referendum: Internet Shock!*

Lord-a-leaping

27.10.99

An errant earl makes a final protest as the old Lords sinks.

To the horror of a packed House of Lords yesterday afternoon, a bearded aristocrat resembling an Old Testament prophet leapt on to the Woolsack in their gilded chamber and began to shout. Peers had not been so startled since demonstrating lesbians abseiled from the public gallery in 1988. In the dying days of the old House, the ill-starred hereditaries were distracted from the contemplation of their own demise.

The shock occurred shortly after lunch. Hereditary peers had crowded in to hear the final set-piece debate on the Bill which eliminates them. They had endured a stunningly tedious half-hour of questions. Baroness Blackstone, an educationist who has never been known to say anything interesting, had lulled everyone into torpor.

The spectacularly polite Lord Boston of Faversham, who has never been known to say anything rude, adjusted his specs and settled on to the Woolsack to moderate the great debate. Peers' eldest sons sprawled and lolled around the throne, as is their right. Peers crowded at the Bar.

And through the crowd slipped a hairy man in his early thirties: the man we now know to be the Earl of Burford, heir to the 14th Duke of St Albans. He mounted the scarlet Woolsack, an operation not unlike jumping on to the lounge sofa. Poor Lord Boston was already on it, and quivered as the wool shook. The intruder started yelling.

The House was stupefied. Distinguished Strangers were stupefied. Tourists were stupefied. The press were stupefied. The Lords attendants were stupefied. Nobody knew what to do so nobody did anything.

'This Bill,' the Beard shouted, 'drafted in Brussels, is treason!' This sounded just like a *Daily Telegraph* leading article. Could it be the Editor?

'What we are witnessing is the abolition of Britain!' he yelled, beard a-tremble. 'Before us lies the wasteland.'

Around him lay a sea of dropped jaws. Lord Boston, sitting next to his feet, tried to pretend nothing was happening and gazed fixedly at his notes as might a commuter from Godalming in a first-class railway compartment when other passengers had begun an act of oral sex.

'No Queen! No culture! No sovereignty! No freedom!' By now, two gartered attendants, shaken from their stupefaction, were making half-hearted attempts to haul the noble bird from his perch.

'Stand up for Queen and country,' he squawked, 'and vote this Bill down!'

The Earl's speech was over. He was ready to go quietly. The hand of an attendant, outstretched to pull him down, was now taken willingly and the fellow was landed courteously from the Woolsack as a lady might be helped down from her carriage.

Black Rod escorted him out. Lord Boston jumped, startled, to life, as if suddenly released from a hypnotist's trance, and began the debate.

Your sketchwriter stayed for the debate. Outside, the Earl was ranting about wastelands, wolves and perdition.

He is descended, I learn, from the 1st Duke of St Albans, whose mother, Nell Gwyn, had threatened his father, Charles II, with throwing her baby from the window as she had no means to raise the boy.

'Throw down the Duke[dom] of St Albans,' replied the King.

Yesterday his descendant threw down the gauntlet. Somehow more fitting than throwing in the towel.

Listen With Patricia   *5.11.99*

What is it about Patricia Hewitt that makes you want to scream? The ever-courteous, well-groomed, well-spoken Kinnockite retread purrs on effortlessly up through the lower ranks of ministers, now translated from the Treasury to the Department of Trade and Industry. She never puts a foot wrong, never concedes the tiniest fault in government, and never says anything remotely informative.

She reverses the usual presumption – that if ministers must read, they at least try to speak as though unscripted – and speaks as though from a script even when she has none. As befits the new 'e-minister', Ms Hewitt reads from a virtual text implanted in her head. Older MPs in her audience are taken back to *Listen With Mother* on the wireless.

She was at it yesterday morning, on the bench for Industry Questions.

Rather bravely, Tony McWalter (Lab, Hemel Hempstead) put it to Ms Hewitt that there might really be a problem with a proposed new tax measure known as IR35, about which the Tories were making a dreadful fuss. McWalter thought it could drive abroad entrepreneurs in information technology.

He might as well have been addressing the wall. Hewitt's reply, though gracious, put me in mind of an aunt who used to interrupt one's flow by raising a well-manicured hand: 'Talk to the hand,' she would coo, 'the ears aren't listening.'

Denis MacShane (Lab, Rotherham), the sort of boy my aunt would have called a clever-sticks, curried a little favour with the e-minister by wondering whether it went too far to call the new, wired front bench 'an e-rogenous zone'. He had also, apparently, been tapping out her praises on the BBC On-Line. Hewitt thanked him prettily. Poor Denis: I doubt whether these jokey little extravagances impress such women. But then what would?

You cannot remember a word she has said, within seconds of her saying it. I think Hewitt messages are transmitted with an invisible accompanying virus which immediately wipes them from your memory disk. Later she hurried away, no doubt to record one of those 'the-number-you-called-is-busy-to-use-ring-back-please-press 5' messages for Telecom. 'I-am-sorry-but-the-number-you-called-is-not-available . . .' To listen to Patricia Hewitt is to hear the 'unobtainable' tone. Sorry. Please try later.

Sheffield Central's Richard Caborn, another minister, is refreshingly unwired: more e-by-gum than e-minister, but even he seems tugged towards the sort of stale business-speak increasingly beloved of ministers.

Brandishing a publication which he claimed made his point, he told MPs that it was dated '3 November 1999'. 'That's yesterday, duckie,' giggled some blessed, insolent soul.

One Day Son, This Won't Be Yours

12.11.99

The end of the Lords.

Not since the gallows were dismantled at Tyburn has London witnessed quite so public an execution. Dukes and earls were jostled into the Lords chamber to sign their own death warrants. This was their last afternoon. At the Bar of the House, MPs from the chamber which has sealed their fate watched, fascinated, like *tricoteuses* at the guillotine.

The Baroness Thatcher came in black. Miladies Buscombe, Rawlings, Park of Monmouth, and Farrington of Ribbleton, came in black. Everybody – every lord and lady, every doorkeeper and police-man – shared a sense of occasion, a sense of melancholy. Well not quite everybody. Not the Baroness Jay of Paddington. The Leader of the House, King Tony's vice-regent in this noblest of his provinces, came without her father, Lord Callaghan of Cardiff, the last Labour ruler before King Tony. A new Labour dynasty is installed as the forces of conservatism are repelled: Lady Jay was arrayed in imperial purple with a purple buttonhole. The Queen hates purple.

Questions were a distracted affair, as the gallows were readied. Lord Grenfell did his best, sticking determinedly to his question. It was his swansong: he declined to stand for mere election, and is for the chop. Baroness Scotland of Asthal, a minister also in black, had the grace to say that he would be missed.

And then the dreadful business. Peers were to consider Commons amendments to the House of Lords Bill: their last chance to spoil the legislation. Lord Stanley of Alderney (for the chop) spoke to an amendment of his own, unacceptable to the Government. The Earl of Caithness (reprieved) supported him. Would they push this to a vote? It could have brought the whole compromise crashing down.

Lord Elton, once one of Margaret Thatcher's senior ministers in the Lords, described the upper chamber's role in restraining governments – even the noble Baroness's. He smiled at Lady Thatcher. She peered bleakly at him, no doubt trying to remember who he was.

As Lord Strathclyde spoke, the penny dropped. He would not be pushing this to a vote. The beguilingly bufferish Tory leader in the Lords was signalling surrender. Hopes fell. Tempers rose. Lord Clifford of Chudleigh, who is for the chop, tried to speak – possibly on the wrong amendment, but everyone was in a muddle. Lady Jay silenced him. He tried again, but she forced the business forward. Peers became upset at her impatience. The popular Earl Ferrers (reprieved) intervened bravely on Clifford's behalf. Everyone was agitated. Jay had misjudged.

She nearly lost it. When it came to the vote, the Labour roar of 'content!' was followed by a scattering of tentative Tory 'not contents'. Jay tried to ignore it. Dissent grew angrier. Could she not just let this fellow speak? Might the discontent that simmers beneath the surface of Tory submission boil over at the last minute? But the minute passed.

Around the throne where the heirs of hereditary peers are by custom allowed to sit, a boy was perched, surveying the gilt and leather. Some day all this will not be his.

Finally, as Parliament was prorogued, came the list of enactments by way of declaration and response. 'The House of Lords Act . . .

'*La reyne le veult.*'

And that was it. There was something brutal in the way they were dispatched, and, in the way they went, something craven.

Queen Splits Infinitive for Blair

18.11.99

The Queen's Speech 1999.

Where did she get that hat? Is there no limit to new Labour's big-head confidence? The headgear said it all. In the Gallery, where Cabinet spouses sat awaiting the Queen's Speech, Cherie Blair's extensive headgear, inky-dark, jostled with something extraordinary in pink (garnished with a funeral feather) on Pauline Prescott's head. Beside them sat a lady wearing a Miro sculpture. Dr Seuss's *Cat in a Hat* concoctions were hardly more fantastic.

And is there no limit to new Labour's command? Yesterday the monarch was arm-twisted into splitting an infinitive, trumpeting 'number one' priorities and 'key' recommendations, crowing about Labour's record, and saying 'pee'.

'Ten pee,' she shrilled. What's wrong with pence? Her Majesty should never say 'pee'. We half expected her to boast that 'thanks to Tony's telly-licence handout, old folk are now set to trouser more than a hundred quid'. It will be 'my husband and me' next. Unless Buckingham Palace gets a grip the Queen will find her Gracious Speech turned into a tabloid voice-over for a party political broadcast – 'joined-up government', 'the many not the few', and 'no return to Tory boom and bust' whinnying through the royal discourse.

She read her text with a kind of loathing. Beside her, hands on his sword, the Duke of Edinburgh wore the glazed expression of a man who could take no more. What His Royal Highness makes of the pledge to curb fur-farming we can only guess.

He had only to look around him to see the harvest of a hundred fur-farms, every pelted robe a personal tragedy for a family of small furry mammals. In the stoat community, mention of the peerage produces the panic that mint sauce provokes among lambs. Acres of ermine stretched before us. And the Carpets were out in force. Lords ceremonial is one of the few circumstances in which it is possible to wear a carpet without inviting derision. Before a trumpet fanfare signalled the Queen's arrival, dozens of men in carpets galumphed in to mill beside the Throne. The entire rug department at Liberty's had got up and walked.

Nor is there any reduction in the tiara-count. New Labour, new tiara. The party's recently ennobled big benefactors have not had to pawn their wives' tiaras to buy their peerages. One of the most ambitious, in gold (dwarfing the lady beneath it), appeared to have been stolen from the stage props of a nativity play – meant for the Three Kings.

Around the Throne, little boys in skirts and ruffs danced attendance on the Queen's robe's train, while a fellow stood holding a huge sword up to his nose throughout. And this was the *modernised* ceremony!

Full-bottomed wigs, Arab ambassadors' keffiyehs, African robes and Maoist tunics rustled and shook as Her Majesty trilled about 'the New Deal' and ground her way through formulations like 'advance the UK's [sic] position', 'compete in the digital market-place' and 'make it unlawful for public bodies to racially discriminate'. Did we only imagine a little fastidious shudder before she ploughed into that split infinitive? It is hard to picture her at breakfast asking about her next 'UK tour'.

It jarred. Our Queen is one of the dwindling few who still rhyme 'cross' with 'horse', so 'fight crawse-border crime' somehow goes off-message. New Labour zap evaporates.

Never mind. Now that Alastair Campbell can tell Her Majesty which words to use, can it be long before he tells her how to pronounce them too?

<table>
<tr><td>24.11.99</td><td></td></tr>
</table>

24.11.99   # Not Down the Tubes Yet

Michael Portillo begins his return to parliament.

Half past seven in the morning is no time to be out on the streets of Kensington and Chelsea. The first grey light was lifting over the smart rooftops, Entryphone gates and magnolia trees as your shivering sketchwriter awaited the arrival of Michael Portillo's campaigning hit-squad for a dawn blitz on Holland Park Tube Station. Will these Portillista desperados stop at nothing?

By 7.45 – Outrage still abed – eager Tories were mustered, assembling piles of blue leaflets bearing smiling snapshots of the great man and anchoring little flotillas of blue balloons to their sleeves. The youngest of these strange creatures sported only stubble on his head. 'Shaved it for charity,' he confessed. 'Last week I was bald.' The biggest Portillista wore a green waxed-cotton coat and curious felt hat. 'Trilby or what?' I asked.

'I go shooting in it.'

But his quarry today were unfeathered: the voters. And these birds were shy. Until El Numero Uno arrived, no commuter had been successfully apprehended.

'He's coming,' hissed an excited Portillista. Down the pavement from Notting Hill steamed a lone Portillo, at a cracking pace. 'Morning everyone,' he growled sternly, in his big Daddy Bear voice, readying himself to press the flesh by the station door. I slunk behind, to overhear. Portillo has a massive neck. People kept slipping by, unapprehended.

Commuters were mostly a mixture of Filipino maidservants (baffled by Portillo's outstretched hand), hungover construction workers hiding beneath hard hats and the occasional rather wealthy looking Suit (who invariably turned out to be a Member of the Kensington and Chelsea Conservative Association already). 'Where are you going,' boomed the Candidate at a group of little boys in school uniforms. They gave him a withering glance.

Anxious to make his mark with more than kids, migrant workers and his own activists, Portillo concealed himself cunningly behind a news-stand. Those heading for the station door could not see him until it was too late. He would jump out, snarling: 'GoodmorningI'mMichael Portillohowareyou?' and grab their hands. One or two hands were withheld ('in a bit of a rush, aren't they?' lamented the Candidate), though there were good wishes from some. Shyer birds seemed anxious to avoid an encounter and drew back. But there was no way into the Tube except past Portillo. Inside the station the lift down to the platform beep-beeped urgently as its doors prepared to close. The pheasants hesitated, then put their heads down and scuttled past him.

For the most part people were not hostile: just uninterested, and late for work: the Central Line had broken down again. This mattered more than any politician. From time to time the Portillista in the shooting hat would capture a passer-by, usually Chinese, and beat them like game-birds in the Candidate's direction, shouting 'Michael!'. Instead of shooting them Portillo would let them scamper off, terrified, with a Tory leaflet. A well-spoken chap caught sight of Portillo. 'How's it going Michael?' They knew one another. After a brief chat the man continued on his way. 'Oh,' he said, departing 'remind me: when's polling day?'

'Thursday,' replied Portillo, but his face had darkened.

'Oh God,' whispered one of the Tory workers.

'What's wrong?' I asked.

'That was the Deputy Chairman of the Conservative Association.' Beep-beep-beep went the lift. I scampered too. The lift-floor was a carpet of screwed up Tory leaflets.

Were You Up for Portillo?   *1.12.99*

Portillo has won Kensington and Chelsea.

Were you up for Portillo? The Tories were yesterday, as he signed the Commons Register. Only trumpets were missing. Not since the Relief of Mafeking has a rescuing force been awaited with such longing. Opposition MPs, packed into the Chamber, had been scampering in all afternoon, in anticipation of the Kensington Conqueror's return.

Michael Fabricant (C, Lichfield), trembling with excitement, leapt up and down to question ministers, unable to concentrate on the answers. John Whittingdale (C, Maldon & Chelmsford E) couldn't keep still. Alan Duncan (C, Rutland & Melton) had blow-dried his hair specially for the occasion.

Already, as Nick Brown, Agriculture Minister, rose for a statement on beef-on-the-bone, the place was abuzz. No Tory could keep his mind on beef. The real beef was pawing the ground beyond those great oak doors. We could almost hear the snort and bellow from the Members' Lobby as Mr Portillo's keepers struggled to restrain him.

For 73-year-old Sir Peter Emery (C, Devon E) it was all too much. Arguing with the Agriculture Minister over England's ancient rights to T-bone steak, Sir Peter totally blew his top. Mount Emery erupted. The snowy-haired MP went pink, then exploded into a deafening yell. Psychotherapists call it displacement. It was really Portillo Sir Peter was agitated about.

In vain did MPs try to focus on the farmyard. In vain did they discuss offal. Infection in the dorsal root ganglia was not where they were at.

Eyes slid sideways towards those doors. Wasn't he leaving it late?

Even Labour's Ben Bradshaw caught the Tory mood. The Exeter MP began babbling excitedly about 'exploding the myth that is being peddled' about something or other. Gorgeous, leggy Julie Kirkbride (C, Bromsgrove) had kitted herself out in gold – a sort of Dralon curtain material – plus a little black skirt. Nails varnished in vampish black, she sat, all a-quiver.

And still no Portillo.

Madam Speaker glanced at the clock. How much longer could she run the Agriculture Statement? The doors opened – but it was only Michael Ancram, the Tory chairman, who looked in then slid out. Was he checking that his side were ready?

Perhaps, for in slipped William Hague next, and sat down firmly in the Tory Leader's place, securing his seat against any usurper.

Then the doors opened again. Tory heads turned. Michael Portillo walked up to the Bar, and stood waiting, flanked by James Arbuthnot, the Opposition Chief Whip, and Francis Maude (the Shadow Chancellor whose job Portillo has made it clear he does *not* covet – oh no). The Statement ended. 'Members desirous of taking their seats,' trilled Miss Boothroyd.

Loose-limbed, laid-back and confident, Michael Portillo swung across the carpet, his proud quiff, sleek at the dispatch box, erect. Every Tory gawped. Mr Hague smiled bravely. Labour wags tried to fill the heckling-deficit left by an absent Dennis Skinner (he has been unwell) but only Skinner could have met the moment.

The new MP belted out the Oath as though dispatching troops to battle, the final 'so help me God' delivered with a kind of flourish. Then out came the fountain pen. Unfortunately it was not possible for Mr Portillo to lean over to sign without thrusting his backside into the faces of the Government Front Bench. Jack Straw, the Home Secretary, took it well.

Finally, a handshake with beaming Betty, and out he swaggered. Tories fell to whispering. Do you remember where you were when Portillo took his seat? They all do.

A Sound Bite is Born
2.12.99

Kennedy – On December 1 to Charles Peter, at the House of Commons, a soundbite, seven words: his first – a sibling, God willing, to many more to come.

It was a real thrill to be present for the birth. All of us had been anxious that Mr Kennedy, though his long-running affair with the Liberal Democrat Party was made legal ages ago, has seemed unable to produce a soundbite. Yesterday he surprised and delighted us.

It was only a little one, emerging shyly at the end of an earnest cross-questioning of the Prime Minister on the financing of London Underground construction.

Kennedy got (for Kennedy) quite cross. Hardly a session passes these day without what is at best a slight misunderstanding, at worst a little fib, falling from the Prime Minister's lips. Last week he told Kennedy that his party had opposed the New Deal. They had not. This week he said that Kennedy's plans for raising public funds for Tube investment meant that the work would be done by the public sector, like (he said) the notoriously problem-plagued Jubilee Line.

But work on the Jubilee Line is not being done by the public sector – nor was Kennedy proposing any such thing. For many years now, little infrastructure work has been done by the public sector, which hires private sector contractors instead. We must charitably assume that the Prime Minister was simply unaware of this.

So perhaps it was mild apoplexy that caused Kennedy's soundbite to pop out. 'From rolling stock to laughing stock,' he protested. Snoozing journalists (for whom infrastructure-finance so soon after lunch was too much) picked up pencils in surprise.

Everyone cheered. All right – it wasn't the biggest, bounciest baby soundbite that had ever been seen in the Westminster ward: but it *was* a soundbite, and a perfectly viable one. We congratulate the proud father. May it be the first of many.

Cook Bombs Moscow – None Hurt

8.12.99

Yesterday in the Commons, Robin Cook began bombing Russians. With adjectives.

The trigger for the Foreign Secretary's fearless attack was Question 21, from a Conservative backbencher, Laurence Robinson (Tewkesbury), whose assault on Russian misbehaviour in Chechnya may become known as the Tewkesbury Raid. Mr Robinson wondered what 'discussions' Mr Cook had had with the Russians. Cook had asked the Chair to move this inquiry to the end of Foreign Office Questions, so that MPs could stage a set-piece battle for Chechnya.

The Foreign Secretary flew the first sortie himself. This was a high-level drop and Mr Cook had armed himself with the full thesaurus. Jets blazing, he roared across the Central European skies.

Bombs away! 'Wholeheartedly condemn'. *Bam!* 'Deplore'. *Crump!* Far below, we could see Russian installations ablaze already. 'The planned visit of the OSCE,' growled Cook, his jet banking into a steep curve, 'may now be pointless.' *Kerthump!* A thin plume of black smoke rose from now-devastated conference facilities at the Kremlin. Cook came back for another assault: a stonker. If Russia were to proceed with the expulsion of civilians from Grozny, he barked, EU leaders might 'review the next tranche' of funds promised to Russia for modernisation. Review? *Wham.* The next tranche? All of it? Ouch. Take that, Ivan!

Cook streaked off, and in roared the instigator of this dogfight, Tewkesbury Terror, Laurence 'bear-baiter' Robinson. He dumped what ordnance he could. Russian behaviour was 'totally unacceptable'. Moscow flinched. Would our Government 'please convey the very seriousness [*sic*] of the situation'. St Petersburg shook.

Mr Cook agreed. And he had words of comfort for the huddled 'elderly and vulnerable' unfortunates still in Grozny: as it was 'impractical for them to escape on foot' Russia must 'withdraw the threat immediately'. Shock-waves rippled through the Duma.

More shocks were in store as Donald Anderson rose with furrowed brow. Labour's hand-wringing cleric of a Foreign Affairs Select Committee chairman was steeled for the nuclear option. Unless Russia provided 'very clear undertakings', the Council of Europe must consider suspending her as a member. This rocked even Robin. We must 'await the report of the rapporteur,' he mumbled.

What was left of the smoking ruins of Russian infrastructure were now peppered by an angry Tory. John Maples, Principal Opposition Spokesman on Foreign Affairs, fired two fearsome word-missiles towards the Urals: 'appalling' and (phew!) 'unacceptable'. Mr Maples's beautifully coiffed hair quivered with his indignation. Shouldn't the West consider 'other measures' gasped daring Maples. Cook promised to discuss this with Ms Albright. Ominous, eh Igor?

Any Russians not tempted to throw in the towel right away will have despaired when a Ming Fighter (Menzies Campbell, Liberal Democrat Spokesman) loosed off his 'outrage' at their 'medieval barbarism'. Stunned Slavs then faced an aerial bombardment of words like 'bloodthirsty tyranny' from the fearsome Malcolm Savidge (Lab, Aberdeen N), spectacles aglint. In vain did that Rusky-sympathising Quisling, Julian Brazier (C, Canterbury) dispatch relief aid in Moscow's direction by suggesting Chechnya's muslim rebels were not saints.

In the Kremlin all hope must have been lost. Or almost. One tiny glimmer of consolation was provided by the faint ack-ack of friendly fire from Tam Dalyell (Lab, Linlithgow) and Alice Mahon (Lab, Halifax). Who taught the Russians to settle disputes by bombing civilians from the stratosphere, they asked? Was it not NATO in Kosovo? Cook spat his indignation and whined off into a darkening sky.

As this anthology goes to press, the Russians are being embraced as our allies against Muslim terrorists.

Vulcans Can Suffer Too

9.12.99

*Prescott returns from India, Redwood sickens, and Portillo makes an
extraordinary speech.*

So he *is* a Vulcan. It was a top Tory spin doctor who gave the game
away – unwittingly. Privately, she was preparing journalists for a muted
performance by John Redwood as he prepared to open the attack on the
Deputy Prime Minister in yesterday's Opposition Day debate.

'Redwood's been ill,' she confided. 'Over the weekend, he was
running a temperature of 110 degrees fahrenheit.'

As *The Times*'s Dr Thomas Stuttaford has confirmed to this sketch,
no human runs a body temperature like this. I rang my Vulcanologist.

'Vulcans do succumb to fever, and it's intense,' he explained. 'It's
called *pong-fah* and brings on a kind of hot-blooded madness, which is
very distressing to a Vulcan. It occurs once every 40 or 50 years.'

The moment Mr Redwood entered the Chamber, it was clear that
pong-fah was upon him. This was lucky for jet-lagged John Prescott,
who himself seemed to have caught buffalo-fever in the Indian rice-
paddies and was bellowing a lot.

Redwood was even worse. The Tory Vulcan simply cannot do
aggression and should not try. It is hard to say which was more chronic:
the personal attacks on Prescott ('from Jags to riches'), the rhetorical
flourishes ('motorists fleeced at the pump') culled from Redwood's
trusty *Earthling Speechmaker's Companion*, or the dissection of
transport policy. To declaim 'When will there be action on the Welwyn
viaduct?' with conviction is more than human – let alone Vulcan – flesh
can manage.

So Prescott's opening line, 'I don't think your speech was worth
coming back from India for,' worked well. Unfortunately it was all that
did.

Like something trying to climb out of a swamp, the Deputy Prime
Minister floundered all over the place. Recording 'Prescottisms' (those
sad casualties of the Secretary of State's friendly fire on his own syntax)
is becoming tedious, so we will restrict ourselves to suggesting that Mr
Prescott's joke – 'of all the trees in the world, the dentist is the
Redwood' – may have muddled 'densest' with 'dentist'; to proposing
that 'vote of no conference' gains intelligibility if for 'conference' we
substitute 'confidence'; to remarking that 'I want to take it out of that

political football' might better be rendered 'I want to stop playing political football with it'; and to wondering what is meant by prefacing an announcement to a House in full session, with the phrase 'tomorrow I'm going to announce that . . .'

Prescott survived not so much through lucidity as by making a confident noise. New Labour poodles had been packed in to cheer him, and fitfully did.

Nobody won. Labour versus Tory spats these days resemble those circus-ring battles between teams of clowns, in which the two teams never quite lock horns, having tripped up on their own shoelaces, assaulted their own neighbour or punched themselves in the head by mistake.

Exit the clowns, or so we thought. Then Michael Portillo rose for his first speech as Member for Kensington and Chelsea. He had carried in with him something weird in a plastic bag, which he now brandished. It was an inflatable portable pillow, he told surprised MPs, imported from Australia, trademarked 'The Portillo'.

To our amazement, the by-election victor then read out the label. 'Portillo for unrivalled comfort. Portillo for ease and convenience. 1001 uses . . . Grab Portillo in right hand; insert thumb into opening and grip firmly; inflate it to its full size and shape.'

This, honestly, is what he said. *Pong fah* – or what?

Oh I *see*

10.12.99

Neil Hamilton sues.

He looked so different from the jaunty politician I used to know. In the raised witness box in court 13 at the Royal Courts of Justice in the Strand, Neil Hamilton stood, yesterday, pale and tense: still dapper, but stress personified. The former MP for Tatton would intermittently run the tip of his tongue around his lips, blinking rapidly.

He faced a hostile inquisition from Mohamed Al Fayed's counsel: that fabled swordsman of the libel duel, George Carman QC.

As fencers, Hamilton and Carman were well-matched. On the merits we cannot comment, but on the swordsmanship we can. Hamilton parried nimbly and with stamina. He was quick and bold. Years of verbal warfare have lent him edge.

He was also witty – his humour arch to the point almost of campery. George Carman put it to Hamilton that if a tailor presented him (Carman) with ten bespoke suits, the gift might be declared to the taxman as worthless because the suits would fit nobody else.

Hamilton's sarcasm was instant: 'I think that if they belonged to you, that would enhance their value, Mr Carman.'

George Carman is remorseless, but he is not fast. You can see an approaching Carman line of attack from the other end of the Strand. Yesterday his theme was greed. He repeated the word often. From the outset, he told Hamilton his questions would be about the former MP's 'attitude to money: the making of it and the keeping of it'.

'To use a simple phrase, this was a fiddle, wasn't it?' he asked at one point. Hamilton had – had he not? – seen Al Fayed as 'a golden goose'. No tabloid journalist has to find the words to bring a Carman question pithily to life: Carman finds them for him: he is a master at fashioning the peg on which to hang an imputation.

And Carman had humour, too. 'Were you known to the garden furniture department at Peter Jones,' he inquired archly, when Hamilton agreed he had bought some garden furniture there, telling the store to send the bill for £959.95 to the lobbyist, Ian Greer.

'Why this elaborate charade?' the lawyer asked about the former MP's efforts to avoid paying directly for garden furniture, a painting and airline tickets. Hamilton explained that in fact he had never needed to engage in 'this rigmarole'.

'Rigmarole?'

Hamilton protested that it was Carman who had used such language. Or was it 'charade'?

'Rigmarole, charade,' Carman murmured, 'we're in the same ball park'.

A battery of Carman's questions established that at the Ritz the MP and his wife had consumed sometimes one, sometimes two bottles of vintage champagne every night, their one-bottle evenings supplemented with bottles of wine. They had also waded into an expensive menu.

'Your wife had a bad back?' Carman inquired. Hamilton confirmed this. And (he added) she had suffered from a chronic viral infection.

'Did they affect her capacity to eat and drink?' Carman asked.

And this lawyer's trademark is his response to explanations he wants his audience to doubt. Who but George Carman can breathe into the simple phrase 'Oh I *see*' such a world of dubiety and scorn?

Hamilton met scorn with scorn. Once, unable to answer, the former MP explained he had not paid 'close attention' to the matter in question. Acidly, Carman asked whether 'you pay close attention to anything you find disagreeable'.

'I'm paying close attention to you,' Hamilton spat straight back at him.

The Wig Meets the Hair   *14.12.99*

Christine comes to her husband's rescue.

For weeks now the audience at the back of Court 13 at the Royal Courts of Justice has been distracted by a golden mound. The mound is the crown of an awesomely coiffed swept-back-and-braided blonde hairdo. It floats like a rising harvest moon over the top of a line of files, just visible above a desk towards the front.

The person beneath the hairdo is hidden, but we know it is Christine. She has been listening from what (to public view) is a kind of pit beneath the high bench on which the judge is perched. Her silent presence has aroused immense and mounting curiosity among press and public. When will she be called? What will she say? Yesterday, the moon rose, and spoke. Christine Hamilton was elevated to the witness box. Or, rather, three Christine Hamiltons. Cross-examination throws the ambiguities of all our natures into unnatural relief and Christine is no exception.

All three Mrs Hamiltons were identically kitted out in a black skirt, immaculate small-check red and black jacket – and that hair. There was Beryl the Peril Hamilton: game, feisty, a one-bottle-of-red-plonk-a-night type of gal (she agreed) and stand-by-your-man chum to Neil.

'I don't think it's any secret that you're 49?' asked a friendly Wig, Desmond Browne, her husband's QC. 'It certainly isn't now,' she shot back. 'Oh crumbs!' the Hair told a hostile Wig, George Carman, QC, who wondered if she remembered a party, 'I certainly do!'

Beryl Hamilton could look after herself. She swung right round in the witness box towards Mr Carman, jutting an elbow forward and eyeballing the elderly lawyer fiercely. She can turn a blink into an act of aggression. Blowing her top at him, she called his accusations 'absolutely grotesque'.

The second version, Ophelia Hamilton, is a woman driven to distraction. Ophelia's story is of relentless hounding by her husband's enemies and the world's media, a life made hell by false accusation. She fought back tears when Mr Browne asked about the effect on her life of Mohamed Al Fayed's accusations. 'I just felt completely desperate . . . We were pushed right back to the bottom . . . it was devastating.'

The Hair would stare at the jury and describe the hell she had been through. 'We were in a fortress: we were besieged' and 'We were just fighting to . . . keep alive.'

Then there is Christine No 3: the dutiful little woman whose husband roams a big world of which she knows little. Cho-Cho San Hamilton knew no more than Madam Butterfly about tax law or alleged unorthodox methods of payment at Peter Jones. 'Not my baby, Mr Carman', 'I can't help you, Mr Carman' and 'I don't get involved'. 'It wasn't my department,' the Hair told the Wig. Repeatedly she would forget the question and, in sweet confusion, ask for it to be repeated. But Cho-Cho San kept a close eye on the housekeeping (checked Neil's pockets for change every night, she said); and Ophelia's tears had not dimmed her watchfulness (I'm trying to think of the exact words, but I know you'll turn them back on me'); and Beryl, Cho-Cho and Ophelia took the interview through to a fighting finish: 'No vouchers, no money, no couriers, no calls and no envelopes. Nothing,' she barked.

And that was that. The Hair had decided to end the cross-examination. Meekly, the Wig sat down.

The Hamiltons lost. This turned out to be George Carman's last famous case before his death.

17.12.99   # Century Ends in a Shriek

And to think the economy is in the hands of such people! A creature rejoicing in the title 'Economic Secretary' – Melanie Johnson – just stood there yesterday, yelling – yelling – complete banalities at the Opposition.

For some sense of the effect this woman had on her audience –
including the poor bemused gaggle of tourists in the Strangers' Gallery
– head for the Westbound platform of the Central Line at Bank Station
on the London Underground, where the train comes in on a tight left-
hand bend and protesting steel wheels screech against steel rails at a
pitch which comes close to intolerable.

Watch the waiting passengers: some with hands clasped to ears;
children whimpering; pain written across every face. Maybe you now
understand what we call the Melanie Effect?

It is not as if the argument merited the anger or the pain. Labour and
the Tories are locked in a silly squabble about whether the overall
burden of taxation is rising or falling under this Government.

The changes involved, whether up or down, are only marginal, but of
the two idiotic sides to this dispute the Government's is slightly more
idiotic. At least technically in the right, the Tories have become
infuriated by the mulish refusal of ministers to acknowledge what
nobody in fact denies.

The squabble, which has been spluttering on for some weeks now,
flared again on Tuesday when Gordon Brown faced the Treasury Select
Committee and wouldn't even admit that 37 per cent was more than 36
per cent. The Tories want him (and the Prime Minister) to admit that the
overall tax burden now is greater than it was when Labour won the last
election.

They are right. The Government insists that the tax burden 'is
falling'. They too are right. The conflict is reconciled as we might
reconcile an apparent inconsistency between the statement that the
temperature now is higher than a year ago, and the statement that at
present the temperature 'is falling'. Both may be true, for heaven's
sake!

But can you get both sides at Westminster to agree to a similar truce
over the tax burden? Not if Melanie and Quentin have anything to do
with it.

Quentin Davies, an Opposition Treasury spokesman, gloated at
Melanie yesterday that Tony – or was it Gordon? – now admits the
burden has gone up. This is not quite the case. Melanie just shrieked.
The Tory Shadow Chancellor, Francis Maude, sneered at the Chief
Secretary, Andrew Smith, that Gordon – or was it Tony? – now admits
the burden has increased. This too is not quite the case.

Andrew just whined, on and on, about '22 Tory tax rises'. Andrew whines in the strangulated tones of someone having his windpipe squeezed by an assailant.

Francis sneers in the adenoidal tones of a pantomime villain. Melanie screams like a demented fishwife. Quentin gloats like a rich kid who has just outsmarted his classmates.

'The Chancellor didn't say that,' whined Andrew. 'Yes he did!' bawled the Tories. 'No he didn't!' yelled Labour. 'Taxes up, up!' bawled the Tories. 'Down, down!' yelled the government benches.

Melanie screamed, Francis sneered, Andrew whined, Quentin gloated . . . and your sketchwriter departed, leaving them all, brawling on towards the millennium, in some kind of a hell of their own creation.

Never mind. It's nearly over.

One Flies Over the Cuckoo's Nest

11.1.00

The Tory defector begins the century in a new party.

The curtain rose on the 21st-century Commons pantomime after Prayers yesterday, discovering a new member among Labour's cast of back-bench elves. Shaun Woodward (Witney) peeped shyly up from behind his fingers, shifting embarrassedly in his new seat.

St Anthony's latest convert couldn't keep still. He inclined to his left to chat awkwardly with the unreconstructed leftie, Harry Barnes (Derbyshire NE). Mr Barnes looked surprised to find himself beside a millionaire former director of Tory communications; almost as surprised as was the soft and sleekly tailored consort of a Sainsbury heiress to find himself grunting alongside a founder of the Dronfield Miners' Support Group whose late Mum, called Betsy, was once a domestic servant.

He inclined to his right for a kind word from the hairy-looking member of Greenpeace and the Co-op Party, Martin Salter (Reading W). A Sainsbury, patronised by a Co-op! Poor Mr Woodward. Passing through the eye of the needle is bruising.

Fingers still spread across his mouth, Woodward craned round to speak to the Formby feminist, Maria Eagle (Liverpool Garston). The

press stared. Some Tories glared. Others tried not to look at him at all.
Government backbenchers shot sly sideways glances. Pity the fellow at
whom half his world cannot forbear to look and the other half is
determined not to. But relief was at hand. Through Mr Salter's hair he
descried the silvery helmet and padded features of Peter Temple-
Morris, the once-Tory Member for Leominster who came over to St
Anthony's cause last year. Mr Temple-Morris smiled in gentle support.
The converts spoke. Woodward relaxed.

It had not been an easy day. At the end of the morning, Woodward
had been forced by Labour's propaganda machine to pose at the
entrance to Parliament and kiss Mo Mowlam. Photographers report a
perfunctory encounter, as between two prim amateur actors obliged to
simulate intimacy before the footlights. The kiss was effected quickly.
Photographers asked them to do it again. They refused.

Mood Swings of Senator Blairochet

13.1.00

As doctors examine General Pinochet, we take a look at General Tony.

Three eminent doctors and an independent neuropsychologist were
yesterday asked to examine Senator Antonio Blairochet to assess
whether he is fit to stand at the dispatch box and answer Prime
Minister's Questions. We cannot divulge their report for reasons of
patient confidentiality, but doctors were minded to recommend the
Senator be spared future Commons ordeals.

To no avail. Oblivious to his infirmity, Blairochet appeared yesterday
at 3pm.

This sketch is worried. Apart from chronic memory loss, Antonio is
suffering from a much rarer malady: the disturbing syndrome discussed
only the other morning on *BBC Breakfast News*. Clinical psychiatrists
call it MPD, or Multiple Personality Disorder.

On yesterday's showing, Blairochet may be the first Prime Minister
to suffer from this. Within 30 minutes, he swung wildly between
character types. The contrasts were stark.

The Senator's first persona was that of a grave and caring leader.

Unprompted, he began his first answer with an expression of deep sympathy for the seven fishermen missing in the Irish Sea, and for their families. 'Our thoughts are with them,' he breathed, a catch not far from his throat, demeanour sombre, face anguished, tone dignified and heartfelt.

But it never lasts. It lasted 15 seconds yesterday. As soon as panting, wet-tongued John Heppell (Lab, Nottingham E), yapping that it was 'an honour' to ask his master the first question of the millennium, had laid his slobbery biscuit of an inquiry at Blairochet's feet and taken a craven little nip at the Opposition to please him, the Senator changed. A new Antonio roared forth. Forgetting that his thoughts had been with the fishermen, he started sneering and bellowing about the Tories.

Voice rising, he railed that they 'always opposed measures that reduce unemployment'. He began shouting. His watery little eyes had taken on a wild, angry look. To witness this abrupt change was scary. He accused William Hague of 'opportunistically seeking to make capital' from the illness of others. Psychiatrists call this 'projecting'. The furious rant continued, very loud and abusive: possibly a touch of Tourette's Syndrome.

Then he changed again, switched to a tone of exasperated rationality. Like a weary teacher, he reeled off lists of NHS statistics. 'These things take time,' he almost whined.

Blairochet switched next to Porky Mode (Münchhausen's syndrome). The patient fibs extravagantly. Yesterday he kept repeating that the Tories want to privatise the NHS, then switched to Panto Mode, reciting a list of accusations and waiting for the cast behind to shout 'Oh!' after each. Hague gave up.

Briefly, Antonio reverted to Caring Mode, to tell Rosie Winterton (Lab, Doncaster Central) about child poverty; then, criticised by Keith Simpson (C, Mid Norfolk) over Jack Straw's attack on English aggression, he momentarily embraced sweet reason ('As one very peaceful English person to another . . .'). For Liberal Democrat Charles Kennedy, he chose Flippant Mode.

You get the picture. So what/who/which is Blairochet? Peter Brooke (C, Cities of London & Westminster) was wondering about this too. 'What is Blairism?' he asked – so baldly that it caught Antonio undressed in any of his personalities. He blurted out the truth. He won the last election, he stammered, 'with a majority of 179'.

Blarism is, er . . . winning.

What Is It About Boateng?

What is it about Paul Boateng that drives normally calm people screaming up the curtains? Though commonly the passport to a political career, the profession of barrister seems to poison a man's power of advocacy anywhere but in the courtroom. It has poisoned Boateng's. How many more bedside clock-radio alarms have to perish beneath fists silencing Boateng's morning fulminations on the *Today* programme, before new Labour communications whiz-kids get the message that, compared with this Home Office Minister of State, Michael Howard was a deeply convincing human being?

No rendering of Mr Boateng's words in cold print can do justice to the repellent quality of his dispatch-box delivery: sneering, blustering, eye-rolling, grandiloquent, false. Performing for the Criminal Bench seems to have wrecked his capacity to sound sincere.

But it isn't just style. In substance, too, Boateng demeans himself. His habit is to choose the low blow. Yesterday Tom Brake (Lib Dem, Carshalton and Wallington) told him he was concerned about over-crowding in Britain's prisons. Boateng told Brake that, 'unlike the Liberal Democrats', the Government was less concerned with prison numbers than with how to reduce crime. It was cheap, and drew some shocked gasps. Any hack politician can get an easy cheer in a village hall by puffing out his cheeks and raging against those who put the welfare of criminals above safety on 'our' streets, but to become Prisons Minister is surely to graduate from this sort of thing?

The minister told MPs that the use of 'hulks' as temporary floating prisons would continue. No doubt it must, but we would have been obliged if Mr Boateng had not sounded quite so joyful about it. One of these hulks, he added, HM Prison *Weir*, had proved 'an unalloyed success'. 'Unalloyed success' is a strong expression. One might hope to hear it used to report human achievement in happier realms than the incarceration of an excess of prisoners; but this may be to underestimate Mr Boateng's enthusiasm for his task. Moments later it carried him away. Boasting to Ann Widdecombe that 30 new prisons were under construction (and more to come) he went on, excitedly, to tell the Tory Shadow Home Secretary that Britain now has '67,800 prisons'. Mr Boateng soon corrected this to 'prisoners', but the slip was creepy.

Spellar Slips, House Rocks, Hoon Sails Away

25.1.00

Still only 52, in mid-career, having reached the level of junior Defence Minister, and on a grey Monday, it must be depressing for a chap to realise he has just said the most interesting thing he will ever say in his life. Even more depressing must have been to realise it was just a slip of the tongue.

Poor John Spellar. Virginia Bottomley struggled to control herself, such was her mirth. Up in the Press Gallery, professionalism pushed past breaking point, journalists heaved with laughter. MPs hardly tried to restrain themselves. Paul Keetch (Lib Dem, Hereford) was even moved to offer 'sympathy' to the minister 'in his first answer'. What Mr Spellar meant to say was 'cuts'. How the errant 'n' crept in, none can say.

The old joke about the difference between Billy Smart's circus and the *Folies Bergère* should signpost the pitfall to any MP, but Spellar tumbled straight in, and emerged blushing. He ploughed bravely on with his answers, stuttering miserably, aware nobody was now listening to a word he said.

The intended sentence – 'those cuts in Defence Medical Services have gone too far' – had acquired quite another meaning, amended by Spellar. Being Minister for the Armed Forces is one thing; adopting the sort of mess talk one might expect in the Armed Forces is another. Spellar quickly corrected himself.

But it was too late. Unfortunately for this minister, he does anyway talk in the most irascible way. As even his most pedestrian answers are spat out like the outbursts of a man provoked beyond endurance, the offending word did not in this case sound completely out of place . . .

But enough. A polite sketch must now draw a veil over the subject, venturing (alongside a modest bet on the prediction that this morning's Hansard will have cleaned up Spellar's prose) the thought that we now know the difference between Prime Minister's Questions and John Spellar's Answers. The first is a cunning row of stunts, the second a stunning row of cuts.

Geoff Hoon, Secretary of State, recovered his composure fast enough. Mr Hoon is a very cool cookie, amiably lowering the temperature with intelligent courtesy. The Emperor Hirohito broke the news of the US nuclear strike on Hiroshima with a broadcast announcement: 'an event has occurred which is not necessarily to our advantage'; the Emperor Hoon is developing a comparable range of understatement. 'Let me first of all question his use of the term "severely",' cooed Hoon, when foam-flecked Julian Brazier (C, Canterbury) suggested that Britain's Armed Forces were hard-put to maintain commitments.

When Richard Ottaway, Tory spokesman, described an under-supplied Royal Navy 'stuck in port' over Christmas, Hoon shuddered at the language. 'There was a point when a significant number of ships were, er, tied up alongside,' he allowed. For turkey and Christmas pudding, apparently.

A secret deal to pool our nuclear deterrent with France's? 'The, er, great majority of that *Spectator* article was based on fantasy.' Massacre and terrorisation of Kosovan Serbs by Albanians? 'There have been, er, difficulties in encouraging Serbs to return to their homes and their jobs.'

I can see the indispensable Rt Hon Sir Geoffrey (as he then will be) Hoon in 15 years: reliable, moderate, pleasant, bright – 'a safe pair of hands'. Every administration needs its Sir Norman Fowlers and this latest is critically short of them. Hoon will go far.

The next day's Hansard *removed spellar's slip.*

Blair Caught Off-message   10.2.00

Hague hears of a resignation before the boss.

Blair off-message! New Labour out-bleeped! Will wonders never cease?

Yesterday at Prime Minister's Questions, something almost unknown occurred. Labour circuitry blew a fuse and the system failed. For all who enjoy the unexpected, the whiff of singed prime-ministerial hair made a moment to remember.

As everybody knows, Tony Blair has a lucky streak. At Prime Minister's Questions it failed him. It was bad luck that at the very moment when the Prime Minister was on his feet declaring that his First

Secretary in Wales was doing 'an excellent job', Alun Michael was resigning.

Had anyone warned the Prime Minister? Why had Mr Blair not found a better way of answering? The creaking Tory machine appeared to get the news to their man before Blair's well-oiled command-control system got the news to theirs. In the dispatch box confusion which followed, Blair's judgement did fail. His scathing description of Welsh democracy as 'fun and games down at the Assembly' will return to haunt him.

It was Sir Archie Hamilton (C, Epsom and Ewell) who lit the Welsh fuse. He defied the Prime Minister not to interfere in the leadership challenge going on at (or 'down at', as Blair was to put it) the Welsh Assembly. Blair yelled a bit about two-faced Tories. Besides, Michael was doing 'an excellent job'. And that was that.

Or so it seemed. But minutes later, sharp-eyed colleagues in the Press Gallery saw a red flash from a small vibrating object tucked under one of the ample thighs of Michael Ancram, the Tory chairman seated near Hague. Both he and Andrew MacKay (the Shadow Northern Ireland Secretary) consulted pagers. A message was passed to Hague. He rose and tackled Blair. Had the Prime Minister not heard that his First Secretary had resigned 'within minutes' of Blair's praising him? Would No 10 now promise not to interfere?

This Prime Minister makes things harder for himself by his habit of refusing to let his opponent score or even draw. He seemed physically unable to admit that his man in Cardiff had fallen. Instead, he flew into what in camp parlance we call a hissy fit. That unwise phrase 'fun and games down at the Assembly' came gibbering out.

Hague picked up on it at once. Was this really Blair's opinion of a structure he had himself set up? Stumped, Blair just shouted back, about the Tories. In most minds the Tories were not the question. Blair spent the rest of the session – and quite regardless of the questions – shouting about Tories. He looked rattled.

By the end of Questions he was still on the road, but it had been a wobble: a palpable wobble.

Some Heckles Are Unanswerable

16.2.00

Hague takes to the road in his 'flat-bed truck' bid to save the pound.

The weirdest heckle that poor William Hague had to face during his otherwise unmemorable truckside address to the shoppers and toddlers of St Albans yesterday was the shout: 'Do you wear dresses?'

We reached for notebooks. How would he respond? 'Certainly not,' risked the headline 'Tory leader denies wearing dresses'. So, ignoring it, he ploughed on. 'Hague ducks "transvestite" charge'.

The occasion was bizarre. To simulate 'real' encounters with the electorate, politics and the media now have to fake it in ever more tiresome ways. Mr Hague did not drive his lorry. He was not driven there in his lorry. He did not depart in his lorry. He did not speak from his lorry. He did not enter his lorry. He never touched it.

In short, Hague and lorry had no connection whatever. They converged briefly in St Albans, and diverged again, Hague driven in a chauffeured Range Rover, lorry driven by the glamorous, polo-necked, casual denim-shirted, fashionably stubbled Ashley Stewart, who was afterwards bullied by the press into admitting that he was not a natural Tory and would not say how he planned to vote. Are many Yorkies called Ashley? Trust the Tories to find the only ideologically shy lorry driver in Britain.

The lorry arrived hours early, pushing out the Dinky Donuts van, whose lady vendor took her candy-floss to the edge of the square while Tories peddled a rival brand. Another lorry turned up, full of the BBC. A van arrived, also full of the BBC. An independent broadcasting van joined them. There was also a small lorry selling crepes to the media folk. As we interviewed each other for a living and munched crepes and Dinky Donuts, the town square boasted a small, short-lived, but perfectly formed micro-economy.

Rumour swept those waiting that Hague was actually inside the lorry.

On hands and knees I peeped through a crack under the tailgate, but saw only an empty space, blue fuzzy-felt, and forlorn metal shelves housing a sad bunch of 'save the £' balloons. Another bunch escaped a Tory lady when, startled, she let go. They stuck up a tree.

A crowd of a few hundred gathered: dragooned Conservative

activists, a rival demo staged by the UK Independence Party, and a significant minority who were just mad. Subtract from the total the media and police; UKIP, Tories and the unhinged (some overlap here); and Ashley, and we are left with very few cases of real people. But one or two of these could be spotted in the crush: aghast pensioners taking cover, and uncomprehending young mums trying to wheel their frightened babies away. Teenagers, spotting media-folk they had seen on telly, hunted for B-list celeb autographs. There cannot be much to do in St Albans.

Hague was late. Michael Ancram kicked things off. 'What a great gathering!' lied the Tory Chairman, continuing (in inward panic) 'I am assured William Hague is on his way,' then filibustering on the history of St Albans. Hague arrived and eyed his lorry for possibly the first time.

With him came Michael Portillo. We had been told to expect him later – maybe (we speculated) in a bigger lorry. Or a tow-truck? Or a flashy Italian car? But the two men arrived together, Hague in one of those tan car-coats they advertise alongside sofabeds, mail-order, in *The Sunday Times*, dark-suited Portillo looking faintly sniffy.

Of Mr Hague's speech, what is there to say? We have heard it before.

So, from his ever-so-slightly weary drone, had he.

My Hero! Ffion Sees Will Club Tony

17.2.00

Ffion Jenkins slipped into the Commons Strangers' Gallery before Prime Minister's Questions yesterday, to see her husband in mortal combat with Tony Blair. She watched intently. What was going through her mind?

In stone-age times, when ape-man went out to hunt, his female mate would often venture from the safety of the cave to sit on some rocky outcrop and watch her naked, hairy partner fight with a raging beast – willing him to win.

So it was with Ffion. True, Dolphin Square SW1 is some cave, and William is less than hairy. True, nobody actually dies after the weekly Wednesday battle between the Prime Minister and the Tory Leader. And true, they wore clothes.

But there remain clear similarities between Neanderthal and parliamentary conflict. The fight is brutal, the weapons primitive and the bellows and grunts the same.

Every night that Ffion's man returns to their cave carrying bits of Tony Blair's skin and fur, William and his blonde mate sleep more securely.

But William had had a bloody time after a bodged scrap near a lorry in St Albans. Now he glanced nervously up at his mate. She gazed tenderly down. Eat your heart out, Tony. Cherie never comes to watch.

How did Ffion's beloved fare?

His first armlock with raging-beast Blair was inconclusive. Even in the British House of Commons, it takes ingenuity to use concern about the sexual abuse of children as a stick with which to beat your opponent, and neither Hague nor Blair tried. The engagement was civil and serious.

Hague fell silent. Ffion pursed her lips. Was her Tory hunk to leave it at that?

At first it seemed so. Hague stayed out of the fray. Blair blustered and whinnied. When the Liberal Democrats' Richard Allen (Sheffield, Hallam) asked an expert question about drug patents and breast cancer, the Prime Minister appeared to lack the least idea what Mr Allen was talking about. Finding it unbearable to admit this, Blair floundered wildly and mentioned everything he knew about drugs and the NHS and other acronyms.

Charles Kennedy mentioned Hague's recent star role with Michael Portillo and a truck in St Albans. Was this not, suggested the Liberal Democrat Leader sarcastically, 'a serious campaign'?

Ffion smiled thinly. She saw the joke but wished she didn't. Kennedy invited Blair to agree that Hague's was the first case in history of dodgy goods falling *on to* the back of a lorry. Ffion grinned naughtily. Her husband (thank goodness) did not see her. And no doubt she felt confident he had something up his sleeve.

He had. As the session's end approached, Hague rose with a string of allegations about Blair's 'broken promises'. He adopted precisely the tactic that so confounded Blair when the Tories tried it last year. Hague confounded him again. Because the Prime Minister cannot bear to give his adversary the last word, Hague fires a series of double-barrelled questions, the first barrel referring back to a previous question, the second broaching a new inquiry. Unwilling to let anything drop, Blair then tries to face all ways at once and ties himself in a knot.

By the end yesterday, Blair was whinnying like a mad thing, and the Tories behind Hague were roaring for more. I looked up at Ffion. The broadest of smiles lit her face. Safe! The beast vanquished again!

Her mate could look forward to a warm fireside welcome back at their Pimlico cave.

18.2.00   # What's That in English?

Twenty per cent of New Dealers start 'below level 1 in basic literacy,' a minister, Tessa Jowell, told MPs at Questions yesterday. New Labour is not doing so well. The basic English of ministers on the Education and Employment bench is a disgrace.

As journalists rolled our eyes and even *Hansard* reporters winced, ministers flippered their way like a colony of penguins through a snow-shower of educational jargon characterised less by an absence of grammar than an absence of sense. Politicians who tangle with educationists get sucked into a sort of communications white-out. In a blizzard of buzz-words and voguish phrases, all meaning is erased.

Take passporting. Jacqui Smith, a minister, told her backbench colleague Mike Gapes (Ilford S) that his local education authority must get government money 'passported through to education'.

Passported? The word seemed to act as a signal to the penguins. All the ministers started to gibber about 'passporting'. Estelle Morris, another minister, told a Tory spokesman, James Clappison, that figures for 'money spent by LEAs and passported to schools' should be published. Then the Secretary of State joined in: David Blunkett wanted 'passporting to schools themselves', he told Labour's Barry Jones (Alyn & Deeside).

As we tried to work out what passporting was – presumably the dedication of funds to specific purposes – ministers fell upon another buzz-word and started jabbering that instead.

'Uplift' (I suppose) means 'increase'. Yesterday there were more uplifts in Labour's education policy than in a brassiere factory.

Teachers should be content, Mr Blunkett told Eric Illsley (Lab, Barnsley Central), 'once they get the £2,000 uplift'. A rise? But there might be inferior results in schools in poorer areas – or, as the MP put it, 'lower educational achievement through local income factors' – because of parents buying fewer books – or, as the MP put it, 'less parental engagement in the purchase of books'.

'We're about empowering parents and that means on this issue as well as on any other issue,' wittered Ms Morris to a Tory spokesman, John Bercow. 'There's bound to be a need to look at the allocation of special needs places at certain points in time.'

The Government would 'drive up achievement: a step change in the available range of attractive and accessible initiatives locally', hoped Ms Smith. By now, Mr Blunkett was in overdrive. 'I lifted the match funding for the excellence in cities programme,' he burbled happily. 'If authorities passport on the additional resources and you then ring-fence, the additional £2,000 uplift will be available on a ring-fenced basis!'

'We have to have additionality!' the Liberal Democrats' Phil Willis (a former teacher) cried to Mr Blunkett, who had hoped to 'uplift the employment and economic activity levels'. Mr Blunkett wanted teachers to 'access salary increases' (uplifts, surely?). Evan Harris, a Liberal Democrat spokesman, thought that mature students 'are deterred by tuition fees from accessing higher education' then used the word 'access' three more times in a single sentence. 'We're being very sensitive to the family dimension of this,' trilled Ms Smith. Blunkett was now yabbering about 'administrative holdback'.

Amid all this vapidity, Ian Pearson (Lab, Dudley S), who, since he was elected, has spoken in tones of increasingly baffled Black Country common sense, wanted extra money 'to encourage the best teachers to work in the worst schools'.

Surely he meant 'incentivise best-practice in schools where low-income factors apply, by ring-fencing salary uplifts for beacon-teachers passported to underachieving schools'?

They haven't found another word for 'schools', yet. But they will.

They did. Mr Blair has started talking about 'academies'.

Apologies and an Amnesty Are Offered

8.3.00

Sketchwriters, if we are not careful, cut off the branches on which we sit. We risk being so impertinent about the most exotic MPs that they go away, depriving us of colourful characters for our columns.

So today this sketch offers an apology, a pledge and one final impertinence. The apology is to John Redwood, the pledge to John Prescott, and the final impertinence about John Prescott.

I am sorry to have been so beastly about Mr Redwood: promise to stop being beastly about John Prescott; and ask leave for one last titter about his English before I reform.

To Redwood first. Come back Spock, all is forgiven: for we have seen your replacement. Archie Norman, the Tories' latest Shadow for Mr Prescott, isn't even lampoonable, he's just dreary. Yesterday it fell to him to answer a statement from the Secretary of State for the Environment, Transport and the Regions about the building of squillions of new houses in the South East of England.

We had not, before we heard Mr Norman, supposed it possible to yell and drone at the same time; to go completely over the top while touching new lows of tedium.

Archie Norman is astonishingly unremarkable, strikingly forgettable, monumentally overlookable, memorably dull. To declare, as he did, that Prescott's plans amounted to 'eight towns the size of Slough' somehow struck the keynote of his address.

So when John Redwood came roaring in on the theme of 'Berkshire Says No', to call Prescott 'two-Jags and one bulldozer' – for 'bulldozing his way across the face of rural England and deeply scarring the countryside' – we recognised the old spark, and missed him.

Norman shadows Prescott. Redwood now shadows Norman, showing how the Tory spokesman's job should be done. Britain's most famous Vulcan has become a shadow's shadow – more's the pity. This sketch repents.

With Prescott, we clowns of the press must not repeat our mistake, but appreciate him before it is too late. This sketchwriter begins tomorrow. For six months from March 9, I pledge not to mock his grammar. What follows, positively my last performance, is a final recital of Prescottisms for a single day: March 7.

Of Archie Norman ('a member of Asda'): 'The whole mistake he makes, which he clearly did not listen to, was the old 20-year protect and build process was one that you set out the target for 20 years then disaggregate the target down so that everything had to observe them based on the build for 20 years.'

Of high-density housing in a model village: 'I would say Poundbury is heavily condensed.'

Of a recent select committee report: 'It was helpful in arriving at some of these deliberations.'

Of planning requirements: 'Local authorities will have to show they are using the brownfield sites before the preference for greenfield sites.'

Of the communities of the future: 'The come-in tease of the future'.

Of soulless estates: 'We have build an awful lot of soulless estates, which is more concerned for building houses than building communities.'

Of a report by Professor Stephen Crow: 'I didn't accept the crow's recommendations.'

Of an apparent miracle of God or nature: 'We have increased the number of greenfield . . . sites since we came to power.'

. . . But enough. So farewell then, John Prescott.

I confess I shall miss your scowling features and tottering syntax, but it is time for a pause.

The mockery stops now.

This was disingenuous. I already knew I would be in the Southern Ocean for the period of my promise.

From March to August I took a break from Westminster to stay on the remote sub-antarctic island of Kerguelen in the Southern Ocean.

Lembit Saves the World   *19.9.00*

It's politics, Jim, but not as we know it. Yesterday, Lembit Opik rescued his planet from giant asteroids. And the Montgomeryshire MP did something much tougher: he rescued the Liberal Democrat conference from itself.

These days, politicians need to show they matter. Mr Opik proved this, big-time. The pale prophet showed us how, by voting Lib Dem, we could save the world from colossal lumps of rock ripping into us from Outer Space and killing everyone. In an epoch when politics has grown small, Mr Opik has found the big picture.

All weekend the newspaper placards had plugged *Big Brother*, fuel frenzy, Olympic dope-tests. In dejected groups Liberal Democrat delegates struggled through the Monday morning rain to the Bournemouth Conference Centre. One more gold for Britain in Sydney and they knew their annual get-together would be wiped from the news.

What could rocket their little gathering into the headlines?

Mr Opik's intervention was as bold as it was bizarre. At the eleventh hour yesterday morning, in a small room, he called an emergency press conference to break the news that the Earth is very likely to be smashed to smithereens, possibly quite soon. They are like buses, he said. 'You wait for one for a long time, then four come along at once.' He told us how, with Liberal Democrat guidance, our ghastly fate can be avoided for £4 billion. A penny on income tax to save the planet? It could be an election-winning pledge.

Prophets are too often without honour in their own party. 'People have tended to snigger,' Mr Opik said sorrowfully, 'when I say that the end of the world could be nigh from Outer Space.' But the paragliding, anagram-cracking Northern Ireland spokesman – mercifully recovered from a serious paragliding accident (some believe he fell off Paddy Ashdown's ego) – knows his subject. 'I have an astronomical background myself,' he told eight astonished journalists.

One of them asked how he answered those who thought he was talking tosh. 'When an asteroid actually does come hurtling at us,' he replied, 'I'll send them an e-mail saying "I told you so".' It did not seem to occur to Mr Opik that at such a moment other anxieties might be distracting them from their laptops.

I am ashamed to report that among press colleagues were cynics and doubters. 'Why don't you concentrate on earthling things like the excise duties on fuel?' asked one. Mr Opik snorted. Trivial! There was certain to be a major asteroid hit, perhaps soon, possibly on London.

'An asteroid,' he explained, 'would incinerate everything and kill everyone within the M25.' He had estimated the cost at £20 trillion. Three or four billion pounds to avert this began to sound like a snippet: 'Peanuts,' smiled Mr Opik. But how, we asked?

'Use rockets as tugs,' he said triumphantly. 'Or explode a nuclear device by the asteroid to give it a tiny nudge.'

Asked if he lost sleep worrying about annihilation, Mr Opik said he was sleeping better now his dire calculations had been proved cogent. If we are indeed sent spinning into oblivion, there will be one very happy Liberal Democrat among us. The MP, whose grandfather was an asteroid scientist, and whose warnings do appear to have been lent weight by a government report published yesterday, insisted that we are 750 times more likely to be hit by an asteroid than win the lottery. One journalist protested that he had seen a lottery-winner but never seen anyone hit by an asteroid. Well obviously, Mr Opik said. If they'd been hit by an asteroid they would have been completely squashed; nobody would be able to see them any more.

Apart from saving the world from annihilation, Liberal Democracy from irrelevance, and Monday from tedium, Mr Opik may have solved the riddle of Lord Lucan.

Welcome to Unreality   *21.9.00*

Re-entry into the political atmosphere proved difficult for me. A Lib Dem party conference was not an ideal place to start.

Dylan Thomas's 'Do not go gentle into that good night,/Old age should burn and rave at close of day;/Rage, rage against the dying of the light' was quoted by fatuous speakers in the debate on pensions.

So here goes. Rage follows. Rage against the dying of debate. Fasten your seatbelt for a brief interruption, for today drollery fails me. Normal service may be resumed shortly – if I have not thrown myself from Bournemouth pier.

What the flipping heck do these conference organisers think they are doing? What planet are they living on? How dare they ask us to report their conference as though it mattered? Are they deaf, blind, insensible to the world outside? These nerds have the balls to sit here – for a week, a whole *week* – holding what they have the cheek to call a political conference, whining, droning, gassing, giggling, squabbling, finger-wagging and nit-picking away about a load of total dog poo while, not a mile from the glass doors of their big, shiny conference centre, fuel frenzy grips Britain, housewives are hoarding bread, the Chancellor's been caught out in a serious fib and half the nation are tearing around like headless chickens.

Public confidence in the maintenance of essential supplies has almost cracked, the Government is in its biggest mess since being elected, the Prime Minister and the Chancellor fight for their political lives – *and the Liberal Democrat conference debates arts policy.*

What must a bemused public think, as they see politicians devote five days to discussing everything but the only thing anyone else wants to talk about? They are so busy holding seminars on listening that they can't hear any more.

What do those who arrange modern political conferences suppose such events are for? I mean – crikey – just look at the facts. Major political storm blows up. PM called back to Downing Street. Country inches away from grinding to a halt. Cabinet in crisis talks.

Newspapers, radio and television go ape. Foreign press describing Britain as descending into chaos. Desperate need for any serious political party to confer, discuss and take a view . . . but hang on! Stroke of luck! Sheer coincidence – one of the two big opposition parties on eve of annual conference. Hall reserved, accommodation booked, news media invited, seats, screens and microphones in place.

And they debate gay marriage. And the disestablishment of the Church of England. There was also a question-and-answer session with the Prime Minister of Belgium.

Snakes alive, it doesn't take an organisational genius to tear up the original agenda, scrap the debate on (say) 'planning policy', offer a representative of the protesting tanker drivers a platform to defend their action, invite an articulate green radical to make the case for fuel tax, challenge the chairmen of the big oil companies to defend their corner, offer the microphone to the NFU – and dare the other two political parties to put forward spokesmen of their own.

But no. All we got on the only national controversy anybody outside this hall is talking about, was a five-minute 'emergency' statement from a somewhat embarrassed-looking Charles Kennedy on Monday declaring that public protest should not dictate policy – before moving swiftly on to a debate on competition and social policy in banking, a policy paper on poverty and social exclusion, and the presentation of an 'award' to Baroness Maddock.

Welcome to Bournemouth: here by the seaside a thousand political journalists are trapped in the only politics-free zone in crisis-torn Britain.

Empty Even of Sound and Fury   *22.9.00*

We should be grateful for small mercies. It was short. There was no swagger, no New Jerusalem and nothing about proportional representation. Indeed there's an impressive list of things it wasn't.

The problem was to suggest anything it was. Charles Kennedy's closing speech was as flimsy as it was intellectually confused. This was sub-Blairite pap, Tony-talk, filleted of the really yukky bits, and pleasingly delivered. It lifted the spirits of a thousand Liberal Democrats, offended few, challenged nobody, and mildly pleased many.

Mildly. An encounter with Charles Kennedy is rather like an encounter with a ginger biscuit: underwhelming but in no sense disagreeable.

Not that we had been encouraged to expect too much. The party's new president, Lord Dholakia, told us he would first like 'to thank Vauxhall for the crash'. He may have meant 'creche'.

Other parties have music and balloons and hilarious warm-up videos. Liberal Democrats have a dreary party political broadcast and a fundraiser called Reg, with a white plastic bucket and a joke about wanting us to put a pee in it.

'Sadly as a party we are not as well endowed as the other parties,' sighed Reg (a number of wistful nods from young Lib Dems greeted the confession) before apologising for himself as a sort of unpleasant preliminary. But 'the leader's speech is the hot sex'.

There was a burst of taped music and the ginger blob came padding down the rostrum. This was not everyone's idea of hot sex. He adjusted his notes, and began.

'I was speaking with the Belgian Prime Minister,' he gurgled. One thrilled to Mr Kennedy's courage. What a risk – to use a reference to the Belgian Prime Minister as a way of firing up one's audience! There was respectful applause as the continental potentate's pilgrimage to Bournemouth was evinced as evidence of Mr Kennedy's international pulling power.

Then began the main body of his speech. 'Potentially,' he breathed, 'politics is at a crossroads.' It is very brave to start a keynote passage with the word 'potentially'. Abraham Lincoln never had the guts to try: 'Potentially, we hold these truths to be self-evident.' In my mind I toyed with 'Potentially, a wind of change is blowing . . .', 'Potentially, I see the Tiber foaming with much blood,' and 'Potentially, the lady's not for turning,' and saw the difficulty.

Kennedy sauntered blithely on. He has a pleasant voice, not unlike the bubbling of porridge on a peat-fired Highland stove. It soothes. He reached his punchline: his clarion soundbite. 'We can improve a lot on Labour,' he cried.

Wow! Who came up with that one? Now there's a tune Lib Dems can whistle! Mr Kennedy turned to doubting Tory voters: 'You have friends in the Liberal Democrats,' he hissed. Scary! A hundred pot-bellied, yellow T-shirted obsessives in the audience nodded menacingly. Great Scot, do they know where we live?

And then policy. 'I asked a panel of experts,' he confided, 'to report on what the Government should be doing.' (Hallelujah! cries a grateful nation.)

Like a lot of hot sex, it was all over too soon. Fair to mock but fair, too, to report that Mr Kennedy palpably won his audience's affection; he looked and sounded secure. He looked and sounded decent.

A limp text was delivered in a relaxed style, without all the crowing and clawing the air that, for a short season, Tony Blair persuaded Britain to confuse with oratory.

Most British party leaders speeches are full of sound and fury, signifying nothing. Charles Kennedy achieved his nullity without the sound and fury. For that, thanks.

25.9.00   # When a Door Isn't

I had just arrived in Brighton. 'This isn't a door,' she said.

It was a door. I could see it. So could she. It had hinges, a handle, it was unlocked, it led out of the conference centre, and I had passed through it earlier. But party officials wanted people to use another door. Fair enough: it's their conference. But it *was* a door.

Of course to say so would have been to admit to a conflict of wills, and in new Labour there is no conflict. There being no door, there could be no dispute. It is an Orwellian solution. There being no questions, there is no need for answers. And so Tony Blair's customary question-and-answer session at the start of the conference has vanished.

A Tory like me remembers the smell of a beleaguered high command, when Prime Ministers are scared of what the town mayor might say in the civic welcome (also wiped from this year's programme); when government limousines slide through the populace as grand persons hunched within – pale, shadowy faces, their electric windows up – turn their eyes away from the newspaper placards; when helicopters buzz in the sky, official spokesmen blame 'tittle-tattle' in the press, and only the bell-boys and policemen are respectful. I smell it again. I know the sound of an angry crowd beyond the crash barriers and tense line of policemen, heard dimly in the conference hall within. I know the smell of a political elite beginning to sense that its time, too, will come . . . for I remember Tory conferences in their last years. Is that the roar of the mob outside, mother? No, just the waves my dear, just the sound of the incoming tide.

I sensed it yesterday. The most tangible sign, a metaphor if you like, is The Bridge – or 'that bloody bridge,' as delegates and pedestrians, arguing with the poor constables on duty beside it, describe the ludicrous structure. A trade union has been stung for funds to construct a clunky overhead pedestrian walkway, from one part of the conference centre to another. Mr Blair can reach the podium from his hotel without passing ordinary people on the way.

Where once one had only to cross a street, huge fences now block the way. Delegates must divert up a sidestreet and climb two flights of stairs (the disabled go through a car park echoing with the barking of alsatian dogs) – to descend not directly to their destination but to an overflow exhibitors' hall where yellow footprints force them past Vodafone, the British Bankers' Association and Mercke, Sharp & Dhome stalls. Ministers, media and delegates are spared the taunts of demonstrators on the seafront and redirected to little plots rented by lobbyists.

In *Animal Farm*, the faithful, loveable horse, Boxer, his usefulness expended, is sent to the knackers by the pigs who took over. Even as the unmarked wagon carts him off to 'retire') the pigs are praising his endeavours to bewildered lesser animals.

Yesterday, in the main hall, Mo Mowlam peeped nervously through a side-door, then charged in, to be fêted by a happy-clappy corporate video (to the accompaniment of Robbie Williams) before making her retirement speech. It was dreadful; limp, tired and dispirited, and a sad swansong. From the unmarked van taking Boxer Mowlam away, some animals thought they heard the faint thud of hooves, desperately kicking the sides. No doubt we imagined it.

26.9.00

Even His Wife Got a Kiss

All at once the clouds parted. On a grey and gusty Brighton afternoon, as anxious Labour delegates looked out towards a stormy political horizon, a great bolt of sunshine burst through. For half an hour it lit the conference in a warm glow.

That sunburst was Gordon Brown. An eclipsed Tony Blair beside him resembled the other figurine on those revolving weather toys where, when the little man slides out, the little woman goes in, and vice-versa. The Chancellor slid out. The Prime Minister went in.

To misquote Wodehouse on Scotsmen, it has usually been possible to distinguish between Gordon Brown and a ray of sunshine, but not yesterday. He lifted Labour's spirits, and his own. He dared to enjoy himself. Once he even smiled.

So carried away did he become with the applause which then engulfed him that he kissed his wife. In public.

It was un-British, un-Gordon, and a tremendous hit.

Whatever happened to the grumpy Gordon we have come to expect at party conferences? Where was that lowered countenance and leaden delivery, that fist smashing down on the lectern?

Gone was the sullen glare, the swallowed words, the bullet-points of economic statistics hammered home like a list of indictments, his audience cowering in the dock.

It was plain before Brown started that the speech would soar. Cameramen scrummed around his new wife sitting in the front row as the Chancellor took the lectern; and from a handful in the hall he got a standing ovation before he had so much as opened his mouth.

Two rotten jokes were greeted with guffaws of delight. A litany of accusation against the Tories, each section ending 'where was Portillo?', found an audience ready to take up the chant. This conference was going to get this Chancellor airborne whether or not he found wings.

But he did find wings. Even Brown's hand movements have been liberated. Where once his gestures were limited to banging things, now his arms were outspread. Hand would go up, fingers extend, and sometimes he seemed to be reaching for his audience. A forefinger would be raised in accusation, a hand would slice the air, and once he clasped both hands before him, fingers earnestly intertwined, in idealistic appeal.

Mr Brown even invented a gesture new to Labour conferences, holding right hand out, with thumb and forefinger forming an O and the three remaining fingers fanned above. In Britain this can indicate precision, but on the continent I think it means something ruder.

One wonders which meaning Mr Blair took. Seated on the rostrum, the Prime Minister maintained a tense smile and led the ovation. From the start he looked drawn, as though life were being sucked from him.

Conference success yesterday was achieved despite the fact that the core of the Chancellor's speech was opaque: few had the least idea what he meant about pensions. Was it a lot of money, or wasn't it? What exactly *was* the difference between Brown's compassionate-sounding 'targeting' and nasty Tory means-testing? The complicated pledge was received with applause, amiable bafflement and (among a few) the suspicion that the wool might well be being pulled over their eyes.

But never mind. This conference – sour, uncertain and a little scared – badly needs someone to love and someone to love them.

After a seemingly unstoppable standing ovation yesterday, Gordon Brown had so much love to give that even his wife got a kiss.

Tony Sweats It Out   *27.9.00*

Dripping with sincerity and gushing with sweat, Tony Blair drenched his shirt and soft-soaped his party.

But Meatloaf got there first. 'I'll Do Anything For Love (but I won't do that)' runs the hit. Tony Blair would do anything for Labour, he told his party conference yesterday. Then, with a sob in his voice and perspiration on his brow, he reeled off a list of things nobody would have dreamt of suggesting he do anyway, and insisted that he would not, should not, simply *could* not do them.

They were incompatible with his 'irreducible core'. Irreducible core? Delegates looked a bit puzzled as Mr Blair launched this mysterious entity at conference. Was it something chewy you find in one of those smart Tuscan soups?

It was brilliant stuff: Clinton-with-a-hint-of-Widdecombe.

Under pressure from the old Labour Left, Mr Blair offered a passionate pledge to resist pressure from the extremist Right. With a mock-spur-of-the-moment delivery, and departing from his text, the Prime Minister cited things such as racism, xenophobia, slashing help for the poorest. 'Ah *can't* do i',' he protested, sweating profusely, accent dumbed down and estuarial glottal stop replacing his t's. The audience, moved, quite forgot that he was actually the Prime Minister and under no such pressure, and roared their support.

'That's right, Tony,' each kindly soul in the hall murmured inwardly, 'don't you let them force you!'

He could have gone on. 'Ask me to rip the ears off me old aunty, and ah've gotta tell yer, ah *can't* do i'.' *Wild cheers.* 'Ask me to legislate for the slaughter of the firstborn and ah've gotta tell yer, ah *can't* do i'.' *Audience weeps with emotion.*

Less effective with this audience would have been, 'Ask me to link old folks' pensions with younger folks' earnings, and put a penny on income tax to pay for it, and ah've gotta tell yer ah *can't* do i'.' But, irreducible as it is, even Tony's core has limits.

Whatever other cores this passage stripped bare, it was undoubtedly the core of his performance.

The rest (as befitted a speech prefaced by the pledge, 'This is not a time for lists!') was a series of lists: more lists, and longer, than in any speech I have heard from this Labour leader. There were 26 lists, containing 161 items and 71 figures. If this was not, as the Prime Minister acknowledged, a time for lists, God spare us when such a time does come.

Mr Blair's leadership of the Labour party began in a speech in Bloomsbury, his audience cowering under a barrage of abstract nouns. To what have we now come! A hail of Post-It notes, bullet points and killer-statistics.

It struck your sketchwriter that this speech won over two audiences.

The catch in the throat, the buckets of sweat, the whinnying insistence by the Prime Minister that he really did have principles, palpably moved his conference, of course. He moved much of the press, too, cynics being suckers for sentimentality.

Whether it will have moved the television audience, I cannot tell.

If only fitfully, few will have failed to thrill (as I thrilled) to Mr Blair's passionate protests and his confessional style. But it was the passion of an actor, not so much deceitful as self-induced.

Blair's is the best kind of acting, where the performer gets right inside the part, believing in and, for a while, becoming the persona he has taken. This is not to lie, but to become – to assume a mantle.

Yesterday the Prime Minister assumed it with energy and skill.

Lucy's Day at the Seaside   *28.9.00*

7am. How I hate party conferences. There's no Pedigree Chum in this flat and David – Mr Blunkett to you – has left my feeding bowl in London.

He may be Education Secretary but my master has no idea of canine psychology. 'Lucy,' he said, 'I've booked us a self-catering flat outside Brighton so you can go for walks and not feel caged in.'

Caged in? We're cut off. The rest of the Cabinet is at the Metropole, where they know how to look after a Privy Counsellor's guide dog.

It's not as if I'm *anybody's* curly-haired retriever. Self-catering – I ask you! And this his big day, too.

7.30am. Uh-oh, maybe not. Nobody on the television seems interested in my boss's Education debate today. They're all talking about a pensions row. Can't understand it.

We passed Alistair Darling, the Social Security Secretary, yesterday. Big man. But I smelt fear. We passed that Baroness Castle. Tiny woman, but I smelt defiance.

8am. I really ought to take David for a walk – he needs the exercise – but he's working on his afternoon speech. Don't know why he bothers. Tomorrow's papers will all be about pensions and the PM stole the boss's best bits for his own speech yesterday.

You should have heard the language in our car! I'd love to sink my teeth into Blair's calves.

9am. *Another* school walkabout. St Peter's, Portslade. These nursery schools are the worst: little brats pulling my tail.

Listened to the radio in our car on way back. All about pensions. Boss furious.

10am. The Grand Hotel. Nice carpets. Terrifying revolving door. Bellboy salutes me as we pass – or I assume it's me; no point saluting the boss.

We go upstairs to work on his doomed speech. Is that John Prescott? Lovely shiny fur, as dark as mine, not a hint of grey – and him all of 62! Maybe that's what Mr Blair meant yesterday about John being proud of his roots?

11am. Pfwoarr! It's Gibson, the golden retriever, in the foyer with his master, Wayne Busbridge, the guide-dog speaker.

Gibson and I trained together. Neutered, poor thing, just like the Cabinet.

11.40am. The rostrum. A thousand eyes upon us. I do love these moments. And they've put a bowl of water out for me. There's that Tony Blair a couple of chairs away. Sniff, sniff – hmm, changed his shirt since yesterday, thank goodness. Someone is talking about the Millennium Embroidery Project but at the back important people scurry in and out, huddling in knots to talk. Pensions, again, I drift off . . .

11.45am Oops! The master's on his feet. I leap to mine and lead him to the lectern. He pats me.

Applause. Shameless. Still, it could be worse: Sarah had to endure being *kissed* by Gordon.

Noon. The boss drones away. You can see the PM isn't listening.

Worried about pensions, I can smell it. Oh no, boss, not that baby Leo Blair joke again! No electricity in this debate.

I'll crash out by that backdrop for forty winks . . .

12.20pm. Come on, dozy delegates, on to your hind legs . . . that's better. Standing ovation – hope the boss realises. I wag my tail.

Cherie's clapping in the front row. The trouble she caused my boss by sending her kids to a posh school! I allow myself a tiny snarl in her direction.

Later we pass Lady Castle: striking little thing, all in green with big gold hair but very elderly, frail, and in a wheelchair. And so tiny!

What's Mr Darling afraid of? I sniff the wind. Boy is he scared! Any dog can smell it.

Mandela Survives Prescott Speech

29.9.00

Only Eric the Eel could have hoped for so rapturous a reception. Nelson Mandela was swept into the Labour conference yesterday more as a guest saint than a visiting politician.

As is the habit of saints, he went straight off-message. The former South African President spoke with restraint and dignity, avoided party politics, and stole into the hearts of every one of his audience. Even Alastair Campbell looked moved.

It must have felt like old times for Mr Mandela as he arrived to find white policemen videoing a chanting crowd of protesters held back by high-security fences. The Countryside Alliance was out in force for Labour's last day.

Before welcoming him, John Prescott, the Deputy Prime Minister, took a generalised swipe at 'the press' and 'the farmers', becoming increasingly carried away as he roared through his speech.

A Prescott speech gathering momentum is as terrifying as a runaway train. You know it can only end in a fearsome accident. 'She takes a lot of whack but she makes the organisation's there!' he cried, roaring to his theme, whatever it was. 'Here's a message to take out on the doorsteps!' 'Tory cuts highlighted in the beer-mat!' 'Free TV licences scrapped for over the four million pensioners.'

Waiting in the wings, what was Mandela making of this? Has word of the Prescott phenomenon reached South Africa? Thank heavens English doesn't have clicks as Xhosa does; the ricochet alone could prove fatal. 'We are poised,' bellowed the great communicator, 'on the greatest historic movement!'"

Upon impact with a full stop in the printed text, Mr Prescott's delivery buckles into itself like a train smashing into the buffers, carriages leap-frogging over each other. Whole clauses jackknife. 'Based on the social provision of treatment the basis of need,' he concluded triumphantly. Then (I think) he introduced the musical accompanist to the video we were about to watch. 'He's remembered for it ain't heavy he's my brother I'm my brother's keeper.' 'I will not pass by on the other side!' he yelled.

The conference loved it – and him. They loved Gabrielle, too, who sang 'Dreams can come true, you know you have got to have them.' Everyone except Peter Mandelson clapped along (Peter doesn't do clap-along) – Alastair Campbell banging his hands together ferociously as though crushing the testicles of an unhelpful journalist. Chris Smith, pink-faced and beaming, clapped blithely, slightly out-of-time. Fanfare over, it was now time for Mr Prescott to introduce the next visitor to the platform, a man (said the Deputy Prime Minister in tones of the deepest gratitude) who 'has just decided to become an honorary member of the Labour Party! So it is my pleasure to welcome Tony Blair' – he paused: grassroots activists looked mildly gratified – 'and Nelson Mandela.'

The hall went wild.

'I am intimidated,' began Mr Mandela, wryly. He then spoke with an almost sombre gravity which quietened at the same time as inspiring the conference. If organisers had hoped for an election endorsement of Tony Blair or his party, Mandela disappointed them at once. Quietly he told delegates that every Western political party had helped to oppose apartheid, each in its different way; and he thanked all allies of whatever party.

The former President then did an unheard-of thing for a visiting celebrity at a party conference: he made a substantial speech, containing real arguments. He held the hall in the palm of his hand.

Out on the conference floor, a home-made placard was held aloft by a delegate. 'We love you, Nelson,' it declared in big letters – 'and Tony'.

3.10.00   # Bunny Girls Witness Boris

Your sketchwriter hit Bournemouth at the same time as four bunny girls in leather trousers and tight T-shirts proclaiming 'freedom of information'.

The hotel porter eyed their fluffy bobtails as he took my case.

'Conservative, sir? I'd steer clear of them if I was you, sir,' he said.

Sadly, the bunny girls lacked accreditation and could not accompany me into the main hall. The place was packed and the mood more excited and confident than I have sensed at a Tory conference in years. This mood can now be manipulated (conference organisers hope) by special lighting, which changes colour according to theme. For the debate on immigration the spotlights will presumably turn white.

First came a fighting speech from Michael Ancram, party chairman.

A fighting speech from Mr Ancram is as about as common as a fierce denunciation by a guinea pig, but he did manage to inject a certain sing-song passion into his normally sepulchral tone, and sounded like a vicar on crack. So fired-up did he become by his own performance and the standing ovation that followed that he rushed at the platform party and kissed Ffion Hague – twice.

Poor Mrs Hague. She is in severe danger of becoming a sort of triumphal habit with senior Conservatives: *'Rousing peroration – standing ovation – acknowledge cheers – victory wave – kiss Ffion – exit.'* If this is the way top Tories are to behave whenever they think they are on a roll, she will have to leave town.

I followed the bunny girls into a fringe debate. We arrived in the middle of a fighting speech by Boris Johnson, the man the Tories have picked to contest Henley, where Michael Heseltine is standing down. Mr Johnson looked momentarily flustered by the bobtails and T-shirts, but then being momentarily flustered is Mr Johnson's stock-in-trade. He has been momentarily flustered for as long as anyone can remember, and his audience love it. Mr Johnson bids fair to become the Mo Mowlam of the Parliamentary Conservative Party.

To say that the blond-mopped would-be MP looked dishevelled, disarranged or unkempt would be to imply that he had formerly been kempt, arranged or shevelled, which is not the case. Nobody has ever seen Mr Johnson kempt and the suspicion grows that he sleeps standing on his head and re-rumples his hair regularly throughout the day.

The prospective parliamentary candidate for Henley had been asked to make the case for the Conservative Party, a task which appeared to baffle him. Britain needed fewer elected politicians, he insisted, 'there are far too many of us as it is'. A rueful smile betrayed some recognition of the internal tensions in his logic. The bunny girls began talking among themselves.

The chairman challenged each speaker to name one brave, unpopular thing William Hague should do. 'Wear a dress?' Johnson spluttered, momentarily flustered.

Then, lest he be thought facetious, he ventured 'call for the reintroduction of crucifixion?' The idea was met by a low rumble of support from root-and-branch Tory activists. Lest he be thought serious, a momentarily flustered Mr Johnson protested that if the challenge was to think of ways to make William Hague more unpopular, then 'my imagination just isn't up to it'. Bunny girls tittered. Aware that his statement might be horribly misinterpreted, Johnson became momentarily flustered, and retreated into a prolonged splutter.

On this man's gravestone will be engraved: '*Here lies Boris Johnson, broadcaster, journalist, and sometime MP for Henley. He was momentarily flustered. RIP.*'

Women With Big Hair Arrive by Car

4.10.00

How dare the media doubt the Tories' claim to be inclusive? Their conference menu yesterday offered the Baroness Thatcher for starters, William Hague as main course and Michael Portillo for pudding. Lady Thatcher scolded us in English. Mr Portillo shouted in Spanish, then translated. Mr Hague whinnied in Yorkshire, offering no translation.

We began with Lady Thatcher. As is the custom in Bournemouth, women with big hair arrive by car. But where poor Pauline Prescott invited national derision, Lady Thatcher simply thrilled. The world had been told to expect her at 09.15. By half past eight the crash-barriers were in place and world-class commentators, TV presenters, serious political analysts – grown men who have written books – were clinging to stairs and parapets in hopes of a better view. And this was just to see her arrive!

She arrived. A small motorcade swept up. She emerged from a deep blue Jaguar. The baroness was in royal blue with big gold buttons and a regal smile. Sir Denis Thatcher, beside her in greeny-brown Country-side Alliance chic, looked less then enraptured. Sir Denis does not do 09.15.

William and Ffion Hague rushed to greet them. There was none of the petting and air-kissing which now characterise party conferences. The Thatchers do not do touchy-feely. Mr Hague tried to shepherd them inside before the lady opened her mouth, for he well knows that, as Lord St John of Fawsley once remarked, 'the danger when Margaret speaks without thinking is that she says what she thinks'.

She intended to. Showing no inclination to be hustled anywhere, the baroness halted and peered at the cartload of media people spilling over the barricade. Selecting at random one half-prostrate figure and deeming this hapless journalist her interviewer, she gave a furious answer to a question nobody had asked.

The cowering hack blinked up from the tarmac as she insisted she had once been Minister of Pensions, then raged about Gordon Brown's dastardly plans to 'means-test' benefits old folk had worked 'all their lives' to fund. 'Outright fraud!' she snorted – and made as to walk in.

'Then why,' called BSkyB's Adam Boulton, 'did you cut the link between pensions and earnings?'

'Tax?' she shot back. '98 per cent when I took office. *Ninety-eight per cent!*' She spun round and made off towards the entrance with small, intent, bustling steps, like a purposeful partridge.

Not long after, William Hague showed us his own way of walking. He strode loose-limbed on to the platform, incredibly relaxed, to answer questions from Tory representatives. The questions were cringingly soft-ball. He was competent, fluent, pleasant and funny, answering every doubt except the most troublesome: what is he *for*?

Michael Portillo is a more troubled performer, and a more interesting one. His brave speech was rewarded by that warm Tory applause, with a hint of 'hmm, what have we here?' The Shadow Chancellor gave representatives a leadership speech.

As this came from the heart, he delivered it without notes. But he did once take out a little prompt-card – for the small part of his address relating to the Treasury.

Widders Hits Trouble

5.10.00

Like a giant, overripe, belligerent raspberry, a cerise-clad Ann Widdecombe promised 3,000 Tories to give their kids a whopping fine and a criminal record. Applause was hesitant.

The morning papers had predicted a thrilling 'Tory crackdown on cannabis' but as the Shadow Home Secretary spoke, some were thinking it through. What might it mean for young James in his first year at Durham?

Ann Widdecombe was billed as the event of the day, not least by Ann Widdecombe. But hers was not the first debate. After breakfast, David 'two-brains' Willetts, the dry-as-dust spokesman on Social Security, emerged blinking on to the podium to be confronted with something he may never have faced: a big, excited audience. They had come early on rumours that the supply of seats to hear Widdecombe would run out.

The lights went out as Miss Widdecombe entered, but representatives had to contain themselves, for the floor-speakers came first. This was the moment Tory hopefuls had been waiting for. What is it that makes perfectly pleasant, slightly podgy and otherwise bland young men in unremarkable suits leap on to a platform and start shouting about handcuffs, criminals and locking people away? What makes thousands of kindly and unthreatened elderly people trek to the seaside every year to applaud them? I do not know.

Or maybe I do, for as the gravity-defying Miss Widdecombe teetered on to the rostrum in brutally chunky Rosa Kleb high heels, and began to bounce about, your sketchwriter eyed the platform's false floor. A thin man could wriggle under from the back, wedge himself beneath the very boards where she pawed and snorted, and lie there with Miss Widdecombe stamping on top of him, her heels smacking into the platform and . . . oooh, stop me, I'm getting carried away.

Her audience this year were less so. Widdecombe badly needs new material. Everybody's doing the noteless 'personal' speech these days. Her jokes worked (though the sound of 3,000 Tories laughing is horribly reminiscent of the din of a massive penguin colony where each bird is guarding its patch) but her manic hand movements have lost the appeal of novelty. Her favourite is an extravagant pumping action with one arm, the other at her side. Widdecombe apart, only hitchhikers in

Africa use this gesture.

So she never quite got going. '23,000 convicts have been let out early!' she cried of Jack Straw's early release policy. '900 robbers!' '200 convicted killers!' 'Nearly 150 convicted of assaulting the police!' And Jonathan Aitken, one thought.

As Miss Widdecombe enjoyed her traditional standing ovation, representatives tried to sing 'happy birthday to you' but started in the wrong key and appeared to fumble for the words.

On the platform the chairman reached for a bottle of champagne as William Hague grinned. For a ghastly moment one feared he was about to break it across Miss Widdecome's bows.

Hague Flounders
6.10.00

After about 20 minutes of crackling humour and before William Hague's speech ran into the sand, I leaned over to the colleague next to me. 'Stop now,' I hissed. But he didn't. On and on it went. One had the distinct impression that Mr Hague had become bored by his own oratory. Everyone else was.

William Hague's speech was an army of lists in search of a theme. After what seemed like hours it seized upon something that almost amounted to one, then, for what seemed like another hour, beat it slowly to death.

The theme, I suppose, was 'people'. I counted 73 occurrences of the dread word. Be grateful for the small mercy that Michael Howard, who says, 'pipul', did not become Tory leader. The speech was peppered with 'people', 'real people', and 'all the people'. 'People' were sprayed everywhere. By the end of all this spraying, Mr Hague looked and sounded exhausted.

In fact he looked fairly exhausted by the beginning. Pale and quiet, the Tory leader sounded like a man who had just had the most monumental row with a friend, wife, traffic warden or railway guard.

At his best Mr Hague can achieve a certain cattle-auctioneering passion, but yesterday the rising cadences never rose. Perhaps he was trying to sound thoughtful, perhaps he was cross, or perhaps he was just tired.

'Didn't Michael Portillo make a fantastic speech and show what a brilliant Chancellor of the Exchequer he'll be?' droned Mr Hague, of the man whose failure to do more than mention in passing his own portfolio had reportedly roused the Tory leader to a cold fury.

'Hmm,' chorused Tory representatives. (Actually they chorused 'yes', but I translate.)

'Wouldn't it be great to have a real Foreign Secretary, like Francis Maude?' Hague bleated. The giant video screen showed Mr Maude, apparently almost in tears. 'The depth of talent that would give us a great Home Secretary in Ann Widdecombe!' he intoned, of the woman from whose wild policymaking on Wednesday morning Mr Hague had spent much of Wednesday afternoon desperately rowing back.

Then, after some good jokes, Hague ploughed into 'the people'. In place of some unifying principle of how government best serves people, the Conservative leader began to make a list of all the people he would help. The British population being quite large, this was potentially a lengthy business.

'We know who we are and what we promise to be!' he cried. 'Glad someone does,' your sketchwriter muttered to himself.

Conference organisers had adopted the risky strategy of screening, for a warm-up, a video of their leader at his best. Sadly, this was followed by a real-life example of their leader at his worst. The comparison was invidious. The video was brilliant: a sort of 'here-is-one-I-prepared-earlier' *Greatest Hits of Hague* in the Commons. We saw him skewering Tony Blair.

It was electric. Your sketchwriter reflected that this was possibly the first time in history that recordings of a leader's parliamentary performance had been used to gee-up a party conference, and it was a good day for the House of Commons, whose chamber Hague uses to such devastating effect.

But Tony Blair had proved easier to face than three thousand grey Tory heads in Bournemouth, who wanted to believe in him as more than just a handy weapon against an unpopular Prime Minister but instead as a positive force in his own right.

At the end they applauded loud and long, but more than a few had to wake up in order to do so.

Reasons a Speaker *Must* Be Found

24.10.00

As Dr Thomas Stuttaford might write: 'Is it healthy for an 84-year-old gent to be trapped for an eternity after lunch in a cramped seat in a hot hall with no evident access to a WC, while 500 MPs pepper him with procedural questions, insist on endless divisions and make him stand up and sit down every few minutes for three hours?'

Poor Sir Edward Heath. As the afternoon wore on and the snowy-haired Father of the House surrendered all expectation of bringing the choice of a new Speaker to an early conclusion, I watched that soft, puffy, sardonic old face. Hope gave way to resignation. Resignation yielded to discomfort. Discomfort turned to despair.

From time to time, bewigged Commons clerks seated beside Sir Edward (an empty chair behind them) would hand the member for Old Bexley and Sidcup little postcards. Some supposed these to be procedural advice but, squinting down from the Press Gallery, I could almost discern the message: 'Hold on old chap, only a few hours now'.

There was a moment's false promise when, halfway through the afternoon, the Liberal Democrats' Alan Beith (Berwick-upon-Tweed) suggested a way out of Sir Edward's dilemma. 'If hon members want an early tea,' he urged, 'elect me now.' But they didn't. Tactful Gordon Prentice (Lab, Pendle) added to Sir Edward's discomfort by suggesting to MPs that Heath had 'one last service to render his country'.

The grotesque procedure MPs adopt for this election is best compared to a coconut shy. Sir Edward surveys the list of wannabe Speakers and asks one of them to be coconut. He chooses another to take a shot. If the latter knocks the former off his perch, then *he* gets the chance to be coconut. If not, another wannabe is chosen to take a shot at the surviving coconut. Eventually, all other coconuts having been dislodged, the surviving coconut wins.

Yesterday Sir Edward selected Michael Martin to be coconut number one. All shots taken, none knocked him from his perch. Mr Martin therefore became Speaker.

In the best traditions of British democracy, the winner had made the worst speech. The Member of Glasgow, Springburn, is not the only drongo in the House, but up there with the most drongoid of the Commons drongos. Commending him, Peter Snape (Lab, West

Bromwich E) told MPs that Mr Martin came from a single-parent family and that his father had been 'torpedoed three times'.

Thus was the challenge laid down for supporters of any rival contender to prove that their man had been abandoned at six months in a telephone kiosk, and his foster father torpedoed *four* times. Ambitious young MPs had better get their dads torpedoed fast. How broken does your home have to be (and how torpedoed your father) to equip you to be Speaker of the House of Commons? The great Victorian constitutionalist Sir Walter Bagehot is silent on this point.

Sir Alan Haselhurst (C, Saffron Walden) aroused some brief support by praising the former Speaker, Betty Boothroyd, for her 'lashings of good sense'. At the conjunction of the words 'Betty' and 'lashings', male Tories stirred interestedly. Might Sir Alan smack them? This looked hopeful.

Gwyneth Dunwoody (Lab, Crewe and Nantwich) made a fine speech: passionate and impromptu, more an aria than a manifesto. Sir George Young (C, Hampshire NW) was civilised, lucid, earnest and funny, impressing all sides of the House. Naturally, both were rejected.

Stop Press: 5.53 – mercy prevails. Sitting suspended for seven minutes. Sir Edward pops out. The *relief*!

Blair Deploys the B-word

26.10.00

Tony Blair torpedoed the Tory High Command at Prime Minister's Questions yesterday, wounding their Commander-in-Chief, Field Marshal Hague.

The damage was inflicted by a single missile: the B-word, 'Bandwagon'.

The Leader of the Opposition was complaining noisily about the price of petrol. The Prime Minister had his answers, but it was when he reminded MPs of the Tory leader's initial refusal to call for cheaper petrol that the lethal weapon was deployed. William Hague, said Mr Blair, used to scorn the idea, refusing (as Hague had put it) 'to ride around on whatever bandwagon comes up'. The Government benches went wild. Tories went quiet.

Blair was in expansive form. Casually he anticipated the next

Budget's proposals for domestic rates on second homes. With a wink he as good as told David Winnick (the Labour MP for Walsall N, who campaigns for compensation for former Far-Eastern prisoners-of-war) that this too was on its way.

The Chancellor was not there to see two crowd-pleasing titbits snatched from his planned announcements.

Poor Gordon: nips off to Montreal for a couple of days and what happens? Tony raids the Treasury's sweetie-jar and hands out toffees to the backbenchers.

Sir Edward Heath missed a surprise too. The Father of the House, on a brief visit to Tokyo, was not in his place to receive in person that rarest of tributes: a kind word from his own party. The unheard-of compliment was paid by William Hague. The end of Sir Edward's 50 years in the House would be 'regretted by all parties', suggested Hague. The two men presumably loathe each other so Heath will be sorry not to have been there to look grumpy in person.

A Parallel Passing World   28.10.00

From the Spectator: *I took time off from Westminster to encounter a world of those I had forgotten . . .*

Welcome to the Hotel California, except that it was not California but Park Lane, and the hotel was the Grosvenor House. Though mirrors weren't on ceilings nor the pink champagne on ice, we were all just prisoners there, of our own device.

Court & Social columns are not my *métier*, but the guest list at the Foyles 70th anniversary literary luncheon last Wednesday, 18 October, was so extraordinary, so gilded, so melancholy as to be a period-piece in itself. A last snapshot of a departing time, you might say, except that the time had long departed. Only the people were left behind.

I am no Samuel Pepys, but public moments that seem indelible in a thousand minds fade quickly if nobody writes them down. There must have been almost a thousand people, of whom nearly 250 were 'guests of honour'. So much honour! Honour's battalions extended across six top tables; a 'top' top table, and beneath it a sort of tournament of top tables.

The seating plan on which I rely charts the field of contest. On paper, the line-up emerges peppered by a hailstorm of decorations. Just a couple for Sir Nicholas Henderson, GCMG, KCVO, a modest three for General Sir Peter de la Billière, KCB, KBE, DSO. At four, the Rt Hon. the Lord Carrington, KG, GCMG, CH, MC was numerically honours-even with Field Marshal the Rt Hon Lord Carver, GCB, CBE, DSO, KCVO; yet in this war of acronyms, both were outgunned by Marshal of the RAF Sir Michael Beetham, GCB, CBE, DFC, AFC, DL, FRAeS.

On the 'top' top table, James Callaghan's last chancellor sat almost next to Margaret Thatcher's first foreign secretary. The Rt Hon the Lord Healey of Riddlesden, CH, MBE and Lord Carrington found them-selves to the left of the principal guest speaker, Mr Ned Sherrin, CBE. The Baroness Thatcher herself was to Mr Sherrin's right. Lord Tebbit had been mischievously seated between Lady Thatcher and the German Ambassador.

Lady Thatcher has never been one for staring around. But had she looked along the seats to her right, her eye – lighting briefly on Lord (Kenneth) Baker and lingering perhaps a moment longer on Lord (Cecil) Parkinson – would have passed three ambassadors, the New Zealand High Commissioner and five peers, as well as her husband and Penelope Keith, before reaching her host, Christopher Foyle, and his wife. Glancing now to her left, she would have noticed two more ambassadors and the Australian High Commissioner – if she were not distracted by Lord (Bill) Deedes, the Duke of Devonshire, Lord Snowdon, Lady (Barbara) Castle, Sir Hardy Amies, Sir Ludovic Kennedy, and others equally illustrious.

And that was just her side of the table. Across it, Katie Boyle, Nigel Nicolson, Dame Norma Major, Sir David Frost, the Lords Cranborne, McAlpine, Biffen, Carr (Robert), Rawlinson (Peter), Mackay of Clashfern, Fellowes . . . oh, where shall we linger? Not by the barons alone, but by the court jesters, troubadours and travelling players too: Harry Secombe, Alan Whicker, Robert Robinson, Thora Hird. Many of the surviving members of the Thatcher, Callaghan, Heath and even Wilson Cabinets were there.

Lady (Mary) Wilson herself was seated between Norris McWhirter and Lord Ryder. Richard Ryder was once Mrs Thatcher's private secretary, later John Major's chief whip, and now sat not far from Uri Geller, looking across at Chapman Pincher. The Thatcher-impersonator, Janet Brown, and Lord Saatchi were close by.

'I've recently become a surrealist,' said Ms Zsu-Zsi Roboz, an artist beside me, and I think I knew what she meant.

Further up the table, Lady Thatcher's head of the Civil Service, Lord (Robert) Armstrong, was within her direct eyeline, though it was Sir Bernard Ingham who will have had the full force. Peering past them (and past Ann Leslie's mischievous eyes), she may have noticed two former editors of the *Times*. Except that she looked a little tired. She hates other people's speeches. She always has.

A certain ennui seemed to dog Denis Healey, too, though when he spoke he gallantly kissed her hand. By the seventh speech it was nearly four o'clock and a number of noble guests were nodding off. It didn't matter. They had nowhere to go. Little that anyone here said mattered any more. Little that anyone here thought was any longer of much account.

In private conversation Mr Sherrin seemed to get on well with Lady Thatcher, though when the jokes in his speech bordered on the risqué, she fixed Norman Tebbit in determined small talk. As Gyles Brandreth began a joke about marijuana the small talk became quite intense.

But she sang along when Larry Adler played the mouth-organ. Nothing in Auberon Waugh's short speech upset; Frederick Forsyth's thoughts seemed to please; and Christopher Foyle was heard with the respect due to our host.

I found the occasion strangely moving and strangely sad. There was almost nobody there representing the 'new' Labour dispensation. Apart from Lord Bragg, seated opposite Lord Mishcon, Tony's cronies do not do the literary lunch. This was the old guard, *l'ancien régime*. One bomb could have taken out most of what's left of the 1970s, almost all of the 1980s and much of the 1990s. Whole lives must have scrolled before the eminent throng as they surveyed their fellow diners in the vast, ornate, yet indefinably tatty dining-hall. Every one had mattered once, very few did now. Thus it must be to die and find oneself in some Elysian field among all the great and the good from an era in which one had spent one's prime. These our actors were all spirits, projected out of air, out of thin air. Their revels were ended. They would soon vanish.

These people had done so much. We owed them – I owed them – so much. On the original canvas their portraits had radiated such potency. Now cut out and glued flat on to the baseless card of a bookseller's fantasy seating plan, the montage was unreal. Elbowed into a new era which they had helped to create but which was not their era, they looked displaced, faded, insubstantial. Bric-à-brac. These were people who could now lunch until tea. They had nothing else to do. The next time many would meet again would be at each others' funerals. I was put in mind of those Russian émigrés in 1920s Paris still toasting the Tsar.

Every age has its monarchs and their courts. Around Margaret Thatcher last Wednesday sat the courtiers, inquisitors, propagandists, scribblers, soldiers, philosophers, jesters, hairdressers and spies who had once dominated the epoch. But the Queen is dead – long live the King! It was a very 20th-century lunch: one of the most glittering, perhaps the saddest, maybe the last.

1.11.00 **Prescott's Warming Warning**

He warned the cockles of MPs' hearts. John Prescott yesterday updated the Commons on 'the global warning'. The warning has triggered what the Deputy Prime Minister called an 'extreme weather event'. This was no government health warming, but might be defined by Mr Prescott as the opposite of the chill wind factor.

The global warning – as Prescott explained to astonished MPs – necessitated pumps for what he called 'water floods'. Other extreme weather events include a coastal battering by sea-waves, and recent snow blizzards and wind gales, but the Secretary of State for the Environment, Transport and the Regions did not specifically mention these in his word-statement.

Nor did he refer to the recent gussets of wind. As Mr Prescott warily circles his lifelong adversary, that Moby Dick of the Hull East MP's political career, the English language, it is as important to make clear what he did not say as to clarify what he did.

Extreme weather events were actually in his prepared text. 'We tend to plan for cases which are a lot less than we can readily expect,' was not.

So we really must stop planning for Deputy Prime Ministers which are a lot less than we can readily expect, because Mr Prescott is a lot more. Prescott is himself a sort of extreme weather event. Terrifying to think that (if Chaos Theorists are right) the flap of a single butterfly's wings in the Amazon tree-forest causes Mr Prescott in the Commons. That butterfly should be found and immobilised at once.

Not least because the Deputy Prime Minister exerts a baleful influence on all around. The junior minister next to him, Beverley Hughes, puzzled MPs when she told Tim Collins (C, Westmorland & Lonsdale) that 'this statement makes a very good case of contrasting the record of the previous government with that of the last'. Mr Prescott glowed like a proud dad beside her.

His Liberal Democratic Shadow, Don Foster, also succumbed to the Curse of Hull. 'Could I just join with the Deputy Prime Minister in joining with him in the expressions of condolence to the bereaved?' droned Mr Foster, more of a light drizzle than an extreme weather event.

'There is a lot more lessons to learn' yapped Archie Norman, the Tories' touch of frost to the Cabinet's Hull hurricane. 'The Deputy Prime Minister said that hardly anyone mentioned the environment,' complained the Liberal drizzle, Mr Foster – then added Delphicly: 'I wonder who he was referring to?' Hardly anyone, surely?

More questions than answers . . . such was the tone of yesterday's statement. As the general election approaches, sentences which in the heady days of Labour's 1997 election victory would have carried exclamation marks are now offered as ruminations on the meaning of life and the extreme difficulty of getting anything done.

Even an event as extreme as Prescott moved to interrogative mode. 'We have to ask ourselves,' mused the Humberside philosopher, 'should our power lines come down every time we have such storms?' Indeed. 'Should one thousand trees fall across our railway lines in the South East?' Most pertinent. 'Are our drainage systems really adequate?' You tell us, John.

Moving from statement to tutorial, Mr Prescott looked alternately fascinated and perplexed by the teasing nature of his own questions. One recalled Tony Blair's recent remark about cannabis: the idea horrified him, he murmured – but could that be because he was out of touch? We await new Labour's election manifesto: 'This Government has achieved much. *Discuss.*'

Dead Verbal Flowers

2.11.00

Can we have a parliamentary ceasefire on condolences to the bereaved and tributes to the emergency services?

Too much Commons time is being taken up with the laying of verbal wreaths and the presentation of verbal posies.

Someone has told Tony Blair that he does funerals well.

Ever since the death of Diana, Princess of Wales, this Prime Minister's talent for the graceful tribute and propensity for the suppressed sob has served him well, and he has noticed. No opportunity for a prime-ministerial squeeze to the shoulder of those who have lost a hero, friend or colleague is now missed.

Last Wednesday, on his first appearance at the dispatch box after the recess, Mr Blair locked straight on to auto-tribute.

There being 659 MPs of whom not many are young, the Great Actuary in the sky can be relied upon to pluck one or two from our midst every year. MPs having set out on a very long summer holiday from July to October this year, two fewer came back.

The tribute to the late Donald Dewar was perhaps expected, but Mr Blair had already given it. He gave it again.

Then there was the late Audrey Wise, a serious leftwinger and no friend of Blair's new Labour project. In death she got a whole paragraph. And of course there was Sir Edward Heath, happily still with us. He had announced his intention not to stand again. He, too, was offered a verbal hug.

The next MP to speak, Andrew George (Lib Dem, St Ives) was then obliged to associate himself with these tributes.

And when the Leader of the Opposition rose it would have looked graceless for him not to do the same. But William Hague, whose style is essentially brisk and unsentimental, does not do ceremony as well as Mr Blair. The switch halfway through Mr Hague's question, from tribute to shin-kick, looked ungainly. Mr Blair looked states-manlike.

This Wednesday at Prime Minister's Questions, Blair was at it again.

We began with a tribute to the emergency services, local authorities, police, etc., who had coped with the effects of the recent bad weather.

Then there was the Prime Minister's sympathy for the many personal tragedies caused by the storms.

Tributes and sympathy were offered with gravity and poise. 'Hear, hear,' murmured MPs. They could hardly do otherwise. Brave would be the parliamentarian who rose to declare: 'That's as may be, Mr Speaker, but what's so remarkable about the emergency services dealing with emergencies?

'Isn't that what they're for? At least these men and women get overtime, which is more than we do.

'As for my Rt Hon Friend's sympathy for the bereaved – sure, he's sorry. We're all sorry. But more than twice as many die every day on the roads as died in that Hatfield train crash.

'We don't start each Commons day by extending our condolences. And, though it's obviously a shame that people have had their lounge carpets ruined by the floods, none of those hundreds of thousands who lost everything – sometimes their lives – in the floods in Mozambique even had carpets to start with, let alone home insurance.

'Couldn't we all agree, Mr Speaker, to take it as read that politicians sympathise with loss, mourn the dead and applaud the emergency services; and instead of parroting the niceties, get on with politics?

'All these tributes don't half cut into the afternoon . . .'

Brave, I say, would be the parliamentarian who spoke thus. Nobody did. Nobody will.

Standard-issue MPs
3.11.00

The modern car, mass-produced for the global market, needs to be easily adaptable for left-hand and right-hand drive. So the body and fascia are designed for either, with a dual set of holes for steering column, gearshift and instrument panels.

Left or right-hand drive can be selected at a late stage in manufacture, and the instruments sited as appropriate. Dummy holes are covered up; but this is cosmetic; it remains possible to make the switch later in the vehicle's life withour serious re-engineering.

MPs are like this too. They are manufactured for use on either the Left or the Right. Before sale to the electorate they are equipped and marketed as 'left' or 'right', but their instrument panels and stick-shifts can be swapped over in a few short weeks in any reputable workshop, by means of a simple socket-set, a few screwdrivers and a Whip.

They just have been.

Labour is now the crisp-suited party of law 'n' order, showing its fist to the unwashed mob; the Conservatives have donned donkey jackets, scrawled home-made placards, and slyly ingratiated themselves with *hoi-polloi*.

Leaders of both tendencies paraded yesterday in their new livery.

Outlining to the Commons his plans to foil the fuel protesters, the Home Secretary, Jack Straw, took his recently right-hand drive Labour backbenchers out on to the road for an exploratory spin as hardline upholders of the Rule of Law. And if Ann Widdecombe didn't quite lead her rabble over to the Left in a shout of '*oggie-oggie-oggie/Oi! Oi! Oi!/6-5-4-3/Gi'us a cut in fuel dut-ee*,' you could tell she would have liked to.

Labour were the disciplinarians now, their backbenchers driving on the authoritarian Right as though they had done it for a lifetime; the Tories have crossed over and happily flirt with the revolutionary mob, thrilling to public anger.

During the poll tax protests a decade ago it would have been the other way round. Your sketchwriter was in the House in those days and remembers the posture of both parties. Yesterday each produced a mirror-image of what the other then displayed. You would have to have had a heart of stone not to smile.

In those poll-tax days, Margaret Thatcher's Tory army barked the slogans of authority. Yesterday it was Jack Straw who (insisting that he did respect the right of 'peaceful' protest) spluttered about the need nevertheless to resist those who would 'prevent law-abiding people from going about their business'. In those poll-tax days, the 'hear-hears!' came from the Tories. Yesterday they came from behind Mr Straw.

In those poll-tax days, the Tory Government knew but could never quite make the Opposition admit that the Labour Party secretly sympathised with the disruption. Labour played the game of wanly deploring disorder, and loudly trumpeting the reasons for it.

Yesterday Jack Straw and his supporters knew, but could not quite make Ann Widdecombe and her Tory gang admit, that they would greatly enjoy the trouble the protesters were threatening. Routinely she agreed that she could not of course condone disorder; fiercely she rehearsed the grievances which had caused it. And sometimes it seemed to be the Labour Left whose fist itched most to smash popular dissent. For circuits wired to crush the class-enemy, substituting one enemy for another requires only the throwing of one simple switch. Gordon Prentice (Pendle) wanted to toughen up the law.

Dale Campbell-Savours (Workington) wondered angrily where we would be if every Tom, Dick or Harry could block the roads in his favourite cause. Michael Connarty (Falkirk East) demanded that broadcasters be censored from publishing information about fuel protesters' gatherings.

How easily memory is blanked. Mr Campbell-Savours ended his rant with the cry: 'Who runs Britain?'

Wasn't that Ted Heath's cry in 1974?

Mini-budget Becalms Tories   *9.11.00*

Seldom in the field of Commons conflict has so much wind been taken from so many sails by a single speech.

As the Chancellor spoke, the Opposition sea across the Commons floor reminded us of a regatta suddenly becalmed. Jibs (and jaws) hung limp; spinnakers (and speech-notes) dropped. Mainsails (and mouths) flapped. As Gordon Brown warmed to his theme and Labour's cheers rolled, only Peter Mandelson on the carpet looked more disconsolate than the Tories.

As soon as Mr Brown began talking about Prudence we knew we were in for a bit of slap-and-tickle. The more a Chancellor mentions this lady, the less he honours her. I counted seven occurrences of her name. 'Stability' got quite an airing (eight references); when a politician speaks of stability, prepare to rock.

Dark-eyed, black-suited and inky-haired, Mr Brown had developed an alarming passion to lock things in. He promised to 'lock in stability', 'lock in fiscal tightening', 'lock in a fiscal stance' and 'lock in a *tight* fiscal stance'. You could almost hear the snap of buttocks clenching along the government front bench as spending ministers complied.

Like some latter-day Calvinist dominie, this Chancellor takes a lip-smacking pleasure in pronouncing words like 'prudence', 'lock' and 'tight fiscal stance'. His jaw works, his tongue explores his teeth and his bitten fingernails scrabble excitedly at the top of the dispatch box. He slips sinful-sounding syllables into familiar words: yesterday we heard about his fight against 'poll-yew-tion', lending it the loathesomeness of the sewer.

As well as sin, there was mystery. Mr Brown wanted to stick 'vignettes' on lorries. Old-Labour MPs on the government back benches looked baffled. *Vignettes?* Wasn't that a variety of spectacles – or perhaps something you put on your rocket-and-radicchio salad in Islington? Or were all continental trucks now to sport poncified little oil-paintings-in-miniature on their windscreens, to show they were French?

I can't wait to hear John Prescott wrestling with that word. Just on the offchance that he's reading this sketch, let's parade before the Deputy Prime Minister's eyes a selection of decoy-words to confuse him: *vinaigrette, lorgnette, launderette, courgette, winceyette . . .*

The Tories, original proposers of this idea for making foreign lorries pay, like to call it a Brit-disc, so Mr Brown needed a different name. It baffled his backbenchers. But then most of his statement did. They could tell it was good because it had upset the Tories but they were a bit hazy as to what it actually meant. Every now and then Brown would throw in a word or phrase his gang could understand; this was seized upon with relief by those behind him, anxious faces lighting up momentarily in recognition, followed by a grateful bark of *hear-hear*!

A Gary Larson cartoon contrasts what we say ('Good dog, Rover, heel, Rover, look after Grandma, Rover') with what dogs hear ('*blah-blah* Rover *blah* Rover, *blah-blah-blah* Rover'). We might likewise contrast what the Chancellor said (there were 17 pages of this) with what Labour backbenchers heard: '*Blah, blah*, statistics, *blah*, contaminated land, *blah-blah-blah*, flats above shops, *blah*, reduce VAT for church repairs, *blah, statistics, blah*, repay Britain's debts, *blah, economics*, 3p off petrol, *blah*, Ford Focus, VW Golf, Astra, Rover 214, *blah . . .*' Every time the poor creatures heard a word they understood, they gave it a great roar of applause.

Michael Portillo never had a chance. Unable to find poise or stride, his attacks on Mr Brown hit home but rarely. Only when they did, did Peter Mandelson smile.

10.11.00   # Every MP's Nightmare

It is a recurring nightmare. The circumstances may alter but the horror stays the same. We awake sweating from a dream in which a curtain is rising and we are meant to perform – but somehow cannot.

Stone Age man, dreaming in his cave, supposes himself drying up in the middle of telling a camp-fire tale. The Druid tosses in his sleep, tormented by images of a Stonehenge ritual at which he was supposed to take a leading role – but failed to turn up, having gone to the wrong stone circle.

The gladiator dreams of forgetting his sword, the newscaster of a frozen Autocue. Each hell is private, but the underlying pattern is stamped into the circuitry of the human psyche. We awake, shaking, until the sweet realisation steals over us: *it was only a dream.*

Except that for Nick Palmer (Lab, Broxtowe) it wasn't.

Dr Palmer stands out from the new Labour replicants who crowd the government back benches. Shambling, stooped and indefinably asymmetrical, he looks a bit odd: the sort of fellow Labour's Millbank image-managers would encourage to stand at the back (not too close to Tony) in 'election triumph' photos of the parliamentary team.

But he speaks thoughtfully and rarely parrots a line or descends to name-calling. Dr Palmer is conspicuously his own man.

So we marked the margin by his name in Questions to the Chancellor. His written Question – 'What representations has he so far received on his Pre-Budget Report?' – would require an answer from Gordon Brown himself. It offered leeway to discuss almost anything. Dr Palmer would have something to say, and the morning after the Chancellor's big announcement was an important time to say it. We made a mental note.

Unfortunately, Dr Palmer hadn't. He had clean forgotten.

There was a reason, and subsequent inquiry has established it. Mrs Palmer had been taken ill earlier, happily only temporarily. Distracted, her husband had then struggled to Westminster. Perhaps he noticed fleetingly from the television monitors that in the Chamber the Chancellor was on his feet for Questions. From whom, however, had slipped his mind.

It did not slip the minds of Brown's aides. As questions proceeded and Dr Palmer's moment approached, they spotted his absence. One tore out to track him down. Far from the chamber and with seconds to spare, Dr Palmer got the call. All this we have learnt since . . .

But what we saw then was a flinging-open of the doors, through which lurched a panting Dr Palmer, face white.

He just made it to his seat as Mr Speaker called his name. Hardly time to sit down before rising. His chest heaved. Gasping for breath, he tried to speak.

It was not clear to this sketchwriter that the MP had had time to think of anything to say. He reeled forward to steady himself on the seatback before him. The whole House – even the Chancellor – was roaring with laughter. Staring wildly round and still trying to breathe, Dr Palmer asked Mr Brown to do . . . er . . . something (*pant*) . . . er . . . more for . . . er . . . (*pant*) disabled drivers.

Ah – the disabled: every politician's default option. MPs cheered.

For the rest of us, another wet Thursday, another Chancellor's Questions. For Nick Palmer, a living nightmare.

Pleasure No Peer Should Be Denied

14.11.00

The Bill equalising the age of homosexual consent must not pass. It must stay in the House of Lords for ever, batted around in perpetual debate.

Talking about unusual sexual practices affords peers such pleasure that it would be wrong to deprive them (or Britain) of the fun. One baron started fantasising about an anal spliff.

The Baroness Young could not stop saying 'buggery': 'far more important', she said, 'than the Dome'. The trim baroness had devised amendments of such fiendish complexity that to explain them she had to say 'buggery' repeatedly.

Buggery in England with men *and* women, buggery in Scotland with girls under 18, buggery at 17 in Northern Ireland with either sex . . . on and on she went. For variety the baroness would sometimes say 'sodomy'.

Then she would toy with 'anal intercourse'. Lady Young coined the phrase 'the age of buggery', which I momentarily supposed to be her grand summary of the epoch, England having made the sad and Gibbonesque decline from the Age of Empire and the Age of Steam to the Age of Buggery.

'Now I turn to girls,' she said, rather severely. The Press Gallery (infested with sketchwriters) was by now giggling disgracefully at imagined double-entendres.

'For girls the position is quite different.' We were unclear what position Lady Young had in mind, but 'my amendments maintain the position'. More giggling. Of all types of love-making (she advised), anal intercourse is 'the most dangerous sexual practice'.

'Not in my experience,' came a fearsome growl from the *Independent*'s seasoned sketchwriter, who has been to New Zealand.

'Let me quote from the manufacturers of Durex,' continued Lady Young, remorselessly. Condoms seemed to excite their lordships and ladyships greatly. One wonders whether the Baroness Seccombe, in her days as a deputy chairman of the Conservative Party, ever realised where it would all end: hitting *www.lovelife.org* on the Web, then leaping to her feet in a crowded chamber to trill that 'condoms are available in all sorts of colours, shapes, flavours and sizes' as peers reeled back, aghast.

Lord McColl of Dulwich, too, wanted to talk about condoms: specifically 'slippage rates'. In trials (he said) the slippage rate was 21 per cent. Peers longed for Lord McColl to tell them exactly how the trials were conducted, but on this he was vague.

And then there was Lord Selsdon, who took the opportunity (these are rare) to share his thoughts on things you could put up your bottom.

Drugs, for instance. You can, he revealed, 'stuff them up your rear end'. Nostrils (he added) were another orifice you could insert things into, though we trust he was only talking about drugs here – and perhaps jelly-babies.

'I find it difficult to use the word "buggery" for the first time in this House,' he said, rolling the word teasingly around in his mouth, 'but then I thought back to my days in the Army and how it used to be a friendly phrase – "well I'm buggered!".'

The Earl of Longford insisted that homosexuals 'should not be condemned'. The earl (94) illustrated what he meant by not condemning: 'homosexualism' was a sad disorder, he said, like schizophrenia and chronic alcoholism. Seduce a girl of 16, he added, and that was a dreadful shame. But seduce a young man and he would 'become a rent boy'.

Lord Selsdon said that he had 'eaten the private parts of a green monkey'.

Please, Mr Blair, don't take this Bill away from them.

Is Hague Losing it?

16.11.00

Is William Hague losing it?

While I was away, from March until the summer recess, word reached me in the sub-Antarctic that the Tory leader was knocking Tony Blair all over the shop. I returned to Westminster to watch the hammering resume.

On MPs' first Wednesday back, there was certainly a hammering: Blair hammered Hague. His taunt about the fuel protests – that the Tory leader jumped on every bandwagon he saw – hit home.

The next Wednesday saw Mr Blair return to this theme. Last Wednesday he accused Hague of 'bandwagonism'. And yesterday, recalling the Opposition Leader's sudden interest in flooding, he mentioned his surprise that 'the Rt Hon Gentleman's bandwagon is amphibious'.

The Tories do not like this. Nor do they like Blair's remarkable success in turning the Dome against the Tories. The PM now cleverly insinuates that Hague used to be a supporter of the project. Yesterday he had a killer quote from a Shadow Culture Secretary, Peter Ainsworth, suggesting that we should all get behind the Dome and join the party. Hague's too-clunkingly pre-scripted gags died.

But, like a cartoon mouse, the irrepressible Yorkshireman pops back up after each mauling to tweak the feline Blair's tail. Yesterday he tried the latest scare about a European 'superpower'. Could he think of a single superpower that has not had an elected head?' Hague taunted.

Hmm. Ancient Egypt? Rome? The Holy Roman Empire? The USSR? China? . . .

'America!' shouted some wag. Hague's onslaught collapsed amid laughter. The Tory leader joked that it was 'easier to get a straight answer from a Florida recount than from the Rt Hon Gentleman', but we could almost hear him scrabbling at the clingfilm in which this drollery had been wrapped. The cold ham curled.

Spending Goes Off-message   21.11.00

Spending has been abolished. According to weekend press reports, a secret Labour memo advises ministers and backbenchers that the words spending, spend or spent are no longer to be used. 'Spending' apparently sets off the wrong vibrations in our feeble little brains. It makes us think that under Labour our taxes may have gone up, or may in future. This, as we know, is a wicked Tory lie.

So instead, Labour's spin-machine is advising MPs to use words which subliminally nudge our thoughts in another direction: away from the movement of cash – *off-message* – and towards the solid results – *on-message* – which will surely come from it.

How, you ask, do ministers talk about spending without saying spending? It's really quite simple. Other words do a similar job but with more productive vibrations.

Chief among these is investment. Any fool knows that an investment has a return. Investing is what wise people do for perfectly self-interested reasons. An investment is made for the purpose of getting back more than you put in. Investing is all about prudence (another of the Chancellor's favourite words). Spending is about recklessness.

In the old days, if a government service cost more to run than it yielded back, the difference was called a subsidy. This was a really off-message word as it suggested loss-making. Subsidy (*boo!*) was paid for out of taxes by a process called 'state spending'. But the word was abolished the day that Labour came to power, and since 1997 there have been no subsidies, only spending.

Now spending, too, has been banned. All we have is investment.

So when Gordon Brown splashes out on an extortionate and gaudy silk tie, and Sarah Brown raises an eyebrow, he has not spent £61 on a tie, he has invested £61 in his public profile. And when Alice Perkins (the wife of the Home Secretary, Jack Straw) nips out to buy a packet of Weetabix, she is not spending £1.79 but investing a further £1.79 of new money in the larder. She is also investing in her family's health.

How do I know this? Because of the Questions Mr Straw's poodles have been submitting for oral answer (by him) at Question Time yesterday.

The thought may strike you that if Mr Straw came up to you and said 'Will you ask me this question next Monday, so I can tell you the answer?' you might reply 'Why don't you just tell me now?' The suggestion betrays your naive ignorance of the British constitution.

Of course, it is not inconceivable that Betty Williams (Lab, Conwy) and Fiona Jones (Lab, Newark) were separately and simultaneously seized with a desire to know how much money the police will be getting in the financial years 2001–02 and 2003–04; but how odd that one asked: 'What resources will be invested in the police service?' while the other wondered 'what real increase in investment in the police service' could be expected.

Straw burbled merrily about investment. Other poodles inquired about (and Straw answered on) the 'allocation of funds'. 'Putting resources into' was another favourite ('into' – like a piggy-bank, see?). Next time you go down the pub, remember, you're putting resources into Whitbreads.

Thanks heavens, then, for old Labour's Tynesider, Ronald Campbell (Blyth Valley), who had indeed been down the pub, to study the Pubwatch scheme. Mr Campbell was impressed. He asked ministers 'to give more money' to the scheme.

Give? More? Money? Off-message, Ronnie.

Road-testing New Model Leaders

30.11.00

Late in the season, three new models of party leader were road-tested at Prime Minister's Questions yesterday. The Hague Mark II was taken for a first spin; results were mixed. The New Blair made an encouraging debut but narrowly avoided a nasty skid; while the latest Kennedy (sports version) left critics scratching their heads.

The Hague Mark II represents a striking change for this familiar Tory marque. The earlier versions (dubbed 'the Tory Bandwagon') has proved a jolly people-carrier, with its shiny top and cheerful joke car-hooter both notable features. But some felt the built-in red nose on the grille detracted from the more serious tone which those marketing the model needed to achieve. And there was a difficulty with the tyres: the PM was learning how to puncture the Hague's jokes. Another problem was that whenever this people-carrier tried to go anywhere (except away from Europe), passengers started baling out.

Yesterday at the dispatch box there were no jokes, little insult and no Europe. William Hague lowered his voice and persisted in the boring-but-important question of reduced numbers of care home beds. Later he tried a seriously pointed question about community health councils, momentarily cornering the Prime Minister.

Reaction was not ecstatic, but at least there were no accidents or punctures. Overall verdict: *are the makers sure that after subtracting the joke-features, enough appeal remains for buyers?*

The New Blair is much toned down on the previous model. 'Classic' Blair has proved a noisy and ostentatious design. The constant revving and triumphal honking irritated road-users; nor did the Blairs' tendency to cheat by sneaking into bus-lanes, please fastidious customers.

Automotive designers had for some time been keen to enhance the authority and command of this marque, reducing the noise. To reposition the Blair it was necessary to replace some of the flashiness with understated torque and a more dignified performance. Consultants had suggested a sleeker car with smoother gearbox and quiet overdrive, better adapted to giving way, merging – and even U-turning – when necessary.

Yesterday at the dispatch box Tony Blair cut out most of the crowing and shouting. When asked whether care bed numbers had reduced, he admitted that they had. He looked relaxed. There was less scrabbling through his notes and finger-pointing; and, when suggesting the Opposition sort themselves out, he sounded almost meditative.

Critics' reaction was generally positive. Once – when the Tories exposed some blatant corner-cutting on community health councils – the New Blair was outmanoeuvred by the Hague Mark II. The Blair had switched lanes, pretending that 'consultation' about the abolition of CHCs meant asking people what should replace them. When the Blair tried to switch lanes back, the car almost lost adhesion; but the spin was well handled, a crash was averted and the vehicle roared off again. Backbenchers cheered from behind the Labour barriers.

Overall verdict? *A much-needed addition to the range.*

The problem with the Kennedy lies in identifying its niche. Do potential customers want an aggressive performance-model designed to burn off the competition, or do we prefer something more sedate, to be garaged alongside the Blair while offering the discerning buyer a marginal advantage over the Labour model? On yesterday's performance, the verdict remains unchanged: *persistent failure to decide its market.*

The latest Kennedy sported a sunroof and go-faster stripe. At Questions the Kennedy tried to cut-up the Classic Prescott, suggesting the Blair should sack him. We cannot say the Blair looked greatly ruffled by the thought.

7.12.00   # Why Does She Bother?

Three famous people seemed differently to express the same question yesterday: 'Why did we bother come?'

The scene was the Palace of Westminster. The occasion was the first Queen's Speech of the millennium. And the first to wonder what on earth she was doing there was Her Majesty the Queen.

She had arrived, after a prodigious amount of the prancing about in fancy dress which the British call History, in her Royal Coach, preceded by about ten car parks'-worth of shiny Mercedes-Benz cars conveying ambassadors of every hue: that class of personage the little people in Africa call the *waBenzi*.

Once the *waBenzi* were sitting comfortably in the Lords Chamber, the lords – or *izinkosi* – arrived, in very great number, swathed in pelts and accompanied by their wives in bangles of dizzying variety and price. Then a witchdoctor dressed in black with a black spear, called Black Rod, was sent to fetch the ordinary warriors – or *impi* – from the Commons. The *impi* are not permitted to sit, but stand at the back looking warlike. And, after a blast on some antique brass horns, and preceded by some court officials wearing carpets and walking backwards, the *Indlovukazi* arrived.

This sketch hastens to point out that in the Bantu languages the expression Great She-Elephant – *Indlovukazi* – connotes authority and wisdom, not physical size.

Be that as it may, speaking from her Lords throne the *Indlovukazi* looked thoroughly bored. They had given her nothing to say.

All that polishing the Royal Coach, all that grooming and braiding in the royal stables, all that clip-clopping down from Buckingham Palace with a veritable cavalry of riders and horses, all that neck-wrenching struggle with the pesky Crown – and for what? A paltry little speech containing a handful of half-baked proposals. And then *clip-clop, clip-clop* all the way back.

As your sketchwriter surveyed the regiment of municipal pooper-scoopers at work after the horses had gone, it struck me that seldom has so much manure been strewn over Westminster's streets in so meagre a cause.

Something of the same distaste seemed to infect the Prime Minister later that afternoon. For the first time in my recollection the House was not full for the Debate on the Gracious Speech. After two ceremonious little speeches from government backbenchers, the Leader of the Opposition opens these debates, and William Hague had got off to a splendid start, cracking jokes, teasing the Prime Minister, haranguing the Government Front Bench and temporarily infusing the Tory troops behind him with the confidence they seem so to have lacked.

Then he got on to policy. And somehow it all slipped away. The old problem arose again: many cogent criticisms and a handful of ideas, but no theme, no tune, no rhythm. Like so much about Mr Hague this was a medley not a concerto, and a cover version at that. Polished to be sure, but what was he there for? As the quarter-hours started to drag, Mr Hague ploughed gently into the swelling hubbub around him.

Tony Blair rose to reply. He sounded confident, dismissive, throwaway. Hand on hip he sauntered through an argument or two, achieved one aphorism ('he hasn't even the courage of his own contradictions') then, noting that the Opposition had lost the heart even to interrupt and his own side were no longer bothering to cheer, laid aside his notes and wound up.

Frankly, my dears, he didn't give a damn.

Number of the Beast

12.12.00

After publication, I was alarmed to receive many inquiries from MPs and journalists who assumed this was true, or partly so.

The most remarkable change has come over Tony Blair in recent weeks. He has stopped shouting. The crowing, finger-stabbing hyperbole has gone. In its place a weary rationality and quiet, almost amused, command is creeping in.

It has never been so strikingly displayed as yesterday, as Mr Blair came to the Commons to report the conclusions of the European Summit at Nice. William Hague was there to tackle him. Never once did the Prime Minister shout at the Tory leader. He just teased him. Teased him into a smoking heap.

To any shortlist – and short it would be – of Mr Hague's big failures at the dispatch box since becoming Tory leader, yesterday's performance will now have to be added. It sounded frankly barking.

Blair flattened him, his victory toe-curlingly, complete. None survived except in pain: Tory wounds were horrible; Labour's sides ached with laughing.

Hague seemed incapable of seeing anything but villainy and surrender in everything Tony Blair had brought from Nice. But to all but the Tory Eurosceptics it seemed more likely that the Nice summit was a messy compromise in which the British position had been more or less maintained.

The lurid colours that Hague tried to splash upon a landscape characterised by shades of grey caused first bemusement and finally hilarity. He walked straight into the Prime Minister's trap. Blair was able to ridicule Hague's fist-shaking defiance towards unnamed 'concessions' by naming a few – like the abolition of the national veto over the European Court of Auditor's Presidents' pension. It left Hague looking simply nutty.

'And isn't it perfectly clear,' thundered a Tory backbencher, puce with horror, 'what's behind all this?'

A hush fell upon the Chamber. What *was* behind all this? Lowering his voice, the Hon Member continued. 'I ask Hon Members to consider that infamous European programme, the Common Fisheries Policy, or CFP. How many letters are there, Mr Speaker, in the word 'common'?'

A pause, for Hon Members to count. 'Six,' growled Dennis Skinner (Lab, Bolsover).

'Correct. And now, Mr Speaker, will somebody tell me what – if we number the letters of the alphabet – is the number taken by the letter 'F' for "FISHERIES"?'

'Six,' came the responding shout from MPs.

'Correct. And now the last of the trio. How many letters in the word "POLICY"?'

An appalled hush fell upon the Tory benches. Bill Cash (C, Stone), Iain Duncan Smith (C, Chingford & Woodford) and John Redwood (C, Wokingham) stared out, aghast at the realisation dawning upon all.

The voice of Teresa Gorman (C, Billericay) trembled as she called: 'Six'!

You could hear a pin drop. 'Well Mr Speaker,' the Hon Member concluded, almost in a whisper, 'what do we have? Six-six-six. The number of the Beast.'

Angela Browning (C, Tiverton & Honiton) fainted. Shouting now above the ensuing din, the Hon Member could just be heard. 'CFP – six-six-six! Number of the Beast!

'And which European Commissioner, a traitor to our own party, shares those initials?'

At first, nobody got it.

'Christopher' (*Hon Members:* 'shame*') '*Francis' (*Hon members:* 'shame') 'Patten' (*Opposition Members scream with rage and horror.*)

Readers, I made that last bit up. But if you think that doing so took much imagination, then you were not in the Commons Chamber yesterday.

I cannot explain (as in another context Sir Edward Heath once remarked) the Tories' approach to Nice yesterday: I am not a doctor.

Mr Patten rang me the following day. The number of his hotel room that night had been 666. Honestly.

Mr Vaz Begins to Wobble   *13.12.00*

Yesterday in Parliament, MPs threw biscuits.

Despite compelling reason to believe otherwise, Keith Vaz is a government minister. Responsible for European Affairs, Mr Vaz is the clown who told us that the Charter of Fundamental Rights carried no greater authority than a *Beano* comic. He has been rather out of the public eye since.

Perhaps to remedy this, at Foreign Office Questions, he tried a few more capers yesterday.

Young Vaz began modestly by insulting the chairman of the

Conservative Party's backbench committee on European Affairs. John Butterfill (Bournemouth West), a man of quiet authority, had asked a difficult question about conflicts between the Nice treaty and other treaty obligations. Mr Vaz didn't know the answer.

When you don't know the answer it's often best to say so.

Mr Vaz decided to mock the questioner. Mentioning Mr Butterfill's committee (and mistaking his post) he said the MP ought to know the answer better than he did.

Well done, Keith. There's one respected senior MP you have managed to antagonise. Mr Butterfill complained bitterly to the Chair.

Next, the Shadow Chancellor, Francis Maude, rose to question Mr Vaz. Mr Maude, a clever, thoughtful, rather vinegary man, had criticisms of the Nice treaty.

Faced with criticisms, it's often best to answer them. Mr Vaz decided instead to insult Mr Maude.

The Foreign Secretary (he said) had worked until 4.30 on the previous morning to get the treaty right. 'The only time he [Maude] is up at 4.30 is when he comes staggering out of the Carlton Club.'

It is just possible to imagine Mr Maude emerging wearily from a reference library at 4.30am. He isn't even a member of the Carlton Club. Anybody less likely than this dry stick to stagger, least of all from a club, let alone in the small hours, is hard to imagine. Sitting beside Vaz, Robin Cook, the Foreign Secretary, looked embarrassed. Go for it Keith! You've irritated your boss too. Lesser men might have thought this enough.

Now, however, came his special stunt. To cheer the Tories up, he sneered, he had brought them back a present from France. The minister then pulled out a packet of Nice biscuits.

Doubtless he planned to fling them dramatically at the Opposition Front Bench, but bottled out. The biscuits fell limply on to the table. Mr Cook winced. It wasn't clever and it wasn't funny.

When you're in a hole it's often best to stop digging.

Mr Vaz dug. Next up was a Tory spokesman, Cheryl Gillan. Mrs Gillan, a conscientious and public-spirited woman of moderate views whose mother has recently passed away after a long illness, asked a serious question suggesting that the Prime Minister might have wrongly informed the House about a removal of the national veto. Right or wrong, it needed looking into.

When a question needs looking into, it's often best to undertake to do this: Mr Vaz decided to deride and patronise Mrs Gillan. She should 'stop getting too excited'. She obviously had 'problems understanding'. She should educate herself by visiting his ministerial website and putting her questions to him there.

A number of new Labour women, sensitive about sexism, looked underwhelmed. Attaboy, Keith – *go! go! go!*

Watching Mr Vaz, it struck your sketchwriter that these were just the sort of flip misjudgements which would have wrecked my own front-bench career, had Providence not intervened and rescued me from that wrong-turning.

Failing Providence, the Prime Minister may have to rescue Mr Vaz. As I left the chamber, the biscuits were still at the dispatch box. They may outlast Mr Vaz.

They did.

Prescott Grapples with His Feminine Side

14.12.00

Is Britain ready for the Browning Experience? It startled MPs yesterday.

Loose comparisons are sometimes made between our House of Commons and a Punch & Judy show, but at Prime Minister's Questions the analogy was exact. John Prescott met Angela Browning head-to-head and there was a lot of bellowing and caterwauling. He bopped her and she bopped him. Nobody lost and nobody won. Nobody emerged any the wiser. It was glorious, pointless Christmas fun for all the children.

Mrs B had been sent to question Mr P because the Prime Minister was away with Bill Clinton in Northern Ireland. Since Prescott was deputising for him, William Hague had sent a deputy of his own: Angela Browning, Shadow Leader of the House.

Never has the word 'shadow' been so misapplied to a woman. Parachuted in at short notice, Mrs B hit the Tarmac screaming. She seemed to be in a permanent high-octane, high-octave rage. There were so many things she wanted to be cross about that they all got jumbled up and came tumbling out in a top-speed, turbo-charged, stream-of-consciousness twitter. In its higher ranges Mrs Browning's voice is audible only to bats, fatally interfering with their radar systems. She must never be allowed to speak in caves.

Prescott's radar went haywire too. The Deputy Prime Minister got his knickers (not to say his parts of speech) into quite a twist and roared and growled and tripped himself up, variously committing the Government to regional parliaments for England, describing himself as an Opposition spokesman, and lashing out violently at the *New Statesman*, probably by mistake. 'Local government finance is a matter of considerable controversial,' he snorted, in one of his more lucid asides.

Our Angela put a number of us in mind of a character in Richmal Crompton's *Just William* series: Violet Elizabeth Bott. The insufferable little girl expressed her profuse and various furies by forever threatening to 'thkweam and thkweam until I'm thick'. Mrs Browning thkweamed and thkwearmed until Mr Prescott was sick. She thkweamed about Europe, thkweamed about the railways and thkweamed about train timetables. Once she got going on the rail crisis, she built up such a head of indignation that she all but came off the tracks. Someone should impose temporary speed restrictions on Mrs Browning, for fear of cracked rails.

Prescott seemed by turns intrigued, rattled and appalled at the Browning phenomenon. He howled, she shrilled. He stumbled, she tripped. He lunged, she bobbed . . .

. . . And all at once it dawned on us. Angela Browning is John Prescott's Tory *alter ego*, four octaves and one socio-economic grouping up. John and Angela – what a coupling that would be! Think of the noises, think of the carpet, think of the damage. As he trumpeted and she screeched, the grisly truth dawned upon their appalled audience: John Prescott was getting in touch with his feminine side.

Come Back Marina – and Bring Your Spike

15.12.00

Your sketchwriter's Thursday morning started with a visit to the dental hygienist to have my gums poked, and continued with a visit to the

Commons to hear MPs arguing about statistics. One sounded like a bit of an ordeal, the other might be rather fun, I thought. I was right.

The dental hygienist was called Marina. Inviting me to sit down she gently reclined my backrest until I was flat on my back. Then she turned on the radio – some light clubby-type music was playing on Capital FM – and got to work. I shut my eyes and prepared for the worst.

And it really wasn't that bad. The little metal spike pricked a bit, but not seriously. The dull vibration of the polishing thingummy which removes tartar was somehow soothing. As I settled back (and Madonna billed and cooed from the radio set) a mood of relaxation crept over me.

Marina, who was wearing a mask and latex gloves, began a serious prodding and scratching between my molars. On the radio, Des'ree began to sing.

I felt increasingly content. Admittedly my posture was undignified and there was always the threat of discomfort – but the matter was out of my hands. I was blessedly released from the need to understand anything or follow what was going on. Relaxed, I began to nod off. The flossing I remember only intermittently. When I left they gave me a free toothbrush. I drifted down from Old Street to Westminster. There was no more pain to fear.

I settled into my all-too-upright bench seat in the Commons Press Gallery. It was 11.33am, time for Treasury Questions.

And they all began shouting at each other. Gordon Brown shouted 'e-commerce' and 'IT' at the Tories. Tories shouted 'Answer!' back. Mr Brown shouted '£180 billion . . . public investment . . . 6 per cent in real terms . . . skills upgrading . . . I'll take no lessons from the Tories . . . 10 per cent . . . 3 per cent . . .'

I was beginning to miss Marina.

Mr Portillo flew into a rage. He accused Brown of lying. '3.1 per cent . . . 1.3 per cent . . .' I tried to take all this down. What did it mean? Who was right? My stress levels were rising. Couldn't someone just floss my teeth?

'Competition white paper!' roared Brown. '. . . 2 per cent, *2 per cent*, 2.4 per cent.'

'No, 3.1 per cent, 1.3 per cent,' whinnied Portillo. 'Fundamental yardstick . . . CBI . . . IoD . . . £5 billion extra taxes!'

'We are proceeding with the Climate Change Levy!' yelled Brown.

I gave up trying to take notes. The attractions of the dental surgery were growing fast. That throbbing de-tartaring thingummy had been so much more bearable than this.

The Chief Secretary, Andrew Smith, rose. Mr Smith speaks as though someone had tied a tourniquet round his throat. 'Appalling Tory legacy . . . share of taxation *this* year, share of taxation *last* year, share of taxation *next* year . . .' Smith's whine rose to the pitch of a high speed drill. Couldn't I have my gums poked with a metal spike instead? Or a tooth removed?

But all at once calm was restored. Stephen Timms, Financial Secretary, was on his feet. Quiet, competent and matter-of-fact, Mr Timms was actually trying to answer a problem an MP had raised. Stress-counts began to tumble: this at least was tolerable, as tolerable as Marina's surgery.

Then I realised why. Timms is no politician: he's too sensible. Alone on his Front Bench, Mr Timms could have been a dental hygienist.

20.12.00   **That Elusive Rubicon**

A commons debate on embryology shows MPs in a different light. The five political senses cease to serve a politician.

Gone is any clear view of the party political street map. Gone are the admonitory noises – the grunts or clucks from whips and business managers – which alert backbenchers to the approved line. Gone too is touch: a Member's feel for how this will play on the constituency doorstep and where the votes lie.

Gone is the taste of power: that salty savour which guides the young hopeful keen to know what's cooking. Gone, even, is the sniff of political ideology: there's no Left or Right in medical ethics. The politician in an MP is left in a state of total sensory deprivation. Chickens would keel over and go to sleep.

Amazingly, MPs don't. They come alive. Debating draft regulations under the Human Fertilisation and Embryology Act yesterday, our Commons became a new place.

It would be tempting here to murmur sagely that when MPs cast aside party and seek consensus we see 'the House at its best'. But the House is at its brain-numbed worst when MPs try to agree. Yesterday they

were not trying to agree. Members divided instinctively into two parties
but they were not political parties. The parties in the embryology debate
were (depending on your view) Science versus the Inquisition, or
Frankenstein versus Faith. Which of those descriptions you choose
would in itself be a good indication of your party.

Leading for Science (or Frankenstein) was Yvette Cooper, a junior
minister whose poise and command is perhaps the only thing on which
both sides yesterday would have to agree. Though never stumped for a
scientific answer, Ms Cooper was anxious to disclaim the mantle of
Frankenstein. In a tear-jerking passage during her hymn to the healing
potential of the 'stem cell' research that this proposed regulation would
permit, she told us that 'this is about the woman with Parkinson's who
struggles with speech so cannot sing nursery rhymes to her children;
this is about the grandfather who cannot enjoy his grandchildren
growing up because of the devastation of a stroke'.

Leading for Faith (or the Inquisition) was a core of MPs which
included a number of Roman Catholics and other convinced Christians.
Ruth Kelly (Lab, Bolton W, RC) intervened to suggest that cell nuclear
replacement (which helped to produce Dolly the sheep) would be
boosted by the regulation. Edward Leigh (C, Gainsborough, RC)
thought that the research pointed towards the cloning of humans.

'Don't clone Tories, whatever you do!' cried an alarmed Dennis
Skinner (Lab, Bolsover).

Lined up on the Labour front bench, silent as Ms Cooper shone, were
two other junior health ministers (John Hutton and Gisela Stewart) like
stem cells, hoping to be selected one day. These cells, sang Cooper, 'are
plenipotent: they have the potential to become anything – and therein
lies their power'. How very new Labour. But this was not a day for
ambition, but understanding. I was amazed at the depth of knowledge
and thoughtfulness that the debate uncovered on the back benches.

Your sketchwriter's bent is towards the Science (or Frankenstein)
side of the argument. But it was hard not to sympathise with the forces
of Inquisition (or Faith) when Ms Cooper told doubters that 'Parliament
is not being asked to cross the Rubicon'.

Parliament somehow never is. Parliament is assured either that the
Rubicon has yet to be crossed, or that the Rubicon was crossed long ago.
The crossing itself takes place always in the night.

Running With Fox and Hunting With Hounds

21.12.00

The loudest sound in all of politics is barely audible to non-politicians, but MPs heard it yesterday as the Home Secretary unveiled his Bill on foxhunting. A soft, slippery hiss filled the chamber, slid around the oak-panelled walls and insinuated itself amongst the rafters. It was sly, it was subtle and it was seductive.

It was the sound of a Government slithering out from under.

Jack Straw had fought his way into the Palace of Westminster through a near-riot of pro-hunt protesters, barred from the precincts by police officers with dogs trained to detect the faintest scent of tweed, corduroy or cavalry twill. Protesters should have stayed their wrath: in his red box Mr Straw carried a Bill that was not so much a draft Act of Parliament as a loose-leaf folder from which MPs and peers could rip out, amend, or insert whatever they fancy – and take as long as they liked about it, preferably a very long time indeed.

'What's the time, Sir Edward?' a colleague once asked the former Tory MP, Sir Edward du Cann.

'What time would you like it to be, dear boy?' Sir Edward replied.

'What does your "Hunting with Dogs" Bill say, Home Secretary?' a young MP might have asked yesterday.

'What would you like it to say, dear boy?' was effectively Mr Straw's reply.

He offered what he called a 'multi-options procedure'. Some people would call this a cop-out. Not content with focus-grouping the voters, before deciding what to believe, the government front bench is now focus-grouping Parliament, too.

'Normally,' Straw told MPs, a minister at Second Reading would explain what the Government hoped to achieve.

But with this Bill 'the content is not decided by Government'.

Then he explained the four options open to the House; by rejecting the Bill they could reject all regulation; if they accepted it they could choose from its selection of measures ranging from self-regulation, through statutory regulation, to outright prohibition. MPs looked variously intrigued, suspicious or just plain baffled.

And Straw's own preference? He told us. He couldn't care less and thought the whole ruddy fuss a bore, a distraction and a nuisance. But as Home Secretary he was forced to take a view on the confounded business – so he'd be voting for the most toothless option with any chance of success. Should this fail in the Commons he'd make sure the Lords got a chance to reinsert it.

Or rather, being a politician, he said: 'Some hold passionate views, but as it happens I am not one of those people and, during my 21 years' membership of this House I have never voted on any Bill on hunting. But since I am the minister sponsoring this Bill I have had to consider it in more detail than might otherwise have been the case.' He would be voting for statutory regulation, and, successful or not, would see that 'the Other Place is given exactly the same choice between the options'.

MPs who cared to amble for half a mile through the winter mist down Victoria Street would have found for sale at Politico's Bookshop a postcard depicting Tony Blair inspecting a range of actor's masks: happy, sad, relaxed, resolved. 'Show me the mood of the people,' runs the caption, 'and I can match it.'

Yesterday Jack Straw offered the House a Bill of a comparably chameleon quality. They can make of it what they will. It's out of his hands now. Phew.

Is This What's it's All For?   *22.12.00*

Not with a bang, but a whimper, or rather a grunt. On their last day before rising until 2001, Members of Parliament yesterday discussed pigs.

Easy to mock, but you will never properly appreciate the way an Hon Member sees things unless you suspend your disbelief and, for a moment, try to enter his world.

Though the great issues of contemporary history flit briefly across his horizon, his gaze is more often fixed on the ground close to his feet. Including pig-sties.

Pigs matter if pig farmers are among your constituents, for pig farmers have had a dreadful year. Thus it was that Nick Brown, the Agriculture Minister, was faced at Questions yesterday, the last before Christmas, with a barrage of MPs as anxious as they were knowledgeable about pigs.

Any minister can waffle plausibly about prospects for the economy or the merits of a European rapid reaction force, but what do you do when Tony Baldry (C, Banbury) asks you to assess, diagnose and prescribe a cure for 'the parlous state of the pig industry'?

Mr Brown rootled through his notes and then launched into a magnificent porcine *tour d'horizon.* We heard about the PIRS (the Pig Industry Restructuring Scheme); about its importance 'to both outgoers and ongoers'; we even heard about 'classical swine fever'. Mr Baldry hit back with the PIDS (Pig Industry Development Scheme) and a gibe about foxhunting.

David Taylor (Lab, Leicestershire NW) waded in with the MPPU (Midland Pig Producers' Unit) and the NPA (National Pig Association). Archie Kirkwood (Lib Dem, Roxburgh and Berwickshire) introduced a new mystery: the 'Pig Reconstruction Scheme', an alarming thought.

To all of them, the conciliatory Mr Brown offered sympathy, information, even hope.

It is a very great achievement in a man's life to have entered the Cabinet and sustained for nearly three years the burdens of the office of Minister of Agriculture. To do it as well as he does, Mr Brown has filled his waking hours, his mental archives and most of his thoughts with a wonderfully detailed knowledge of the Pig Industry Restructuring Scheme and everything an Agriculture Minister needs to know about Hill Livestock Compensatory Allowances. If Nick Brown ever had a rich interior life or a busy and fulfilling social existence, he does not have them now.

He lives, breathes and dreams pigs, sheep, bullocks, sugar-beet and council of ministers meetings in Brussels; his weekdays are filled with Whitehall meetings, interminable briefs, and spiky MPs' questions; his weekends are spent being shouted at by farmers' representatives up and down the country and sneered at in the Sunday newspapers.

If he is very lucky, he may move up a notch in Cabinet before retiring. More likely he will be Agriculture Minister for a few years more, or move sideways to Overseas Development or Wales. In a decade or so his name will appear in *Who's Who*, along with dozens of other Browns, followed by a shortish paragraph mentioning that, like innumerable forgotten former politicians, he was once Minister of Agriculture. 'Hobbies: walking.' He will not have made much money.

Is this what it was all for? Is this what an ambitious young would-be politician sweats and claws his way up through the ranks of commonplace or disobliging people for twenty or thirty years to achieve?

Mr Brown looks like a nice and rather thoughtful man. I wonder whether, during a few snatched days of leisure over this Christmas, he thinks it has all been worth it?

After the election, Mr Blair made up his mind for him.

War of Laura's Leg

10.1.01

Darkness falls over the Commons. Unreason descends. Anger mounts. Fists shake. Men and women who once aspired to rational discourse shout pure gibberish. Ploughshares are beaten into swords, statistics hammered into weapons of destruction. The lights are going out all over Parliament as with sinking hearts we see the shadow of a looming election back towards us at the year's beginning.

What else yesterday could explain the sight of scores of MPs, their little faces contorted in rage and indignation, turning a discussion about the replacement of a limb lost by a little girl caught in a bomb outrage, into a venomous scuffle about the honour of ministers making promises?

Readers with longer memories may remember from the election before last the War of Jennifer's Ear: a violent engagement between Labour and the Tories over the use by the former for a party election broadcast of a little girl's operation for glue-ear. Unless Dr Julian Lewis (C, New Forest E) or John Hutton (a sunken-cheeked junior Health Minister who puts one in mind of a starving Victorian serial-poisoner) backs down, then Health Questions yesterday saw the first shots in the imminent War of Laura's Leg.

Dr (he has a PhD in strategic studies) Lewis had put down a question about progress made by the Health Department in making 'artificial limbs with lifelike silicone coating' available on the NHS.

Frankly, for Dr Lewis, lifelike limbs would be too little, too late. Until lifelike silicone coatings become available for the production of lifelike faces, and audio-synthetic techniques capable of turning the whines of mosquitoes into lifelike voices, there is little hope for this

MP. But his ostensible purpose yesterday was to bring hope to a young constituent, Laura Giddings, who (he said) lost a leg in a terrorist explosion at Planet Hollywood in South Africa.

A genuinely moving case, and not one we should employ for mockery if Laura's MP had not tried to employ it for party advantage, to attack Labour.

Mr Hutton replied that next year silicone coatings would become available on the NHS.

This was good news. But Dr Lewis had ready only an angry blast at Labour for failed delivery and phoney promises. Laura's case was thrown in as evidence of the human misery to which new Labour ministers were callously averting their eyes while beguiling voters with 'warm words'. Admittedly Hutton's positive answer had hardly been matched by his gloomy delivery, but there was no evidence in Dr Lewis's comeback that he had listened at all. Dr Lewis launched into a sustained and angry whine.

Some sympathy is due to the minister, but not much. In a cynical display of electioneering, Hutton accused Dr Lewis of a cynical display of electioneering. This is normally followed by the Liberal Democrats, easily the most cynical of the lot, accusing both sides of cynical displays of electioneering. Somewhere in all this, Laura Giddings was forgotten.

I hope she gets her silicone-coated leg. Her parents should be advised that there will never be a better time to bid for a limb of any description.

When Coiffures Meet

19.1.01

Drawing himself up to his full (Imperial) 5ft 5½in at the dispatch box yesterday afternoon, Alan Duncan (C, Rutland & Melton) declared: 'drawing myself up, Mr Speaker, to my full Imperial 5ft 6¼in . . .'

The Tory spokesman on Trade and Industry moved to less disputable ground, however, when he complained that the sledgehammer of trading standards legislation was being used to crack the nut of a small trader selling bananas by the pound: 'absurd and unnecessary,' said Duncan.

'I'm happy, Mr Speaker, to stand at my full height of 1.6m' replied Helen Liddell.

If, as this sketch suspects, Mr Duncan was including his heels in his height, Mrs Liddell must have been including her hair. Without this extraordinary, lacquered, honey-coloured helmet, the Trade and Industry Minister may be about only 4ft tall.

Not yards away on the government front bench sat the Leader of the House, Margaret Beckett, also 1.6m, most of it hair. Mrs Beckett's, a steel soufflé of light butterscotch, is not so much manageable as drilled, each enamelled strand standing proudly to attention.

From beneath her own gilded carapace, Mrs Liddell had little to say about bananas, and what she said was lost on me. I was absorbed in a horrifying speculation . . .

What if Mrs Beckett's and Mrs Liddell's hair should meet? What if, brushing accidentally together, the hairdos should touch?

It could so easily happen. Both creations are wider than the heads they crown. Just as we car drivers may forget our wing mirrors when judging how close to pass an oncoming vehicle, so these two ministers might forget their hair. And what then?

Once, restringing a wire fence, I got two balls of old barbed wire tangled together. It was hell to separate them. As they touched, they locked into each other like burrs to a sock. Stags lock horns; was there a danger that these does might lock hairdos?

When ministers cross each other to change places on the front bench, it is an unavoidably close crossing, like trying to swop seats in the theatre. Beckett must pass Liddell to take up position at the dispatch box. One imagined their brisk crossover suddenly arrested as, with a dreadful jerk, two prickly helmets engaged and Velcro-like, stuck. For a moment, legs would keep walking in opposite directions, but heads would be going nowhere and the two bodies would form an opening pincer, joined at the head.

After that there would be nothing for it but to sit side by side. Whenever Mrs Beckett wished to rise, Mrs Liddell would have to rise with her, and vice versa. This would probably be ruled out of order. The two MPs would leave together (or not at all) to try to disengage their heads behind the Speaker's Chair, probably with the help of two of Mr Speaker's bewigged parliamentary clerks-at-the-table, each pulling one MP. There would be a ghastly ripping sound, as when Velcro is separated. Necks might crick. The static electricity generated could spark a lacquer-blaze. And damage to the hairdos would be extensive, quite possibly rendering them insurance write-offs.

Lost in appalled conjecture, I failed to notice Trade and Industry Questions winding up. It was 12.30pm. Next up would be Mrs Beckett.

I saw the Leader of the House rise and move towards the dispatch box, just as Mrs Liddell started edging her way between the front bench and the table, towards the exit.

I watched aghast as the two ministers edged nearer, *almost* touched . . .

And passed without entanglement. Another Thursday, another narrow squeak.

25.1.01 **When Best Friends Fall Out**

Mandelson falls – again.

As after a death, which in a way it was, tributes to Peter Mandelson in the Commons yesterday were more dignified than ardent.

Fortitude in adversity is always brave and on the front bench, as the Prime Minister and his Northern Ireland Secretary sat together for the last time, Gordon Brown was taking the bad news with wonderful composure. Geoff Hoon looked positively perky. The Home Secretary radiated a massive calm.

One rung down from that on which a vacancy had so unexpectedly appeared, junior ministers hid their grief and made their calculations: 'If x moves sideways to y, p moves upwards to q . . .'

'*Big fleas have little fleas/Upon their backs to bite 'em,'/And little fleas have smaller fleas,/And so ad infinitum.*'

Only David Blunkett made much of consolation, reaching out across Mr Hoon and holding Peter Mandelson's hand in a minute-long grip.

Mr Mandelson himself remained as dignified as is possible when you're gutted. He handled his final Northern Ireland Questions with patience, earnestly arguing his corner over the proposed name change for the Royal Ulster Constabulary. The packed Chamber and press gallery, and a palpable buzz, must have mystified tourists; were Northern Ireland Questions such a big deal?

Tributes from back and front benchers were courteous – no more – but only Mandelson's Tory shadow, Andrew MacKay, failed to pay any tribute at all to his work.

As the House moved towards Prime Minister's Questions, the buzz intensified. Gordon Brown came bustling in at speed then broke his momentum towards his usual place near the Prime Minister when he saw Mandelson there, skidded to a halt and sat down on Geoff Hoon, who crawled out from under and squeezed a place for Mr Brown.

Tony Blair looked shattered, his face more than pale: waxy and hollow. He stood stiffly for a while by the Speaker's chair, almost at attention, sucking his cheeks. Taking his seat he turned to Mandelson and tried to smile.

Mandelson's face knotted – into an attempted smile, or what, it is not possible to say: comradeship and reproach wrestled there.

Throughout Questions what struck this sketch about the scene on the government benches was the singularity of the Prime Minister's mood. In a sea of faces, choppy with excitement and speculation, Mr Blair's was a still, central focus, radiating – as from Edvard Munch's screaming woman – waves of shock. For some of Blair's comrades this event was a nuisance, for others an opportunity. For Blair it was a personal tragedy.

William Hague's response delighted all his supporters save the best.

It's an old maxim of party politics, of course, that when your opponent is down, that's the time to kick; and the Tory leader kicked.

Every so often we are reminded that in the end people act in their natures. You can make a politician over, tweak his image or redesign his profile, but sooner or later the old Adam will out. That has been said often enough of Peter Mandelson but, remembering how Mr Hague hardly waited for John Major, the man who made him, to bow out before attacking his predecessor for 'constantly shifting fudge', I reflected on the recurrence yesterday of this trait: a small lack of grace.

For my part, and for half the House, *hodie mihi, cras tibi* were the watchwords of the afternoon. *To me today, tomorrow to you* should be emblazoned across the main gate of the Palace of Westminster.

Lady Macbeth Takes Scotland   *31.1.01*

Anne Robinson watch out: Helen Liddell is on her way. The new Scottish Secretary did not so much hit the House running yesterday as run at the House hitting. She was awesome. No one else got a look in as, fists flailing and hair glinting like a crème brûlée, Scotland's Steel

Thistle marched in and gave Question Time a good kicking.

In her days as a Treasury Minister, the civil servants' codename was Lady Macbeth – but is the Member for Airdrie & Shotts soft enough for that role? As a gooey-eyed Malcolm Savidge (Lab, Aberdeen N) sucked up to the new boss, her withering smile suggested she might without compunction have pluck'd her nipple from his boneless gums/And dash'd his brains out.

A lesser minister might have felt herself under some disadvantage that afternoon. In Edinburgh, Scotland's First Minister, Henry McLeish, had just defied London's orders and promised free personal care for the elderly, north of the border. The idea is a big headache for the Cabinet at Westminster. Opposition MPs made pathetic attempts to wring the admission from her. But could anyone make her squirm? Mrs Liddell is about as squirmy as a pterodactyl.

When Alex Salmond (Banff & Buchan), scourge of the Scottish Labour Party and former leader of the SNP, ventured a rare Commons appearance to scare her, she flashed him an iron-clad grin and tore into him. 'What a pleasure,' she hissed, 'to see him here in London. Evidently Edinburgh isn't big enough for the Hon Gentleman.' Mrs Liddell played with him for a while, as though with some half-eviscerated rodent, then spat: 'He is the weakest link. Goodbye.'

The line the new Scottish Secretary was sticking to was that the distinctive policies being adopted in Scotland were a thrilling demonstration of devolution in practice. Let a thousand flowers bloom, she implied. The fact that her department had tried and failed to pull up this particular flower by its roots and was now examining a range of patent weedkillers, was something all knew (and knew she knew we knew) but nobody could pin on her. Her effrontery is little short of magnificent.

And Great Scot can Mrs Liddell patronise! The gutsy Eleanor Laing, a Scottish-educated Scotswoman representing an English seat (Epping Forest), and a Tory spokesman on Scotland, opened hostilities with a generous tribute to her prowess. Liddell eyed her. 'A fine product,' she smiled menacingly 'of St Columba's & Kilmacolm. Her teachers will be proud of her good manners. *Better* manners than some of her honourable friends.'

Charles Kennedy rose and tried a friendly welcome too. Mrs Liddell met it with more condescension.

It struck this sketch that when the Commons discusses Scotland the Liberal Democrat leader is on tricky ground and, as he distances his party from Labour in London, it's getting trickier. Liberal Democrats are governing in coalition with Labour at Edinburgh.

As a Scottish Liberal Democrat representing Ross, Skye & Inverness W, therefore, he should dance into the chamber wreathed in goodwill. As national leader of the overwhelmingly English Liberal Democrat Party, who are now barely on speaking terms with Labour, Mr Kennedy should stalk in scowling.

But Kennedy is so bland that the disjunction is barely noticeable: a transition not so much from hosannah to curse, as from simper to pout.

Yesterday being Tuesday, we got the simper. Watch today at PM's Questions for the pout. It might help us to distinguish if Kennedy would actually cross and recross the floor to underline the distinction.

Tread Softly on Their Pebble-dash

1.2.01

'Good God,' exclaimed the tenth Duke of Devonshire when Stanley Baldwin compared press barons to prostitutes: 'That's done it. He's lost us the tarts' vote.'

At Prime Minister's Questions yesterday, while William Hague was scoring points off a rattled Tony Blair, Charles Kennedy was losing the Liberal Democrat Party the pebble-dash homeowners' vote.

This sketch had not realised that Liberal Democrats regard pebble-dash as an inferior finish for external walls, or that they reserve any special contempt for those whose homes are clad in this way, but there was no mistaking either the Lib Dem leader's meaning or his tone when he invited Tony Blair to join him in sneering at what had been called 'pebble-dash populism'. The implication was clear. People who live in pebble-dashed houses have unpleasant opinions, to which it would demean a politician to pay heed.

Is this suggestion wise? In Mr Kennedy's own Highland constituency, crofts may outnumber pre-war terraces, but a glance at some of his party's Westminster marginals – Twickenham, Kingston & Surbiton, Colchester, Southport – suggests constituencies in any one of which the pebble-dash vote would vastly exceed the Liberal Democrat majority.

I have checked Liberal Democrat manifestos of recent years. There has never previously been a party policy on the exterior finish of houses, nor any suggestion that this one is associated with an unacceptable class of person or repugnant point of view.

I have called a range of housebuilders to explain that Britain's third party now seeks to distance itself from a building method – and met bewilderment and dismay. Nobody can put a figure on it, but the consensus is that millions of homes in the United Kingdom, especially those built before the First World War, are pebble-dashed.

Contacted by this column, an indignant Andrew Littler, author of the standard work *Sand and Gravel Production* (Institute of Quarrying, £23.50) protested: 'The use of natural gravels for facing a building can be an attractive alternative to block or brick.'

One colleague points out that (where in-keeping) the finish is now retro-chic; another adds that to those millions who are proud to own pebble-dashed houses we should add millions more whom we might call 'pebble-dash aspirational': upwardly mobile wannabes who dream of moving from a 60s tower block or Peabody estate to a solid pebble-dashed semi with a garden of its own.

Still more (your sketchwriter among them) have happy childhood memories of suburban life in a world of flowering laburnums, net curtains, pebble-dashed walls and *Welcome* doormats.

From all these people and their hopes and dreams Mr Kennedy yesterday cut his party adrift.

But then parties, like people, can themselves be upwardly mobile.

By allying itself to 'new' Labour and the Islington set, does the Liberal Democrat Party now seek to move up from the inner-city and suburban pavement politics of terrace, towerblock and semi, towards the gravel drives, yew hedges, or Georgian facades of the cranberry-juice and Tuscan holiday classes?

If so, whom else does Mr Kennedy plan to denigrate? Vauxhall owners? Lambrusco drinkers? DIY enthusiasts? People who fly from Luton airport?

To his despised pebble-dash populism does he plan to add package holiday Poujadism, the Babycham bourgeois or rum and coke reactionary? Where is Kennedy on caravanning, MFI furniture and the link between PVC double glazing and political incorrectness?

Can you have a reproduction of Constable's *Haywain* on your lounge wall and still be intelligently committed to proportional representation?

Is patterned wallpaper compatible with an enlightened attitude to Third World debt?

I think we should be told.

'RIP' – The Only Missing Initials

2.2.01

The road to Damascus led through Agriculture Questions yesterday. Suddenly, I understood the Third Way.

Barbara Follett (Lab, Stevenage) asked how the Government will support 'farm diversification', ie, finding something else for farmers to do. The Agriculture Minister, Nick Brown, rose.

I was unprepared for what hit us next. A deluge of initiatives, acronyms, task forces, reports and brochures erupted from the minister's folder and spewed over the dispatch box, inundating the Chamber.

Did Mrs Follett know about the Rural Enterprise Scheme? Were MPs up to speed on the Environmental Crops Scheme? Mr Brown wanted to tell us about the Tree Planting Scheme, too, adding a word on the Action Plan for Farming.

He went on to remind us about his free Guide to Farm Diversification – oh, and had he included the Rural White Paper recently unveiled?

Struggling to keep up – RES, ECS, TPS, ACP, GFD, RWP – I almost missed the only hard number seriously discussed, when the Tories' James Paice reminded Brown of a scheme he had omitted to mention: the Farm Business Scheme. Of the £6 million allocated for the FBS, two per cent had been allocated, said Mr Paice. A fair complaint: £120,000 won't even buy you a place in the House of Lords these days, let alone fast-track your passport application. Joan Ruddock (Lab, Lewisham Deptford) wanted new uses for farmland too. A junior minister, Elliot Morley, discussed the Countryside Stewardship Scheme. The CSS was part of the English Rural Development Plan.

To Tim Boswell (C, Daventry), who mentioned a backlog of payments under the CSS, Morley said that he had just returned from a Regional Advice Centre (RAC). He commended the ESAS: Environmentally Sensitive Areas Scheme. On the disappearance of hedgerows, he looked to the CSS for help. He began burbling to David Taylor (Lab, Leicestershire NW) about the Arable Stewardship Pilot Scheme. For a moment, I though that the minister was proposing to retrain farmers as pilots, but the ASPS turned out to have nothing to do with aeroplanes. What I did have to do with never really emerged.

There was also a Meeting of Devolved Ministers. MDMs consider RDS 'initiatives', Morley explained to the Liberal Democrats' Richard Livsey (Brecon & Radnorshire).

Briefing in hand, Joyce Quin, a junior minister, was ready to tell Eric Martlew (Lab, Carlisle) about the Milk Task Force Government Action Plan; besides the MTFGAP she had news about a School Milk Scheme; and advice for Peter Pike (Lab, Burnley) about the findings of the CC (Competition Commission) on milk.

All this within four Questions. Then a postscript, an afterthought from Miss Quin, stopped me in my tracks. The problem really, she remarked, was the price.

Ah! The price. So *that's* why dairymen are going under. Nobody's going to do much about the price. So, when the suicidal farmer has nipped down to the RAC to find out about the MTFGAP, the ASPS, or the ECS, TPS or RES under the APF; and when he's read his free GFD in hopes of better understanding the RWP; and when, despairing of rescue by the SMS, the CSS or the MDM, and realising that nobody is offering to retrain him as a pilot after all . . . the penny drops. Milk's too cheap to make a living, and there's no way out.

The Left say 'Subsidise milk'. The Right say 'Bury the dairy farmer'. The Third Way says 'RIP' and sends flowers.

There were plenty of flowers from the Front Bench an hour later, for sacked steel workers.

9.2.01   # Beacons That Give No Light

A grey minister with a grey voice was saying: 'We will have regard to the pilot programmes when addressing the issue of a national rollout.' A whip on a front bench was picking his nose. Nobody was listening.

This could only be Education Questions.

Few venture into the educationists' camp and return alive. They

sucked the daylights from Mark Carlisle and defeated the late Keith
Joseph. They stymied Rhodes Boyson, bloodied Kenneth Clarke and
knocked the stuffing from Kenneth Baker. They drained Gillian
Shephard.

Their latest victim, David Blunkett, is still conscious, but if he isn't
winched out soon he'll be a goner too. Yesterday he began wittering
about 'schools facing challenges' – the educationists' term for failing
schools. 'I'd like to see this piloted right across the United Kingdom so
that the uplift can be mirrored,' he told an MP who had inquired about
some fatuous scheme.

They have names, these 'initiatives', but none remember them and
nobody is meant to, for the Department for Education and Employment
is a parallel, hologram world. Task forces, reports, New Deals, projects,
pilots, schemes, ventures and agencies bob along the horizon like a
flotilla of *Mary Celestes*, bedecked with gay strings of acronyms and lit
with pretty words like 'beacon' and 'excellence'. Approach, however,
and you'll sail slap through and out the other side, appearance leaving
no mark on reality. Even the recollection will be wiped from your
consciousness.

'Will Job Points be rolled out nationally?' trilled Rosie Winterton
(Lab, Doncaster Central), a sunnily loyal backbencher forever agog for
further evidence of the Government's wonderfulness. This sketch
confesses we do not know what Job Points does, nor whether it is a pilot,
a beacon or an agency, nor what 'rolled out nationally' means. But
Tessa Jowell, the Minister for Employment, was enthralled by it. Ms
Jowell told Labour's Jim Fitzpatrick (Poplar and Canning Town) that
her department's innovative Employment Service Direct was an
'award-winning' scheme. Subsequent inquiry reveals that the award –
the 'Government Computing Award' – was awarded by another branch
of Government. And Employment Service Direct has won a second
prize: it has been awarded Beacon of Excellence status. By the Cabinet
Office. Thus does government conjure into existence a plethora of
meaninglessnesses all rejoicing in the name of action, and – behold! –
they start giving each other awards. There's probably an Awards Co-
ordination Task Force being piloted somewhere before being rolled out
nationally.

And the curse of meaninglessness which haunts the Department for
Education and Employment afflicts the Opposition, too. Theresa May,
the Tories' chief education spokeswoman (in chic black trouser suit

yesterday, and gaudy pink new Labour scarf) bucks and whinnies at the dispatch box, her hair perfect; but her meaning vaporises as the echo dies. Her young sidekick, Graham Brady – bland, big-boned, vacantly handsome – looks and talks like a minor member of the Royal Family. He sounds mildly sensible and nice but the instant he has spoken you forget everything he has said. 'Looks like Prince Andrew!' shouted Dennis Skinner yesterday – and it was true.

Through all this warm fog, one sharp outline, that of the Liberal Democrats' David Heath, often looms. Mr Heath at least is forceful and clear. Yesterday he asked David Blunkett whether he could promise that a future Labour government would not introduce top-up fees for students – 'Yes or no?'

'Yes,' said Blunkett.

Politicians reeled. Civil servants fainted in their box. So Blunkett's not dead yet. Or the corpse is still twitching.

13.2.01 MPs Fight Shy of Bazookas

Are you a forces beauty who'd like to be on Page 3? Call the *Sun* today on 020 7782 4105. We'll call back.

. . . Or so yesterday's *Sun* was promising. Stunning Melanie Cotton, based by happy chance at SHAPE, had already taken up the news-paper's offer, and was showing her 'devastating firepower' across a page headlined 'Another saucy services special'. Beside Mel was a reprise photograph of Lance Corporal Roberta Winterton – 'the first to drive Page 3 fans Army barmy' – pictured naked but for a red feather boa, sensitively arranged. A poster of Roberta is to be published; now Mel was opening up 'a second front'.

'What's so bad about showing your knockers?' commented Mel.

And you'd think that Gerald Howarth would agree. We cannot imagine anyone more insistently heterosexual than the Tory MP for Aldershot. A fierce critic of the idea that homosexuals should serve in the Armed Forces or (judging by his habitual tone) anywhere else, except French restaurants, Mr Howarth has been loud in his anxiety lest the promotion of homosexuality divert young people from healthier pursuits. We last encountered him flanking Baroness Young in a press conference, calling for new laws to criminalise buggery.

Howarth first came to public notice in the early 1970s in a political broadcast for the Liberal Party. He was with a panel of young people asking critical questions of Jeremy Thorpe, who was the Liberal leader. The teenage Howarth wore flares, long hair and a ludicrously huge collar and tie.

For Defence Questions yesterday he was more quietly dressed, but no less noisy. He took the first opportunity available to raise what he called 'the activities of two army women'.

Presumably he was going to commend them? Wasn't this a timely bit of corrective therapy for squaddies in imminent danger (as Howarth has warned) of being distracted in their tasks by the inclusion of open homosexuals in their ranks? Were Roberta and Mel not exotic reminders to our troops of where their duties lie, and wholly consistent with the Howarth world-view?

Not a bit of it. According to Howarth this was all part of the folly of 'women in the front line'. It is becoming difficult to work out what, or whom, Mr Howarth does approve of. The MP's ire seemed to extend beyond poor Mel and Roberta, to their sex generally. 'Women,' he huffed, 'shouldn't be able to treat' the Armed Forces this way.

John Spellar, the minister unlucky enough to reply, failed to take this opportunity to compliment the Army on its new bazookas. He looked scared. Ever since Mr Spellar convulsed the whole House (and Press Gallery too) by tripping on the word 'cuts' in 'army cuts' (an uninvited 'n' crept in) the whole subject of sex has unnerved him. He has not, for instance, been allowed to answer questions on our missiles' depleted uranium tips.

Who Cares What She Said   *14.2.01*

Gathered in the Press Gallery at the Commons yesterday, five parliamentary sketchwriters gazed into space. It was Questions to the Secretary of State for the Environment, Transport and the Regions. Nothing was happening, as usual. It was all very Third Way: paltry sums of money, copious quantities of jargon, and a hell of a lot of fiddling around. Nothing of any consequence was being said.

But push the inconsequential too far and it tips into absurdity. As a junior minister, Hilary Armstrong, ground on, and the Tories began to titter, then laugh, and finally roar, five sketchwriters cocked an ear and listened – actually *listened* – to what Miss Armstrong was saying.

The minister had moved from saying nothing much of interest to talking such unmitigated gibberish that suddenly we were in Edward Lear territory. This was nonsense. This was comic. This was scary.

Five sketchwriters gathered later over a tape recorder. Sometimes, all you need is the record. Take a moment if you will, simply to read what they *said*. No words can express the unreality – no words better than theirs.

Mrs Joan Humble (Lab, Blackpool N & Fleetwood): *To ask if [ministers] will make a statement on the new local strategic partnerships.*

Miss Hilary Armstrong: 'Mr Speaker, local strategic partnerships will provide a single, overarching, local co-ordinated framework which will enable local stakeholders to address issues that really matter to local people. They will prepare and implement local community strategies and local neighbourhood renewal strategies. They will allocate local neighbourhood renewal funds which will double to £200 million and rationalise local partnerships working to deliver better services . . .'

May I chip in here to explain that this was the *prepared* part of Miss Armstrong's answer? Somebody in Whitehall wrote that stuff. Would it be indelicate to point out that suicide is an option?

But we interrupted a new Labour love-fest . . .

Mrs Humble: 'May I thank my Hon Friend for that statement? [Can she confirm that] successful existing partnerships the Blackpool council has developed are the basis of the new local strategic partnerships, so this very welcome inward investment can be part of my constituency?'

Miss Armstrong: 'I congratulate her on her commitment to ensure that deprivation is tackled in Blackpool and indeed elsewhere. It is this Government that has recognised the importance of targeting effectively deprivation wherever it occurs, and I can assure her that local agencies should be seeking to build on local arrangements that have already worked well rather than starting again from scratch and this cross-sectoral cross-agency umbrella partnership offers real opportunities for stream-lining both existing partnership arrangements and to make them more effective by making better connections between individual initiatives.'

Sir Patrick Cormack (C, Staffordshire S) could contain his indignation no longer. He asked whether Miss Armstrong could put her
answer 'in English?' Po-faced, she refused to see a lighter side. She
seemed to think Sir Patrick's problem arose from a difficulty in hearing
her, rather than the gibberish she spoke. So she recast the gibberish. She
spoke of effective overviews and strategic priorities, but spared him the
cross-sector, cross-agency, overarching umbrellas.

Miss Armstrong went on to congratulate Ivan Henderson (Lab,
Harwich) on 'the very tendentious way' he had put his case. The
national strategy, she explained, 'aims to deliver faith communities'.

Or I think that's what she said. What is a 'faith community' and how
does government 'deliver' any such thing? Is it an issue to be
addressed?

Oh heck, who cares?

Nick Brown Puts Foot In Mouth

27.2.01

The livestock disease hits Britain.

As the Agriculture Minister, Nick Brown, took his place at the dispatch
box yesterday, something mysterious lumbered in and sat down behind
him. It was a hulking great MP with no neck, beefy and red-faced. None
of us had ever seen the Member before.

Could this be a bovine fugitive from the ministry's foot-and-mouth
humane-killer patrols? A classic evasion technique, of course: the lion's
den ploy. The creature sat very still as Mr Brown rose to speak, and
slipped silently away behind him.

Brown has only two Commons styles: soothe, sulk. Yesterday his
soothing soothed few and his sulk outraged the Tories.

And with reason. There can be few in Britain who have not seen the
Agriculture Minister on television, heard him on the radio, or read him
in the newspapers in recent days, talking about foot-and-mouth disease.
We could be forgiven for wondering what else the minister had had time
to do but court the media.

So you can understand the Conservative fury. Mr Brown had been asked (after a short, uninformative statement to the Commons) about further Commons discussion of the outbreak of foot-and-mouth disease. The Opposition has called a debate for tomorrow because the Government has refused to.

Brown flew into a massive sulk. 'Frankly,' he pouted, 'I do not welcome it.' Tories howled.

'Debate,' said the minister, 'will divert resources.'

Tories gasped. And this from a politician who has spent the past five days touring the nation's broadcasting studios!

Which resources was Mr Brown worried about diverting? Do teams of scientists gather outside the chamber every time the great man rises at the dispatch box in case a medical hypothesis has to be urgently tested? Are lorry-loads of vets carted in from the countryside to attend Mr Brown at Westminster for pit-stop briefings or an unanticipated veterinary diagnosis?

As the minister pouted away about this tiresome diversion, by a mere legislature, of terribly important people in the Ministry of Agriculture, a cloudy picture arose of a Whitehall department operating like a sort of kibbutz. Here, it seemed, were no reserved occupations, but permanent secretaries doing overnight stints bulldozing carcasses, meat inspectors on standby in Herefordshire to draft Mr Brown's speeches in London, weary laboratory technicians frogmarched from their Cambridge microscopes to attend the minister in London.

If so, Mr Brown must surely be right. Was it not all but unpatriotic for MPs so much as to ask the minister questions, in case he had to 'divert resources' to answer them? It was really very good of Brown to come down to the Commons at all for this short statement, and a damned cheek to expect him to attend a whole debate on Wednesday. He has pigs to slaughter.

But some of us knew better: the only resource in really short supply was Mr Brown's airtime. Upon this the news media have first call. He put it candidly. 'That is the way the modern world works,' he huffed, explaining how hard it was to keep up with the teams of cameramen and reporters tearing around the country in pursuit of new cases of the disease.

'*They're* probably spreadin' it,' growled a morose Dennis Skinner.

Truly, an Altered Toad

28.2.01

At the end of *Wind in the Willows*, Mr Toad is forced by the Rat and Badger to turn over a new leaf. He is no longer to be a proud Toad. Henceforward he will be a humble Toad.

As this Parliament draws towards the end, and after some unpleasantness in the newspapers, Mr Keith Vaz, Minister for Europe, has been forced by whips and colleagues to make a similar change.

With only one relapse (when Toad was goaded past endurance by a Tory weasel) we saw yesterday, at Foreign Office Questions, Mr Vaz's first public appearance in his new role.

'Mayn't I sing them just one *little* song,' Toad pleaded piteously in *Wind in the Willows*.

'No, not one little song,' replied Rat firmly . . . 'It's no good Toady; you know well that your songs are all conceit and boasting and vanity; and that your speeches are all self-praise and – and – well, gross exaggeration and – and –'

'And gas,' put in Badger.

'It's for your own good, Toady,' continued the Rat, '. . . a sort of turning point in your career.'

And so it was for Mr Vaz, who had heaved 'a deep sigh; a long, long, long sigh . . . He was indeed an altered Toad.'

Or Vaz. The alteration to the Minister for Europe was profound. He was a couple of stone thinner. And he spoke quietly! The self-praise and gross exaggeration and – and – gas which we have come to expect from him had quite disappeared. In place of bombast, we had restraint.

The Foreign Secretary was away so Vaz took the trickiest questions. And if yesterday is anything to go by, these will become tricky indeed after the general election.

To all, the Altered Vaz cast down his eyes, and burbled modestly that it was too early to comment, there was 'ample scope for consultation' and 'I have listened to what my Hon friend has said and I will pass it on'.

Previously he would have puffed himself up and gurgled boasts and certainties. Yesterday, like Toad, 'he only smiled faintly and murmured "not at all", or sometimes, for a change, "on the contrary".'

Only once did the modesty slip. Poked at mercilessly by the Shadow Foreign Secretary, Francis Maude (who accused the Prime Minister of saying one thing to Mr Bush on missiles and the European rapid reaction force, and another to domestic and European audiences), the Altered Vaz began to quiver. There is something weaselly in Mr Maude's manner. All at once Vaz cracked. He likened Tory spokesmen to weasels.

Challenged by Maude on Europe, he exploded. 'He doesn't understand. I'll have to invite him to see me in my office, and explain. He simply *doesn't* understand.' Tory weasels squealed mockingly.

And the Vaz subsided. Attacked (on British aid for a Turkish dam project) by almost every Labour backbencher who intervened, the Altered Vaz, murmuring tributes to each colleague's expertise, 'only shook his head gently, raising one paw in mild protest'. Truly, this was an altered Toad.

A Budget for Broody Browns

8.3.01

Over in the House of Lords they were debating Potentially Hazardous Near-Earth Objects. In the Commons, a leaden lump of basalt was making the closest approach Gordon Brown's annual orbit offers our planet. The Chancellor was explaining baby-credit. 'For the first year of a child's life I propose . . .'

Babies were cheering. The rest of us were bemused. This was a too-clever-by-half Budget, a fidget-Budget. We British like our bribes simple. Who, please, apart from babies, was being bribed? Where was the promised cynical election ploy? It was enough to make you cynical. 'Spectrum tax proceeds'? 'Locking in the fiscal tightening'? Government backbenchers grinned in a vacantly supportive way, like admiring grans as the junior prodigy presents his dissertation on astrophysics and Doppler effect. The Tories just looked clueless.

Only when the Chancellor mentioned Escorts, Astras and Micras, unleaded petrol and 1.5 litre engines, did MPs perk up. At last some technical terms they understood!

There was no unified response to this Budget, no tune to whistle, no sense the House had got the drift. Tony Blair, fingers locked, maintained a tight smile and series of tense little nods, like an overwrought organ-grinder's monkey. Stephen Byers looked prim, Alistair

Darling impassive, Margaret Beckett glazed and Ann Taylor bleak. Chris Smith managed a brave grin. Alan Milburn was alert, sniffing the wind for cash.

David Blunkett had been evicted from his place by Andrew Smith, the Chief Secretary – a blind Cabinet minister pushed out of his seat by one of Brown's bodyguards: sign of the times.

As the Chancellor chuntered somewhat oilily on, the spectacularly loyal nodding-dog impersonator, Ben Bradshaw (Lab, Exeter), seated near the press in the MPs' overflow gallery upstairs, seeemd to coach us in our responses. 'Yes!' he hissed, as Brown mentioned fiscal tightening or somesuch: then '*very* good!'

Debt repayment was '*whoooarrh*!', the Tory legacy an ostentatious sucking of the teeth. 'That's right!' cried Mr Bradshaw when the Chancellor expressed himself broadly in favour of families; then 'yup! yup!', 'ho-ho-ho-ho' (at the Budget surplus), 'good!', '*excellent!*' and '*har-har-har*', 'tch-tch-tch' at alleged Tory folly! 'Quite right!' he kept yelping.

The sketch cannot recall what in particular Bradshaw thought quite right in Brown's Budget. Just about all of it, we gathered. The Chancellor seemed pretty pleased with it too, but the budget was only one of things Mr Brown was pleased with; heading the list was himself. There was a distinctly smarmy patina to the performance.

And Brown delighted himself with a new rhetorical technique he was trying yesterday, learnt from London barrow-boys. 'I'm raising it not to £10 million – but to £15 million,' he declared. 'Not £57 million but £68 million!'

These were gratifying figures, but why the preliminary news about the amounts he was not announcing. He mystified MPs by announcing 'I'm not able to give Nightingale wards £100,000.'

'No?' we thought.

'I'm giving them between £½ million and £1 million.'

What would William Hague make of this? The Tory leader had to speak next. It's a tall order to unpick, by stunning analysis and in stirring language, a 52-minute treatise on spectrum tax proceeds. Tories looked glum.

Hague lifted their hearts. Truly this man is the P-Y Gerbeau of opposition politics. Fate bops him down and he bops right up again, cocky as you please. By the time their leader had finished, cheering Conservatives believed they had seen how a shapeless mess was, after all, a shameless fraud, a coiled python. Gordon Brown stared queenily at the ceiling.

Four months later, the Chancellor and his wife announced the expected arrival of their first child.

9.3.01   Mr Brown and Dr Rorschach

The Rorschach Test – or Ink Blot Analysis – is famous among psychiatrists. The technique involves folding in half a leaf of paper at whose centre lies a wet splash of ink. The patient is asked to study the splodge and tell his analyst what picture he sees there.

Some see a butterfly, some a twin-headed eagle, some a sea-monster. Others discern a pelvis. The key is to appreciate that *there is no right answer*. The splodge is all those things and none: everything that anyone in his madness or caprice may choose to see in it.

The picture discerned tells us more about the person doing the discerning, then about the splodge. So it is with Budgets. A Budget is a sort of splodge. Ink goes everywhere. The result has no objective meaning and no agreed effect.

The forces which drive the Chancellor's ink in various directions are familiar enough: buoyancy of revenue, debt, inflation, cries of pain, an impending general election – these are just a few.

But it is the relative strength, one to another, of these forces, and in the end the Chancellor's digestion at any given moment, which determines the budget's shape.

So complex is the interplay that the result is to all intents and purposes random. Like any splodge it neither 'means' nor reveals anything. Except about the patient who claims to interpret it.

Yesterday at Westminster it fell to three different patients to describe what they saw in Gordon Brown's recent splodge. Over at Smith Square, a chap with big hair saw in the splodge a snarling beast. Far from offering to repay national debt, the beastly splodge had been calculated to add to it. Hidden within the splodge's ink were numberless secret imposts called 'stealth' taxes. The splodge's claws menaced business, industry, enterprise and the whole of Middle England. The beast's maw was wide open to devour the fruits of citizen's labours and pensioners' savings.

The picture tells us little about the splodge, a great deal about Michael Portillo. Here is a man who needs to frighten us. Upon our anxieties he wishes to rest the ladder of his own ambitions. Back in the Commons chamber, another Tory was interpreting the Brown splodge. David Heathcoat-Amory had risen to open the Budget (Splodge) Debate. The creature whose picture the Shadow Industry Secretary saw in the Chancellor's ink was less sensational than Mr Portillo's beast. 'In some ways,' droned Mr Heathcoat-Amory in his listlessly fair-minded way, 'this was not the worst of the Budgets presented by this Chancellor in the last five years.' Then he tried to get worked up about it, succeeding intermittently.

This picture tells us about an essentially honest man who, obliged in his job to frighten the world, is trying to frighten himself first. After the Shadow Industry Secretary the real thing spoke. Stephen Byers, his manner (as ever) concerned, saw in the Chancellor's splodge a host of angels, come down from heaven to rescue Britain from the Tory legacy. Their wings were feathered with helpful initiatives for business. Their harps twanged melodies of hope for single mums. Their tidings were of a golden age to come. There were ten pages of this.

This picture tells us that Mr Byers fears a sideways move in the next reshuffle.

Mr Heathcoat-Amory had talked about 'the Budget emerging from the mist'. No Budget emerges from the mist. The Budget *is* the mist. From it emerge only the ambitions of the speaker.

Balls Rolls Out Plums   14.3.01

The Government, Yvette Cooper told MPs yesterday, is 'rolling out' free fruit in infants' schools. Fantastic news! The oranges and plums should roll very nicely, though the redcurrants may take some time and large melons could prove a danger to small kids. Bowling pears and bananas does, I find, present problems.

That this junior Health Minister (married to the Chancellor's adviser, Ed Balls) is in fact Mrs Balls only adds to the curiosity. 'Balls rolls . . .'

would make an intriguing start to any headline.

For readers out of touch with fashion in ministerial claptrap, 'roll out' is a new Labour buzz-phrase designed to impart a spurious air of boardroom whizzkiddery to statements whose honest meaning is that a start has been made in some places. 'We are rolling out these changes' sounds better than 'We're trying them in East Wittering'.

But that's incidental. This sketch has another purpose: to ask at what point, as power corrupts a government's ability to see itself as others see it, ministers lose their sense of their own absurdity.

We knew that Margaret Thatcher had passed that point when, somewhat late in her administration, she attended a Lord Mayor's banquet in a dress so elaborate that a train-bearer was needed. The spectacle dismayed, but in the then Mrs Thatcher's defence it might be said that she had more or less ruled discovered space for almost a decade, so it was not altogether surprising when, at 65, she began to lose sight of how silly she could look.

But Yvette Cooper is only 31. This slip of a thing is just a sparky parliamentary under-secretary with a couple of years' experience in the most junior ranks of government. Sally Keeble (Lab, Northampton N) asks her about measures to prevent coronary heart disease, and already Ms Cooper is looking humourless and talking about rolling out fruit and expecting us to take her seriously.

Not that her boss, the Secretary of State, sets much of an example. Alan Milburn is about as self-deprecating as Louis XIV. '*La santé, c'est moi.*' The Sun King of Elephant & Castle deports himself these days as though his cupboards contained more robes than lounge-suits. Even his face seems to have turned a different colour from other men's: a sort of tanned tangerine.

In the course of informing the Opposition front benches that their future was finished, and that 'I can tell the House that the NHS now has the fastest-improving cancer services in Europe' (what does that statement mean? How does he know?) Mr Milburn found time yesterday to claim credit for the fact that 'we're growing our own nurses'.

Has Milburn any conception of how preposterous he sounds? 'Growing' nurses indeed! A vision swims to mind of hundreds of little upturned trainee nurses' faces, waiting for Mr Milburn to come and water them. Lest he be thought nurse-ist in his horticultural condescension, Milburn went on to tell the Tory dream-team duo, David

Amess (Southend W) and Dr Julian Lewis (New Forest E), who had asked about hospital consultants, that 'we're growing more' consultants.

Accused by a Tory spokesman, Desmond Swayne, of authoritarianism, Milburn barked 'stop hollering and I'll answer'. If the meek shall inherit the Earth then, post-Judgement Day, Milburn's in for a thin time.

I escaped, returning during the Budget debate to hear Kenneth Clarke take about six minutes to make the Conservative Party sound electable. He sat down and the impression passed.

V1, V2, E1, E2, E3 and The Big M

15.3.01

'Hacked off' is the best description of Tony Blair at Prime Minister's Questions yesterday. Not that the Prime Minister was having much trouble with Questions. He seldom does now. It was the world which was refusing to behave.

There were Mr Blair's V-problems, for a start: virus and Vaz, V1 and V2, the germs spreading foot-and-mouth disease and the not-quite-exonerated Minister for Europe, Keith Vaz. V-problems have been spoiling Blair's sleep. It showed in his pale, taut face, knotting fingers, bad hair and irritable gabble.

Take that pestilential virus. Viruses aren't like the Conservative Party. A controlled cull, a torching of political carcasses and a big splosh of disinfectant – and the Tories go away for ages.

But this new virus is more elusive, pluming in the wind, travelling on the soles of shoes and the tread of tyres. Tory election leaflets don't do that.

V-threatened sheep aren't like Charles Kennedy's Liberal Democrats, either. The Kennedy flock is easily lured into a barn and – kept in the dark and offered (in the form of dark hints about proportional representation) the merest whiff of silage – Liberal livestock stay docile.

There was no trouble from their leader at PM's Questions yesterday, just a bleat about threatened bed & breakfast businesses. Real sheep are different. They lamb at inconvenient times, they wander the moor and heath unchecked, and their desperate owners rage against ministers.

If only (Mr Blair must reflect) it were Liberal Democrats, not sheep, who were susceptible to foot-and-mouth. The problem could be eradicated in days.

As for Vaz, this V, too, refuses to go away. The only time yesterday when William Hague had Blair seriously rattled was over Mr Vaz. The Prime Minister couldn't decide whether to shout or mutter, so he muttered and then shouted. Neither convinced the House.

Then there are Mr Blair's E-problems. No, not the euro, but the economy and the election. E1, the economy, had been coming nicely to the boil in time for E2, the election – with E3, employment, hitting an all-time high yesterday.

But now the economy is looking less secure as America falters and Japan stumbles – and, due to V1, it's becoming possible that E2 might have to be put off until the autumn – by which time, if E1 has been knocked off course, E3 might be moving sharply upwards, and . . . who would be Prime Minister?

Scariest of all, there's the M-problem. Mandy was not present for Prime Minister's Questions – and it is a sign of the times that there can hardly have been a journalist in the packed gallery who did not spend a good few minutes not listening to the Prime Minister, but scanning the Chamber for the Big M.

Might Peter Mandelson be skulking behind the Speaker's Chair? Behind the crowd standing by the door? Tucked away in a shadow at the back? Is the former Northern Ireland Secretary really happy to toil obscurely on the back benches for the next four years? Few believe it. How can Mr Blair neutralise the threat? What's a bean-spilling biography from this arch-insider worth, with serialisation and television rights? £2 million? After all, Betty Boothroyd secured nearly half that sum.

What if V1 spreads, E2 is delayed, the press get their teeth into V2, E3 rockets and E1 goes belly-up – and then M goes nuclear . . . ?

As a distracted Tony Blair eyed his Tory opponent yesterday, he might have mused that Q1 from WH at PMQs was the least of his problems.

One Wagging Finger Tilts The Balance

21.3.01

Doubts about the wisdom of a May election grow, as foot-and-mouth rages.

Labour's Dale Campbell-Savours is one of life's finger-waggers. Tall, stooped and sallow, he wears a sour look and a certainty that all kinds of people, mostly Tories, are up to no good.

But, however occasionally skewed the Workington MP's view, nobody doubts that he paints the world as he honestly sees it. When he seems to rebuke not the Tories but his own colleagues, Commons-watchers sit upright.

Yesterday Mr Campbell-Savours told the House – but effectively his own side – not to make light of what he called 'a real, real crisis' in the countryside. His annoyance was not unprovoked.

Government benches were half empty yesterday, and Conservative and Liberal Democrat benches almost full, for a statement from Michael Meacher, the Environment Minister, on the work of the Rural Task Force set up to help the countryside to weather the foot-and-mouth storm.

Whatever the scale of foot-and-mouth, a severe outbreak of the word 'consider' is taking place. According to Mr Meacher, the national parks are 'considering' whether and where footpaths might be reopened; the Government 'will consider' extra rate relief to local authorities; local authorities 'will consider' whether and where to defer payment of rates; and ministers, banks and the Small Business Service 'are considering' how to help those in financial trouble.

Meacher spoke ve-ry, ve-ry slow-ly, imparting to his statement a gravity its proposals lacked. To their cornucopia of 'packages of measures' ministers now add the package of potential measures.

The Tories wanted more, and sooner. Emphasising the advantage of a bipartisan approach, their chief spokesman, Archie Norman, stopped short of a scrap, but, urging the need for haste, declared that the countryside was threatened with 'meltdown and permanent loss'.

'Meltdown' may be a silly word, but Mr Norman did intend to suggest calamity and by 'permanent loss' he meant just that. To the mostly rural MPs behind him, such language did not sound absurd.

But to the Parliamentary Labour Party it did. They hooted, laughed and jeered, convinced that the Tories were going (as they saw it) over the top.

The mockery enraged – for once, genuinely – the Tory benches, who shouted 'Yes! *Yes!*' at the Government. It was a moment of real anger, of instinctive division: a revealing moment.

As Mr Norman continued, Labour backbenchers sat with arms folded, shaking their heads in disbelief, occasionally shouting 'No!' and sometimes laughing. One consulted his wristwatch in pantomime fashion. When Gary Streeter (C, Devon SW) asked the minister whether 'he really understands the depth and extent of alarm and despair and sense of crisis?' some backbenchers opposite went 'tch, tch'.

Wisely, Mr Meacher did not join this. Though he urged that we 'keep it in perspective', he called Norman's approach 'sober'. But Tory tempers were fragile. When Mr Meacher caricatured the idea of postponing some local elections as 'suspending democracy', Tories shouted 'No!'

And when Labour backbenchers rose to question the minister, it emerged that a hitherto silent minority shared the Opposition's alarm. Jack Cunningham (Lab, Copeland), the former Minister of Agriculture, used the words 'urgent' and 'crisis', said the countryside was 'suffering very, very seriously' and wanted ministers to be 'more aggressive' and commit 'more resources'. Dr Cunningham has a rural seat.

So does Mr Campbell-Savours. It is hard to put into words, he said, the sense of shock there. Tourism was 'almost wiped out'. Towns were hit too. Government must recognise this.

'Join us,' shouted a Tory.

It must be the first time that they have ever said that to Dale Campbell-Savours.

Your Task, Should You Choose to Accept It . . .

22.3.01

Government whips (one of them once told me) keep a little list. Her Majesty's Brigade of Expendables consists of that small band of backbenchers who combine, to an unusual degree, the qualities of courage and stupidity. In a crisis a name is drawn from the list and the unlucky fellow summoned for a drink with the Chief Whip. He bounds in, panting with excitement.

'Sit down, Giles,' grunts the Chief, as a massive slug of Mr Speaker's Selection sloshes into the young chap's trembling tumbler. 'I'll be straight with you. You'd be a fool to accept this assignment. You'll be on your own – you know that.

'You'll probably sink with all hands – and we won't be there to help you. You can me to **** off now,' (whips use filthy language) 'and I'll understand. Or you can ask me to elaborate . . .'

'Go on!' Giles's eyes are bulging with excitement.

'It was the PM who thought you might do it. He knows the risks. He knows *you'll* know why he can't be associated with this. But he won't forget.'

'I'll do it!' Giles bursts out. 'Whatever it is. Just tell me, and I'll do it.'

As my whip-informant added, it then remains only to make sure the chap throws the grenade and not the pin.

Thus it was (at least in this sketchwriter's imagination) that young Jonathan Shaw (Lab) came scampering in, wide eyed and hairless, for Prime Minister's Questions yesterday. At 30 the surprise winner in Chatham & Aylesford in 1997, the oval-faced Shaw has nothing to lose.

And his mission? To market-test for Tony Blair the viability of an electioneering strategy leaked to Tuesday's *Times*, appearing on our front page under the headline 'Blair bid to scare voters to the polls'.

The Prime Minister must within days decide not only whether to call an election but (if he does) what style to adopt. But in the hours since, as foot-and-mouth spreads, the national mood has darkened. Will a gung-ho 'kick the Tories in the nuts' scare campaign strike the right note? Blair must find out fast.

If evidence were needed that the mood has darkened, Prime Minister's Questions provided it. It was almost all foot-and-mouth, and when it wasn't it was doomed steelworkers.

Except for Jonathan Shaw MP. But to him in a moment.

William Hague was good: serious, lucid, insistent, without trying to score points. He was full of news about unburied carcasses and absent tourists, and ideas for sorting things out.

Tony Blair was good: tired, well-briefed, unpartisan. He was full of news about water-tables, vets' wages and that wonderful and mysterious reason why man-plus-spade doesn't equal hole: 'logistics'.

Most backbenchers picked up the sombre, fact-based mood. This was no time for . . . well, electioneering. The Chamber sensed this.

Jonathan Shaw didn't. Called by the Chair, the young trooper came whooping over the top with a bizarre question whose punchline was 'save the pounds!' – a hustings-style attack on Tory 'investment' cuts, threatening the collapse of schools and hospitals if the Tories win, etc.

Shaw's colleagues cheered bravely, but few can have missed the question's shrieking inappropriateness to the moment. It jarred. Badly. It looked even worse on telly.

Shaw sunk. Mr Blair sailed briskly on by. But the Prime Minister will have taken note.

The election was postponed.

Whips' Firebreak Quarantines Vaz

27.3.01

Keith Vaz has been quarantined.

As the Prime Minister led ministerial colleagues on to the front bench for his report from the Stockholm European Council meeting, a sorry figure tagged limply behind them. The Minister for Europe was under orders to keep his distance.

Cabinet members took their seats, Gordon Brown to Tony Blair's left. To Mr Brown's left sat an Agriculture minister. To her left sat an Environment minister. To her left sat a government whip with a big red book, arms grimly folded.

The whip was a firebreak. Between the whip and the Prime Minister were political livestock, filling the wide band which Labour spin-vets now require to separate the PM from possible media contamination with Vaz.

As a result there was no danger that the tight camera shots which the Commons imposes on television coverage of the chamber should, however momentarily, include Blair and Vaz in the same picture. Even the extreme tip of Mr Vaz's right elbow was outside the frame of any shot with Blair's left ear in it. Blair gave no indication of having noticed his colleague's presence.

Most surprising however, was the Prime Minister's sudden and weird reference to the common cold. The contain-and-slaughter policy was difficult to operate, he explained. It was 'like tracking the common cold'.

What can Mr Blair be hinting at?

Troubled by a persistent cough? Annoying sniffle? Go into hiding at once.

After the election, Vaz was dropped.

Ben Bradshaw Begins To Shake   *28.3.01*

Fiona MacTaggart (Lab, Slough) was educated at Cheltenham Ladies' College, as a baronet's daughter ought to be. She sailed into the chamber yesterday in a polished cotton trouser suit of burgundy hue, a beige silk blouse, an immense medallion of copper and brass and, tossed over the shoulder, a russet scarf in crushed velvet.

She asked about Kashmir. I half-expected Robin Cook to suggest Angora.

But Questions to the Foreign Secretary are a rich field for misunderstanding. What did Robin Cook mean when he told Ben Bradshaw (Lab, Exeter) that he saw Tchaikovsky on Sunday?

'Splendid,' I thought; 'and I saw Rossini.' One had always thought of the wild-eyed, troll-like Mr Cook as more inclined to Grieg or Mussorgsky than a fan of swirling romantic angst – but never mind; only when a Foreign Secretary gets heavily into Wagner need alarm bells ring.

The Tchaikovsky whom Mr Cook saw last week turned out to be Trajkovsky; gabbling, the Secretary of State had slightly mispronounced the name of the President of the Former Yugoslav Republic of Macedonia. For all the difference it will make to the future of the Balkans, Mr Cook might as well have seen Brahms.

I suspect ministers just make up these names. Backbenchers embarrassed to admit not having the faintest idea what the front bench is talking about, simply shut up and look impressed.

From this uncomprehending docility we must, for once, excuse fresh-faced Ben Bradshaw. Normally he nods whenever a minister speaks. It's Pavlovian. He nods immediately. He nods ferociously. He nods regardless of what the minister is saying. When the minister is the Prime Minister there is a severe danger of Mr Bradshaw dislocating his neck.

But yesterday something unprecedented happened. A particularly manic minister (bearded John Battle) was answering a particularly fatuous question (from Labour's Adrian Bailey) about 'initiatives' to 'tackle' the international drugs trade.

Mr Battle was spluttering and steaming away about 'alternative crops' (urging Bolivian peasants to grow tomatoes at 10p a pound instead of coca at a hundred times that price; a brilliant wheeze about as feasible as the 'international community's' other masterplan, revealed yesterday by the junior minister Keith Vaz: to spread 'the message of multi-ethnicity' in the Balkans).

And then Mr Bradshaw's head did what it has never been seen to do before.

It began to shake.

It was only a little shake, a gentle shake, a sorrowful hint of a shake.

But it was a beginning.

After the election, Bradshaw was appointed a junior minister.

Off-the-wall Ideas For Graffiti

4.4.01

Her Majesty's Unofficial Opposition, otherwise known as Eric Forth (C, Bromley & Chislehurst), hit the Commons yesterday for Dr Jenny Tonge's debate on graffiti. He wore a tie which, were such a gaudy thing to be sprayed by vandals on to a carriage window, would cause the entire train to be condemned.

Jenny Tonge was in vengeful mood yesterday expounding plans, in a Graffiti Control Bill of her own devising, '*to prohibit the sale of spray paint to minors*'. The punishment, she cried, 'must fit the crime!'.

Was the Lib Dem MP proposing that vandals be stripped and spray-painted? Sadly Tonge's plan was less exciting: culprits must scrub things clean.

Like many in her party, Jenny Tonge sees her role in politics as what

Winston Churchill called the promotion of 'happy thoughts' into legislation. A kindly and industrious soul, Tonge had written herself the first known wholly self-imploding speech.

The MP got off to an awkward start by contending that graffiti can be 'much-admired,' even 'brilliant', as art. Liberal Democrats find it hard to sneer at social-worker-types, so having allowed that 'some people say this is an art form' she could not dismiss them. We should distinguish, she thought, between good and bad graffiti. She was within an ace of suggesting that a new public body be set up to adjudicate graffiti, before any decision whether to prosecute the perpetrator as a vandal or commend him an artist. This is not party policy. Yet.

Next she revealed the shocking cost of paint-removal: £10 million, she gasped: how many classrooms would that provide? The answer being 'about three', she chose to leave the question hanging.

Defending her ban on paint sales to minors, Dr Tonge asked 'what legitimate purpose a young person of 15 or 16 would have buying spray paint?' This was meant to be rhetorical, but the thought then struck her that there might indeed be lawful reasons. Ah well – young people could get notes from their art-teachers, she proposed.

One possible cause of graffiti had occurred to Tonge: paint was too cheap. 'You can get five or six cans for £1!' she exclaimed. Resale Price Maintenance for paint is not her party's policy. Yet. Unwittingly she suggested why. Paint is so easy to shoplift. People 'can scoop cans off the shelf and into a bag' she pointed out. The drawback in prohibiting sale of paint to those planning to steal it did not seem to have occurred to her.

Further (she concluded), some people buy spray paint to sniff. There was a law against the sale to minors of other solvent substances: why did one never hear about prosecutions being brought?

Why indeed? But was this a subsidiary, 'anti-solvent', argument for banning spray paint sales? Why then was she saying that such laws don't work?

If, on the other hand, her concern was with graffiti, wasn't it preferable for minors to sniff rather than paint with the spray they shoplift rather than buy, in the shops which would anyway have refused to sell it, even too cheaply, without a note from a certified art teacher?

'Who will prepare and bring in this Bill?' called Mr Speaker.

'Mr Vincent Cable' (Lib Dem), 'Mr Edward Davey' (Lib Dem), 'Mr Paul Burstow' (Lib Dem), 'Mr Tom Brake' (Lib Dem) 'and myself,' cried Dr Tonge, triumphantly.

'What a shower,' barked Eric Forth, mentally inking h-a-t-e on one set of knuckles, l-i-b-s on the other.

Tory Turmoil? Call in the Troops

5.4.01

For some weeks now, William Hague has been calling in the Army. As he is not Prime Minister this has had limited effect, but as an opposition policy it's a brilliant wheeze.

The party itself is in a heck of a state, with mutinous mutterings in the Tea Room and policy differences popping up everywhere – but whatever their disagreements, any Tory can at least agree that soldiers are better at getting holes dug than civil servants.

The policy covers a multitude of uncertainties. We don't actually know what the Tories think the Government should do differently in the foot-and-mouth outbreak. We don't even know whether they want a campaign of mass vaccination, though they keep calling on the Government to make a decision on this.

But we do know they want to call in the Army. The Army, says Mr Hague, could 'sort it out'.

The Tory idea has wider application. The National Health Service seems to be in rather a mess and the Tories lack inexpensive policies to remedy this – so why not call in the Army?

Muggers stalk the streets, the police are understaffed, but the Tories don't want to propose spending increases – so why not call in the Army?

Railtrack keeps delaying the date by which it hopes to have the railways fixed, the Tories maintain an embarrassed silence, so . . .

You get the drift. At Prime Minister's Questions yesterday Hague celebrated what he claimed to be an early success in his campaign to hand Britain over to the generals, crowing at Tony Blair (never knowingly out-crowed) that two weeks ago he had proposed calling in the Army to deal with foot-and-mouth and now – lo! – the Army had been called in. Rather like Orpheus who played his lute just before sunrise every day, the young leader hopes to acquire a reputation for causing the dawn.

As the Tory search for alternative policies grows more desperate, expect more Tory calls for military intervention. But nobody expected Dennis Skinner (Lab, Bolsover) to outflank even the Tory right in a bold new plan to inject a splash of khaki right into the heart of the British constitution.

Up jumped the notorious socialist and fabled Beast of Bolsover yesterday, as sharp as mustard. Blair stared at him with that pleading 'look, y'know, Dennis, I'm all for a bit of knockabout but do just keep in mind which side you are on' expression.

'Will the Prime Minister ask the Army to take overall control of the Tory party?' he demanded.

Journalists and tourists in the galleries upstairs are not supposed to laugh out loud, but the guffaws came from high and low. Even the parliamentary clerks, who keep lemons in their mouths, smiled.

And, strange to relate, the laughter from the Tory side was, if anything, louder than from the Labour benches. Even the butt of this, William Hague, could not conceal a grin – as ever the opposite of Tony Blair, who is always trying to feign one.

But this time Mr Blair hit it right in his response. 'I yield to no one,' he smiled, 'in my admiration for the Army, but some logistical tasks, I fear, are beyond them.'

They Gas Britain   *10.4.01*

Journalists entering the Press Gallery above the Commons chamber yesterday were alarmed to see two young men sitting there with what looked like an array of miniature *Star Wars* hardware.

A giant yellow vacuum flask with dials on the side sat on the desk, alongside a sinister black receiver set and, attached to it by a wire, an air-intake wand with breathing holes at one end.

What could this mean? Were we being tested for foot-and-mouth? Had Tony Blair found the perfect excuse for culling awkward journalists?

Gingerly I approached the two operatives to inquire. Apparently the object of their investigations was not us media folk, but the air which MPs breathe. The yellow flask thing was a microbial air sampler, which sucks in air then filters out the bacteria, which are placed in little glass agar plates to be grown.

As I examined the device, Jack Straw, the Home Secretary, and the bouncy and irrepressible Tory MP for Buckingham, John Bercow (Labour Members shout '*boingg!*' whenever he jumps up to speak), started screaming at each other about something. I swear I heard the microbial give a little gasp as it sucked in the fetid air.

I turned my attention to the black receiver. This, explained the chap from RPS Consultants, was an IAQ Surveyor. 'It records temperature and humidity, and the level of gasses in the air,' he said. He waved it. As he waved, the majestically implausible (and implausibly majestic) Paul Boateng, who likes to describe himself as the Deputy Home Secretary (he isn't), opened his unbelievably wide (and widely disbelieved) mouth and began gassing about the Government's wonderful success in reforming prisons and turning them into centres of learning and personal character development. He mentioned the sum of £130 million – surely about what we're spending every week on foot-and-mouth?

Attacked by Ann Widdecombe, the chief opposition spokesman on home affairs, Mr Boateng puffed: 'The Right Hon Lady doesn't do the seriousness of the subject any service by approaching it in this way.' This is new Labour-speak for 'You've got me there, guv'. Then he called her 'cheap'. That's new Labour-speak for 'Ouch!'

And here's a funny thing. As Boateng spoke, I'll bet my bottom dollar I saw the dials on the machine go haywire. It was suffering from input-overload. There's only so much stale gas a machine can take. As for us journalists, we inhale it daily for hours. We are suffering from passive gassing. We may have to sue.

11.4.01   # What are Milburns *For*?

The House rose yesterday for the Easter recess. After that the days before the election will be just the butt-end of new Labour's first term in office.

Significant that Questions on this rather final Tuesday should have been to Alan Milburn, the Health Secretary.

Mr Milburn is new Labour without the charm. Subtract from Tony Blair his likeability and you have Mr Milburn.

Critics may call Mr Blair hollow, may question the substance of his policies, may mock his mania for presentation and his instinct to sidestep debate and news-manage 'events' out of harm's way; they may shudder at the control-freakery; but few can quite escape the impression of personal idealism: a sense that Anthony Charles Lynton Blair genuinely wishes to do good in the world.

This is Blair's secret weapon. It is why we keep forgiving him. When he said 'I'm a pretty straight kind of a guy' – and although he said it (over the Bernie Ecclestone affair) in a dodgy cause – it was believable because we really do suspect he means well. His aims being virtuous, we overlook the skulduggery employed to further them.

When all the nonsense now being written and still to be written about spin has lined the cat litter for which such newsprint is destined, it will remain the case that new Labour's super-durable honeymoon owes less to spin than to two truths: that we were fed up with the Conservatives; and that Blair seems well intentioned. Strip these truths from new Labour, and the residue is unviable.

Time will deal with the first. Within weeks 'the last Government' – always to blame – will be the Labour Government of 1997–2001.

And the second truth? Never underestimate the importance to Blairism of its garnish: Blair. The alternative is Alan Milburn: on-message, managerial, mealy-mouthed, uncontemplative, bullying, triumphalist and content-free. Milburn is new Labour ungarnished.

He rose scowling at the dispatch box yesterday with the swaggering menace of a bouncer in a Co Durham casino. MPs inquired about cancer services, but Milburn preferred to discuss 'decades of shameful neglect'. Under the Tories 'not a penny piece' had been 'earmarked for cancer'.

This was not honest. He meant that the last Government had left health authorities to decide how to slice the cake.

Another backbencher asked him about cancers attributable to asbestos, but Milburn moved swiftly to his preferred topic, cancers attributable to the Tories.

Someone asked about heart disease. Milburn said the Tories failed 'to earmark a single penny piece for heart services'.

The Health Secretary betrayed no trace of originality or even thought. There being no evidence of what Mr Milburn was in politics *for*, it mattered that he should be likeable. He was not.

'It is one of the recurring phenomena of politics,' writes John Peyton

(Lord Peyton of Yeovil) in a fascinating new biography of Harold Wilson's Chief Scientific Adviser, Solly Zuckerman, 'that new governments seem like rockets propelled upwards into the sky, not so much by great new ideas as by a rather older and simpler one, that it is Buggins's turn. Reaching their peak, they spread both light and sound to the chagrin of their opposition who, crushed, disappointed and at odds with each other, make premature and ill-conceived attacks which hurt only themselves . . . In this first phase of upward climb, governments seem to carry all before them. Although not every minister loves his neighbour, the sounds of friction are muffled.'

The trajectory is still up. But as the rocket falls, ministers like Milburn will speed its descent.

The Last Government Will Soon Be Their Fault

24.4.01

Whether a minister or a backbencher, there is one pleasure that Parliament still affords a Labour MP. It must be enjoyed soon, before it dies on June 7. These are the last days in which it will be possible for Labour to blame anything on the last Government. They may well win on June 8, but thereafter the last Government will be Labour.

Even in Defence Questions yesterday, ministers were thumbing their noses at the previous administration while they could. Was there a problem (as the Tories alleged) about recruitment to the Armed Forces? If so, John Spellar told John Bercow (C, Buckingham), this was a problem born 'under the previous administration' which *this* administration was tackling. And that was a tougher task than 'under the levels of unemployment your Government left us'. But soon we may hear the first Labour minister tripped in mid-crow about the horrors of the last Government, by Tory cackles of 'yours!'.

Labour need a plan. During Margaret Thatcher's second term, the Tories made famous a simple phrase, 'the Winter of Discontent', and let that serve. Labour needs something equally striking. 'The last Conservative Government' is not vivid enough. It is beginning to sound like 'the last Liberal Government'.

Memo to Millbank: the politics of inheritance needs resloganing.

Hazel's No Bike and Etonians Don't Piddle

A June general election looks inevitable . . .

Dr Johnson was wrong. For MPs, at least, the approach of a day of reckoning does not concentrate the mind. They go all giggly. They cannot concentrate at all.

At Questions to the Secretary of State for the Environment, Transport and the Regions yesterday the House seemed less like a legislature than a class for disruptive adolescents.

Poor Mr Prescott had to pretend not to hear as the kids on the government benches (furious about America's rebuff to the Kyoto accord) thumbed their noses at the United States. Nigel Griffiths (Edinburgh S), a former minister and present cheerleader for Gordon Brown, called President George W Bush 'the toxic Texan', Jane Griffiths (Reading E) called him 'the fool on Capitol Hill'. The Chair bawled for order. Unruliness ruled.

Mr Prescott seemed unconcentrated, too. He accused David Rendel (Lib Dem, Newbury) of 'piddling around on the sides, as Liberals tend to do'. Tall, dignified and faintly grand, it is hard to imagine the Old Etonian Mr Rendel piddling around, or indeed piddling at all. Etonians piss. Harrovians piddle.

The tone was lowered further when a Tory, Gerald Howarth (Aldershot) tried to make a point about flashing rear lights on bicycles.

It was Anne Campbell (Lab, Cambridge), looking rather extra-ordinary in leather, who had first got them fired up about cycling. She wanted more of it. Replying, an unlikely-looking chap with a stubby moustache called Bob Ainsworth, said to be a minister, made a baffling reference to 'the bowler-headed Member on the back benches opposite', which most of the kids took to mean Desmond Swayne (C, New Forest W), a keen cyclist who wears a bowler-shaped polystyrene helmet, though not in the chamber. Mr Ainsworth hummed and hawed about flashing rear lights.

''E's a flasher!' shouted Dennis Skinner (Lab, Bolsover) – about whom we were not clear.

'Of course,' said Denis MacShane (Lab, Rotheram), an independently wealthy cyclist and polyglot smartypants who, as he fades like the Cheshire cat, will leave behind only a sneer, an Asprey's cycle-clip and a lingering suspicion of manicured fingernails, '*all* Tory cyclists are well-known flashers'.

The kids fell about. Mr MacShane went on to complain about 'those little yellow lines' indicating cycle lanes, 'which only serve as an attraction for motorists to knock down cyclists like me'.

Denis, Denis – are you reading this? The attraction wouldn't be the little yellow lines.

By now, Tony Blair's little ray of sunshine, Hazel Blears (Lab, Salford), had become aerated about two-wheelers, too. Up she bobbed to question another minister, Keith Hill.

'As chair of the all-party motorcycling group,' she chirped. Mr Hill craned round excitedly, baring his enormous teeth. Like the Mona Lisa's eyes (another sketchwriter has observed) Keith Hill's teeth follow you round the room.

But something in the bizarre Hill brain short-circuited. How what escaped his teeth ever made it through, we shall never know. He blurted out: 'Blears the Bike!'

Clutching her tiny bosom, Ms Blears shook her head in amazed disbelief. John Prescott was almost wetting – sorry, piddling – himself. Knights of the shires chortled pinkly. Half the government back benches shook with suppressed laughter. All the Tory benches shook with unsuppressed laughter. Even Mrs Campbell smiled.

Decency compels me to point out that Ms Blears has no such reputation. Fairness compels me to point out that Mr Hill did not mean to imply it. What, though, he did mean to imply is anybody's guess. Possibly he's under some kind of stress at home.

General Gordon and Sgt Major Blair

26.4.01

Even as Tony Blair glides through Prime Minister's Questions, swatting the Opposition for easy fours as he did again yesterday, a slow shift is taking place. Mr Blair is losing altitude. Not fast, but imperceptibly the magnetism weakens. There are no knockout blows; it's more a matter of aura-fatigue. Something is ebbing.

There he was at the dispatch box yesterday, shuffling fast and furious through his reams of notes, tackling questions about hospitals in Kettering and interest rates on emergency loans for rural businesses.

But where was Gordon Brown? Running the Government, the Chancellor's friends would reply, winking. Mr Brown does not look in on the Commons too often these days.

Impertinent questions from Tories he considers *lèse-majesté*; fawning questions from his own side he suffers – barely. The Chancellor does not see why he should articulate phrases like 'the burden of taxation has risen' just because some pipsqueak English Tory asks him to. There isn't much Mr Brown feels obliged to articulate.

The Commons has not, for instance, had the benefit of his thoughts (or presence) during debates on the foot-and-mouth disaster, though he was good enough to mention in passing that the outbreak was 'unexpected, unwanted and most unfortunate'. You cannot imagine Brown swotting up on a demand from Laurence Robertson (Con, Tewkesbury) for a public inquiry into an explosion at a chemical plant.

But there was Tony Blair, teeming with information about imminent reports from the Environment Agency. Some would think this is a matter for the departmental minister, the Deputy Prime Minister. Others think Mr Blair *is* the Deputy Prime Minister.

Brown turns up here and there, on a whim and regardless of who the appropriate minister might be, to unveil a plaque or cut a ribbon on a sexy new Government initiative. Or he'll flex a bicep in the face of pesky Europeans telling him how to run the economy. Or, by the slightest twitch of an eyebrow on that leaden countenance, indicate a disposition to loosen the purse-strings here, crack the financial whip there.

Hands in pockets he looks away, whistling a Highland air, while John

Prescott twists on the rack of London Underground's hated Public-Private Partnership – as Prescott did after savage criticism from Jim Fitzpatrick (Lab, Poplar and Canning Town) at Questions on Tuesday. Brown made the rack. The Mayor winds it. Brown could let Prescott off it.

And how about the fate of the other Brown, one of the Chancellor's protégés? Sad heads shake. Gordon has decided to let Nick go. Meanwhile, Tony runs around like a headless chicken trying to sort out foot-and-mouth.

Like a regimental sergeant-major, the Prime Minister was in jaunty form in the Chamber, tearing strips off William Hague, bawling out John Redwood, blanking Charles Kennedy and boosting morale among the Labour squaddies.

The General, however, was not present – probably back at HQ poring over maps.

Who's Been Eating *His* Porridge?

2.5.01

Could the *Daily Star* be right? Yesterday, beneath a snapshot of the bearded Foreign Secretary, juxtaposed with one of the false-bearded impressionist Rory Bremner, appeared the headline 'THROBBIN' ROBIN COOK – He lowers voice after TV send-up'.

One doubted this. Had our ethical statesman nothing better to do than watch comedy programmes and then experiment with his voice to stop them making fun of his squeaky delivery?

The *Daily Star* had no doubt. 'Gossips,' the paper said, 'claim the Foreign Secretary was hugely peeved when the television impressionist ruthlessly mimicked his high-pitch twang.'

As Mr Cook always sounds as though he is hugely peeved, how did they know? It is that capricious see-sawing of the voice, forever skipping up an octave in pique, quivering dangerously between a sulky squeak and a petulant trill, then descending again into an irritated grunt, that has attracted the phrase 'hugely peeved' in the first place. The man has been peeved since the pram. Should he now have become peeved that he sounds peeved when his voice may reach a pitch audible only to bats?

So sketchwriters scampered into the Chamber yesterday for Questions to the Secretary of State for Foreign and Commonwealth Affairs. We could check for ourselves.

Michael Fabricant (C, Lichfield) asked when the Foreign Secretary would next meet his American counterpart to discuss the future of Nato.

The hugely peeved statesman rose. 'I regularly meet . . .' he began.

Sketchwriters gasped. It was true! Cook was trying to growl. 'I expect we will discuss . . .' came a low, fog-horning sound from the general directionof the Foreign Secretary's wispy ginger beard.

How did it sound? Recall your nursery days when your mother used to read *Goldilocks and the Three Bears* to you before bed. 'And the *big* bear said,' she would read – then, lowering her voice to a daddy-bear grunt – 'who's been eating *my* porridge?'

That was how Mr Cook was speaking. As if someone had pressed his tummy.

Very well, we thought, anyone can do this for a while. But sooner or later – and when his infuriating Tory Shadow, Francis Maude, begins tormenting him – the voice will slip, or rather skip.

Mr Maude rose. Maude has a voice like vinegar. He enrages Cook. He sneered at the Foreign Secretary for a few minutes.

Cook's beard waggled perilously and his head began to move in a series of involuntary jerks. 'For an Opposition,' he began, quite angry and low, 'which has *claimed* to believe . . .'

On 'claimed' there was an awful tremble in the *basso profundo* and for a second we thought the *epiglottis Cookensis* was about to flip. But from somewhere in the caverns of his elfin brain a small voice was warning: 'Keep it down, Robin, keep it down', and he did. 'I would have thought . . .' he continued, gravel-toned.

Paul Robeson it was not. But it was no longer Bremner.

Chasing the Soap   *3.5.01*

Trying to pin down Tony Blair is like chasing one of those slivers of soap beneath the suds of a warm bath. You think you know where it is, or was; you plunge a hand in its general direction – and it slips away, to

brush lightly against your left toe; until, that is, you make a grab for it –
but there it goes again, slithering past your right buttock.

It's infuriating. For the Tories at Prime Minister's Questions
yesterday, so infuriating that the Opposition threw its rubber duck out
of its collective bath. Unfortunately it hit the Chair. The Speaker, Mr
Michael Martin, then threw a wobbly of his own.

But to begin at the beginning . . .

Nobody could lay a finger on our self-lubricating Prime Minister.
William Hague made a plucky attempt to discuss the Wembley fiasco
with him. Blair's response? 'Not a government project.'

Andrew Robathan (C, Blaby) asked about John Prescott's alleged
grace-and-favour London flat provided (he said) by the RMT union, and
the cool million given (he said) to Mr Prescott's constituency
association.

Blair's response? 'Not correct.'

Charles Kennedy asked whether and why this Government was
spending less than the last on health, education and pensions.

Blair's response? 'No.'

Jacqui Lait (C, Beckenham) called for an inquiry into the affairs of
the former Labour Paymaster General.

Blair's response? None of the Prime Minister's business.

The Liberal Democrats' transport spokesman, Tom Brake, asked
how Blair responded to savage criticism of Labour's plans for London
Underground, from Bob Kiley, the Transport Commissioner.

Blair's response? 'Not the advice we received.'

Crispin Blunt (C, Reigate) asked about defence cuts.

Blair's response? 'Not true.'

Mr Hague asked about Blair's attitude to US proposals for a
missile defence system. Blair's response? 'We don't yet have a
proposal.'

As Tories chased the soap, Blair slid beneath the bubbles with
insouciance. Tory tempers wore thin. Blair accused Hague of band-
wagoning – an astonishing accusation, as Hague pointed out, from the
Downing Street saviour of Phoenix the calf.

Hague pressed Blair on Wembley. The Prime Minister ignored the
question and started quoting from a leaflet he claimed had been put out
by a prospective Tory parliamentary candidate somewhere.

The row continues. We must tiptoe away. Mr Hague is smarting, the
Tories are snarling, the clerks are scratching their wigs . . .

And the Prime Minister? Wasn't that him, slipping between the loofah and your left thigh, just beneath the Timotei?

The Invisible Glass Shield

So long as a minister remains useful to the machine, an invisible glass shield protects him.

Nobody sees it lowered or knows by whom. Nor is it easy to describe its operation. Let us just say that, in the buzz and whisper which is as much a part of the ambience of Westminster as are shrieks and gibbers in the night air around London Zoo, criticism of this minister finds no echo. Snigger about him to any insider, and you meet the blank stare of the Zanzibar police.

Journalists like to stay on the winning side of argument and prophecy. It's not enough to be insightful: events must prove you right. The commentator who unfairly criticises a minister who, in the event, falls, is a more useful member of his profession than the commentator who justly criticises a minister who goes on rising. We are subliminally alert for the half-official winks which encourage us in a line of speculation – and for those slightest of shrugs, which warn us off.

For ministers (often the last to know) the experience must be creepy: *why* is the word on the street that colleague A is thriving? And why, all at once, are people snorting whenever the name of colleague B is pronounced?

Glass slides silently into place – or away. It's like having plainclothes security cover so discreet that you don't even know who your bodyguards are; but one morning you wake up and something in the wind tells you protection has been withdrawn. You walk out of your front door alone, suddenly vulnerable to any passing sniper.

. . . All of which may help to answer a teasing question: how does Robin Cook survive?

He's frightful. Nobody believes a word he says. People don't even bother to contradict him any more: they just look, aghast, frown and walk away.

Fretting, preening, clucking and cooing to himself, and scuttling importantly around like a cockroach in its Sunday best, the Foreign

Secretary is about as plausible as Liz Hurley's lips.

Yet he stays. You ask why? Sources close to Downing Street will tell you. The answer is Because.

We are therefore unlikely to read elsewhere in the press or hear on the breeze that, hauled into the chamber by the Speaker yesterday to explain Britain's position on the US nuclear defence proposals, Cook put up another perfectly ludicrous performance.

Everybody knows Britain's position. It is as set out by the Prime Minister's Press Secretary, Alastair Campbell, on Wednesday. The decision in principle has been taken: we will co-operate with the Americans. For months the Defence Secretary, Geoff Hoon, has been signalling as much (for that dwindling band of obsessives who watch the Commons these days) at Defence Questions. Unfortunately it is not what Tony Blair said at Prime Minister's Questions this week, not hours before Campbell said otherwise. Mr Blair pretended to be awaiting details with an open mind.

Tormented by his own backbenchers, kneecapped by Tony Benn (who reminded Cook of his 'passionate' commitment to CND), the Foreign Secretary – had he been unable to make a clean breast of things – might at least have had the decency to be uncommunicative. Instead, he danced around like a little circus dog, barking at Tories, jumping and snapping at every distraction, then standing on his hind legs to inform us gravely that Blair and Campbell had said the same thing.

The Tories laughed. They have given up on Cook. We all have.

So, it turned out at the next reshuffle, had the Prime Minister.

St Anthony's Chariot Swings Low

9.5.01

Blair calls a general election.

Tony Blair, who last year ran into trouble with women at the WI, yesterday chose girls of a more gullible age.

With a Cross behind him, sacred stained glass above him, the upturned faces of 500 schoolgirls in pink and blue gingham before him, and to the strains of a choir singing 'I who make the skies of light/I will make the darkness bright/Here I am', Mr Blair launched his campaign at the St Saviour's & St Olave's church school in Southwark.

In these dark days, life remains bearable by grace only of the conviction that one day this kind of thing will surely be swept away on a great wave of national revulsion. Yesterday that conviction faltered.

It was nauseating. It was breathtakingly, toe-curlingly, hog-whimperingly tasteless. It was unbelievably ill-judged. Just when one is teased by the thought that Blair might not be all bad, he does something which nobody with a grain of sense or sensibility could even contemplate.

If the PM sanctioned the arrangements for this dire event, and if there is a Hell, he will go there.

To prepare for his entry, the choir sang an ethnic song whose predominating lyric was wah-wah-wah. In new Labour this passes for an argument. The wah-wah-wah increased. Cameras swivelled.

Wild rumours swept the audience that Phoenix the calf was coming on with Blair. Then, to girlish screams normally reserved for adolescent pop idols, Tony Blair strode calfless on to the chapel stage, positioned himself between the Cross and the cameras and beneath the motto 'Heirs of the past, makers of the future', flung off his jacket to further screams, and sat down in shirtsleeves, legs apart, arms spread like a sumo-wrestler. A girls' choir sang 'We are the children of the future', which was not the case.

Blair grinned soupily. Mobile phones trilled. Flashguns popped. I moved closer. A Labour aide warned me off. 'You will end up in the cutaways, Matthew,' she hissed.

'*A time to love, a time to share,*
A time to show how much we care,'
sang the girls. Alastair Campbell clapped caringly.

Of Mr Blair's speech, the less said the better. We are not used to seeing a Prime Minister, with a Cross behind him, to an audience of children in their own school chapel, attacking the Opposition. 'What did you think of that?' my *Daily Mail* colleague said to a small black girl after the speech.

'Bunch o'lies,' said the perceptive child.

Something amiss with the chapel sound-amplification caused Mr Blair's voice to sound as though he had just inhaled from a helium tap. Listening to it made us feel as though we had. But the speech was for television. Few of the children looked riveted by his thoughts on negative equity.

Most did not try. When the Prime Minister told them he had come to win not just votes but hearts, one girl, drawing her blouse up at the midriffs, placed the collar over her head. It was an eloquent response. The speech was vapid. Seldom have so many clichés of sound, vision and song been dragooned together in so dismal a cause.

'What I say to my country,' said Mr Blair, extemporising in monarchial fashion from a speech we were told was not a speech but 'remarks' – but which was pre-released to the press. Even the remarks are scripted.

Beside me, and before the closing hymn – yes, *hymn* – Alastair Campbell sneezed. I tried to say 'Bless you'. The words stuck in my throat.

11.5.01   Hague Was . . . Well, *Fine*

The music was heroic. The venue was historic. The atmosphere was electric. And the geometry of the backdrop recalled the angle of the *Titanic* as she sank beneath the waves. The Conservative Party was launching its Manifesto 2001 at the Institute of Civil Engineers.

In a hall that witnessed the launch of Neil Kinnock's election-losing 1992 Shadow Budget, and to music specially written for the Tories by the composer of the Wombles theme, members of the Shadow Cabinet marched on to a stage-set in which everything seemed to be at 45 degrees except the mysterious slogans 'through our lives' and 'knowing who we are', which were vertical and to be read from the bottom up. The lectern, which has been salvaged from last year's Tory conference platform at Bournemouth (times are hard at Central Office) was all triangles and spiky microphones. The whole set was dominated by a great sinking cube at a crazy slant, constructed in glass panels suggestive of a flatpack double-glazed conservatory home-assembled by an amateur DIY enthusiast. Aimed, no doubt, at the pebble-dash vote.

Backstage, where senior Tories had gathered, I joined a group of journalists chatting to a key member of the Shadow Cabinet.

'We shouldn't be here,' said a journalist, 'this is for top Tories. Don't go,' pleaded the Tory, 'or I won't have anyone interesting to talk to.'

As Ann Widdecombe, the Shadow Home Secretary, sashayed in to a swelling chord, we regretted that, for her entry at least, the composer had not reverted to *Remember You're a Womble*.

She sat down and tried to look statesmanlike. Beside her, Michael Portillo, the Shadow Chancellor, now road-testing the spectacles of a French intellectual, tried to look gritty. Beside him Francis Maude, the Shadow Foreign Secretary, tried to look sexy. Then in walked William Hague and tried to sound like the next Prime Minister.

He was introduced by Michael Ancram, the party chairman, trying not to sound like a decent cove cursed with the thankless task of sounding the ship's whistle for a doomed voyage crewed by earnest no-hopers – but too much of a gent to jump ship now.

Mr Ancram exhorted us to etch into memory a luminous phrase of Mr Hague's at PM's Questions on Wednesday, and misquoted it. The Conservative leader was, said Ancram, 'quite simply inspiring'.

Then Hague spoke. And that was the problem. Hague was fine – quite simply fine – *not* inspiring.

It was bravely and competently done, though. What Hague said was neither nonsense, nor unintelligent, nor without point. He delivered his speech in relaxed and lucid style, and with confidence. He answered some cruel questions from the press quick-wittedly and with grace. He was pleasant, bright and funny.

But whatever quality it is that inspired that assembly of Davidian next-worlders in Waco, Texas, to set themselves alight in the firm belief that Heaven's gates were about to be opened to them . . . Hague didn't show it. The Tory leader is no David Koresh, and the better man for it; but something extra was needed; something inflammatory; everyone was anxious for it; and it didn't quite come.

Instead we witnessed a performance that was wholly sure-footed. That it was only slightly flat-footed should not normally matter; but my eye kept straying from the very earthbound figure at the lectern, and my ear from the very earthbound speech he was making, to that sickeningly tilted rectangle behind him, ready to dive into the floorboards. This was an emergency. This man was not an emergency measure.

Wheel Comes Off Strong
14.5.01   # Leadership

Yesterday in Sedgefield, the wheel came off strong leadership.

Strong Leadership is the name of a bus: one of Tony Blair's three battle buses. And while the Prime Minister was busy pressing the flesh inside the Trimdon Labour Club, your sketchwriter spotted the bus, parked so that its wheel-change was hidden from the press. 'Damn,' a Labour organiser supervising the wheel change said to me, 'we didn't think you'd see this. Puncture. Nail gone straight through.'

But Mr Blair's speech was anything but flat. To feel obliged to like anything a politician says is painful for a sketchwriter, but this was Blair's finest, most thoughtful, least strutting performance in many years. Maybe coming up from London to real people in a real place has that effect.

I had not emerged from my minicab into this hard-bitten little village in the breezy Sunday afternoon, with high hopes. *The Times*'s news editor had telephoned the night before. 'Blair vision, tomorrow, Sedgefield, 2.30,' he said. Many through history have had visions, but these have tended to come as a surprise. It seemed remarkable that this vision could be so accurately predicted that the pilgrims were able to arrive before the visionary, rather than, as has been the custom, the other way round.

'What do you think of the media circus?' a journalist asked a lady whom he assumed to be local. 'I don't think I qualify,' she said: 'I've driven here to *look* at the media circus.'

It was out in force. Gazing in wonder at the three menacing battle buses with their darkened windows – *The Work Goes On, Strong Britain*, and the ill-fated *Strong Leadership* – a small crowd witnessed the descent of the linen jackets with bright ties, the T-shirts with fluffy mikes, the hard-faced women in black trouser suits, and a hundred miles of trailing cables. Sketchwriters were whipped into line behind crash barriers.

Lonnie Donegan had been the last big name at the Trimdon Labour Club and when the quasi-royal couple strode up the concrete path, Cherie wearing some kind of sari and Tony that tense lower-face smile from which the eye-muscles have been wholly detached, we braced ourselves for another load of skiffle.

In he walked. And somehow this time it was different. The place was nothing to do with Millbank, and it was as if the place took over. Blair's constituency agent, John Burton, set the tone with a homely, unscripted introduction.

Describing the Prime Minister as 'someone we love very much' to local Labour Party members assembled to readopt him as their candidate, he added: 'I gotta tell you it'll be a bit of a problem if you don't.'

Then Blair spoke. He looked tired. But his speech took wings. It sounded – how can I put this and be believed? – meant. It contained real arguments. It was defensive – 'I honestly do stand for something' was the subtext – but the defence was convincing.

Explaining how some of Thatcherism had seemed right and necessary for its time, while some had repelled him, Blair charted his own ideological journey, and his growing recognition of where his party had gone wrong in the last century. 'I do not conform to the traditional political stereotypes because I don't believe in them,' he said, and it rang true.

For 15 minutes I was able to feel on this man's side. Then, speech over, I tried to leave through the club's lounge. 'You have no access here,' a Millbank-type advised me, barring my way.

'Stay and be a crowd,' I heard another Labour minder advising a local person.

'On Wednesday Tony Blair will put policy meat into this sandwich of philosophy,' I heard a Sky reporter telling his camera.

And the spell broke.

A Brave Face – But Does He Weep?

18.5.01

'Any of you got any eggs?' asked William Hague in the rain yesterday. He was descending from his helicopter, *Common Sense*, in one of those car-coats they advertise in *The Sunday Times Magazine* at £39.95. Ffion was with him.

Egg-throwing? It was a forlorn hope. Arriving out of a grey cloud, the Tory leader was struggling to be interesting enough for anyone to want to hit him.

The touchdown of *Common Sense* on a waste of wet grass somewhere near the A1 was not auspicious. The helicopter flew in
confidently enough, but then seemed to hesitate about where to land. It
hovered over what seemed a likely patch of grass, then changed its mind
and hovered somewhere else. Then a gust of wind blew it sideways.
Finally it hovered back to where it had started and, very tentatively,
settled in a puddle. A metaphor for Mr Hague's leadership.

Out came Ffion, looking fabulous. Out came William, looking – well,
fine. Riding the Tory battle bus to Peterborough, we had heard him
interviewed on the *Today* programme and he had been – well, pretty
good really. Watching his tour of Peterborough and St Albans yesterday
was a lesson in keeping your head when all around you are losing theirs.

Yet still the polls slide. How this man stays so jaunty is a modern
wonder. 'It's not my policy to hit voters during elections,' he grinned to
reporters anxious for his views on John Prescott. He was funny, quick-
witted and, apparently, relaxed.

But it's not enough and you can tell he knows it.

With Ffion you cannot tell. She has glamour, presence and a feline
confidence. She draws eyes and applause wherever she goes. Even old
Tory ladies squeal as a Jaguar door opens and an elegant Welsh leg
extends kerbwards.

There were many such old ladies yesterday. The doughty couple were
met at the Bull Hotel by a brave little posse of septuagenarians, some
with sticks, many with hearing aids, a couple quite unsteady on their
feet, and one in a Panama hat. These were good, brave people but they
ought not have been carrying the weight of their Tory candidate's
constituency campaign.

A morning street-meeting in the town had been cancelled. Instead we
proceeded to what appeared to be a backyard of the Bull Hotel for
Hague to unveil a mobile billboard before a minuscule crowd. Even this
furtive ritual was wrecked by a posse of Labour demonstrators shouting
him down. The old ladies looked dismayed. Hague looked unperturbed.

The sound system failed. Hague carried on as best he could. As
supporters tried to make a joyful noise, a UK Independence Party infil-
trator wrecked the speech's end with a sustained harangue. Everybody
started shouting. The pair left, Hague calm, Ffion looking as though she
couldn't remember when she had enjoyed herself so hugely.

Undaunted, the pair sped to St Albans for a rally in the square. The
weather turned icy. The rain bucketed down. The rally was cancelled

and a meet-the-party-workers in the Town Hall hastily arranged. A claque of supporters were spooked by protestors with pillowcases over their heads. Ffion ignored them and looked overjoyed as shivering Tories attempted an ecstatic cheer in the rain. Upstairs the couple staged Britain's first centrally heated, indoor walkabout in a half-empty hall. Hague threw himself at his speech like a *Just a Minute* contestant, the candidate, Charles Elphicke, nodding and grinning like a zombie.

William and Ffion left, for all the world as though they were having a perfectly lovely time – to brave cheers and a group outside shouting: 'You're not welcome here!'

This campaign was to be William Hague's finest hour, the journey he has been planning for 20 years. It must be scary to grab the wheel, hit the gas pedal, and feel no response. Alone in the dark with Ffion in the small hours, does he weep?

Ginger Nut Inspects Bananas   *16.5.01*

''Ere's that ginger bloke – you know – wazzisname'. South London was greeting the arrival of Big Banana, the Liberal Democrats' bus, containing Charles Kennedy.

Big Banana caused quite a stir. Mr Kennedy caused something closer to bewilderment. The media herd caused total mayhem.

It had been the Liberal Democrat leader's intention to press the flesh on the streets of Camberwell and Peckham with the constituency's earnest and nervous Lib Dem candidate, Donnachadh McCarthy. Kennedy arrived on a yellow bus. McCarthy arrived on a yellow bike. Both were greeted at East Street Market by a posse of troublemaking Tory youths waving 'Save the £' placards on sticks.

In moved the cameras – a battalion of them. Grinning Tories stuck their placards in front of the lenses. Despairing Liberal Democrats stuck their orange placards in front of the Tory ones, TV crews jumped on fruit boxes and stuck their enormous fluffy mikes in front of everything. Cameramen tripped, photographers clicked, reporters jostled, sketch-writers chortled, Tories and Liberal Democrats remonstrated with each other, police constables circled like anxious sheepdogs, TV anchormen stared meaningfully into lenses and belted out banalities . . .

. . . And South London gawped in amazement. 'Can I be on telly?' shrieked one woman? 'What's it all abaht?' wailed another.

'Tell 'im to buy something 'cos we're skint,' a stallholder selling lacy black bras and panties bawled.

'Hi, I'm Charles Kennedy,' cooed the ginger nut at the centre of the storm, moving down through the market as the media fell over each other in pursuit and women with pushchairs cursed. 'Justice! Honesty!' cooed Kennedy. 'Rubbish,' shouted a chap behind a greengrocer's barrow, selling tomatoes by the pound. The ginger nut looked sheepish.

Some Liberal Democrats tried to pull down the Tory placards. 'Keep the pound,' shouted a Jamaican accent. 'But what's it all abaht?' insisted the first woman. 'I don't know what they're tryin' to do.'

'This is killin' my business,' complained the proprietor of a barrow-load of tat as the ginger nut was borne helplessly on a wave of fluffy mikes. 'Ah fort 'e wuz interested in 'elpin' the small entre-manure.' 'It's all bullshit, innit?' said a woman with kids.

'Hi, I'm Charles Kennedy' repeated the ginger nut, showing sudden, desperate interest in a reggae music stall. Its proprietor, in shades, eyed him suspiciously. Kennedy bought *Reggae Revolution* for £3 'Three pounds? Bootlegged' muttered a colleague. Kennedy fumbled for loose change.

'I don't want any of that foreign single stuff,' growled the shades.

Kennedy remonstrated. 'Nah, that don't win ya a vote mate,' said the shades.

'Drivin' us all mad the next four weeks,' muttered a flower seller.

'I think that Hague looks like he's gonna start anuvva war,' opined the shades. ''E scares me. I prefer Nigel Portillo.' The pack stumbled on, camera bags knocking the sticks from under cursing pensioners.

'Good business today?' hummed the ginger nut to a fruit seller, displaying his wares in imperial measures. 'Could I have some bananas?' The fellow cut a bunch. 'Our bus is called Big Banana, you know,' remarked Kennedy. The fruit seller handed him his bunch, wordlessly.

'Let it dangle, Charles, let it dangle,' called a cameraman urgently. 'I beg your pardon?' said the ginger nut.

'Five teachers missing in every school in the constituency,' said the candidate, '70 policemen short . . .'

'Anyway, Labour's gonna win again,' said a passing shopper, 'not as big as last time, but big.'

A Royal Train

It was almost medieval. Tony Blair took his court, his unruly knights, a handful of jesters and his most trusty bodyguards on a procession. In stately formation they moved across England from the Palace of Westminster to a great hall in the Midlands, where a ceremony was performed in the sight of special subjects summoned to attend. Then he visited the sick and processed with his entourage back to London.

King Tony's court was his entire Cabinet, led by his favourite, a blind minister called David Blunkett. His unruly knights were most of Fleet Street's most important political editors. His jesters were sketchwriters, licensed to mock. The bodyguards were from the Special Branch. The ceremony was the Unveiling of the Manifesto. The special subjects were favoured members of the local Labour Party. And the great hall was the International Conference Centre in Birmingham.

And the procession went by train. The 07.37 from Euston to Birmingham yesterday resembled nothing so much as a royal train. It was a metaphor for new Labour. Like his Government the destination was a mystery: not until it left were we allowed to know officially where we were going. Where might it stop? Court attendants were not allowed to tell us. How long would it take? Like Labour's manifesto promises, the timescale was not within our knowledge. As with new Labour patronage, so ticketing: you couldn't buy a ticket but if you knew the right person they waved you on.

Be at Euston at 6.45, they said. When did the train leave? They could tell you – but then they would have to kill you. Which platform? 'When you need to know, you'll be told'. It was a sort of special train, put on by Virgin. Pretty damn special as it turned out, for it arrived without delay.

A royal departure requires cheers. These were provided by a claque of gimlet-eyed Labour activists, with their placards. These were handmade affairs. One had been decorated with homely flourishes. 'That's a sweet poster,' I said to its lady bearer, 'did you make it yourself?'

'No, we were issued with them,' she said.

To tiny squeals and joyful applause from the claque, the King strode down the platform in shirtsleeves, cloak flung informally over his shoulder. The rest of the court were already aboard as the royal personage boarded, liveried Virgin servants in attendance at the carriage doors.

Uniformed policemen guarded the access between carriages as the royal train pulled out of Euston, the cheers fading behind us. King Tony was installed with his Lord High Steward, Gordon, seated opposite. Tony faced forward: Gordon got the backwards-facing seat. The rest of the Privy Council spread themselves through the carriage, the King's hired assassin, Alastair Campbell, seated very close. We journalists were in the next carriage, supervised by court officials, mostly women in black. 'May we film him?' a colleague asked one.

'Apparently not.'

'Why?'

'Bids are in.'

'But what's the point of this train if we can't film him?' Silence.

Still, it was a privilege to know our carriage was hooked up to one in which the greatest in the kingdom were travelling. One of these soon came through to talk to us.

Like a ticket inspector recently retrained in the art of customer relations, Gordon Brown was all smiles and small talk. He stopped at every table. On and on he chatted, with time for even the most humble. Frankly, he just wouldn't go away. Hadn't he work to do?

Then the answer dawned. He had been seated opposite Tony. So this is how you make Gordon socialise with the rabble: give him no alternative but socialising with the Prime Minister.

At Milton Keynes the royal train stopped. Puzzling. Surely nobody was getting off? But soon we saw the crowd of Labour disciples with their happy posters, eyes aflame, dancing around outside the royal compartment and cheering. Some pesky Tories with 'Save the £' signs had broken through to the platform and were being repulsed. I made for the door to see them. 'Journalists aren't allowed off', said a woman courtier, barring my way. This may be contrary to railway bylaws, but what's a bylaw when the Lawgiver-in-Chief is on board?

The Chancellor, having now conversed with everyone in two carriages, passed us on his way back to his seat. Two minutes later he shot back into our carriage. Tony still in his seat, then? Brown began a second series of consultations with hacks.

At Birmingham New Street, virtually the entire Virgin workforce seemed to be lined up in uniform, hands behind backs at the doors of carriages, for the alighting King to pass. He passed. He was conveyed in a Jaguar, we in buses, to the hall, for the Unveiling of the Manifesto.

There, an elderly man with glasses was suddenly pinned to the wall by a Labour Party marshal. It was done with huge violence and took the old man by surprise. He must have been in the wrong place at the wrong time. The Prime Minister was about to arrive.

And in walked Tony Blair. A Labour claque cheered and cameras flashed.

Oblivious to the old fellow now shaking on the sidelines Mr Blair smiled, shook hands, moved forward, and moved off. Ordered joy resumed. The man was cleared away. In a perfect world the small incident could have been wiped also from the memory.

Ways to Straighten Chesterfield Spire
19.5.01

In Wales, the Deputy Prime Minister has punched a protester. In Chesterfield they like that . . .

'He did right,' the Chesterfield shopper was telling her Labour candidate. 'Tell that John Prescott we support 'im. I mean, 'e *retaliated*, didn't 'e?' In Chesterfield that clinches it. It would be considered a halfway decent defence to murder.

Chesterfield was always a hard-bitten town, no better than it ought to be. Local legend explains the crooked spire in the story that the spire used to be straight but, centuries ago, a virgin from Chesterfield entered the church to be married. The spire bent down in amazement for a closer look. Townspeople say that if another virgin ever marries in their church the spire may straighten up again.

But the town is changing. Mines are shut and heavy industry shrinks; in their place a post-1980s economy – of lighter industry, smaller businesses and modern trading estates – has started to thrive.

Frankie & Georgie's American Diner greets you as you arrive from the M1; there's a new cinema complex, out-of-town shopping centres, and smart former council estates with top-of-the-range front doors and double-glazed conservatories.

The shift is reflected in the town's politics. The Tories have never done well there – for even the most aspirational in North Derbyshire there are limits – but at every election since 1987 the Labour vote has sunk and the Liberal Democrats' increased. Labour lost ground there even in 1997. Had he not decided to retire, Tony Benn, their former MP, would have faced a tough fight this time.

Reg Race will have a tougher one.

What shall we say about local Labour's odd choice of candidate to replace Mr Benn? A left-wing hardliner as a NUPE official, often accused of helping to bring down James Callaghan's Labour Government in the strikes of 1978–79, he was elected in that year as a London MP, for Wood Green. In the House with him then, we always thought of Race as somewhat to the left of Trotsky.

So it was odd to encounter him yesterday campaigning for new Labour in Staveley market. All the angles had dropped out of his face. He was plumper, milder, rounder, with big, bland glasses. I inquired after his former ideology as one might about a missing grandmother, suspected sold. 'Still Trotskyite?' I joked, 'or Blairite now?'

Race fixed me with a regretful look. 'Not an "ite" of any kind, Matthew,' he murmured. 'We've some very important local issues to deal with in Chesterfield.'

Was Tony Benn canvassing for him?

'He did my adoption meeting.'

But would he actually be canvassing for his successor?

'He did the meeting very nicely.'

I asked Harry Barnes, Labour candidate for NE Derbyshire, out canvassing his own voters in the same market, about his new colleague's leanings. Barnes is a consistent, old-fashioned leftwinger ('some of my voters are asking "How do we vote for you without voting for Tony Blair?"').

'Reg?' he replied, a little guardedly. 'We work together on local issues. We'll have to see where he stands ideologically.'

'Nice to talk to thee,' I overheard Race saying to a shopper. Hmm. He didn't learn to talk like that in Wood Green. Mr Race has his work cut out to win Chesterfield over. The Lib Dems, I noticed, are winning the poster war, but then they always do.

So I sped over to Brimmingham to meet Paul Holmes, the Liberal Democrat, a history teacher in a Derbyshire comprehensive, and local councillor. With 20,300 votes, his party were 5,775 votes behind

Labour in 1997. The Tories, who have now been wiped right out of local government in the town, came nowhere with 4,752. Mr Holmes was talking to some roadworkers when *The Times* arrived. 'Please don't photograph us,' their foreman said. 'It's a Labour council we work for.'

Mr Holmes seems like . . . a teacher and local councillor; solid, keen and brimming with facts, some of them relevant. He introduced me to a woman who did vote Liberal Democrat and to her baby, Mackenzie, who would if she could, as might so many babies. Holmes seemed optimistic but by no means confident.

Chesterfield has for decades been taken for granted by the Labour Party. But the town has changed, and is now capable of surprising its old masters. It is possible that townspeople may awake on June 8 to see their spire upright again, in shock. Holmes might win.

He did.

Come Fly with Ann   *23.5.01*

'Would you like to fly with Ann?'

What journalist who calls himself an Englishman could refuse such an offer? The Tory Shadow Home Secretary's campaign organiser was speaking to me in London early yesterday. 'Could you get yourself to Birmingham,' he said, 'and join her helicopter there?'

I indicated that I would like very much to fly with Ann, and would get myself to Birmingham, or anywhere else, if that was what was entailed. And so it was that your sketchwriter found himself some hours later at the National Exhibition Centre where, in a hall with subdued lighting, Ann Widdecombe was stalking the rostrum and giving the conference of the Association of Chief Police Officers what for. Her audience was subdued – not as the lighting was subdued but as the Gauls were subdued.

Their chairwoman tried to bring questions to a close. Miss Widdecombe stopped her. 'My helicopter will wait.' She made her way to the exhibition hall, retinue trailing behind.

Leaping from an emergency vehicle, she was almost sliced by a sliding door – if any door would dare. 'That would have been the photograph of the campaign,' she said grimly.

Next, Miss Widdecombe's attention was caught by a police car-chase simulator. She leaped into the pod. Police sirens wailed. Her eyes flashed. The 'car' accelerated.

Conversing with voices audible only to herself over her headphones – 'tango Mike one four' – she drove straight over the middle of a roundabout at about 60 mph. 'I love these,' she announced, emerging from the pod. 'In an airforce simulator I shot up all the allied bases.'

Now she (and I) boarded the Twin Squirrel (or Widdecopter), which had whirred her to the Midlands. 'Food,' she said, as the blades spun. She attacked four defenceless little sandwiches.

It was a glorious, cloudless day. The West Midlands slid shimmering beneath us as Miss Widdecombe described all the means of travel that she had employed in her campaign blitz on the electorate. 'That 1948 De Havilland Dove,' she said, 'which took us to the Police Federation in Blackpool – with the rain coming in. Marvellous!

'And then there was the Mini Metro tour of South London, which we had to cancel because we couldn't all fit in it, what with ITN. And my Popemobile in the constituency.'

Popemobile? 'It's a D-reg pick-up truck,' she explained, chomping her sandwich, 'fitted up by a local farmer. We've created a special glass bit I stand up in, and harangue Maidstone.'

As we dived towards a green field outside marginal Shrewsbury I saw a tiny group of ant-like people with white hair waving. They grew into the local Conservative Association and their candidate, Anthea McIntyre.

The whirr slowed and died.

Photographers were outside. 'Gotta be careful how I get out,' said Widdecombe. 'Not the most elegant of operations, from a helicopter – and the press these days wouldn't hesitate.'

'It must be dreadful being a woman,' I said.

'It's great. Just *great*.'

'Ah Ann!' gasped Gyles Brandreth, waiting on the grass. 'You've descended. A vision has come among us. And some angels too,' he added, glancing at *The Times* sketchwriter. 'The air smells sweeter.'

'Grass-mowings, more like,' said Widdecombe; then, to the Shrewsbury Tory candidate: 'You're gonna win this one Anthea. Aren't you.' Miss McIntyre, who seemed bright and nice, did not demur. It was not a question.

Tory Cheated of Amazing Day   *24.5.01*

The Dome, said Peter Ainsworth, the Tories' Dome spokesman, as he posed for photographs yesterday in front of the monstrous spiky construction at Greenwich 'is a symbol of Time'.

'The Dome,' a Conservative handout says, 'is a symbol of new Labour.'

'The Dome,' Tony Blair said, in days best forgotten, 'will be the first paragraph in my re-election manifesto.'

'The Dome,' the publicity for the New Millennium Experience used to say, 'is one amazing day.'

The Dome yesterday was none of these things. It was as cruel an illustration as you can find of the profound hopelessness of the Tory campaign. Everybody knows the Tories are right about the Dome.

Everybody knows the Government has made a ghastly hash of it.

And nobody cares.

There is, as Mr Ainsworth's brave, despairing smile half betrayed, something even more dejecting than losing the argument: winning it hands down – to see your adversary grin, whistle, and walk away.

The Tories had planned the morning as a showdown over the history and future of the Dome. Their amiable, decent, energetic, slightly gormless Peter Ainsworth was to stride into an on-site meeting with the Chairman and members of the Government's New Millennium Experience Company, tell 'em what for, stride out, and lambast the Government before a crowd of waiting newsmen. The meeting was arranged and the press briefed.

So the company cancelled the meeting. Mr Ainsworth was barred from the site and left prancing around on a patch of grass near a pub with the Dome behind him, a claque of plucky Tory-boys with placards beside him, two standard issue, pencil-thin, bossy PR women with mobile phones from government agencies telling him to go away, a forlorn Tory candidate for Greenwich and Woolwich with his wife feeding their baby, and a couple of giggling parliamentary sketch-writers. This was billed as a High Noon between Government and Opposition; it more resembled a trespassing picnic.

You can see it from the company's point of view. Ainsworth ain't going to be the next Secretary of State for Culture, Media and Sport, so why give the Tories their fun?

Even on a beautiful spring day the North Greenwich peninsula is a sad place.

In the background was the great Dome itself, security-fenced, being stripped of exhibits. 'The heart was recently taken out of the Body,' one of the PR stick-women informed me. In the foreground, as Ainsworth struggled for new adjectives to describe the fiasco, stretched acres of empty car park.

The Underground station was as deserted as it was grandiose, row upon row of ticket machines standing idle, the huge integrated transport exchange on its forecourt a waste of steel, glass, tarmac and kerbstone.

This is a bonfire of statist vanities. The whole scene breathes massive balls-up. A monumental error of judgement has been made. We know the names: Mandelson, Blair, Falconer . . . laughing spirits, wraiths, who have vanished into the May sunshine like so many dancing Thames waves. Was that Peter Mandelson's fleeting gossamer smile, Blair's grin, Charlie Falconer's courtly smirk . . . or just tricks of light reflecting off water by the empty boulevard where happy families on their One Amazing Day were to picnic?

Argue about the past? 'Sorry,' says new Labour sniggering behind its hand. 'The argument's been cancelled, didn't you know? Tony's written that one down to experience.'

So the Tories won the debate? What debate? Who's debating? High Noon has been dropped: we are the timekeepers now. The future not the past. The many not the few. No more Tory boom and bust. Tough on crime . . .

The ashes of half a billion pounds of public money smoulder in heaps around us, Tory pups bark, the new Labour's caravan moves on. Peter Ainsworth, barred from the Dome, is left to yap and caper on the grass outside.

With Honour in His Own County

28.5.01

In flight from the smirks of new Labour parliamentary candidates, now let loose across the land, I scoured the by-ways of leafy southern England yesterday in search of a Conservative who was still loved. Was there any Tory canvassing out there who still met cheers and hand-shakes? Is there such a thing as a popular Tory any more?

Finally I found one. Everyone seemed to adore him. Pity he isn't a candidate any more.

We tracked down John Major in St Neots. He was on the stump in the marketplace accompanied by Norma. The former Prime Minister, who is retiring from political life, was canvassing with Jonathan Djanogly, his successor as Tory candidate for Huntingdon, the safest Conservative seat in Britain.

'Isn't he lovely?' a lady said to me as Mr Major passed. 'He's just . . . just *lovely*,' said another, older woman at the pedestrian crossing. The only strong language came from a man outside the Conservative Club. It spoilt the saccharine moment – but he added 'that Labour shower, I mean'.

'He can ask me out for the evening any time,' giggled a well-endowed young woman at a table inside.

'The thing is,' said a man in the local bookshop, 'he's genuine. He talks to all types. He crosses boundaries.'

'A good man,' said the woman behind the hot-dog counter in the market, raking over a tray of frying onion rings.

Nobody in St Neots, so far as I could establish, had a bad word to say of him – except for a skinhead-looking type with Union Jacks on his barrow, speaking for the new ascendancy in the Conservative Party. 'Thatcher was the one,' he said.

Mr Major? Not afraid to meet people,' said one passer-by. Another added, dutifully: 'We 'ope the new gennelman does jus' as well.'

For the new gennelman, Mr Djanogly, this was not an easy morning. Not only does he labour under a miscellany of consonants and vowels that my *Independent* colleague described as more like a nightmare hand in Scrabble than a surname, but also under the bitter duty, too, (I remember it from my first campaign) of smiling enthusiastically each time the umpteenth voter tells him how much his predecessor will be missed.

But Jo Dangly, or Jan Godly, who looks about 14, was wearing his temporary eclipse with good grace.

We saw John Major intervene quickly and unobtrusively when the manager of the bookstore asked the young candidate to pose with a copy of Mr Major's autobiography in his hand.

'No, no,' said Mr Major gently, moving the book aside, 'not needed.'

He had sensed his successor's hesitation and acted to spare him the embarrassment. It was a touching moment and typical.

'That autobiography,' said the manager of Barretts, 'helped our book section take off. There were queues all the way round the block – 400 people – in the rain, when he came here for a signing. We sold nearly a thousand.'

'It began a revival of reading, generally, in St Neots,' said a member of Mr Major's staff, 'an upsurge'. In promoting the miraculous powers of the Prophet John, her enthusiasm had perhaps run away with her.

Everybody said they would miss him. Relaxed in pink shirt, shirtsleeves and sky-blue tie, Mr Major looked as though, yes, he would miss *them* but that frankly he would not miss *it* – the game of politics.

Will the game miss him?

'They'd be doing better if he was still leader of the Tory party,' said one white-haired lady, echoing the sentiments of a number. 'They won't win with that wimp.'

She was not referring to Djanogly. 'Ooh, *sshh*,' said her friend, tittering – as though such things were not said in St Neots.

I relayed to Norma Major what people had been saying about her husband's much-missed leadership, and wanting him to carry on.

Mrs Major used to be, if anything, more hurt by the attacks on her husband by his Tory colleagues than he was himself.

She looked not flattered but a little sad.

'I'd have supported him whatever he did, if . . . I could have stood it.'

She added quietly: 'People who say all that, about missing him as leader . . . they've forgotten, they don't remember . . . you know . . . why he isn't there any more.'

She paused. 'You can't undo all that.'

She is right. But whatever vituperation her husband may have had to endure in 10 Downing Street, this is a prophet with honour in his own county.

Tiny Haystacks Fights For Survival

29.5.01

'It's totally pagan!' shrieked an irrepressible little blond haystack, as what appeared to be a sizeable grove of birch trees came dancing through the centre of Lichfield with bells on their ankles, on a warm Bank Holiday morning yesterday.

The blond haystack, who was carrying a plastic bucket, turned out to be Michael Fabricant, who hopes that this tiny, quirky city in Staffordshire will return its tiny, quirky Tory again next Thursday.

The birch grove turned out to be Morris dancers dressed all in green leaves and waving branches. This was the city's annual Bower Parade.

'Aren't you dancing along with us this year?' called one of the Morris men to their former MP, plonking a leafy boater on Mr Fabricant's extraordinary hair.

'Lower profile required this year,' sighed a rueful Mr Fabricant, glancing up enviously at a petal-strewn Bower Queen perched on an immense purple float drawn by a tractor. 'It's the election. I'm collecting for charity instead. A bit of dignity was called for.'

At the word 'dignity' a suppressed splutter was heard from Mr Fabricant's friends, gathered to wave him off at the start of the parade. 'Dignity,' conceded the candidate, 'is perhaps not my middle name.'

'He's always at the forefront of things,' a lady whispered. 'Bit of a figure of fun at times but he's in there doing a lot for us. Nothing's too much trouble. You'll not fault him.'

'He's a good sort,' said her husband.

Michael Fabricant needs to be a good sort. His majority last time was 238. 'But we think they may have died,' he said.

This sketch can confirm what his constituents supposed: that at Westminster, Lichfield's MP has been a bundle of energy: always in his seat; always ready to chip in; always bright; often original. Your sketchwriter can also confirm that he's a bit of a figure of fun at times: totally his own man, and fatally unwilling to take the Commons as seriously as it takes itself.

I asked him about his new, lower profile. 'You missed me on Saturday,' he said, 'handing out balloons.'

And Sunday? 'I was in a parade with two gold maces.'

The band was striking up and Mr Fabricant twirled his bucket. 'We do canvassing too.'

I inquired after his Labour challenger, Martin Machray, but failed to find him. He appeared not to have insinuated himself into the parade.

'How about the Liberal Democrat, Phillip Bennion?' I asked.

'He isn't here.'

The drums beat, the sun came out, and the parade moved away. 'Off we go!' whooped Mr Fabricant with another twirl of the bucket, 'doing my bit as Mr Nobody.'

The *Times* photographer and I gave chase. It proved impossible to keep up with him.

Darting almost under the wheels of the Bower Queen's tractor and in intermittent peril of being trampled underfoot by the bearskinned guardsmen, Mr Fabricant rushed, waving his bucket, at a crowd of startled folk. '*Hello* there! Get your money out. It's not for the Conservative Party.'

'Ooh, it's 'im,' squealed one constituent, 'Hello Michael,' another, and 'Good luck Mr Fabricant,' a third. A fourth rather spoiled it: 'That's what those bloody Tories do,' he snorted, 'get all your money.'

Zigzagging in front of a vintage fire engine and pink-faced with the effort, the Tory candidate brandished his bucket, now too heavy to wave, along the lines of onlookers. Many seemed to know him. None seemed to dislike him. Not all were taking him entirely seriously.

Lichfield has produced some rare and strange talents – Erasmus Darwin, Charles's scientist grandfather; Samuel Johnson; George Fox, the founder of Quakerism, who, awaking from a dream in which he saw the city's vast, weird cathedral engulfed in blood, fled barefoot, crying 'Woe unto bloody Lichfield!' – so Mr Fabricant and his adopted city are not unsuited to each other.

Watching him, you might wince at the indignities to which a man will subject himself to stay their MP. But we know him better – and it's worse than that. He enjoys it. For this candidate, the carnival is for life, not just for a general election.

Eat your heart out, Bower Queen: to Mr Fabricant, every day is a parade.

He won.

Positively Her Last Appearance   *30.5.01*

She was so close I could see the white of her face powder.

Some images, fleeting as they are, will stay with us the rest of our lives. Standing on a rubbish bin in the market square in Northampton yesterday I watched a tiny figure in blue brocade, a face so pale it was almost a death mask, mobbed by friend and foe.

She was almost at my feet. All around her was a kind of frenzy. Cameramen jostled, reporters scribbled, Tories cheered, protesters booed and an agitated crowd of the committed and the curious pushed and surged for a glimpse.

And she was still. Still, but not calm. She was the centre of all this furious energy. Nobody I have followed in this campaign – not Tony Blair, not William Hague, and certainly not Charles Kennedy – has aroused such spontaneous passion.

The Baroness Thatcher of Kesteven had arrived after noon in a Jaguar Majestic so blue it was almost black. Television crews and journalists had been positioning themselves there for most of the morning.

Supporters of Shailesh Vara and John Whelan, the Tory candidates for Northampton's two marginal seats, carried 'Save the £' placards and a life-size cardboard cut-out of Lady Thatcher, with handbag. The replica swayed sickeningly above the mêlée as the real thing pushed her way purposefully into the middle of the throng. Admirers shouted, 'Hurrah!'

One woman shouted 'Rubbish!' The Baroness, hearing this, moved not away from but towards the protester – who shrank hastily back to shout 'Rubbish' from a safer distance.

Like a dangerous animal suddenly attracted by the movement of a prey, Lady Thatcher fixed her eye on the brightly coloured tie of Central Television's Peter Hayes. Momentarily oblivious to the hands of worshippers reaching out to touch her, her expression said: 'Make my day sonny, ask me a question.'

'Why are your afraid of the euro?' asked Hayes.

'*What* a question!' she snapped. 'What a *question*.' Mr Hayes flinched. 'As' – she stabbed him in the chest with an index finger – 'a *broadcaster*' she stabbed again – 'you should *protect*' – stab – 'the pound'. Hayes began to back away into the crowd. She pursued him! Then she grabbed his mike like some kind of trophy and brandished it in front of his own crew's camera, in much the same way the tribesmen of the Danekil in the Horn of Africa sport, on a necklace, the withered penises of the men they have killed in battle.

She had finished with him. She turned her attention to a girl with Down's Syndrome, who was clasped, a little boy with flowers, who hand was held, and an old gent in grave danger of losing his stick, whose shoulder was gripped.

In a burst of sunshine I could see the gold lacquer in her hair, and the papery skin beneath.

Lady Thatcher began to move through the market. A karaoke girl-band sang 'Mama Mia'. 'I came face to face with her,' gasped one Northampton woman. 'She's so tiny!' From the fringes of the scrum a gaunt, angry Scot shouted: 'Show us your bank account.' The police pushed him back. 'She gets police protection and she's not even an MP,' he bawled.

'She's a baroness,' an indignant Tory corrected him.

'She's a pain in the butt,' snapped a stallholder.

Lady T spotted me and fixed me with a gimlet eye. I didn't know what to say. 'You seem to be attracting a lot of attention,' I stammered.

She glared. 'Are you surprised, Matthew?' I blushed. 'You should be ashamed of yourself.'

'And you should be Prime Minister,' called an admirer. Thatcher leant over. 'Did you hear that, Michael [*sic*]?' she said to me. Off she went, the riot around her backing, stumbling, a child's hand forced into its candyfloss. 'We must move,' she explained. 'We're affecting their profits.'

Someone challenged her about the euro. The very idea, she harrumphed. '*We*,' she added, as though completing the argument, 'have a much older history.'

As Lady Thatcher moved back towards her waiting Majestic, the girl-band sang 'Thank You for The Music'.

She paused at the car door, almost pinned to the side. So many faces – so much attention – pressing round. She seemed to hesitate. Something in her face said: 'I don't want to go. Ask me another question.' It was as though they were taking her away.

And she went. A Tory with a megaphone continued his harangue about the euro but the crowd drifted off. It had been the singer, not the song.

Mr Vara just failed to make it.

Riveted By His Own Show

It has become almost obligatory for 'colour' writers covering famous trials to observe that the accused 'sat impassively in the dock, sipping occasionally from a glass of water'. But in Court 8 at the Old Bailey yesterday, Lord Archer of Weston-super-Mare hardly touched his water. Nor did he appear impassive. He looked absolutely fascinated.

The famous author, politician, impresario and comeback kid had arrived at court that morning accompanied by his wife, Mary, and their son, William. As they entered and heads turned, your sketchwriter was having a spot of difficulty of his own – gaining admittance. So accustomed am I to Lord Archer's fabled ability to pull a string here, smooth a path there and open a door where necessary to help a pal, that I was a split-second away from asking if he would have a word with the court officials and get my entrance pass sorted out, when it struck me that he was the accused.

'Following Lady Thatcher yesterday and me today, I see,' he said, sounding chuffed by the association.

With Lord Archer was his co-accused, Ted Francis. Where Lord Archer looked brisk, Mr Francis looked miserable. It was he who first accused his former friend of drawing him into a planned conspiracy to pervert the course of justice. The two men placed themselves almost as far apart as it was possible to sit while remaining in the same dock. I never saw them exchange so much as a glance, let alone a word. Both were observed intently from the press gallery by Michael Crick, author of a book on Lord Archer and persecutor-in-chief of the famous peer.

Most of the day was taken up with legal argy-bargy between counsel and the judge, almost all of it 'in camera', as they say. It might be possible to explain what the arguments were about, but as a new millennium begins, it becomes increasingly clear that what the legal profession needs is not explanation but a stick of dynamite up its *obiter dicta*.

All of this, Jeffrey Archer observed with the same rapt attention. He looked riveted, and when counsel for the prosecution began the opening address, he opened a notebook and began to write, looking up sharply from time to time like an exceptionally motivated student.

The case for the prosecution was begun, in the habitual manner of British law courts, in a sort of Gilbert and Sullivan stage-villain 'Mr

Nasty' voice, full of courtesy – 'if you will forgive me', 'if I may ask you to register in your minds' – that is so elaborate as to be almost mocking, as well as calculated, one supposes, to impress fellow lawyers.

Jeffrey Archer did not object. He was having a sort of out-of-body experience, keenly observing himself sitting there in the dock as might an author observe in his imagination the central figure of his new novel, caught in the intricacies of an emerging plot. For years the rest of us have seen Lord Archer as theatre. Yesterday it struck me that he may see himself in the same way. Will our hero be acquitted and achieve a sensational third come-back in his roller-coaster life? Or might he be convicted and go to prison? What a novel. What a memoir. What a film.

Taking a break from the mumbo-jumbo, I found a noticeboard in the lobby. Here the Court Service invited comments and suggestions from 'customers'. Results from the week commencing May 14: 'Comments/ Suggestions: NONE. Action: NONE'.

It was announced that we were all to be sent away. Some sort of procedural cock-up had occurred. Lawyers sat there like so many ticking taxi-meters, clocking up the bucks.

Back in court I watched an attendant carry in a bundle of papers, plus an envelope, and present both to a bewigged lawyer. She opened the envelope and took a little peek. It contained a cheque. She slipped it quickly into her bag.

The following morning in court the judge complained about this sketch, I am pleased to report.

Heath Lunches as a Political Statement

1.6.01

At the White Cross pub in Bexley yesterday, the former Prime Minister Sir Edward Heath unveiled a new campaigning tool. Lunch. The old bear came out of his cave for a prawn basket and chips, at £7 – or as Sir Edward would prefer, €11.25.

'Ted,' his campaign secretary had told me politely when I telephoned from London earlier that morning, 'is not intending to make any *public* appearance for his successor as Conservative parliamentary candidate; but today he is planning to lunch with him. It's a means of demonstrating his support. The idea is to show solidarity. The lunch will be private. I'm afraid you can't come.'

What a splendid idea. Candidates can cease knocking on doors and arguing with voters, and instead attend lunches designed to demonstrate their opinions or affiliations. But it seemed to me that lunching as a form of electioneering did need to be visible. Pointing out that holding the repast in secret severely limited its effectiveness as a campaigning tactic, I asked if we might at least know where this meaningful lunch was to take place. *The Times*, I said, would like to observe – no more – the great man's arrival. I promised not to talk to him.

'I'll have to ask Sir Edward.'

Ten minutes later my phone rang. Sir Edward did not wish the national press to observe his arrival. His secretary was not to tell me where the lunch was to occur.

I had to find out for myself.

In the heart of Sir Edward's former constituency of Old Bexley & Sidcup, the White Cross pub was called the Red Cross until the First World War, when it was ordered to change its name lest casualties be carted in. The pub is a pleasant, cosy little place, but then Sir Edward always did have good taste. 'He's often here,' said Roy Kennedy, the publican, a tremendous German shepherd called Fred growling at his feet. 'Fred don't like Ted,' he added. 'Ted calls him a "specimen".

'Likes his single malt, does Ted – Glenmorangie. He don't pay for it neither. Offers to, of course. We like him. Mind you, when the Labour candidate holds his meetings here I have to place a square of cardboard over the photo of Sir Edward. Tactful like.' Surprisingly, this is a marginal seat where Sir Edward's would-be Tory successor, Derek Conway, is looking at a 1997 majority of just 3,569.

Awaiting their arrival in the pub car park, I hid behind a big horse-chestnut tree. The *Times* photographer concealed himself behind a wheelie-bin near the kitchen. We knew Sir Edward well enough to know him capable of spotting the press and driving off, leaving his lunch guest behind. A photographer from the Kent press turned up to lurk with us. His first Heath photo-op? 'No, he unveiled a bench last year.'

The genial, roly-poly Derek Conway arrived. It is unusual for Eurosceptics to be either: they are almost always thin, stressed people.

Mr Conway saw the press but looked relaxed. A blue-grey Jaguar swept up. The door opened. The old bear surveyed us with a weary, pained forbearance, and got out. 'I'm here to welcome Derek Conway,' he said, a quite extraordinarily effusive statement from Sir Edward, not least because Mr Conway is a convinced Eurosceptic. It was good of Sir Edward even to acknowledge the man's existence, let alone share a prawn basket with him. This point was put by a journalist, backing as Sir Edward advanced. He looked balefully at his questioner but maintained his pace. 'If you don't watch out you'll knock something over,' he rasped, and walked on with his roly-poly friend.

At 84, and after 51 years in the Commons, Sir Edward is now quite lame. Watching him it occurred to this sketchwriter that we were perhaps witnessing the last electioneering performance of his life.

Which we are nevertheless confident, will be much-prolonged. After all, Sir Edward has something big to live for: a final, unfulfilled purpose to existence. He wants to be around to fail to turn up at Margaret Thatcher's funeral, on the grounds of a previous engagement.

He could do worse than make it lunch at the White Cross.

Conway won.

Women on the Verge of a Nervous Countdown

5.6.01

This is a story of Gillian, Christine and Lisa; Judy, Eileen and Margaret; of Marion, Maggie and Emma; and of Marlene, Gwen, Chantal and Debs . . . But to begin at the beginning: Gillian is the Labour parliamentary candidate for Lincoln. Christine is her Conservative challenger. Lisa is standing for the Liberal Democrats.

Margaret (Mrs Beckett to you and me) was the Labour MP for a city which had almost always been Labour. Gillian Merron recaptured the constituency for the party, and has represented Lincoln since the last election. Christine Talbot is a Tory local councillor and though (as she calls herself) 'a local girl for 23 years', this is the first time she has stood for Parliament.

The likeable Lisa Gabriel also lives locally. 'I used to be on the alternative cabaret circuit in the 80s,' Ms Gabriel, a musician, told me. 'I played the bass guitar for an act in which the *Titanic* sank and 1,500 people drowned.' I wished her luck, turning to pay my driver, Marion Quant, the proprietor of Bee Gee's Taxis in Newark. 'When I'm waiting for a fare,' Marion told me, 'I knit.'

Gillian had fled; Lisa and I were joined outside BBC Radio Lincolnshire by Christine. Christine and Lisa seemed to get on fine – but Gillian is their common enemy. Even added to the Tory vote last time of some 14,000, the Liberal Democrats' 5,000-odd does not reach Labour's 25,000 plus.

Gillian's campaign team (her assistant is Eileen) was slightly sniffy about gathering with Christine and Lisa. 'There's no *personal* animosity,' Lisa assured me; but the sisterhood had limits. I regret to report that we did hear Ms Merron described as 'lethal Gillian' by one of her rival's teams.

Maggie (Curtis), at the radio station, had arranged for this sketch to meet the three candidates after they had shared a studio together for an hour's election debate. Their interviewer, Emma (Bough) then asked if she could interview the sketchwriters of *The Times* and the *Guardian* for her afternoon show. After that, Christine took us shopping.

Like two little boys in tow behind a purposeful lady we visited Chantal's, a shoe shop, where Christine asked about the co-owner, Debs. Next we visited Flowers By Suzanne, then called in for a chat with the woman running The Arbour flower shop. After that it was lunch in a pub with her agent, Judy.

Mrs Talbot left to a call of 'Good luck, Christine!' from Marlene and Gwen, dining there. She is a strong local candidate, and the Tory vote should hold up well. But she is unlikely to beat Gillian.

By 3.30pm Gillian was outside the Westgate school, surrounded by women come to collect their children. While waiting for Gillian to arrive, we were eyed suspiciously by one or two of these. But Gillian made it clear we were all right and we were allowed to stay.

I had remarked to the Tory team campaigning with Christine that Gillian had the most beautiful reddish-raven hair, quite pre-Raphaelite. 'Huh!' said one of Christine's friends, 'not her natural colour. Straight out of a bottle.'

The remark came from a man. Bitch.

Gillian won.

Faces of Tory Defeat

The faces said it all. As William Hague spoke from a makeshift podium in the market square at Abingdon in Oxfordshire yesterday, me at his feet, I swung on my heel and watched his audience instead. For all of ten minutes, back turned on Mr Hague himself, I studied the scattering of upturned Tory faces stretching away from him. I saw what none of them saw. I saw what he saw: them.

None of them believed. All of them supported, all of them wanted to believe, none of them could.

Something in the set of a person's mouth, something uncontrollable, gives the game away. Mouths were fixed, eyes expressionless, faces blank.

And arms were folded. Try standing with your arms folded across your chest to feel what the posture is saying. Thus we might stand while giving a Mormon a hearing.

Others had placed their fingers across their mouths. You could almost hear the sound of sucking teeth. A toddler in a pushchair at my feet, mistaking his moment, tried to clap but his mother restrained him. A nearby woman held her save-the-pound placard aloft with one hand and bit the nails on the other. Everywhere among the crowd eyes wandered.

On the unlucky Hague ploughed. It was, like every performance in his brave campaign, a marriage of energy with passionlessness. The Tory leader took it at full tilt without hesitation, deviation or repetition, like an apprentice tightrope walker fearful lest in pausing he should teeter and fall. But his face stayed blank.

There had been just enough supporters awaiting him to line a 50-yard corridor across the market square to his plywood platform. Mr Hague was to arrive by the car bringing him from a landing pad where his helicopter, *Common Sense*, was to drop him.

Common Sense flew over the square, high above. The crowd below barely looked up. I have seen more interest among penguins. Ten minutes later *Common Sense* flew over again. From up there the crowd must have looked even smaller than it was. Was its principal passenger entertaining second thoughts about bothering to land?

But he did. On arrival at the square there was a small Tory cheer and feeble boos from Labour supporters, roused more to curiosity than anger. Only Ffion caused a flutter. Shaking hands as he went, William made his way to the platform.

His speech was, like all he does, workmanlike. But it breathed more of the business-management course than of the rally. Although the delivery was noisy the content was flat. Hague's eyes were without fire as he shouted his way through a key-point by key-point set-piece presentation: '. . . burst Blair's bubble . . . Labour sleaze . . . Vaz . . . Mandelson . . . political correctness . . . higher taxes . . . soft on crime . . . all spin no delivery . . . bring back matron . . . more police . . . save the countryside . . .'

You could almost hear the click-click of an automatic slide-change monitor as he spoke.

Mr Hague was rewarded with a brave cheer; spoke briefly to media interviewers, then sped off. His helicopter awaited.

'You'd better not look down/Or you might not keep on flying,' runs BB King's blues classic. 'You'd better not look down/Or you might just end up crying.' If poor William Hague had paused just once on his podium during his speech in Abingdon market square yesterday and looked down at the faces of his own supporters, he might have been unable to start again. He would surely have wept.

Pants To Politics

7.6.01

On the eve of poll . . .

The ties summed it up. You could have skipped the whole campaign, looked in on Labour's final press conference yesterday in Nottingham-shire and read their victory strategy in two neckties, plus a string of pearls and some underpants.

Gordon Brown wore a pink tie with blue dots; Tony Blair wore a blue tie with pink dots; and Margaret Beckett wore pearls. We had just learnt from that morning's *Mirror* that Mr Blair was in designer underwear.

So that's their secret. Compassion, conservatism, class – and Calvin Klein. The Chancellor's socialist compassion was specked with the blue beads of conservative prudence. The Prime Minister's Christian conservatism was dotted with caring pink. And Mrs Beckett, chairing the conference as haughtily as she commands the Commons, decked out her authority in a classy string of pearls.

As for the underpants, ask a chap skulking at the back of the hall, the bloke who keeps the tabloids sweet, the cynic who knows that at the heart of any successful campaign must lie a core of utter shamelessness. For Calvin Klein read Alastair Campbell.

The brand of Blair's pants, claimed the *Mirror*, had been revealed by chance, and Campbell was appalled at the triviality. Appalled? Campbell was the man who spread the story that John Major tucked his shirt into his underpants.

'Men,' gasped the *Mirror*, 'who wear Calvin Klein are cool. They just are. This simple fashion statement spells confidence, poise, good sense, sound judgement, style. Its oozes class and statesmanship! And modernity. And SUCCESS. *Now vote.*' In short, Tony was cool.

Gordon was grumpy. Nobody was talking about his underpants, except to speculate that they were tartan, emblazoned with a £ sign at the front, and massive.

The two men could not have presented a sharper contrast. Blair was mobile, his face, like an actor's face, alive to every fleeting mood. Humour, irritation, conviction, perplexity, slyness, anger chased their way across his tired features like squalls over water. As Brown spoke Blair tried on the mask of adoration then, suddenly bored, allowed his eyes to dart around the audience.

Brown was solid, impassive, real. Blair was fey. One belonged to the air, the other to the earth. Something about Brown dulls the spirits, yet reassures. Something about Blair beguiles, yet disturbs.

An innovation is the planting at press conferences of claques of Labour supporters, to clap Blair's answers to journalists or laugh derisively at unhelpful questions. A Sky man tried a question intended to be helpful – how much had Cherie's companionship meant to Tony during the campaign? – without realising this was a Wednesday.

On Mondays, Wednesdays and Fridays the Prime Minister complains about the trivial personalisation of politics. On Tuesdays, Thursdays and at weekends he brings his son in on the campaign, gets Cherie into every camera frame and jokes about bringing up baby Leo. It being a Wednesday, Blair decided to sneer at the questioner, whipped up the Labour claque into sneering at him too, and then came back for a second swipe as the claque laughed. He reminded me of a playground bully. Then he reverted to breathing platitudes about values, vision and 'schoolsnhospitals'. After this he took several further swings at the Conservatives and William Hague.

His aides have been briefing that Tony is worried lest this election be about rejecting the Tories instead of embracing his own positive vision for Britain. What an infernal construction this man is. I used to think Blair was aware of the contradictions, but cynical. I now believe he *is* the contradictions, and unreal.

Reality, in the form of Gordon Brown, plodded off: for Birmingham, Edinburgh, and meetings in his constituency. It struck me as one of the nicer things one knows about the Chancellor, that he almost certainly cannot remember what sort of underpants he is wearing, and certainly doesn't care.

Widdecombe Explodes   19.6.01

And the Tory leadership struggle begins.

Sadly, Ann Widdecombe is unable to offer Michael Portillo her support for the Tory leadership. Her hair has turned quite gold with grief.

Mr Portillo chose the English National Ballet School as backdrop to his photo-opportunity last week. To rub in the contrast, Miss Widdecombe chose a run-down council estate in Hackney. The press were called urgently to the Ardley Estate on Hoxton Road where, we were told, she would announce the collapse of her leadership bid.

For perhaps the first time in history a politician had created a ceremony around the declaration of what she was *not* going to do. Leadership bids are two-a-penny in the Tory party these days and one is invited often enough to witness the balloon going up; but to be summoned to witness the balloon going down was a novelty.

We had been brought to Hackney to watch the Widdecombe inflatable deflate.

Not that the event lacked its thrilling side. The rapid bursting of Miss Widdecombe was always going to be a dangerous affair. There was a risk that she might at any moment fly off diagonally, up and over a tower block, and scream sideways into a bus queue, rubbery bits of her wrapping themselves around innocent cameramen, obscuring windscreens or taking a shopper's eye out. Or another leadership contender's career out.

She certainly arrived looking wicked. Dozens of media folk and more policemen than would otherwise dare hang about in this unsavoury corner of North London were waiting for her. One speculated on the number of drug deals cancelled that morning on her account alone; the GDP of Hackney probably blipped downward by a half point. 'There was a killing here last Thursday,' said the man from the *Hackney Gazette*.

Miss Widdecombe too had murder on her mind. She stepped from her car in powder blue, her hair on an autumnal cusp between gold and russet, just opposite the Macbeth Public House. Was this a dagger that she saw before her? Two women lovers holding hands had just sashayed past; mercifully, Widdecombe missed them by minutes.

An elderly Londoner with a small tangled terrier in her arms, observing the tiny, half-limping figure at the centre of the media storm, remarked to a baffled friend: 'She's gonna sigh wevver she's gonna stand fer the leadership of the Tory or not.'

She was not. How can I describe her expression – her half-determined, half-tormented demeanour – as she plonked herself on a dog-fouled patch of grass in front of a wrecked postwar mansion block and, facing about ten dinner-parties'-worth of urban liberal professionals in the form of the national press and television corps, began railing not just at us but at the entire sophisticated world for not taking her, and her politically incorrect concerns – concerns for those she called the 'Forgotten Decent!' – seriously? She looked as might someone on a quest for martyrdom: tense, grim, happy. And I think she meant it.

But she had not, she told us, found it any easier 'to engage Michael Portillo' in problems like the Ardley Estate's, than she found it to engage us. And that was all the assassin of Michael 'something-of-the-night' Howard was saying about the other Michael.

For the moment.

On a wall nearby was mounted a plaque. 'In a house near this site,' it read, 'on 12 October 1605, Lord Monteagle received a letter unmasking the plot led by Guy Fawkes to blow up the Houses of Parliament.'

Centuries hence, will there be another plaque? *'In a housing estate near this site, Ann Widdecombe launched a campaign which led her to blow up Michael Portillo'*? Time will tell.

All Stand For Capt Duncan Smith

20.6.01

Iain Duncan Smith and David Davis announce their candidatures.

Were you up for Iain Duncan Smith?

The question took on a new meaning after Mr Duncan Smith declared for the Tory leadership at 8am yesterday at Church House in Westminster. Most of the small group of yawning media folk present had made a dawn start to get there. As the former Captain Duncan Smith strode into the hall, a trumpet reveille would not have been out of place. 'Good morning ladies and gentlemen!' he barked.

He paused. Rubbing our eyes we dimly sensed we had been expected to chorus 'Good morning captain' in response. But he let it pass.

To set the appropriate tone for a Duncan Smith leadership bid, your sketchwriter was wearing a brown tweed jacket, fawn twill trousers, brown lace-up shoes, checked cream shirt and a green wool tie. Once you've got the clothes right the opinions come naturally and you know instinctively what to think. If this man does not become the *Daily Telegraph*'s choice for leader, I will eat the tie.

He spoke.

The joy of being Iain Duncan Smith is that you do not need to spell out your views for it to be known by osmosis what they are. As befits a gentleman he began with a tribute to the 'outstanding' William Hague. Why, in that case, Mr Hague was departing was not a question which arose; praising the last chap is good form. A Tory gent (a sadly diminished species) would say as much if taking over from the Devil himself: 'Mr Beelzebub has done a splendid job with the central heating.'

Duncan Smith said he was 'proud' of Hague's record, which was an achievement 'to build on', adding that the party needed a 'break with the past'. There was no need to reconcile these two statements. Both were volunteered 'frankly' – the key word in Duncan Smith discourse; nine franklies were recorded yesterday.

Frankly, a gent does not bad-mouth the competition. Frankly he does not have to. Asked whether being less well-known than his principal rival was a problem, Duncan Smith murmured that 'being well-known sometimes comes with difficulties'. Frankly we knew what he meant. Only as we left was the text of his speech given us. Mr Duncan Smith is of the old school to whom – frankly – the idea of releasing a speech before making it is, frankly, not on.

David Davis is of the new school, of 'modern conservatives', 'modern' appearing (like 'David') in yellow, and 'conservatives' (like 'Davis') in indigo, on the slick backdrop behind challenger number three, out of the starting trap at 2, Carlton Gardens, at the modern hour of 10.30am. With him were a good half dozen of his MP supporters, at least one of whom was perfectly sane – an encouraging harvest, given the current composition of the Parliamentary Conservative Party. This launch attracted a buzz where Duncan Smith's had invited a zizz.

Mr Davis talks sense and talked it yesterday. Everything known about him is good, except that he speaks as though delivering a managing director's report at the AGM of an East Midlands light cardboard packaging company.

Davis dropped an *ad hominem* into his remarks, then, on hearing that he was Alastair Campbell's choice for Tory leader, protested '*au contraire*'. On Kenneth Clarke he refused to be drawn, pointing out that he was not here. Indeed not; in Vietnam, we hear. *Reculer pour mieux sauter*.

Behind Davis's logo was that of the Royal College of Pathologists, whose hall this was. '*Sedes invenire et causas morborum*' has been translated as 'seek to find the causes of disease'. If only the Tories knew. Davis is undoubtedly not the disease. Whether he is the cure remains – frankly – uncertain.

Like a Groom at the Wedding Feast

22.6.01

In Africa yesterday there was a solar eclipse. In London, Michael Portillo launched his leadership campaign. Both events inspired wonder.

The second inspired perplexity too. To kick off his bid to reconnect the Tory party to the concerns of ordinary people, Mr Portillo chose as a venue a millennial-chic bar restaurant – all glass tops, cherry veneer and recessed lighting – in fashionable St James. Outside The Avenue (as it is called) was the establishment's logo on a purple (or, this being London, mauve) flag: a simple @ sign – *über*groovy or what?

Among those shire activists whose votes Portillo will shortly need will be those more familiar with the '@' on an agricultural supplier's invoice – '*200 fencing posts @ £1.12 – £224.00*' – than outside a swanky purveyor of small pieces of papaya and kiwi fruit on big white plates. The paintings were abstract, the pain was *au chocolat*, the scrambled egg came in pastry thimbles, the coffee in cafetières and the bacon in *nouvelles* butties.

I was tempted to ask for a cup of tea but feared being frog-marched from the place by young men in black with earphones. The decor screamed metropolitan elite. The mirrors were huge. The waiters were gorgeous. The place breathed self-regard.

Why, Michael, *why*? It was a small, key misjudgement of the type that has characterised Portillo's career. One recalled the time when he hired an entire cinema for a fringe meeting at his party's conference in Bournemouth.

And he came among us like a bridegroom at a wedding feast, walking from elegant table to elegant table and remembering first names. The aspirant leader had ensured that the guest list of journalists was leavened with camera-friendly political supporters to applaud whenever he spoke.

Francis Maude, happeningly jacketless, opened the meeting. The party needed, said Mr Maude, 'a *big* leader'; a man, he said, of '*high* intellect' who would also have '*abundant* energy' as well as '*deep* convictions' and '*broad* appeal'. Who could this colossus be?

Big, high, abundant, deep and broad, Michael Portillo stepped forward. He was also gruff.

'I want the Conservative Party,' he growled, 'to be four things!'

'Great,' I thought, 'abundant indeed. Actually, two or three would do. Or even one . . .'

'Not against things,' he continued. My heart sank.

Not Nicholas Soames's, though. The expansive former Armed Forces Minister, surely more at home at Boodles Club up the road, was led on to tell us what a jolly good Defence Secretary Michael had turned out to be – contrary to initial prejudices.

This was the bride's uncle testifying to the fact that the groom was by no means the cad he had at first seemed.

As for the groom himself, his greatest asset was presence, which

Portillo has in bucketloads. The other thing which came in bucketloads was froth. Because he is no orator, we noticed. Nobody who promises 'a better tomorrow' should be at liberty.

Michael Ancram promised a better yesterday too. Yesterday's second Tory campaign launch took place in the more traditional setting of a little park near the river where, against a background of lawns, statues and fading ceanothus bushes, the party's faintly patrician former chairman did his emollient best to persuade us that his party's immediate need was to calm down.

As the BBC's Andrew Marr had pointed out earlier, the genial heir to the Marquess of Lothian makes his pitch to the 'all this is doing my head in' section of the Tory party. Mr Ancram has (and displayed yesterday) two modes of delivery: indignant guinea pig and well-fed guinea pig.

But he also has (and displayed yesterday) two smashing daughters and a wife called Jane.

Nobody whose wife is called Jane ever fails in the Conservative Party.

Marlboro Man Blows Smoke in Their Eyes

27.6.01

Kenneth Clarke returns from selling cigarettes in Vietnam with a late bid.

With Kenneth Clarke it was never a matter of 'may I be perhaps of any help?' He breezes off to Vietnam to flog cigarettes with an airy murmur of 'call me when you're ready'.

Yesterday they were ready. They had called, long-distance.

Mr Clarke bowled into the Institute of Directors not as a petitioner but as a long-acknowledged chief prepared to receive a petition from a wretched party on its knees before him. Yes, he would be their leader so long as they were truly sorry for their idiotic behaviour and prepared to do as they were told from now on.

It's always a shock in politics when somebody doesn't beat about the bush. When the punch is landed, in a totally genial way, right in the middle of the stomach, the shock is intense.

After a fortnight of leadership launches awash with ums and ahs and coded language about, ahem, family – and stuffed with stardust, renewal and the need for a great and searching debate – Kenneth Clarke waded into the elegant Nash Room after lunch and told the Tories that their party was a shambles, its last four years a waste of time – and serve them all ruddy well right. All other candidates for the leadership were unpopular and most of them were kids – not up to the job. The Tories' obsession with Europe was a disaster. The Conservative Party had better make him leader, do as he said, and shut up on the euro. Otherwise he'd go away again.

Nobody, including the press, knew quite what to say. It was not what we had expected. Iain Duncan Smith had offered us a dawn reveille at Church House. David Davis had offered us a new logo. Michael Portillo had offered us filter coffee and little savoury canapés. Michael Ancram had offered us his daughters. What would Mr Clarke be handing out? Free packets of Lucky Strike cigarettes or State Express 555s?

But there was no implied bribe. Except, of course, the big one. Asked whether he thought the parliamentary Conservative Party would suffer a leader imposed upon them by the Tory rank-and-file, all the bluff bonhomie suddenly fell from Clarke's face. His eyes narrowed, and met his questioner's direct.

Rather quietly and with a terrible intensity, he said he'd learnt a thing or two about the Tory Party in his time. It had its internal differences. But one thing united it. 'It does want to win elections.' *That* would bring them round.

Clarke discussed Tory policy on the euro rather as might someone who, at a wake and amid company anxious to tiptoe around the tragedy, suddenly bangs the table, knocks over the sherry, and begins a long and grisly post-mortem at maximum volume. They'd asked for his views and they were going to get them.

These provided uncompromising. Both sides would have to tone down their language, he said, making not the least attempt to tone down his.

I looked around the room. There were some unexpected people there. Lady Olga Maitland had positioned herself at the door like a society hostess. Boris Johnson was doing his best to persuade friends that he had just wandered in to the IoD, possibly by mistake. Several young men whom one had seen at another launch skulked at the back, maybe as turncoats, maybe as spies.

Spotting another MP whose Clarkite leanings had been hitherto unsuspected, I raised an eyebrow. 'Ah,' he said, flustered, 'what you're seeing from me is a case of sheer, naked careerism.'

Perhaps, then, Clarke is right. Being a winner is all he needs to be. Winning is all he needs to do.

Is This Me? Is This All? Was That It?

21.06.01

And Robin Cook awakes from a long dream.

It was more than human flesh could bear. The lid of one eye rolled fractionally down, gingery eyelashes descending a tad closer toward the gingery beard . . . 'Improved patient care within the NHS . . .' droned Tony Blair, after lunch.

A muscle on Robin Cook's other eye began to fail. The second lid rolled halfway down.

'Labour's proudest creation is the National Health Service . . .' read Mr Blair from his script. But where was the National Elf Service when one of its members was in urgent need of resuscitation? Would the new Chief Whip sitting beside him, Hilary Armstrong, not come to his aid? She stared glassily ahead, mired in her own internal struggle against Morpheus.

'. . . Treatment must not depend on the patient's ability to pay,' burbled the Prime Minister.

Mr Cook's eyeballs seemed to have swivelled up under their lids. We could see only the whites, like marble half-moons on a Greek statue.

'Seventeen thousand extra nurses . . .' The half-moons waned to crescents.

'. . . Recruit and retain new doctors . . .' Mr Cook's eyelids came to rest in the fully shut position.

'. . . A policing system fully equipped to tackle modern crime,' the Prime Minister said in a perfunctory way. Across the tortured, crumpled face of the new Leader of the House flooded an expression of sudden peace.

'. . . Double the assets seized by drug dealers,' announced Mr Blair, like a bored building society clerk quoting current interest rates. The Cook kop began, fractionally, to loll over sideways in a rightward direction.

'. . . Car crime down . . .' The angle of incline reached danger point.

'On welfare reform there are already, after four and a half years, 850,000 fewer claimants . . .' The Cook head was approaching the Cook right-hand shoulder – or, worse, Ms Armstrong's left breast.

With a sickening jerk, Mr Cook snapped his head back into the upright position. His eyes popped open with a momentarily startled expression.

Where was he? Who was he? What was he? The dream, in which he was returning to the Commons to describe to an incredulous House how he had just saved the Nice treaty single-handedly by marathon overnight summitry in a foreign capital, fled.

And it all came back. He was not Foreign Secretary any more. Tony had shafted him. He had been forced to return to work in the kitchens as Leader of the House. And this was Tony's opening address on the Queen's Speech, 2001.

Mr Cook lifted a notebook that was lying useless on his lap and began pretending to take notes.

Victory, But Not in Front of the Children
14.09.01

On the steps of St John's, Smith Square, an unkempt gentleman of a certain age in a frayed baseball cap, startled by the television lights, rolled up his well-worn sleeping bag and made off, leaving the media scrum behind. The media were there to hear the result of the Tory leadership contest.

Over the road and inside Conservative Central Office, an unkempt gentleman of a certain age in a crumpled suit rolled up his well-worn hopes of becoming party leader and made off, leaving the media scrum behind him. Ken Clarke had been roundly defeated.

It was done in a gentlemanly way, after a bare announcement from the chairman of the Tory 1922 Committee, Sir Michael Spicer, and the shortest of speeches from Mr Clarke. The vanquished Clarke was followed by the victorious Iain Duncan Smith, who, generous in victory, made a short and low-key speech of his own.

This was the most subdued accession of a new leader I have seen in the Conservative Party. It also felt like the bitterest.

There was something strange in the way that, though the outside world had gathered in the square to hear the result and see the rivals, the two men slunk inside to a room in the bowels of the building for what passed as a victory ceremony. It was as if it hurt too much to be acted out in front of the children. In every sense this was a very inward moment for the Tories.

Nobody's behaviour can be faulted, except that of a small claque of Clarke supporters who booed Mr Duncan Smith's speech to the waiting crowd milling about outside Central Office.

For Anthony Steen, the MP for Totnes and a keen Clarke supporter, to call Duncan Smith 'a former army officer and estate agent' was perhaps a little sour, but the two principals, Clarke and Duncan Smith themselves, were the model of what to the outside world looks like courtesy, and within the Conservative Party is recognised as suppressed loathing.

Clarke wished Duncan Smith luck. He said he 'hoped' his rival would lead the Tories to victory. The hope sounded like something less than an expectation. If Mr Clarke did not actually add 'and pigs will fly' then he left the thought hanging in the mind.

Duncan Smith thanked Clarke for that very 'warm' endorsement. It was not said sarcastically but as the endorsement had been cool it was hard to take it in any other way.

Mr Duncan Smith spoke with dignity and deliberateness. His face was tense but composed, like someone lowering himself into slightly too hot a bath.

Between his two front teeth your sketchwriter noticed a distinct gap. Among Zulu warriors this is taken as a mark of courage and virility, and the new Tory leader can be confident that he would receive an enthusiastic welcome in the African bush.

From the Tory jungle, however, some of the noises were less encouraging. How big was this beast? Or might he grow?

The room was not quite full. The journalists were not quite riveted.

The losing side was not quite reconciled. The winners were not quite cock-a-hoop.

Neither side was quite confident that the other would not cut up rough – in time. Nobody was quite expecting trouble – yet.

A band of UK Independence Party activists with their leader had joined the Tories outside to cheer Iain Duncan Smith. Their cheers were as ominous as the Clarkeites' boos. Sooner or later, the new Tory leader knows that he must forfeit the company of one or the other.

MATTHEW PARRIS
Off-Message
New Labour, New Sketches

Matthew Parris has spent the last thirteen years laughing at parliament from his birds-eye seat in the press gallery, as political sketchwriter for *The Times*. Running through the humour, though, has been a vein of sharp observation. He spotted Tony Blair's talents when he was just a workaday opposition spokesman; he saw his flaws, too, the minute he stood up to become party leader. And he watched in horrified amusement as the Conservative Party, for whom he was once an MP, roller-coasted from triumph to disaster.

Setting the scene with some earlier sketches from the days when the Tories could do no wrong, this book centres on the four years from 1997 to 2001 – a time when New Labour seemed to be doing (almost) everything right. But with Parris it is not the policies but the performances that count. These include William Hague's often sparkling but doomed leadership, Blair's strutting, Charles Kennedy's awkward Lib-Lab straddle, Robin Cook's fretting, Ann Widdecombe's extraordinary pantomime dame and Peter Mandelson's watch, silent and pale from the wings.

Matthew Parris is also the author of the bestselling *Great Parliamentary Scandals* and *The Great Unfrocked*. He will be quitting his perch as sketchwriter at the end of 2001. *Off-Message* could not come at a more apt moment.

COVER ILLUSTRATION RICHARD WILLSON

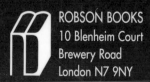 ROBSON BOOKS
10 Blenheim Court
Brewery Road
London N7 9NY

£12.99

ISBN 1-86105-479-3

9 781861 054791